# Beethoven's
# Ninth

# Beethoven's Ninth

## a political history

### Esteban Buch

Translated by Richard Miller

The University of Chicago Press

Chicago and London

The University of Chicago Press, Chicago 60637
The University of Chicago Press, Ltd., London
© 2003 by The University of Chicago
All rights reserved. Published 2003
Paperback edition 2004
Printed in the United States of America

12  11  10  09  08  07  06  05  04
2  3  4  5

ISBN: 0-226-07812-4 (cloth)
ISBN: 0-226-07824-8 (paperback)

Originally published as *La* Neuvième *de Beethoven:
Une histoire politique,*
© Éditions Gallimard, 1999

Library of Congress
Cataloging-in-Publication Data
Buch, Esteban, 1963–
     [Neuvième de Beethoven. English]
     Beethoven's Ninth : a political history /
Esteban Buch ; translated by Richard Miller.
                    p.    cm.
     Translation of: La neuvième de Beethoven.
     Includes bibliographical references (p.        )
and index.
     ISBN 0-226-07812-4 (alk. paper)
     1. Beethoven, Ludwig van, 1770–1827.
Symphonies, no. 9, op. 125, D minor.
     2. Beethoven, Ludwig van, 1770–1827 —
Influence.    3. Music — Political aspects.
I. Title.
ML410.B42 B8213 2003
784.2'184 — dc21
                                        2002014831

The University of Chicago Press
gratefully acknowledges a
subvention from the government of
France, through the French Ministry
of Culture and Centre National du
Livre, in support of the costs of
translating this volume.

# contents

# introduction

## The States of Joy

One of the early critics of the *Ode to Joy,* perhaps made uncomfortable by its rugged grandeur, remarked that for Beethoven, deaf and nearing the end of his life, the act of composition had become very like dreaming. He may well have been right. Yet Beethoven's dream, rather than hinting at the composer's alienation from the world of real sounds, took the form of a kind of political fantasy, the creation of a monumental work that would constitute a statement about ideal power, that would itself be an act of power — concrete and embodied technically both in its score and in the strategy surrounding its creation. Schiller's poem, *An die Freude* [To Joy], was its basic component. Written in 1785, the poem had quickly become an Enlightenment manifesto, and the young Beethoven had wanted to set it to music early on. With regard to the musical composition, the course of events was to be similar. In the Ninth Symphony in D Minor, op. 125, which had its premiere at Vienna in 1824, the expansion of symphonic form first noted in the *Eroica* Symphony was accompanied by a rhetorical gamut of musical genres, from military to religious, culminating in the ritual of a hymn (sacred or profane) in which the chorus of mankind celebrates its unity: "All men will become brothers," proclaims the best-known line of the work, in which, for the first time, the human voice breaks into a musical form that had hitherto been purely instrumental.

The work demonstrates Beethoven's awareness both of the baroque tradition, in which the King of Heaven was linked with the earthly king, and of the revolutionary experience that had found in the people a subject for its poetry. Indeed, the Ninth Symphony was composed at the height of the Restoration, a period that witnessed the birth of modern political musical compositions. In the eighteenth century, *God Save the King* had been the first national anthem, its words expressing a subjective relationship between the members of the national community. Soon afterward, the secular ceremonies of revolutionary France, drawing upon the works of Jean-Jacques Rousseau, began to make an innovative use of symbolism and created — through the *Marseillaise* in particular — the myth of the nation speaking with a single voice. This new kind of political hymn was rapidly adopted by the counterrevolutionary Austrian state with its own imperial anthem, the *Emperor's* Anthem, which was commissioned from Franz Joseph Haydn by an official in the country's police services. Later, Beethoven was to combine the people's voice and the baroque sublime in his cantata *Der glorreiche Augenblick* [The Glorious Moment], op. 136, composed in 1814 for Metternich's "Concert of Europe." Thus, while the new rhetoric did sometimes serve to express a form of opposition and even to propagate revolt or revolution, it was also employed to buttress the legitimacy of constituted power and express attachment to the established order by means of official or state music — in other words, music seen as gesture, as political discourse, music produced and interpreted by the state itself.

If, therefore, in composing the Ninth Symphony, Beethoven was able to succeed in realizing his monumental dream, it was because the evolution of musical language enabled him to push to the limit the narrative possibilities latent in various instrumental forms and also because he was fully familiar with preexisting political and official music. In addition, he was quite aware of the position that a great musician could occupy in a nation's life. At the time the British anthem had been produced, the works of George Frederic Handel had firmly rooted in English minds the notion that a composer could in some way represent the identity of a whole people. In composing the Austrian anthem, Haydn had acted as the faithful servant of the emperor, the "father of his subjects," and was himself honored as the "father of harmony." The Congress of Vienna marks the moment at which Beethoven, already recognized as the greatest composer of his time, emerged as a true public figure in the eyes of the establishment. At the premiere of the Ninth Symphony he was showered with praise that turned him into a civil hero on a metaphysical level: to his admirers, he embodied national grandeur far more convincingly than did the men who were actually wielding power. His death, on 26 March 1827, marked his accession to immortality, an apotheosis created by the biographies that were published and the commemorative ceremonies that were held, in which every political tendency joined in hailing him as the greatest musician of modern times.

Yet there were some reservations. The Congress of Vienna, for example, is generally viewed as having been the least glorious moment of his life, a period in which he composed the worst works of his career. With the decline of the aristocracy, nothing was more unfavorable than to be viewed as having been the "official musician" of one regime or another, and especially of that of Metternich, the embodiment of everything that stood in the way of modernity. The creator of the *Ode to Joy* would be far more highly praised, for it was composed at a time in his life when his admirers were less numerous and he himself less closely linked to the political power structure. His official music would be relegated to the periphery of his output, whereas the Ninth Symphony was to be hailed as a glorification of human freedom in which any trace of the state is, by definition, absent. Such value judgments are difficult to argue with from an aesthetic point of view, but we must also recognize in them an ideology requiring the artist to be close to the people or nation while maintaining a distance from power. This holds true for reactionary or oppressive states, but it holds true as well for liberal or democratic states, which may be hailed as guarantors of artistic freedom but never as its inspirers or interpreters.

The question of Beethoven's relations with the political powers of his day thus also comes to include the relationship that his image has with posterity. "Whatever the state touches, it kills," Romain Rolland wrote in criticizing the composer's being made into "glory's official compost heap."[1] Yet it is precisely in support of such discourse that Beethoven was to be honored by politicians and official bodies in the bourgeois era. Bourgeois governments looked at the life and work of this great deaf creator, who had risen above his physical infirmity and overthrown the musical rules of the ancien régime, and saw in him a musician who answered to their ideals of struggle and progress, a positive embodiment of the individual will and of the aspiration to universal reconciliation. Indeed, it was this duality — public vocation and private communion, symbolized respectively by his final symphony and the late string quartets — that made Beethoven's entire oeuvre a political metaphor. In the face of such canonization, few have dwelled on Beethoven's relationship with official music: exceptions are Thomas Bernhard, who stigmatized "the stupidity of the military march even in his chamber music,"[2] or certain Nazis who, taking the opposite stand, viewed that very military element as the main reason for admiring him. Given the desire to attract both the masses and the elite to worship at his monument, however, this issue has usually just been ignored.

The Ninth Symphony has become the work that has done the most to create its composer's unique public status. Yet that does not mean that it has always been viewed as his finest composition. The depiction of joy is one of the greatest challenges an artist can take up, and even when he succeeds, failure is always lurking. In 1855, Richard Wagner wrote to Franz Liszt to tell him that he considered the last movement of the Ninth Symphony to be its weakest section, just as — he added — the "Paradiso" was the least successful section of *The Divine Comedy*.[3] That, however, did not prevent Wagner from constructing around the work a whole musical theology that reflected his own dreams of redemption. Others would follow his example and silence their own reservations in order to promote the flowering of the myth. For aside from any dispute about its aesthetic value, the *Ode to Joy* is still today the most convincing depiction of utopia in sound. And utopia is a concept that haunts private unhappiness just as it does political ideas, it is a concept to be found linked with the Ninth Symphony from its premiere down to the present day. A comment, a quotation, some new lyrics, an arrangement, a ceremony, a special concert, a commemorative act, or merely a few sentences in a familiar biography or analysis — all are a means of saying that the work's ultimate principle is the embodiment of a political idea, that this idea is what reveals its deepest meaning and gives us the best reason for performing and listening to it.

There are of course many who challenge the "appropriation" or "use" of a work of art for ideological ends, many who believe that music should be beyond or apart from politics. For them, music is a universal language in which men can take refuge from words or from the world's misery. And it is true that the Ninth is, above all, a work of "pure" music, an integral part of the classical repertoire whose performance in the lay ritual of the public concert allows each of us to be at once alone and part of a group, in line with the principle that aesthetic pleasure carves out an almost sacred space for individual freedom. Yet whether or not we accept this view, we are forced to recognize that even the most passionate defense of the autonomy of absolute music or the most systematic refusal to make social or historical considerations a part of technical musical analysis still implies taking a position with regard to the social role of the work of art. And it is precisely this latitude in artistic concepts, between language and form, between the hearing of suffering and the contemplation of beauty, that has made Beethoven's Ninth into a kind of aural fetish in the Western world.

Consider this: The romantic composers made it a symbol of their art. Bakunin dreamed of destroying the bourgeois world, of wiping out everything but the *Ode to Joy*. German nationalists admired the music's heroic power, and nineteenth-century French republicans found in it an expression of 1789's three-word motto, *Liberté, Égalité, Fraternité*. The communists hear in it the gospel of a classless world, Catholics hear the Gospel itself, democrats hear it as the voice of democracy. Hitler celebrated his birthdays with the *Ode to Joy,* and yet the same music was used to oppose him, even in his concentration camps. The *Ode to Joy* resounds periodically at the Olympic Games, and it was also heard not long ago in Sarajevo. It was the anthem of the racist Republic of Rhodesia, and it is today the anthem of the European Union.

That brief listing may serve to illustrate the breadth of the consensus. Yet it also suggests that that consensus can, at times, present a problem — a moral problem, a problem that the work's appropriation by the Nazis, for example, exemplifies but does not exhaust. On quite another level, we can ponder the fact that in certain cases the Ninth has been employed as an official state anthem. For many, of course, this may not seem especially significant. Yet whether it is done on behalf of artistic autonomy or because of the antinomy that exists between state and utopia, the linking of the *Ode to Joy* to any form of "official culture" can be denounced as a corruption of its original meaning and therefore as a form of betrayal: this is the position of Agnes Heller, a philosopher and music lover, who views the "European anthem" as representing the "death of the Ninth Symphony."[4] And that is not merely an example, for the European anthem, while only a minor episode in the work's history, brings together a number of the questions that arise when music is made part of a political plan, not only because it turns the *Ode to Joy* into a state anthem, but also because it links it with a form of "European" identity.

It is true that, at first glance, there is nothing unusual about this latest event. The European anthem can lay claim to a long historical trend connecting the idea of Beethoven to that of Europe as a single entity — one that has played an important role in the Ninth Symphony's history, without however dictating the orientation of its political reception — a subject, let it be said at the outset, that this book does not pretend to deal with exhaustively. Indeed, from the very beginning, statements about Beethoven were voiced within the context and sphere of nineteenth-century Europe. In 1845, the erection of his statue in Bonn, a turning point in the establishment of an international memory linked to music, was the fruit of efforts by the cultured European elite. And it was another elite group, most of whom were European, including several heads of state and the great figures of the artistic world, that assembled at Vienna in 1927 to celebrate the hundredth anniversary of the composer's death. Thus, the link between Beethoven and a certain "European community," already embodied in an established musical repertory and a body of interpreters engaged in celebrating the shared ritual of the public concert, has been made concrete in a specifically political way via public commemorations.

Yet only rarely did the speeches heard on such occasions exalt the composer's "European" character. In Austria and Germany, the Beethoven cult was above all based on nationalism, and its promotion often included polemics against the influence of foreign — Italian or French — art. At the same time, from early on, this national aspect served as counterpoint to another notion no less important to the nascent modern period, namely, the idea of Mankind. Of course this twofold allegiance was not confined to the composer of the Ninth Symphony. Just as the French revered a Mankind raising its "hymns to freedom," a freedom created by a nation believed to be the incarnation of the universal ideal, so the Germans praised the universal significance of a music that was also specifically national in character. The Beethoven myth was to burgeon in the force field set up by these two poles of thought. And although the cult had adherents in most Western countries, the argument was carried out for the most part in Germany and in France. In Paris, towards the end of the nineteenth century, there were those who went so far as to call the *Ode to Joy* the "Marseillaise of Mankind," while in Germany pains were taken to praise its essentially German character. However, the equation has often been inverted as well, whether by German communists hailing it on behalf of the proletariat of every land, or at events associating it with France's historical patrimony, such as Francois Mitterrand's visit to the Pantheon upon being elected president in 1981.

Within this dual tradition, national versus universal, the figure of Europe itself has been singularly absent. This was true at the Bonn commemorative ceremony in 1845, when "Europe" was subsumed in a cosmopolitan undertaking and sabotaged by nationalist tensions, just as it was almost a century later at Vienna, when the worldwide scope of the event went far beyond the "civilized world" so recently engaged in the Great War. In both instances, the result was dictated by the problematic nature of the "European notion" itself, a very different matter from the objective creation of a cultural sphere on a continental scale. This notion, which since the Enlightenment had been linked to that ancien régime overthrown by the impetus of revolution and nationalism and fleetingly restored at the Congress of Vienna, had long been viewed as outmoded. The notion of Europe as a possible political and ideological entity emerged with the decline of its world hegemony, and thus it was not until the second decade of the twentieth century that the idea of a European anthem, composed by Beethoven, the "Great European," begins to be significant. The notion truly crystallized with the establishment of the institutions set up in the aftermath of the Second World War, when decolonization and criticisms of cultural Eurocentrism led to the continent's coming to be regarded as an actual entity and not as a mere universal figure. The adoption of the European anthem in 1972 went hand in hand with an emphasis on Western values that reflected the limits of a Europe that had excluded, de facto, all of Eastern Europe throughout the cold war period. The possibility that the *Ode to Joy* might become a shared European symbolic monument remained subject to such hybrid pressures — half national, half universal — which influenced and which continue to influence the ideological matrix prepared for its reception.

That being said, throughout the twentieth century the work's reception has also been influenced by the simple fact that, as time continues to elapse, the person and music of Beethoven become increasingly distant. Political readings of his work will always have to contend with his ever-greater anachronism in a rapidly, sometimes dizzyingly evolving world. It is hardly surprising that the voices raised, even those calling for revolution, are often highly conservative ones, particularly among the cultural elite who have given allegiance to the avant-garde notion of perpetual aesthetic renewal. In the Romantic era, the most advanced musicians had made Beethoven their idol and model; at the time of his centenary, the same group was not in the vanguard, their place being taken by politicians, musicologists, and a few academic composers. Following the Second World War, when some contemporary composer happened to show an interest in Beethoven it was as an icon of mass culture and not as an impetus to his own artistic experiments. In 1987, Andy Warhol, exploiting an image everywhere recognizable and everywhere the same, produced a *Beethoven* to signal the fact that the composer had more to do with Marilyn Monroe than with John Cage. This illustrated the banalization of the Beethoven mythos, a process that had, indeed, already bothered the Romantics even as they were creating it and that, with Nietzsche in particular, had succeeded in making the composer himself slightly suspect.

Warhol brings us up to the present day. It goes without saying that as long as Beethoven's works continue to be performed, the aesthetic pleasure they afford will be, by definition, contemporary, as music lovers the world over continue to experience it on a daily basis. Indeed, his status as an icon of classical music may itself continue to be an incitement to artistic creation and an object of historical research. Yet the question remains as to whether the immortal Beethoven is, in some way or another, already dying, or in danger of dying. Whatever the reply, an investigation into the relationships between the *Ode to Joy* and politics must today take that change into account if it is to be anything more than a mechanical repetition of clichés.

# The
# Birth
# of Modern
# Political
# Music

# 1

## God Save the King and the Handel Cult

The principal musical avatars of English political life appeared nearly simultaneously: 1739 first heard the official funeral music, with the "Dead March" from Handel's oratorio *Saul;* the following year came James Thomson and Thomas Arne's *Rule Britannia;* 1742 produced *Messiah,* with its "Hallelujah" chorus; and three years after that came *God Save the King,* a tune by an unknown author that no one yet thought to refer to as the "national anthem." It was no happenstance that such symbols all emerged within that short, six-year period, resounding out of a rapidly changing culture in which music was "a major metaphor for politics."[1] It was a time when the German Georg Friedrich Händel, naturalized in 1727 as Handel, had already been hailed by poets as the "English Orpheus" and his statue erected in London's Vauxhall Gardens by its impresario. Although the triumph of *God Save the King* was in part the work of the press — it was published in the first newspaper ever to have printed the records of parliamentary proceedings — the consecration of the composer of *Messiah* was the work of an elite who, with the support of modern notions of freedom and of public opinion, were awakening to the political implications inherent in discussions of national identity.

This did not turn the new melodies into pure embodiments of the "new." The tune of *God Save the King* goes back to at least the sixteenth century, and it had already been sung to honor a number of earlier rulers. Handel's admirers drew inspiration from men of the preceding century, men like Milton, Bolingbroke, or Pope. In 1698, a collection of Henry Purcell's songs had appeared with the title *The English Orpheus.* Made in a society marked by the rise of the bourgeoisie, Handel's career was to owe a great deal to his close connections with the monarchy. Shortly after his arrival in London in

1711, Queen Anne, the last reigning descendant of William III, had commissioned him to compose some works of an official nature. However, it was principally in association with the succeeding Hanoverian dynasty from Germany that the German Händel, former Kapellmeister to the court at Hanover, was to forge his career as Handel, the composer of British state music. Ever since the Glorious Revolution of 1688 against the Catholic Stuart dynasty, the dominant element in the concept of the English nation had been its Protestantism, which had worked in Parliament in favor of the Elector of Hanover, a Lutheran prince actually rather far down in the line of succession. Handel contributed to George the First's festivities, beginning with the *Te Deum* performed at his coronation in 1714. Three years later, an outing by the king on the River Thames occasioned a commission for the *Water Music,* a large-scale outdoor instrumental work. Appointed as composer to the Chapel Royal and awarded a life pension, Handel's role in the Hanoverian dynasty extended into the succeeding generation: he was professor to the royal princesses, and in 1727 he composed the *Coronation Anthems* for King George II and Queen Caroline. In 1749, to celebrate the signing of the Treaty of Aix-la-Chapelle, he composed the *Music for the Royal Fireworks.* To the end of his life, he was to turn out official compositions at regular intervals, and upon his death, in 1759, he was given the country's highest honor when his remains were laid to rest in Westminster Abbey.

For several decades, therefore, Handel was the principal purveyor of music to the British Crown. He exalted its greatness in highly skillful works of monumental scope whose style and genre have inextricable links with religious music. Of all of this output, in principle fated to become ephemera, *Zadok the Priest,* one of the 1727 anthems for chorus and orchestra, was to become most durably connected to subsequent royal ceremonies. Its text was drawn from the first Book of Kings:

> Zadok the Priest, and Nathan, the Prophet,
> Anointed Solomon King.
> And all the people rejoic'd, and said:
> God save the King, long live the King,
> May the King live for ever!
> Amen, Alleluja![2]

This biblical passage invokes the collective voice of the people in the form of a quotation of a prayer for the king on the occasion of his coronation — an utterance that the music renders via the brief and massive phrase of *God save the King, long live the King,* which is sung by the entire choir after a brief pause and prior to the contrapuntal jubilation leading to the concluding Alleluja:

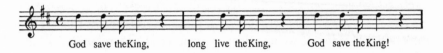

God save the King,     long live the King,     God save the King!

In one's mind, the collective voice is inseparable from the religious congregation, expressing itself through biblical quotation. As a practical matter, these accomplished works are always performed by professional musicians and in a strict ritual context, set off by orchestral fanfares. Thus, in principle, they represent the concrete participation of the subjects of his or her sovereign majesty — often at some distance, excluded as they are from the confined spaces where such ceremonies are held, in this case Westminster Abbey. Apart from the musicians themselves, who are not of course regarded as expressing their individual or personal feelings, there is nothing in Handel's official compositions to suggest that the English themselves should express their fidelity to the monarchy by actually raising their voices in song.

Indeed, although Handel came to assume a political dimension hitherto unknown in musical history, this did not happen because of his position as Crown musician but, rather, because of new ways and practices that made art more widely accessible and that gradually freed contemporary artistic production from aristocratic control and made it subject to the market laws of supply and demand. In 1720, the creation of the Royal Academy of Music, the opera company led by Handel under the king's patronage and with the backing of a group of noblemen, illustrated the adaptation of traditional patronage to a new kind of commercial enterprise. The emergence of a market for contemporary works immediately led to the establishment of a musical canon — a body of noncontemporary works which, forming a repertory interpreted by a trained and knowledgeable elite, came to be viewed as a paradigm of legitimate musical productions and practices. This was a conservative reaction that enjoyed the support of members of the upper aristocracy, who attributed to such works a moral value that could be extended to public life in general. In this regard, Handel's success was due principally to the way in which he managed to effect a link between the accepted canon and innovative works, beginning from a point that — both because of his German background and because of the style of his works —

was at the outset relatively ambiguous. Indeed, during the 1720s, the period of his rivalry with the Italian composer Bononcini, he was identified with Hanover and Germany, and thus with the official Protestant regime, in a contest with a rival who was backed by Catholic circles; yet both composers were vying for supremacy in the realm of "Italian" opera. The "foreign" and "effeminate" character of certain of the works performed at the King's Theatre under Handel's aegis, which featured castrati like Senesino, was to be denounced by a segment of London's elite who were eager to promote an art that would employ the English language and be more in keeping with the virility of the British character. "Would it not be a glorious thing to have an Opera of our own, in our most noble Tongue, in which the Composer, Singers, and Orchestra, would be of our own Grown?" as Daniel Defoe was to write in 1728.[3] Another author nostalgic for "the olden days when the English were men" and "their music grave and simple, like themselves" was to write in 1735: "We are in treaty with all the Princes of Europe to furnish us with Performers of every Country — in twenty unknown languages at least, so that we shall have Performers of every Nation in Europe — but our own."[4] And, in 1737, the newspaper *Common Sense* condemned Handel's theater as a "Sanctus Sanctorum of Nonsense," although that did not prevent him from going on to produce his Italian opera *Faramondo* there the following year.[5]

The criticisms aimed at Handel are remarkably parallel to the tensions that beset the reigning dynasty itself, founded by a monarch who did not speak English and who had little interest in English affairs. Some went so far as to attribute the decadence (real or imagined) of English dramatic poetry to the Hanoverian succession, which had set upon the throne princes who, ". . . not understanding our Language, have been very instrumental in introducing Sound and Show" — i.e., Italian opera.[6] The first Hanoverians were confronted with the so-called Patriot opposition, which, although basically loyal, engaged in a campaign — waged in newspapers like *Common Sense* — to give the monarchy a more "national" dimension. Thus, in a way, George II's and Handel's German accents, reflecting their shared geographical roots, had comparable effects at the political level. Where the composer was concerned, the polemic did not die down until he began to compose his large-scale English oratorios. If those works, however, met the expectations of the "religious nationalists" and went on to enjoy a great and lasting success, they did not do so solely because they were in English; they did so because they also offered a kind of "Biblical sublimity,"[7] in the form of large-scale epic tales enhanced by richly orchestrated music and, above all, a virtuosic handling of choral masses. The most famous of these monumental choral works is of course the "Hallelujah" chorus that closes the first part of *Messiah,* performed first in Dublin in 1742 and in London the following year. The text unfolds progressively, introduced by homophonic or unison phrases which then explode with powerful dramatic logic into a great contrapuntal rejoicing. There is a close relationship between the collective voice of *Zadok the Priest,* performed in public places to honor the king, and that raised in theaters to adore the Savior, "King of Kings, and Lord of Lords."

Reflecting the admiration of the period's intellectuals for Greek tragedy, the chorus thus moved to the forefront and became a collective character playing an important role in the story and often entrusted with voicing its moral. The notion that the biblical image of the people of Israel could be a metaphor for the English was daily announced in the Anglican liturgy, and it was easily grafted onto Handel's oratorios. Simply put, the English public found in monumental works such as *Israel in Egypt* an additional reason to believe that Providence protected them above all others. And that feeling was centered on the people, not the monarch; for, in keeping with the often hazy image of the Hanovers, in the oratorios the monarchs are invariably figures that are, to say the least, ambiguous. There is *Saul,* in which the king, eaten up with envy at David's triumphs, attempts to assassinate the young hero before being himself murdered, along with his son and his soldiers, by the Philistines. The funeral march sets the seal on the tragic end of a sovereign who had dared disobey God to satisfy his own desires, and it precedes the succession of David himself, who will himself execute the divine will — including the massacre of the Philistines, *one and all.*

Thus, the oratorios play out on an allegorical level that is constantly open to political readings, the latter a decisive element in their reception. Such readings were often contradictory, arising as they did out of differing political sensibilities, but this paradoxically gave rise to a consensus with regard to their deeper meaning, making the composer a kind of "catalyst of national unity."[8] Debates in which questions of musical aesthetics were linked to questions with moral and political import were naturally reflected in a press that claimed to deliver "common sense" to the public. On 14 October 1738, the newspaper *Common Sense* published an article on Handel's ode *Alexander's Feast,* which had been premiered at Covent Garden a short time before. The subject of that work, inspired by Dryden's 1697 *Ode to*

*Saint Cecilia,* was the power of the musician Timothy over Alexander the Great, conqueror of the Persians — an episode familiar to eighteenth-century musical experts. With regard to Alexander, we read:

> And Mr. Dryden, in his celebrated *Ode upon St. Caecilia's Day,* represents that Hero (Alexander), alternately affected, in the highest Degree, by tender or martial Sounds, now languishing in the *Arms* of his *Courtesan, Thais,* and anon *furious,* snatching a *Flambeau,* and *setting Fire to the Town of Persepolis.* This we have lately heard, set to Musick by the Great Mr. *Handel,* who, for a Modern, certainly excels in the *Ortios* or *Warlike Measure . . .*

Along with Plato and other classical writers, the author supports the idea that, working directly on the passions, musical modes and rhythms are a means of acting upon men, especially powerful men. Extending this observation from individuals to include nations, he applies his discourse on the *ethos* of music to the contemporary English scene:

> The Swiss, who are not a People of the quickest Sensations, have at this Time a Tune, which, when play'd upon their Fifes, inspires them with such a Love of their Country, that they run Home as fast as they can . . . Could such a Tune be composed here, it would then indeed be worth the Nation's While to pay the Piper . . . I would, therefore, most earnestly recommend it to the Learned Doctor Green [*sic*] to turn his Thoughts that way. — It is not from the least Distrust of Mr. *Handel's* Ability that I address myself preferably to Doctor *Green;* but Mr. *Handel,* having the Advantage to be by birth a *German,* might probably, even without intending it, mix some Modulations, in his Composition, which might give a *German* Tendency to the Mind, and therefore greatly lessen the National Benefit, I propose by it.[9]

In the eighteenth century, many others were bemused by the Swiss folk tune known as the *Ranz des vaches* [roughly, Bringing in the Herd]:

It could not be more different from official British melodies, whether from the pen of Handel or the aforementioned Maurice Greene, who was the organist at Saint Paul's Cathedral and musical director of the Chapel Royal. The two composers were rivals less out of nationality or musical style than for personal and political reasons. Greene was close to Horace Walpole, the prime minister, while his rival enjoyed the direct favor of George II. Nonetheless, Greene's "natural mode of expression, like Handel's, was founded on the cosmopolitan *lingua franca* of the day, an essentially Italianate style," and both men's anthems displayed a "spacious polyphony and massive grandeur which precisely typify the robust, self-confident spirit of the age." [10] That has little to do with the simple and pastoral old Swiss tune that was capable of inspiring love of country and was rooted in everyone's habits and memories, or — more concisely — in the national tradition. Yet how does one devise a traditional symbol? The article in *Common Sense* appears to suggest that such a tune can be created ex nihilo like any other piece of music, and that one need only call upon the composers producing official music — a logical reaction when it is a question of the link between music and nation. However, it also makes the creator's origins the key to the national "tendency," linking tradition to heredity and heredity to the national interest. The affair is one of the nation itself, seen as the true commissioner of the tune in question.

The 1738 article has been regarded as presaging *God Save the King* some seven years prior to the appearance of that melody on the public London scene. [11] In calling for an English *Ranz des vaches*, the author is aiming for something on a much larger scale: he envisions the piece being played at the opening of sessions of Parliament in place of the present prayers, regarded, he says, as "ineffective." From this point of view, even if he intends an instrumental composition and not a collective hymn, his proposal can be regarded as the first concept of a national anthem as state music. However, we must beware of such a retrospective reading when examining the actual history of the British anthem; we do not know that the article had any effect at all, for example, on Maurice Greene. [12] The emergence of *God Save the King* as the piece of English political music par excellence owes nothing to Greene, nor to Handel, nor yet to the proposal set forth in *Common Sense*. It is a direct outcome of the Jacobite rebellion of Charles Edward Stuart, the Young Pretender, thirty years after the first attempt led by his father, the Old Pretender. In the summer of 1745, Prince Charles landed in Scotland and, at the head of an army of highlanders, began a march on London with the aim of reclaiming the crown for the Stuart dynasty, which had been driven out in 1688. The military adventure posed little danger for George II, urgently summoned back from his estates in Hanover, but for a time London was gripped by panic. Loyalist resistance was organized throughout England, and volunteers signed up to defend the Protestant dynasty against the "Papist representatives," tacitly supported by France, the traditional absolutist and Catholic foe. Although waging war had hitherto been the business of professionals, principally mercenaries, both of the Jacobite rebellions planted the seed of a new notion of civil defense, of a "nation in arms," which was to become widespread when it came time to face the threat of a Napoleonic invasion.[13] And this activism was accompanied by a completely new kind of political propaganda to which Handel was to contribute with *Stand Round My Brave Boys,* a song for the London volunteers.

Such was the context in which, on 28 September 1745, following a performance of a comedy by Ben Jonson, the company of the Drury Lane Theatre first sang *God Save the King.* This ancient tune, of unknown origin, had already been sung in honor of the Stuarts in the days of the Glorious Revolution; later, it had been sung in secret for the same two Pretenders whom it was now intended to combat.[14] In deciding to draw upon a common patrimony, the theater's music director, Thomas Arne, may have been hoping to express just such a twist in meaning. In any event, the tune's pro-Catholic significance was soon forgotten in the wake of the Young Pretender's defeat at the hands of the Duke of Cumberland in February 1746 — an outcome hailed musically in the accepted forms of biblical allegory and state music — in this instance Handel's *Occasional Oratorio* and a *Te Deum* and anthem by Greene. Protestant tradition, indeed, was to retain only the first rendition of *God Save the King* for the Hanovers, in an arrangement for three soloists, chorus, and continuo. Here is the first verse:

God save our noble King
God save great George our King,
   God save the King.
Send him victorious
Happy and glorious,
Long to reign over us,
   God save the King.

*God Save the King* begins with the same biblical phrase as *Zadok the Priest,* representing the voice of the people, but it is now pronounced by the song's subject. It is still a prayer, but now it is a prayer by "us," addressing God for the safety of "our" King and asking for collective well-being. Second verse:

> O Lord our God arise,
> Scatter his enemies
>     And make them fall:
> Confound their politicks,
> Frustrate their knavish tricks,
> On him our hopes are fix'd
>     O save us all.

Divine protection of the king's person is invoked in the face of a political and military threat posed against the community as a whole, which, in 1745, was a direct reference to the Jacobite crisis. Third verse:

> The choicest gifts in store
> On him be pleased to pour,
>     Long may he reign.
> May he defend our laws,
> And ever give us cause,
> With heart and voice to sing,
>     God save the King.

The last verse is the only one dating from 1745. In praying God to preserve the king as the guarantor of law, *God Save the King* voices the principle that, replacing the old doctrine of divine right, had inspired the Glorious Revolution and the Hanoverian succession itself: "A religious foundation of monarchy and the idea of a contract between ruler and ruled were thus, at least in theory, satisfactorily squared." [15] *With heart and voice to sing:* the idea of a British nation protected by Providence and supporting its king only insofar as he remained faithful to his constitutional mission is embodied in a collective anthem that allows each individual voice to project its personal feelings into the public sphere. *God Save the King* is both a "necessary anthem," a product of the crisis, and the musical and poetic synthesis of a whole political culture.

The public greeted the anthem with an enthusiasm inspired by the country's situation, as the *Daily Advertiser* reported:

> On Saturday Night last the Audience at the Theatre Royal in Drury Lane were agreeably surpriz'd by the Gentlemen belonging to that House per-

forming the Anthem of God save our noble King. The universal Applause it met with, being encored with repeated Hurras, sufficiently de-
noted in how just an Abhorrence they hold the arbitrary Schemes of our
invidious Enemies, and detest the despotick Attempts of Papal Power.[16]

A few days later, *God Save the King* was also sung at Covent Garden in
an arrangement by Charles Burney, Thomas Arne's young pupil, who was
to become one of the earliest music historians. In October, the *Gentlemen's
Magazine,* the first publication to have printed Parliamentary debates, included it in one of its issues, and shortly thereafter, the *London Magazine*
followed suit. Those two publications were to mark an important turning
point: henceforth, members of the public were no longer content merely to
listen to the new tune but began to sing it themselves. Thus, through the
dual agencies of theater and press, as both political manifesto and economic
commodity, *God Save the King* worked its way into the heart of English political life. The phenomenon's novelty is brought out by the use of the term
"anthem," which cannot be explained solely by the tune's generic nature.
The word "anthem" was used, in principle, to designate religious music
employed as part of the ritual and not sung by the congregation — unlike
the psalms and hymns which began to abound during this same period,
largely thanks to the Methodists.[17] On the other hand, the use of the word
to describe a song honoring the king is a direct reference to the "anthems"
of a Handel or Greene, which had always implied an indissoluble bond between kingly ceremony and religious ritual. The transfer of the term "anthem" from the domain of religion to one that was entirely political
"confirms just how closely patriotic identity in Great Britain was yoked to
religion."[18] At the same time, it signals the creation of a discourse in which
the nation is regarded as sacred, a discourse with links to a religious realm
but henceforth adopted and employed by the public sphere. Indeed, apart
from a few isolated attempts (roundly denounced by the Puritans), *God
Save the King* has never become a part of the liturgy.

Having said that, *God Save the King* was not accepted first and foremost
as a truly communal anthem; under George II, for example, we have no
record that describes congregational singing, nor do we find it used as a
communal anthem in any form of civil religious ceremony. Although the
tune began to be played fairly early on — at least by 1749 — when the king
was present, becoming a de facto element in various ceremonies, its use for
official purposes would seem, in the beginning, to have been fairly haphaz-

ard — and, indeed, it has to this day never been formally sanctioned for such use, the English preferring in this instance — as in so many others — to rely on tradition.[19] English historiography readily claims that "on that Saturday night in September 1745 the British 'invented national Anthems,'"[20] but the date is fairly arbitrary and linked to the founding myth of the Protestant nation in its final victory over the Catholics. Instead of bursting onto the scene on a specific day during the Jacobite crisis, the real adoption of *God Save the King* as the national anthem occurred gradually throughout the reign of George III, who was crowned in 1760 after his grandfather's death. It spread almost inorganically through both society and the state. Nearly a half century after the Jacobite rebellion, this lack of formal acceptance was to be described by Franz-Joseph Haydn, who copied out the score and noted:

> Lord Clermont [Claremont] once gave a large Soupé, and when the King's health was drunk, he ordered a wind band to play the well-known song "God Save the King" in the street during a wild snowstorm. This occurred on 19th Feby 1792, so madly do they drink in England.[21]

Such excessive enthusiasm shows that *God Save the King* was obviously, by definition, a manifestation of loyalty to the king and the political system. However, the French Revolution was to inspire a number of parodies of it, both for and against the Jacobins, and with a spontaneity that foreshadowed what was to become its widespread usage: as a sign to be brandished in the political arena, taken over and adapted by any one who wished to make use of it. True, the earliest of such agencies was to be the Crown. In 1809 and 1814, George III's golden jubilee and the centenary of the Hanoverian succession were both celebrated throughout the realm. Directly based on the *fêtes* of the French Revolution, parades and performances were staged at which *God Save the King* was sung by young women clad as Britannia.[22] The inclusion of the tune in state ceremonies was confirmed in 1821 during the coronation of George IV, when it was quoted in the *Coronation Anthem* composed by Thomas Attwood — a way of paying a tribute to its already traditional status while continuing the tradition of large-scale official state compositions. Having said that, in 1819, *God Save the King* was sung in Manchester at a demonstration in support of universal male suffrage that the authorities regarded as seditious. Henceforth, invocation of the symbol was to afford a kind of legitimacy to anyone seeking to identify themselves with the nation, even when it was used to question the prevailing concept of that nation. It was during that period that the term "national anthem" began to gain currency, and the first attempt was made to record its history when, in 1822, Richard Clark published a pamphlet, *An Account of the National Anthem Entitled God Save the King.*[23]

The work spread abroad in a similar manner. From 1760 on, the tune was played at theatrical performances in America, although often twisted by the insurgent colonists, who used it to hymn revolution with, for example, the words *God save great Washington* or with the simple title *America*.[24] It was also well known on the Continent in a number of versions, which, while remaining faithful to the monarchical spirit of the original, varied according to political and ideological circumstances. The oldest of these translations is probably one dated 1763, in Dutch, which appeared in *La Lire maçonne* printed in the Netherlands.[25] In 1782, in Kiel, the student August Niemann wrote the first German version, *Heil, Kaiser Joseph, Heil!*, in honor of the emperor Joseph II. *God Save the King* was thus absorbed into the Enlightenment and into one of its more important elements, the Masonic lodge. Fourteen years later, Niemann was to produce a new version with a nationalistic slant in which, in the final verse, the figure of the fatherland replaced that of the king: *Heil, Deutschland, Heil!* At Flensburg, in 1790, Heinrich Harries, another student, published an anthem honoring Christian VII, king of Denmark and Norway, based on the melody, which he described as an English *Volkslied;* in it, the king appears not as the guarantor of the law but as "father of the people." Three years later, Balthasar Gerhard Schumacher adapted Harries' verses to fit Friedrich Wilhelm II, the king of Prussia. Now called *Heil Dir im Siegerkranz,* the tune was sung in public for the first time, on 5 May 1795 at Berlin's Nationaltheater. The occasion was a fitting one: it was the king's birthday, and his troops had just won a fleeting victory over Bonaparte's army, which explains the reference to the victorious crowning in the first verse:

| | |
|---|---|
| *Heil Dir im Siegerkranz,* | Hail to thee, victoriously crowned, |
| *Herrscher des Vaterlands,* | Leader of the Fatherland, |
| *Heil, König, Dir!* | Hail thee, o King! |
| *Fühl in des Thrones Glanz,* | In the splendour of thy radiant throne |
| *Die hohe Wonne ganz* | May thee fully realize the glory |
| *Liebling des Volkes zu sein.* | Of thy peoples' favor. |
| *Heil, König, Dir!* | Hail thee, o King![26] |

Thus, with a few "Germanizing" variations, *God Save the King* was soon being utilized in other German states — in Bavaria, for example, to honor Maximilian I, whom Napoleon placed on the throne in 1806. However, *Heil Dir im Siegerkranz* was not actually to be adopted as the Prussian state anthem until the wars of liberation in 1813–1815, after which Hanover, Saxony, Brunswick, Weimar, and Luxembourg followed suit; thus, the melody of the British anthem, whose origins were often forgotten, was to be the symbol of the German states throughout the nineteenth century. In Switzerland, the German-speaking cantons adopted a version entitled *Rufst du, mein Vaterland?* [Are you calling, my Fatherland?] written in 1811. As was the case in the United States, the image of the king was replaced by that of the fatherland, whose "children" respond "with heart and hand" (*mit Herz und Hand*) — a pact to defend the country militarily replacing the "heart and voice" of 1745. This highly republican promise, which probably indicates the spread of *La Marseillaise* beyond French borders, was also made in the country's French-speaking regions:

| | |
|---|---|
| *Ô monts indépendants,* | O free mountains, |
| *Répétez nos accents,* | Echo our voices, |
| *Nos libres chants!* | Our songs of freedom! |
| *À toi, patrie,* | Thine, our homeland, |
| *Suisse chérie,* | Beloved Switzerland, |
| *Le sang, la vie* | Are the blood and lives |
| *De tes enfants.* | Of thy children.[27] |

Yet at a time when the French foe was threatening every monarchy in Europe, the tune of *God Save the King* continued to be more firmly linked to thrones than to republics. In Russia, the tsar adopted it as his official anthem. It is that dynastic logic, rather than some notion of nationhood, that appears to have inspired the continental spread of the English tune in a nascent public sphere still tightly controlled by police states. *God Save the King*, in all its translations and variations, can thus be said to embody a type of music that is totally political and to be a patriotic or loyalist manifesto closely tied to the dynastic universe that, in 1814, was to gather at Vienna to set the seal on the Concert of Europe.

At the time, however, there were long-standing doubts about the "national" character of the Hanoverian dynasty. George III was the first of his line to have been born in England, and, from his coronation on, he took

pains to emphasize this in a number of ways. They became even more evident after America's declaration of independence in 1776 and the ensuing
war, a setback that had the paradoxical and indirect effect of strengthening
British identity via "a far more consciously and officially constructed patriotism."[28] This development assuredly played a part in Handel's definitive
consecration as the symbol of national greatness. His cosmopolitan nature,
far from posing a handicap, was now viewed as an additional guarantee of
his ability to remain above parties; following the loss of the American colonies, he was to be hailed as "the harmonic strength of Europe."[29] In 1780,
a pastor "found" that the custom of standing for the "Hallelujah" chorus —
extended to the *Dead March* and *God Save the King*— had been begun by
George II's enthusiastic reaction to the piece at *Messiah*'s first London performance in 1743; although it is based on the flimsiest of evidence, the anecdote became a part of the legend as final proof of the English monarchs'
devotion to the composer's cult.[30] Handelian fervor was to crest in 1784
with a huge festival for the hundredth anniversary of his birth: there were
five days of concerts, which opened with *Zadok the Priest* and culminated
in a performance of *Messiah* in Westminster Abbey in which five hundred
musicians took part, an unheard-of number at the time. The event inevitably aroused some suspicions; one poet ironically took note of the thousands
of "commemoration-mad" spectators who, taken in by the weird mixture
of music and religion, were praying to Handel rather than to the Messiah.[31]
However, the Puritans notwithstanding, it was "a broad-based political
spectrum of an essentially conservative nature" that rallied around the composer in 1784; the aristocratic members of the *Concert of Antient Music,*
nearly two-thirds of whose repertoire consisted of Handel's compositions,
thus joined the bourgeois who had become familiar with the oratorios at the
many local festivals with their strong religious flavor.[32] And at their head
was George III, "the nation's leading Handelian," intent on redefining the
British monarchy in national terms.[33] Such a redefinition implied not only
an emphasis on the monarch's nationality but also on his private life and artistic proclivities, in short, on his humanization. Thus, a basically private
pleasure based on a music held to be superior to mundane pleasures —
which still meant the Italian opera — was presented to society as a veritable
lesson in morality. The king himself entrusted Charles Burney with writing
a history of the Great Commemoration of 1784,[34] which was to be repeated
in succeeding years, interrupted in 1791, and taken up again in the nineteenth century, reaching its apogee in the Victorian era — a period when, it

should be recalled, the splendor of official ceremonies far outshone those held under the Hanovers.[35] At the death of George III, however, just as Great Britain was about to become a hegemonic power on a world scale, the linkage of the monarch's image with Handel's enthronement, as well as the fundamentally conservative spirit underlying the idea, were stated with almost startling clarity in an obituary published in the *London Magazine:*

> The true constituents of Handel's style were in perfect accord with the element of the King's faculties, constitution and habits. Robust by nature, his pleasures (even his intellectual pleasures) were all manly; his sensations were too hearty and sincere to admit much sophistication — too healthful to need the provocatives exhibited by modern art — too regulated to endure the invitations which such words and music, as have lately been most admired, administer to vice in its most dangerous and alluring forms. The King was moral, even in music.[36]

# 2

## La Marseillaise and
## the "Supreme Being"

Jean-Jacques Rousseau, in his *Essai sur l'origine des langues* [Essay on the Origin of Languages], wrote that the primal power of music, prior to its inevitable degeneration, was its ability to move us. Song was the fusional instant in which individuals gathered together "around the fountain" to give free expression to their emotions.[1] Within the primitive community, the contradiction between law and liberty was dissolved in the primal fusion of music and poetry. "The earliest songs of every nation are canticles or hymns," Rousseau wrote in the *Dictionnaire de musique.*[2] We can almost say that his social contract itself is based on anthems. The idyllic picture Rousseau paints is similar to the vision of "public entertainments" he described in his *Lettre à d'Alembert,* a vision of ideal republican fêtes inspired by Plutarch and by Rousseau's memories of his own Geneva childhood.[3] The "spectator become spectacle" reveals his most intimate thoughts to the compassionate ears of his fellow man, and joining in are the elderly, men, and children, creating and ensuring unity among the generations and the permanence of common values. Music, viewed as the language of the emotions, is both the symbol and the instrument of a utopian social order in which subjective emotion assists in the establishment of the collectivity.

This bond between the personal and the social is expressed most vividly in song, preferably in unison song, for, as Rousseau says, "it is the most natural, and, hence, the best."[4] However, it can also be created by an instrumental melody, as evidenced by the *Ranz des vaches,* "that tune so beloved of the Swiss that its performance before the military audience [composed of hired mercenaries] was forbidden on pain of death, for so keenly did it inspire the troops with a burning desire to see their country again that, hearing it, they burst into tears, deserted, or perished on the spot." The reasons for this were not to be found in the nature of the tune itself: "Such effects, which have no influence whatsoever on foreigners, arise solely from custom, memories, the thousand circumstances of which the tune reminds those who hear it, recalling to them their country, their former pleasures, their youth and all their ways of life, and awakening within them a bitter sorrow at having lost it all."[5] Love of country, exacerbated by music, outweighed in the mercenaries' hearts their obedience to any foreign sovereign. Tears, desertion, and death are extreme forms of fidelity to a republican law, making this community kin to those that raised their voices in song around the fountain of languages. And Rousseau adds: "Thus, *Music* does not act merely as *Music,* but, rather, as a memorative sign." The statement is a prelude to the relegation of political music, a "memorative sign" performed in the communal sphere, to the outskirts of the artistic realm.

Rousseau's picture becomes less idyllic when, inspired by Greek and Roman antiquity, he turns to ways in which symbolism can be manipulated within a real society. The concept of civil religion adumbrated in *The Social Contract* is set forth in more detail in his *Considérations sur le gouvernement de la Pologne* [Thoughts Regarding the Government of Poland]. The state is to be responsible for the development of the national character, conceived as the counterpart to some uniform European character: "Today, no matter what they say, we no longer have Frenchmen, Germans, Spaniards, not even English; all that we have are Europeans. They share the same tastes, the same passions, the same customs, for none of them has been set in a national mold by some particular institution." This creation of the national, made permanent through its monuments, includes the cult of past heroes and the commemoration of important historical events. The mechanical reproduction of patriotic feelings calls for uniformity in the subjective relationship to the collectivity: "When an infant opens its eyes it should see the fatherland, and only it, until its death."[6]

The contrast between the spontaneity of the *Essai* and the strict formality of the *Considérations* forecasts the paradox of patriotic republican song. True, the later text does not explicitly proscribe communal singing, which suggests that Rousseau regarded it as more closely connected to some mythical happy past than to contemporary society, which had departed from the state of nature. However, the men of the French Revolution, who were directly inspired by Rousseau, were to make anthems an essential part of their republican celebrations or fêtes. "Let there be no mistake: it is not a question of mere tunes, but of the communion of souls, represented by voices raised in unison," wrote Julien Tiersot.[7] His words go to the heart of the Revolution's musical plans, which culminated in the *Fête de la Fédération* of 14 July 1790. They also directly concern the myth surrounding *La Marseillaise*. Those plans and that myth both entailed creating for the nation a single voice.

Just as in England, the nation's voice is that of a "we," an "us"—a pronoun that eschews the established genres of monarchical state music and becomes the grammatical indication of the people's transformation into a political subject. It is this, perhaps, that *God Save the King* and the *Marseillaise*, both of which are models for every other modern national anthem, have in common. However, the anthems that proliferated in revolutionary France were very different from the English prayer, which is firmly anchored in tradition. Reflecting an event that ushered in a new era in world history, the French contributions all emphasize the break with the ancien régime. The Revolution represents the replacement of royal sovereignty by a new ruling figure, that of the people-nation, the body that will, according to the law drawn up to express the general will, constitute a Republic that is "one and indivisible." The nation's one voice is directly linked to the "revolutionary religion of unity."[8] And in that, the *Marseillaise* was to play a most decisive role, even though it was not, a priori, included in the musical programs of the Revolution's fêtes — which featured anthems by Gossec, Méhul, Lesueur, Cherubini, and other composers of the Institut National de Musique that had been established in 1793. It has been noted that the distinctive feature — and in a way the key to the success — of Rouget de Lisle's tune, in contrast to other traditional songs, resides in a new formal element — the lead-up to the refrain — which gives the line "Aux armes, citoyens" [To arms, citizens] the performative effect of a "political rallying cry."[9] It was this cry that official musical utopia was to attempt to incorporate, bringing it into the repertory as a popular expression that would extend to all state music. That being said, it is no easy matter to make an entire people sing in unison. The singing of revolutionary anthems was to oscillate between the representation of the collective voice in works composed for professional musicians and attempts to bring the populace itself to raise its voice in song. The various attempts were often colored by practical questions, but they also all bear the trace of political debates about popular participation in general and, consequently, about the status of democracy.

The idea of a people hymning liberty in unison because of the Revolution predates the *Marseillaise* and was, at least in the beginning, independent of the state. This was clearly expressed in the press on the eve of the *Fête de la Fédération.* While work was underway to prepare the Champ-de-Mars for the celebrations and the revolutionary song *Ça ira* was being sung everywhere as a rallying cry, one newspaper suggested that "there be sung in French an anthem in praise of liberty set to music by a famous composer," adding that "the *Te Deum* might precede the swearing of the civil oath and the anthem would conclude the ceremony," so as to connect the old with the new.[10] On 8 July, the *Chronique de Paris* took up the notion, for the day was near when "twenty-four million men would pledge themselves, at the same hour, to liberty." At this juncture, however, it was suggested that the *Te Deum* be eliminated, since that work, in Latin, "had been ordered sung by tyrants, sung for crimes, sung for petty trifles." The author called for the composition of a new hymn in French, following the example of Jewish and Roman antiquity, "a canticle as simple and forceful as the oath itself, great and majestic as the 14th of July": "Let its performance be a simple one! Young boys *untonsured;* young girls as innocent as liberty, will sing the hymn to the God of liberty. A refrain will be taken up by the choir, a chorus of twenty-four million men."[11]

In these 1790 newspaper articles, the whole notion of the voice of the people is already present, especially in the vision of a choir twenty-four million strong. We find several breaks with traditional practice: a linguistic one, Latin being replaced by French; a thematic one with the transition from invoking the Christian God to invoking the God of liberty — or indeed "god of liberty"; a stylistic one, calling for a "canticle" with the classical virtues of grandeur and simplicity; and, lastly, a difference in performance or utterance with the elimination of the barrier between musicians and nonmusicians and the establishment of a collective subject of the anthem, the united voice of the people composed of its individual members all assembled. Those individuals were to swear an oath, that classical "sacred act of social contract" which, foreshadowed in 1785 in Jacques-Louis David's *The Oath of the Horatii,* was to be part of every revolutionary rite from the Tennis Court Oath on.[12] Of course, the radical novelty of such a plan did not escape the notice of contemporaries: "A regenerated people, a people celebrating the conquest of liberty, must speak in a new tongue," proclaimed the *Chronique de Paris.*[13]

In the aftermath of the *Fête de la Fédération,* however, the newspaper *Les Révolutions de Paris* was forced to note, with a touch of disappointment: "It would have been a revolution in a religious and civil ceremony to substitute our mother tongue for Latin, and a beautiful hymn by one of our poets for the old *Te Deum!*" [14] That revolution was not to occur in 1790. After Talleyrand had celebrated mass and the solemn oath had been taken by King Louis XVI and the president of the Assemblée Nationale, the people listened, just as they had in the past, to a religious work sung in harmonized Gregorian chant, and in Latin. François-Joseph Gossec's *Te Deum* was performed by professional musicians and students from the École Royale de Chant, led by the composer, who was described by *Le Moniteur* as "the religious precentor." [15] The assembled *fédérés* were not invited to join in. The *Te Deum* itself, however, sung and played in the open air, was hardly the same one that had been performed in churches under the ancien régime. The huge choir and wind orchestra were backed by a large percussion section that was augmented at the end by a discharge of artillery. The final apotheosis also saw a significant addition to the text: the image of the nation, *Domine salvum fac gentem,* was added after *Domine salvum fac legem* and preceding the traditional *Domine salvum fac regem* — introducing a new trinity of nation, law, and king that we can read as an echo, albeit fleeting, of the spirit of *God Save the King.* The national community thus made its entry into official state music, even though a great deal more would have to happen before a "chorus of twenty-four million" would actually be brought together in any literal sense.

However, the poet Marie-Joseph Chénier, in keeping with the wishes expressed by *La Chronique de Paris,* had already written, in French, a *Hymne pour la fête de la Fédération,* an ode of twenty-six quatrains: its length and style make it clear that Chénier's idea had not been to rouse the people to break into song. Indeed, his text is unsuited to singing, even by professional musicians. Nevertheless, three of its verses were set to music a year later by the omnipresent Gossec. The *Chant du 14 Juillet* is a far different matter than the *Te Deum:* it includes no Gregorian chant, nor are there any instrumental interludes. Instead, after a short introduction, we find a single melodic line over a very basic harmony and an accompaniment whose fanfares give the work a typically military flavor.

This composition, which still praises "the God of the people and of Kings," presages the anthems that were to proliferate under the Republic. Those revolutionary hymns were strongly influenced by the music of Gluck's operas, especially his "reformed" choruses composed to conform to the prosody of the texts. Yet the orchestrations for wind instruments, the use of military flourishes, the need to ensure that the words would be understood, the open-air performances — the whole performative function itself as part of a participatory liturgical exercise — made such music markedly different from that of opera. Indeed, the anthems cannot be reduced to a single form, their main common characteristic being a negative one related to their avoidance of Gregorian chant and Palestrinian polyphony. The various influences they exhibit, from military music to a certain religious background, including pastoral forms and the "terrible fervor" of which the composer Grétry made mention,[16] not to mention some of the elements to be found in Masonic music, are fairly good evidence of the ideological oscillations of the revolutionary cult, all within the overall framework of neoclassicism, which David was employing in the plastic arts and which was to become the official art of the republican government.

None of this, however, necessarily made such works suitable for communal singing. The melodic line of the anthems Gossec composed to Chénier's texts, which make up the bulk of the official hymns composed up until 1793, does not exclude popular participation a priori, but the works were not composed with that in mind. In the early days, the revolutionary authorities do not appear to have made any great effort to facilitate "popular" participation, either by adapting the new pieces to popular modes of performance or by incorporating popular music into the official canon — despite the fact that in France at that time there was a wealth of such tunes, a virtual boom in political music. However, the question of participation in revolutionary celebrations began to be a subject for discussion and to reflect political differences. In the spring of 1792, the sans-culottes and the patriotic clubs organized a celebration in honor of the Swiss uprising at Châteauvieux at which the *Choeur à la Liberté* and a *Ronde nationale* were sung. *Les Révolutions de Paris* reported the event: "There was no question of marching in cadence; only the choirs kept together, but that was sufficient."[17] The almost orgiastic note was in contrast to the outright militarism that the same newspaper reported a short time later during the Fête of the Law that had been organized by the Feuillant-controlled government to honor the mayor, Simonneau, who had been killed during a riot. Both the *Triomphe de la loi,* to a text by Roucher, and the two poems of Marie-Joseph Chénier written for the Chateauvieux celebrations were set to music by Gossec, and it cannot be said that the first piece is the more difficult of the three. So far, music seemed to be flirting with popular participation, appearing to solicit it while at the same time keeping it at a distance, but without actually abandoning the carefully planned nature of performances or the professional status of the musicians who took part in them.

This state of affairs began to change with the declaration of war on 20 April 1792, which presented new challenges for the civil liturgies, and with the appearance of the *Marseillaise,* which set a new model for political music. The link between the two events is obvious, not only from the work's tone, its title, and the circumstances surrounding the composition of Rouget de Lisle's piece on 25 April 1792, but from the actual text of the *Marseillaise,* the *Chant de guerre pour l'armée du Rhin* [War Song for the Army of the Rhine], which contains a similar call to arms to the people of Strasbourg: "Aux armes, citoyens! L'étendard de la guerre est déployé; le signal est donné. Aux armes! il faut combattre, vaincre ou mourir. Aux armes, citoyens! Si nous persistons à être libres, toutes les puissances de l'Europe verront échouer leurs sinistres complots" [To arms, citizens! The flag of war is unfurled; the signal is given. To arms! we must fight, conquer or die. To arms, citizens! If we persist in freedom, every power in Europe will find its sinister plans foiled!].[18] The political tenor of the refrain mentions a trumpet call, evoking the performative nature of musical signals in the military. Such an apparent abandonment of "art," emphasized by the fact that its author was an amateur composer, played a part in the spread of the *Marseillaise* at the time of the Revolution and in the legend that was to grow up around it. Its spread from Strasbourg and Marseilles to Paris, from Valmy and Jemmapes to every revolutionary battlefield, reveals how promptly it was put to military and political use, an incorporation that was accomplished not only by the authorities but by the republican populace as a whole, the latter embodied in the famous Marseilles battalion that, according to legend, burst into the Tuileries on 10 August 1792 singing the anthem's fearsome, terrible couplets.

Yet the *Chant de guerre pour l'armée du Rhin* had its origins within the power structure itself. The mayor of Strasbourg, a solid, upper-middle-class citizen from a noble Protestant family and friendly with the philosophes, loathed the revolutionary *Ça ira* and deplored its popularity; it was, therefore, a recognized authority figure who commissioned a well-known musician and a poet known for his mastery of the new trends in patriotic music to create something to counterbalance a hugely popular tune — Rouget de Lisle had already, in 1791, written a *Hymne à la Liberté* that had been set to music by Ignace Pleyel. A few days later, the new tune was performed in the public square at Strasbourg by the band of the national guard. Thus, the revolutionary tune par excellence began its public career as official music. An observation by the mayor's wife helps to explain its successful reception at the stylistic level: "It's Gluck but better, more lively, brisker." [19] Although the song was immediately to find favor with the "people," it had been composed by an officer in the engineering corps, a man of aristocratic birth. "*La Marseillaise* is the point at which the two principal trends in revolutionary music — anthems and popular song — were to meet. An anthem owing to its strongly ideological words and its rapid acceptance; a song because of its magnificently simple music, so perfectly wedded to the text and, as a result, highly expressive." [20] It presented no competition either to Gossec or to the *Ça ira,* it was "different": different in a geographical sense, because it had spread throughout the hinterlands before its triumphant success in Paris; different in a biographical sense, because of its author's ambiguous standing, half amateur, half professional; different in an institutional sense owing to its having been semiofficially commissioned; and, lastly, different in the stylistic sense, "Gluck but better," which meant that, with some few adjustments, everyone could join in when it was sung at official celebrations. To complete the catalogue of what made it different, Rouget de Lisle's words, with their open glorification of victory and annihilation of one's foe, deviated from both the Strasbourg proclamation and large-scale revolutionary rituals by omitting the famous portion of the oath that called for a willingness to perish for the fatherland.

During the summer of 1792, the *Marseillaise* invaded the street, the press, the theaters and even the private sphere in Paris. However, it was in Gossec's arrangement of it as part of the patriotic tableau entitled *L'Offrande à la Liberté* [The Offering to Liberty], which was performed at the Opéra on 30 September 1792, that "the religious aspect of the 'sacred love for the Fatherland' was brought to the fore, a pendant to its bellicose side." [21] In October, the newspaper *Feuille villageoise* referred to the *Marseillaise* as the "national anthem" — probably the first use of the term — and remarked that the anthem "brings together so many great ideas that it should truly be sung with a kind of religious decorum." [22] This religious connotation coincided with its inclusion in official ceremonies. Following the battle of Valmy, the minister of war proposed that the army of Belgium sing the *Marseillaise;* on 14 October 1792, in Paris, the celebration of the victory over Savoy saw the tune's first integration into an official republican celebration: "The song of the Marseilles warriors, now the Republic's anthem, was enthusiastically intoned," reported *Le Moniteur*.[23] It was also on that occasion that the so-called *strophe des enfants,* or "children's verse," was heard for the first time, the final lines of which introduce the "oath" theme absent in the original: "Nous aurons le sublime orgueil / De les venger ou de les suivre" [Ours the sublime pride / Of avenging or of following them].

The reception of the *Marseillaise* outside the borders of France was to contribute directly to its new status as a republican symbol: the song became a symbolic rallying cry for republicans everywhere — English, German, Austrian, Italian, and Polish — who had it translated and printed in countless editions and who sang it at gatherings that were more or less clandestine. In 1794, the musical score arrived in Buenos Aires, where it became the model for all revolutionary music in a Latin America in revolt against the Spanish Crown. Thus began the process that was, throughout the course of the nineteenth century, to make it the republican anthem par excellence as well as the centerpiece of a whole ream of political musical compositions as varied as Belgium's *La Brabançonne* and the communist *Internationale.* The sacralizing imprint of the Republic did not save it from being subjected to some anti-republican and anti-French transformations: as early as 1792, a German translation changed it to the *Schlachtlied der Deutschen* [German Battle Hymn], an imitation of the original French title;[24] at Valmy, the Prussian crown prince had taken great pains to obtain a copy of the music, remarking to the person who managed to bring him the complete score (according to legend): "You could have forgotten the words."[25] At Mainz, the *Marseillaise* was still being sung before six thousand men drawn up on parade eight months after the town had fallen to the Prussians and, according to Norbert Cornelissen, "in the presence of more than one hundred and fifty Prussian officers of all ranks, some of them generals, who had it performed three times or more, apparently unaware of the irritation and embarrassment it was creating among the French émigrés in attendance."[26] In 1798, a man named Karl Herklots wrote a poem to the tune of the *Marseillaise* for the coronation of the Prussian King Friedrich Wilhelm III. And although none of these anti-French versions ever truly caught hold, we cannot ignore their significance. The *Marseillaise* is, and will remain, the republican musical symbol par excellence; at the same time, it also proposed a new model for political music to the subjects of Europe's other monarchies, called upon to wage a symbolic combat that was in some ways similar to the one waged by the French revolutionaries. The story of

Mainz shows that, for the Prussians at least, the piece was not, at least not originally, solely reminiscent of the revolutionary period so loathed by the French aristocracy but, rather, something that piqued their curiosity and, indeed, aroused their admiration. There followed a stream of political musical compositions that, anti-French as they were, still brought touches of the *Marseillaise* to various parts of Europe. The tune's political connotations were also to seep into so-called pure music: as early as 1795, instrumental variations on the melody were published in Germany, the first of a long series of clever appropriations and quotations in a list that would eventually include, among many others, the names of Schumann and Wagner. "It is most disingenuous to say that this anthem is only sung in France; it is sung wherever one finds friends of liberty: the tune and its accompaniment are sung wherever men are sensible of the charms of music," Cornelissen was to write in 1796. The musical charms of the *Marseillaise:* the work is a truly European object, one that characterizes the era of revolutionary wars.

In France, the appearance of the *Marseillaise* markedly changed the landscape of civil ceremonies and gradually led to the notion of a single, unique musical symbol. To begin with, its circulation was far wider than that of any other song, both with its original text and set to other words (some two hundred different versions have been recorded in France alone), which made it at once an aide-mémoire and gave it legitimacy. Secondly, it was to furnish a new model to the organizers of revolutionary celebrations, eager to find a way to connect the abstract exaltation of the universal values of liberty or equality to a thematic or bellicose theme directed against an outside enemy often bundled into the single word "Europe." The tenth of August 1793 saw the *Fête de l'unité et de l'indivisibilité de la République* [Celebration of the Republic's Unity and Indivisibility], the first of the large-scale celebrations to be stage-managed by David, who laid before the Convention a plan in which popular participation in the festival's musical portion was officially specified for the first time.[27] There was still provision for the premieres of several Gossec anthems composed along the accustomed lines, but the ceremony was also to include a gigantic five-part procession ending up at the Champ-de-Mars with the *Air des Marseillais* to be played in an arrangement by Gossec and with a new text by Varon that concluded with the refrain: "Courage, citoyens, formez vos bataillons / Du sang des rois abreuvez vos sillons!" [Courage, citizens, form your battalions / Let your gutters run with the blood of kings!]. The overturning of the monarchy thus became part of the text of the *Marseillaise,* bringing the symbolic status of the "republican anthem" into line with its literal meaning, and the resultant symbol was now to be performed at the culminating moment of the republican rite, preceding the sermon to be delivered from the altar of the fatherland by the president of the Convention Nationale: "Now, as we are creating France, Europe attacks it from every side; LET US SWEAR to defend the constitution until death! The Republic is eternal."[28] Republican anthems were to retain their central role during the period of the so-called Cult of Reason, when they were explicitly utilized to replace Catholic plain-chant; it was also at this time that the plan for regular communal singing at the national level began to take shape with the appearance of "militant an-thems" to be sung at tenth-day (the so-called *décadaire*) ceremonies. At the Fête of 20 Brumaire, the *Journal de Paris* described an anthem to Reason by Chénier and Gossec, sung "by the entire Convention" and by "every Section."[29] There is no way of knowing how the Convention managed to participate in singing this music, which had probably never been heard prior to the event; the uniting of representatives and people in joint song, a metaphor for the Republic's institutional health, is too idyllic not to be taken with a grain of salt. Indeed, a few weeks later, Danton — who had nev-ertheless willingly accepted the notion of music being used to "decorate" the Revolution — rebuked some Parisian Section members who had burst into the Convention chamber and begun to sing the *Marseillaise:* "I respect the civil feeling of the petitioners, but I ask that in future they reason in speech only."[30] Irony aside, Danton points to a political use of music that, in times of political crisis, was incompatible with parliamentary procedure. In the tensions created by the struggle between the representative principle and sans-culotte demands for direct democracy, collective song became — especially for the latter group — a weapon in the militant's arsenal that was to strengthen its already widely recognized status as a metaphor for national organization.

It was under Robespierre's hegemony that the notion of en masse com-munity singing was to reach its highest embodiment. The "chorus of twenty-four million" envisaged in 1790 came closest to becoming reality at the *Fête de l'Être Suprême* [Festival of the Supreme Being]. The person be-hind that true technical achievement was of course David, although he was only acting in the spirit of the "system of recognized national celebrations" that Robespierre had enunciated on 18 Floréal, Year II. David's *Plan* in-cluded a musical accompaniment for each of the high points of the celebra-tion; however, neither in that document nor in its accompanying *Détail des cérémonies* is there any mention of precisely who was to sing the *Hymne à l'Être Suprême* when it came time for the president of the Convention to deliver his speech.[31] The explicit instruction that the populace should participate at that crucial moment appears to have come from Robespierre himself, who four days prior to the celebration ordered Bernard Sarrette, the head of the Institut National de Musique, to replace Marie-Joseph Chénier's anthem, which was already on the program, with another piece to be sung by all present.[32] The next day, the Committee of Public Safety officially adopted the *Hymne à l'Être Suprême,* text by Théodore Desorgues and music by Gossec, and provided that the score be distributed to every département so that the celebration could be as uniform as possible. This meant that the state's highest authorities had taken action to realize the idea of a simultaneous and collective songfest to be held throughout all of France. In their enthusiastic response to the order, the musicians stated: "The free people of France will thereby prove to enslaved Germany and Italy that they too possess the genius of this art [i.e., music], but that they devote it solely to hymning liberty."[33] It goes without saying that some preparation was required to bring this off. Two days before the celebration, members of the Institut National de Musique were instructed to teach Desorgues' anthem to the populace for its performance in the "Jardin National" of the Tuileries along with Chénier's verses to the tune of the *Marseillaise,* which were to be sung on the artificial *monticule* that had been created on the Champ-de-Mars.

David's *Plan* provided that the first two verses were to be spoken in unison by the two thousand four hundred men and women to be stationed on the *monticule* alongside the authorities, and that the refrains were to be taken up by every man and woman present; the final verse was to be sung by everyone on the *monticule* and the refrain sung by the entire assembly. Here, we recognize the kind of stage management that was so dear to Rousseau and that was so in keeping with the spirit of the *Réquisition Générale* [Blanket Requisition] decreed by the Convention in August 1793: "Young people will go to war; married men will forge weapons and transport supplies; women will make tents and uniforms and serve in hospitals; children will make lint [for bandages]; the elderly will speak in public places to urge on the fighters, teaching hatred for kings and the unity of the Republic."[34] This division of labor, which was shortly to reappear in *Le Chant du départ* of Chénier and Étienne Méhul, was implemented on a monumental scale during the *Fête de l'Être Suprême* prior to the voices of each group joining together in the single voice of the nation. David's *Plan* specifies that, at the end, "all of the French will mingle their emotions in a fraternal embrace: they will have but one voice, whose common call of *Vive la République* will rise up to the divinity."

The *Hymne à l'Être Suprême* of Desorgues and Gossec has a simple melody, almost pastoral in mood, with the indication "très gracieux et religieux" [very graceful and religious]:

The first verse is to be sung in unison; the second is in four-part harmony to be sung by the chorus of the Institut along with the general public:

| | |
|---|---|
| *Père de l'univers, suprême intelligence,* | Father of the Universe, Intelligence Supreme, |
| *Beinfaiteur ignoré des aveugles mortels* | Benefactor unknown to blind mortals |
| *Tu révélas ton être à la reconnaissance* | Thou revealest thyself to the gratitude |
| *Qui seule éleva tes autels.* | That has raised up thine altars. |
| | |
| *Ton temple est sur les mots, dans les airs, sur les ondes,* | Thy temple is built on words, melodies, the waves, |
| *Tu n'as point de passé, tu n'as point d'avenir;* | Thou hast neither past nor future; |
| *Et sans les occuper, tu remplis tous les mondes,* | Without using space thou fillest the world, |
| *Qui ne peuvent te contenir.* | Which cannot encompass thee. |

On 20 Prairial, the mass singing of the *Hymne à l'Être Suprême* was to be led and accompanied by a large body of musicians under Gossec's direction. It was to occur between the two parts of Robespierre's speech — which was described as "Orpheus instructing mankind in the principles of civilization and morality"[35] — and after the incineration of an allegory of Atheism, whose ashes — it would appear — were accidentally to blow onto and singe the white allegory of Wisdom that was revealed by its immolation. In any event, the ceremony on the Champ-de-Mars was designed to be imposing in the extreme. To start with, the men on the *monticule* were to sing, to Rouget de Lisle's melody:

| | |
|---|---|
| *Dieu puissant, d'un peuple intrépide,* | Powerful god of an intrepid people, |
| *C'est toi qui défends les remparts;* | It is thou who defends the ramparts; |
| | |
| *La victoire a, d'un vol rapide,* | Victory in its swift flight has |
| *Accompagné nos étendards.* | Accompanied our standards. |
| *Les Alpes et les Pyrénées,* | The Alps and the Pyrenees, |
| *Des Rois ont vu tomber l'orgueil;* | Kings have seen pride brought low; |
| *Au Nord, nos champs font le cercueil* | To the north, our fields are the coffins |
| *De leurs phalanges consternées.* | Of their routed troops. |

Following the refrain, the women were to take over:

| | |
|---|---|
| *Entends les vierges et les mères,* | May you hear virgins and mothers, |
| *Auteur de la fécondité;* | Author of fecundity; |
| *Nos époux, nos enfants, nos frères,* | Our husbands, children, and brothers |
| *Combattent pour la liberté;* | Are fighting for freedom; |
| *Et si quelque main criminelle* | And if some felon hand |
| *Terminoit des destins si beaux,* | Should end such fine fates, |
| *Leurs fils viendront sur leurs tombeaux* | Their sons will come to their tombs |
| *Venger la cendre paternelle.* | To avenge the paternal ashes. |

After the repetition of the refrain, the two thousand four hundred men and women were then to join in singing the third stanza:

| | |
|---|---|
| *Guerriers, offrez votre courage;* | Warriors, offer up your courage; |
| *Jeunes filles, offrez des fleurs;* | Young girls, offer up flowers; |
| *Mères, offrez pour votre hommage* | Mothers, offer as your homage |
| *Vos fils vertueux et vainqueurs.* | Your virtuous and victorious sons. |
| *Vieillards, dont la mâle sagesse* | Old men, whose masculine wisdom |
| *N'instruit que par des actions,* | Teaches only by deed, |
| *Versez (versons) vos bénédictions* | Let thy benedictions fall |
| *Sur les armes de la jeunesse.* | Upon the weapons of the young. |

Finally, everyone present — several hundred thousand people — was to sing the refrain one last time in unison. It was a true oath taking. Unlike the oath sworn at the *Fête de la Fédération,* however, the oath at the *Fête de l'Être Suprême* was taken by all — or, rather, by all the men, since the women had to be content with abetting their sons, husbands, and fathers in their promise of sacrifice:

| | |
|---|---|
| *Avant de déposer nos/vos glaives triomphants,* | Before laying down your triumphant swords, |
| *Jurons, jurons (jurez, jurez)* | Swear, o swear |
| *d'anéantir le crime et les tyrans.* | To wipe out crime and tyrants.[36] |

Four years after the idea of a "choir of twenty-four million French" had first appeared in the newspapers, that same image, under the aegis of *fraternité* [brotherhood] thus became a reality at the *Fête de l'Être Suprême:* "It is a sight worthy to be viewed by the universe and of being remembered down the centuries to see a family of twenty-five million brothers rise together before dawn to lift their souls and raise their voices to the Father of nature."[37] Of course, "thousands" of people is a far cry from twenty-five million, but the assembled chorus became a good metaphor of the nation's mystical togetherness thanks to a melody that, once its difficulties had been ironed out, had become the key element of the republican pact. With the oath that now concluded the *Marseillaise,* the French sang in a single voice — a voice that was both a hymn and a summons, a voice that was both political and religious, an anthem that was both liturgical and warlike — in short, they became what David was to describe as "the common call" of the nation. This oath sealing the social contract in song realized the plan to "crown the Revolution with the inauguration of a state religion."[38] The celebration of 20 Prairial concentrated the implications of revolutionary music into one single event, an event in which official aesthetics made its closest approach to the experience of the sublime that had formed the kernel of so much philosophizing throughout the eighteenth century. Neither before nor after was the utopian "voice of the people" to be so nearly a reality. It would be nugatory to dwell on the exceptional nature of this event: a few weeks later, when preparations were under way for a celebratory ceremony in honor of Barra and Viala, two teen-aged soldiers of the revolutionary army who had been killed in combat, David had planned another mass communal performance of an anthem, by Méhul to a text by Davrigny; however, on 10 Thermidor, Parisians who had been prepared to honor the child heroes were to watch Robespierre's head fall instead.

Because it played a central role in Robespierre's "state religion" in that spring of 1794, the voice of the people raised in unison has been historically associated with the Terror. The link is strengthened by the realization that the practical execution of such a large-scale project could not have relied on spontaneous participation alone but must necessarily have entailed a fair amount of coercion. It was that authoritarian aspect that was to make David's celebrations a target of the Thermidorians' criticism, as when Marie-Joseph Chénier declared to the Convention: "Where public celebrations are concerned, when an entire people is supposed to rejoice, it is absurd to prescribe their every move as though they were soldiers under orders."[39] And indeed, this link between bringing a nation to speak with a "single voice" and simultaneously managing to maintain discipline is one of the problems inherited from the French Revolution and one that reemerges whenever repressive or totalitarian regimes come to discuss policy. Yet it is not merely a Jacobin invention but, rather, a recurrent revolutionary fantasy, the ringing conjuration of an enemy that represented despotism and Europe. Although Robespierre was the only leader who set out to make the common voice of the nation actually heard, other revolutionary leaders were to dream of doing so and to use the concept to bolster ideologies and institutions. On the very day of Robespierre's execution, Chénier himself again raised the question of anthems, their theory and practice, in a speech that was to lead directly to the creation of the Conservatoire National de Musique et de Déclamation. Noting that "Germany and proud Italy, conquered by France in every other realm but still victorious in this single field, will at last have found a rival," he referred to Rousseau's concept of memorative signs in the "anthems that adorn our civil ceremonies, that even yesterday aroused the due enthusiasm of the National Convention and that French republicans will forget no more than the proud descendants of William Tell will have forgotten the rustic and popular melody which, on foreign soil and into their old age, brings back to their wakened imaginations sweet memories of childhood and even sweeter memories of their native land." [40]

Such continued interest serves to explain why the repertory of republican anthems continued to increase following Thermidor, producing some of the more noteworthy examples of the genre, inter alia, Cherubini's *Hymne au Panthéon:*

France, by stepping up its war, was to multiply the fronts on which its symbolic combat was being waged: the minister of the navy sent collections of republican anthems to the colonies to be sung by the slaves being freed there, described as "Africans become French," in order to encourage, as the minister put it, their "fanatical devotion to liberty."[41] Under the Directory [1795–1799], the nationalist trend toward republican universality was also at the heart of other projects that were more civil and less warlike. Jean-Baptiste Leclerc, a Theophilanthropist and member of the Conseil des Cinq Cents [Council of Five Hundred], impressed like everyone else by the power of the *Ranz des vaches* and concerned at the noxious effects of current "fashions," attempted to create the foundations for a "national music" in the hope of forming a "unique national character" based on an "anthem type" that could include the *Marseillaise* as well as divers romances and songs.[42] La Révellière-Lépeaux, the president of the Directory and author of an *Essai sur les moyens de faire participer l'universalité des spectateurs à tout ce qui se pratique dans les fêtes nationales* [Essay on the means of achieving the participation of all spectators as a whole in all that takes place during national celebrations], was to envisage a collective hymn with several vocal parts, to be realized with Méhul's technical assistance.[43] Indeed, those years were to witness a new attempt to establish community singing on an organized basis, but now, not for some sublime moment of mass unity but, rather, in the more discreet surroundings of the *culte décadaire,* or tenth-day cult, one of the Revolution's substitutes for the erstwhile Sunday services, into which the Theophilanthropists intended to introduce the Protestant tradition of congregational hymns. The shift in emphasis from large-scale special events to small-scale restricted practices found literal expression in the inclusion of Desorgues and Gossec's *Hymne à l'Être Suprême* in every décadi hymnal.[44] However, in the long run, the décadarian hymn was to have a short life, and in large-scale ceremonies the movement towards monumentalism was to give less and less attention to active popular participation — final, and extreme, evidence of this would be provided under the Consulat by Méhul's *Chant pour le 14 juillet 1800,* composed for three choruses and orchestras. The empire was then to sweep away the remains of the republican musical utopia and, with it — and for some time to come — the *Marseillaise.* However, the discourse and practices of community singing under the First Republic would survive the vicissitudes of that period and eventually become an integral part of the French republican tradition. Thanks to the spread of the *Marseillaise* beyond France's borders, such discourse and practices would play an important role in the creation of a body of republican political music upon which various revolutionary and nationalist elites would continue to draw throughout the nineteenth century, and even up to our own time.

# 3

## The *Ode to Joy* and the *Emperor's* Anthem

On 11 July 1785, Friedrich Schiller wrote to Christian Gottfried Körner, who had invited him to move in with him: "I have never gone along with the great Rousseau's negative response to the letter that Count Orloff sent him, in a burst of enthusiasm, offering the exiled poet asylum. To the degree that I feel that, compared to Rousseau, I am smaller, I should like to act in a bigger way. Your friendship and kindness hold out an Elysium for me. . . ."[1] Indeed, some twenty years earlier, Rousseau had replied as follows to the Russian aristocrat who had suggested that he come to live on his estates: "You are expecting a kind of Man of Letters, full of eloquence, who would repay your generous hospitality with wit and fine words, and all you would get would be a very simple man made solitary by his taste and misfortunes, one who botanizes all day and whose sole amusement resides in finding with plants that sweet peace which human beings have denied him."[2] Schiller's letter reveals his admiration for the author of the *Essai sur l'origine des langues* as well as the personal and philosophical differences between them: where Rousseau believed that culture entailed an irretrievable loss of human happiness, Schiller cherished the Elysian dream that the beautiful, aesthetics, could make man better. Shortly after the letter to Körner, the author of *Die Räuber* [The Robbers] left Mannheim and moved in with his friend, near Dresden. His poem entitled *An die Freude* [To Joy], written in 1785 and published the following year in the review *Rheinische Thalia,* was a homage to the friendship he had found with Körner and his circle. The first verses of this original version are as follows:

> *Freude, schöner Götterfunken,*    Joy, lovely divine spark,
> *Tochter aus Elysium,*    Daughter of Elysium,

| | |
|---|---|
| *Wir betreten feuertrunken* | Drunk with fire, we enter, |
| *Himmlische, dein Heiligtum.* | Heavenly one, your shrine. |
| *Deine Zauber binden wieder,* | Your magic spells reunite |
| *was der Mode Schwert geteilt;* | What convention's sword has sundered; |
| *Bettler werden Fürstenbrüder,* | Beggars become the brothers of noblemen |
| *wo dein sanfter Flügel weilt.* | At the gentle touch of your wing. |
| Chor | *Chorus* |
| *Seid umschlungen Millionen!* | Embrace, you millions! |
| *Diesen Kuß der ganzen Welt!* | This kiss is for all the world! |
| *Brüder — überm Sternenzelt* | Brothers, up there in the star-filled vault |
| *muß ein lieber Vater wohnen.* | A loving father surely dwells! |
| *Wem der große Wurf gelungen,* | Let whoever has had the great fortune |
| *eines Freundes Freund zu sein,* | To encounter true friendship, |
| *wer ein holdes Weib errungen,* | Whoever has found a beloved wife, |
| *mische seinen Jubel ein!* | Join in our jubilation! |
| *Ja — wer auch nur* eine *Seele* | Yes! if there be just *one* other soul |
| sein *nennt auf dem Erdenrund!* | That is *his* in all the earth! |
| *Und wer's nie gekonnt, der stehle* | And whoever cannot achieve that, may he |
| *weinend sich aus diesem Bund!* | Steal weeping from the group! |
| Chor | *Chorus* |
| *Was den großen Ring bewohnet* | Let all who dwell in this vast circle |
| *huldige der Sympathie!* | Honor Sympathy! |
| *Zu den Sternen leitet sie,* | For it leads to the stars |
| *wo der* Unbekannte *thronet.* | Where the *Unknown* is enthroned. |
| *Freude trinken alle Wesen* | All creatures will drink Joy |
| *an den Brüsten der Natur,* | At Nature's bosom. |
| *Alle Guten, alle Bösen* | All the good and all the wicked |
| *folgen ihrer Rosenspur.* | Will tread her rose-strewn path. |
| *Küsse gab sie* uns *und* Reben, | She has given *us* kisses and the *vines*, |
| *einen Freund geprüft im Tod.* | And a friend faithful unto death. |

| | |
|---|---|
| *Wollust ward dem Wurm gegeben,* | Even the worm is given pleasure, |
| *und der Cherub steht vor Gott.* | And the cherub stands before God. |
| | |
| Chor | *Chorus* |
| *Ihr stürzt nieder, Millionen?* | Do you bow humbly down, ye millions? |
| *Ahnest du den Schöpfer, Welt?* | World, do you *feel* your Creator? |
| *Such' ihn überm Sternenzelt,* | Seek him up there in the star-filled vault, |
| *über Sternen muß er wohnen.* | He surely dwells among the stars. |

Social differences lead to the violence of convention, of fashion, whereas joy denotes membership in the community of mankind, in friendship or love. It is also the transcendent principle of the natural world. The ode's praise of Nature leads up to an invocation of God which the chorus emphasizes by questioning acts of obeisance and urging mankind to lift its gaze to higher things. The 1785 version, in its final verse, set forth a veritable program:

| | |
|---|---|
| *Rettung von Tyrannenketten,* | Delivery from the tyrants' chains, |
| *Großmut auch dem Bösewicht,* | Magnanimity even to the scoundrel, |
| *Hoffnung auf den Sterbebetten,* | Hope at the bedside of the dying, |
| *Gnade auf dem Hochgericht!* | Mercy at the place of execution! |
| *Auch die Toten sollen leben!* | Even the dead shall live! |
| *Brüder trinkt und stimmet ein,* | Brothers will drink and sing together, |
| *Allen Sündern soll vergeben,* | Every sinner will be forgiven, |
| *Une die Hölle nicht mehr sein.* | And Hell shall cease to be! |

*An die Freude* is one of several odes to joy, a traditional eighteenth-century form typified by the conviviality of the many *Trinklieder* or drinking songs. Schiller, however, was among the first to have linked joy to a *Weltgefühl,* a "world sense or feeling";[3] mankind's earthly happiness has an essential role in the poem's text. Here, we find embodied the same social and political concerns of the author who at the same period was at work on *Don Carlos,* the drama which — particularly in the character of the Marquis de Posa — was to embody a whole cosmopolitan concept of liberty or freedom (*Freiheit*). True, the word *Freiheit* does not occur in the Ode to Joy — indeed, there is no solid basis for the hypothesis that the poem is a politically "adjusted" version of an earlier ode entitled *An die Freiheit* [Ode to Freedom].[4] However, in *Don Carlos,* liberty or freedom is viewed as a fundamental element of the natural world and a symbol of "mankind's lost nobility," in words that are often very close to those of the *Ode to Joy:*

> *. . . Sehen Sie sich um*
> *In seiner herrlichen Natur! Auf Freiheit*
> *Ist sie gegründet — und wie reich ist sie*
> *Durch Freiheit! Er, der große Schöpfer, wirft*
> *In einen Tropfen Tau den Wurm, und läßt*
> *Noch in den toten Räumen der Verwesung*
> *Die Willkür sich ergetzen [. . .]*[5]

[Look around you, see the splendors of His nature! It is based on freedom . . . and in its freedom, how rich it is! He, the Great Creator, spawns the worm from a drop of dew and allows free will to flourish even in death's charnel house!]

Thanks in part to its overtones rich with notions of liberty, the *Ode to Joy* has always been open to different overtly political interpretations, although they were not to become current until the nineteenth century. In Schiller's own lifetime, the poem was principally considered from a religious viewpoint — for example, to denounce the non-Christian sentiments expressed in the line "Hell shall cease to be!" In 1793, Wieland wrote in Schiller's defense in the *Neuen Teutschen Merkur,* and, although he expresses sympathy for the man he had helped to set himself up in Weimar in 1787, as a good and tolerant Freemason, he does not refrain from criticizing the exclusion of the solitary man from the circle of rejoicing.[6] From a fairly mundane celebration of wine and friendship to the cosmic lyricism of a literary generation at the threshold of the romantic movement, there were many who, like the poet Magenau, viewed the poem as a harbinger: "The punch bowl had already been set steaming on the table when Hölderlin demanded that everyone join in a preliminary lustral purification: singing that anthem, he said, required that one be cleansed of all stain."[7] The author himself attested to its popularity among German intellectuals in a letter to Körner dated 21 October 1800, in which he wrote that the ode "has had the honor of becoming almost like a piece of folk poetry [*Volksgedicht*]."[8]

Even so, Schiller, embarrassed by the "defective taste" of the period in which the ode had been written, was to omit it from an anthology of his poetry.[9] Three years later, however, he changed his mind and, for a new edition, reworked the text into what was to be its final version. The final verse disappeared, and the words in the first verse about beggars becoming the "brothers of noblemen" were replaced by "alle Menschen werden Brüder," [all men will be brothers], perhaps the most famous line he was ever to pen. These changes have often been viewed as reflections of the evolution of Schiller's personal politics: the poet had been made a French citizen by the Assemblée Nationale in 1792 as a tribute to *Die Räuber*, but because of his position at the court of the Duke of Saxe-Weimar, an "enlightened despot" who was to ennoble him in 1802, he had scant sympathy for the Revolution. In any event, it is clear that the changes he made in 1803 take the edge off the poem's political tone while making it into a manifesto for an ideal of universal human brotherhood, one shared by men of the *Aufklärung* [Enlightenment] as well as by the French revolutionaries.

That ideal is also one of the precepts of Freemasonry, and it is expressed here by a man who, although not himself a Freemason, was nonetheless of the same mind as his hero, the Marquis de Posa,[10] and Freemasonry was to be the principal conduit through which the *Ode to Joy* spread, with the added support of music. In fact, a number of composers had immediately seized upon the poem, starting with Johann Christian Müller, who published his setting of it at Leipzig in 1786. These early settings, strophic in form, are generally *lieder* in the *style galant* mode favored by the German *Empfindsamkeit* or sentimentalist movement; when composers like Johann Friedrich Reichardt employed a cantata-like form the result was usually overly reminiscent of their academic roots. It was in Bonn in 1792 that Ludwig van Beethoven, no Freemason himself but at the time being taught by the Freemason Christian Gottlob Neefe, first had the idea of setting Schiller's poem to music — all we know about this early project is that he had intended to set the entire poem — this from a letter from a friend of the poet which describes a young musician on the eve of his departure for Vienna, "wholly devoted to the great and the sublime."[11] In 1799, however, there appeared in Berlin a collection of song settings of the *Ode to Joy*, which included one that was anonymous but that later was to be attributed to Johann Gottlieb Naumann, a close friend of the Freemason Körner and the composer of many Masonic hymns:

Freu-de  schö-ner  Got-ter-  fun ken    Tochter  auf  E  ly  si-  um

The following year, the same tune was again published at Berlin, still unsigned, with the text in English translation and designated as "a masonic song." Unlike earlier versions, this is a simple melody, easily sung by amateurs, which included most lodge members — but many others as well in bourgeois society who were beginning to awaken to the idea, itself academic, of "popular" or folk melody. Thus, it was as a Masonic hymn placed at the beginning of many song collections aimed at the bourgeois audience that Schiller's poem moved out of a strictly intellectual orbit: shortly after the poet's death in 1805, a Berlin music journal was to note that the *Ode to Joy*, beloved and enthusiastically sung by "thousands," had become a true folksong, a *Volksgesang*.[12] The change occurred at a time when Mozart's *Die Zauberflöte* [The Magic Flute] had already achieved an artistic synthesis that was both cultivated and accessible, a time in which Franz Joseph Haydn — who had since 1780 been composing *lieder* to popular verses such as Gottfried August Bürger's *Gegenliebe* — had created "a popular style that abandoned none of the pretensions of high art," the style that was to characterize his late, great works.[13] In 1794, the young Beethoven in turn composed his own *Gegenliebe*, a song in praise of mutual love, preceded by another of Bürger's poems describing the sorrow of loneliness (*Seufzer eines Ungeliebten* [Sighs of One Unloved], WoO 118):

This simple, tuneful melody of Beethoven's was to the first of a series of "popular" songs containing images of happiness, a series that would culminate in 1824 with the *Ode to Joy*—which is not without a touch of irony, since, for Schiller, the poet Bürger, in love with the "joys of the real world," had made the mistake of "becoming one with the people rather than condescending to them with dignity." [14]

However, a decisive role in Beethoven's departure for Vienna in 1792 was to be played by an interview with Haydn, who was impressed not by one modest *lied* but by the young composer's first excursions into monumental music with a political tinge — just as Haydn's trips to England had whetted his interest for large-scale works on the Handelian model. In 1790, Beethoven had composed two works for soloists, chorus, and orchestra to texts by Anton Averdonck: a *Cantata on the Death of Joseph II* and a *Cantata on the Coronation of Leopold II* (WoO 87 and 88). These had been commissioned by the "reading club" of a group of intellectuals in Bonn, a city over which the Elector Maximilian Franz, brother to both emperors, exercised a tolerant rule reflected in the growth and development of the city's university and the spread and availability of the works of the French philosophes. The group's leader was Professor Eulogius Schneider, who shortly afterwards joined the ranks of the revolutionaries in Strasbourg, although he went on to lose his head under the Terror. Beethoven's two cantatas, whose texts contain paradigmatic references to "enlightened despots," were intended to be performed at ceremonies organized by the *Lesegesellschaft.* The first, for Joseph II, is the best known, particularly for its opening funeral chorus in C minor, which, under the influence of Gluck, is an early example of Beethoven's tragic pathos. The central section, an aria for soprano and chorus, describes mankind moving upward toward the light. Although the subject of the text remains abstract, and although the F-major melody does not progress stepwise, as in the *Gegenliebe,* the passage marks Beethoven's first use of a chorus of a "noble simplicity" inspired by antiquity. Following a threefold salute to the monarch — "Heil! Heil! Heil!" — the cantata for Leopold II also concludes with a final chorus to a verse by Averdonck that might be a reply to Schiller's question, "Do you bow humbly down, ye millions?" with its imperative: "Stürzet nieder, Millionen, an dem rauchenden Altar!" [Bow down, ye millions, before the incensed altar!]. A Handelian *fugato* is followed by a D-major apotheosis, which concludes another "first" in Beethoven's work, namely, a piece of celebratory music exalting a political power figure, in this instance the emperor of the German Holy Roman Empire, in the baroque tradition of large-scale official state music.

Although the Bonn cantatas, for reasons that are still unclear, were not

performed at the time, the young Beethoven, in composing them, was helping to legitimize a regime in which the ruler was often portrayed as a "servant of the state" and "benefactor of the people." In the development of
such symbolism we note the part played by intellectuals like the Freemason
Joseph von Sonnenfels, who proposed as early as 1771, in his treatise entitled *Über die Vaterslandliebe* [On Love for the Fatherland], what was described as a "lay cult, one inspired by antique religions, to increase state authority," and who in the reign of Joseph II was to tell his students at the
university of Vienna that all of the emperor's subjects were now "citizens." [15] It goes without saying that, in Vienna, terms like "citizen" and "patriotism" did not have the revolutionary connotations they were to acquire
in France; the body in charge of censorship was supervised at the time by a
recognized leader of the German-speaking Enlightenment, Baron Gottfried
van Swieten, and the police, under Count Johann von Pergen, had for the
first time become a politicized body. Even those authoritarian measures,
however, indicate the importance that was attached to establishing a kind of
consensus based on the ideals of humanity and fraternity, a consensus that
the Masonic lodges played an important part in promulgating, and whose
best musical embodiment is probably the character of Sarastro in *Die
Zauberflöte*. It was also this same elite that preached the moral value of an
older musical culture whose "truth and grandeur" was to serve as a rampart
against "artistic decadence." [16] It was at this period in Vienna that the first
attempts were made to organize regular performances of both older masterpieces and of new works that were deemed worthy of that past tradition. In
1786, Gottfried van Swieten, along with Schwarzenberg, Lobkowitz, Dietrichstein, Apponyi, and other members of the aristocracy, founded the
*Gesellschaft der associierten Cavaliers* [Society of Associated Knights], a
club principally devoted to the oratorios of Handel, often in arrangements
by contemporaries such as Mozart. In contrast to the situation in England,
this initiative was not a response to increased commercial activity but rather
a response to the sentimentality of the *style galant*. The tenacity of tradition
is illustrated by the Austrian career of Franz Joseph Haydn, Kapellmeister
to the Hungarian prince Esterhazy, whose duties often kept him away from
the capital. The development of the music-publishing industry, however,
enabled him to win an international reputation that can truly be described
as "European," if we take that term to mean simultaneous fame in Paris,
London, Berlin, and Vienna. In 1791 and 1794, Haydn was able to witness
firsthand the different situation that prevailed in England; there, he was

welcomed not only with commercial success but also with such honors as an honorary Oxford degree of Doctor of Music and a reception by the royal family. "Indeed," Charles Burney was to write, "it seems likely that the productions of Haydn will be admired and imitated *all over Europe,* as long as those of Handel have been in England only." [17] The trips were a decisive spur to the composer's reputation in his own country, where he was henceforth to be regarded as "a great creative and ever-productive genius" of whom "his Fatherland can be proud." [18]

Haydn's first return to Vienna in 1792 coincided with two events that were to affect the Austrian political landscape for decades to come. First, the sudden demise of Leopold II and the coronation of Franz II marked the introduction of a new political policy that was to put an end to the regime of "openness" practiced by Joseph II. Secondly, the declaration of war by France ushered in a long period of hostilities that was to exacerbate the new regime's regressive tendencies by provoking widespread instability throughout the Hapsburg territories. The abandonment of Enlightenment attitudes had a profound effect on Vienna's cultural life, replacing the Josephist elite with a new conservative hegemony dominated by the church. At the center of this new state of affairs was the reorganization of the Ministry of Police, which led to intensified secret surveillance, direct control over censorship, and periodic interference in the educational sector. The changes began to take place in 1793, under the direction of Count Pergen, who had been recalled to power, and Count Franz Joseph von Saurau, the vice-minister of police and confidant of the new emperor. The following year, Saurau played a prominent role in breaking up the so-called "Jacobin conspiracy," a process during which both committed republicans and Josephists were arrested, including a close friend of van Swieten. Saurau did his best to make the trial of the accused into a propaganda circus, although they "had done little more than sing the *Marseillaise* and dance around 'liberty trees' that they had planted in and around cities like Graz and Vienna." [19] In fact, the most successful of the Austrian "Jacobin" propaganda efforts was to be a song, the *Eipeldauerlied,* influenced by French revolutionary music.

Franz II's officials were, however, forced to recognize that it was impossible to effect a total return to the former absolutist practices. "There were, of course, those who turned like straws in the wind, and abandoned enlightened principles as soon as they realized that they were no longer favored in government circles. Lorenz Leopold Haschka, once the bard of limited monarchy, now tried to stir up enthusiasm for the war against France. On the whole, however, the reign of Joseph II and Leopold II had brought about too great an evolution in political consciousness to make possible a mere passive or fatalistic acceptance of the new policies."[20] Such a situation, in which expressions of political opinion were acceptable only to the extent that they echoed official policy, was also reflected in the new genres of political music that began to appear on the artistic scene in Vienna. Trumpeted in the press, often composed for war-related charity functions, the countless works composed to exalt the Hapsburg and "Austrian" patriotism during the so-called wars of the Coalition were to remain relatively independent of the state's official music, and especially of the control of the Imperial Kapellmeister, Antonio Salieri. Although they were generally in the classical form of secular cantatas or stage music, some of the compositions also sought to reach the individual fighting for the international community. In January 1794, a funeral cantata in honor of Louis XVI by the composer Theresa von Paradis was performed in the Burgtheater; a few weeks later, Franz Xavier Süssmayr — a pupil of Mozart's who had completed his unfinished *Requiem* — presented at Prague a cantata to celebrate the emperor's birthday. On 19 September 1796, the return of Archduke Charles from his campaign against the Army of the Rhine was celebrated with a concert at the imperial palace at which, following Haydn's Symphony no. 94, another cantata by Süssmayr entitled *Retter in Gefahr* [Savior in Peril] was performed. It was also at this time that Joseph Weigl, Haydn's godson, produced a cantata entitled *Österreich über alles* [Austria Over All] to a text by August von Kotzebue; at its performance in the Leopoldtheater, the audience was invited to join in the final chorus.[21] Also in 1796, the war itself was reflected in Haydn's *Missa in tempore belli* [Mass in Time of War], which concludes with an *Agnus Dei* in which the composer calls upon the kettledrums to play "as though one could already hear the enemy advancing in the distance."[22]

Nevertheless, the government's repressive attitude did not enable it to enjoy total control over public opinion. In 1796, during the Italian campaign, the confrontational policy being implemented against France by Baron Franz von Thugut, the minister for foreign affairs, was greeted by a wave of discontent by a sector of the aristocratic elite. The policy was a particularly sensitive one because its critics had a representative at the very heart of the dynasty, namely, the archduke Charles, who was skeptical about Austria's chances for victory despite his own military successes.[23]

Archduke Charles's prestige was in sharp contrast to the unpopularity of his brother the emperor, whose contemporaries often portray him as a mediocrity. In July 1796, with highly placed members of the elite, supported by a part of the population, bringing increased pressure on the government, Baron Thugut was to write: "I continue to fear Vienna more than the enemy in all its fury, and it will be the source of our ruin. I intend to have a meeting on the subject tomorrow with Monsieur de Saurau, for, indeed, the police above all are the ones who should advise on ways of controlling opinion, especially in public places."[24] The meeting between Saurau and Thugut was to have several direct consequences: the church was called upon to preach war against France from every pulpit; a decision was taken to form a volunteer battalion in Vienna to defend the country; and, lastly, an anthem was commissioned to honor the emperor, with words by Lorenz Leopold Haschka and music by Franz Joseph Haydn.[25]

The formation of the Vienna volunteers inspired the poet Friedelberg to write an *Abschiedsgesang an Wiens Bürger* [Song of Farewell to the Citizens of Vienna] and, six months later, during the mass call-up of men decreed by Saurau as Napoleon began to close in on Vienna, a *Kriegslied der Öster-reicher* [Austrian War Hymn], beginning with the words, "We are a great German people." Both of Friedelberg's texts were set to music by Beethoven, a newcomer to Vienna's cultural scene, and both employed simple melodies sung by a soloist and replied to in martial tones by a unison men's chorus (WoO 121 and 122).

These anti-French songs, with piano accompaniment, were intended above all to inspire patriotism at the domestic level; nonetheless, they too, in their nationalistic and egalitarian purpose —"virtue makes us like princes"— bear traces of the emotional model of the *Marseillaise*, here redirected to serve the Hapsburgs. As for Haydn's anthem, it is likely that the vice-minister of police's experience with the "Jacobin conspiracy" had given him the idea of finding a kind of "counter-*Marseillaise*," a propaganda tool that would respond to the French at the symbolic level. However, the model he had in mind was not the anthem of the French foes but that of the British ally. Although Saurau never mentions Rouget de Lisle's tune, he does hold up *God Save the King* as an example. Unlike those two predecessors, the Austrian anthem did not rise out of the populace to find favor in official ceremonies: here, we have a high official taking the initiative to impose the rite of collective song. The Austrian imperial anthem is the first to have been official state music from its very beginnings. Its difference from the traditional forms of state music — from the religious works for official ceremonies — denotes the recognition of a new type of political subject by the very people who had the greatest interest in combating its spread. And, in fact, the anthem does not buttress any national affiliation in the modern sense of the term. Its true purpose is to express fidelity to the king of Austria and Hungary, the emperor of the Holy German Roman Empire — who, shortly before the dissolution of the latter in 1806, would, as Franz I, assume the title of emperor of Austria — a head of a State conceived on a supranational principle and ferociously opposed to national movements. The tension between an "Austrian" identity, which in the beginning had meant fidelity to the Austrian Royal House, and the feeling of belonging to a culturally defined "German" nation is reflected in the presence of two trends in the era's political music — symptoms of a conflict that was to persist throughout the rest of Austria's history.

Sometime between October 1796 and January 1797, therefore, Haydn composed the anthem *Gott erhalte Franz den Kaiser* [God Save Emperor Franz] to words by Lorenz Leopold Haschka:

Following Count Saurau's instructions, the poet had written his text with a German translation of *God Save the King* before him, as the prayer in the first stanza reveals:

| | |
|---|---|
| *Gott! erhalte Franz den Kaiser,* | God! save Emperor Franz, |
| *Unsern guten Kaiser Franz!* | Our good Emperor Franz! |
| *Lange lebe Franz der Kaiser* | Long life to Emperor Franz |

| | |
|---|---|
| *In des Glückes hellstem Glanz!* | In the bright eyes of good fortune! |
| *Ihm erblühen Lorbeer-Reiser* | May laurels flower for him |
| *Wo er geht, zum Ehren-Kranz!* | On his path and form a crown! |
| *Gott! erhalte Franz den Kaiser,* | God! save Emperor Franz, |
| *Unsern guten Kaiser Franz!* | Our good Emperor Franz! |

The second stanza projects the image of the "good sovereign," an echo of the enlightened despotism that Haschka had praised under Joseph II:

| | |
|---|---|
| *Lass von seiner Fahnen Spitzen* | May the points of his standards |
| *Strahlen Sieg und Fruchtbarkeit!* | Glitter in victory and fruitfulness! |
| *Lass in Seinem Rathe Sitzen* | May his councilors be |
| *Weisheit, Klugheit, Redlichkeit;* | Wisdom, Intelligence, and Honesty; |
| *Und mit Seiner Hoheit Blitzen* | And from his eminence may only |
| *Schalten nur Gerechtigkeit!* | Justice flow! |
| *Gott! erhalte Franz den Kaiser,* | God! save Emperor Franz, |
| *Unsern guten Kaiser Franz!* | Our good Emperor Franz! |

The third stanza, like that of the English anthem, cites the law; but it is not "our laws" that are being referred to but, rather, the law of God, the source of human law via the mediation of the sovereign's will:

| | |
|---|---|
| *Ströme Deiner Gaben Fülle* | May Thy abundant gifts stream down |
| *Über ihm, Sein Haus und Reich!* | Upon him, his house, his kingdom! |
| *Brich der Bosheit Macht; enthülle* | Crush evil's power; expose |
| *Jeden Schelm- und Bubenstreich!* | Every roguish and knavish trick! |
| *Dein Gesetz sey stets Sein Wille;* | May Thy law be his will; |
| *Dieser uns Gesetzen gleich!* | And may it be ours as well! |
| *Gott! erhalte Franz den Kaiser,* | God! save Emperor Franz, |
| *Unsern guten Kaiser Franz!* | Our good Emperor Franz! |

From a musical standpoint, *Gott erhalte* is obviously close to the English anthem, which Haydn had written down and probably arranged while in London. It is a slow tune, easy to sing, composed in the key of G major. Although a secular piece, it is not incompatible with a certain religious tradition — a stylistic similarity later to be confirmed by the use of the tune in English religious services.[26] On the other hand, the *Emperor's* Anthem is totally devoid of the panache of the *Marseillaise* and the rest of the musical rhetoric of the day, so redolent of war and the effects of war, a rhetoric that

Haydn himself was able to employ to perfection when he so chose. In this respect, the composer had been faithful to the implicit requirements of Count Saurau's commission: his anthem is indeed a counter-*Marseillaise* insofar as it rejects the epic notion of "we as a nation," preferring, on the English model, to express a devoted relationship to the monarch under the aegis of religion. However, whereas the English anthem is in three-quarter time and asymmetrical, Haydn's is in four-quarter time with the four-measure phrases typical of the classical style. The introduction of a second motif in the fifth line, which lends it expressivity while preserving its utter simplicity, has no equivalent in *God Save the King*, which is rooted in the monothematic mindset typical of the baroque. On the other hand, the refrain does bear a relationship to that of the *Marseillaise*.[27] The imperial anthem and the revolutionary song share the same, basically dynamic, musical code; here, Haydn is clearly a contemporary of Rouget de Lisle and not of the anonymous English composer. We can even say that to a certain extent the Austrian "counter-*Marseillaise*" sprang from the suspicion that the emperor's subjects might well have felt some affinities with republican rhetoric and that it would therefore be well to give them something else to occupy their minds.

The anthem *Gott erhalte Franz den Kaiser* was sung in public for the first time on 12 February 1797 to celebrate Franz II's twenty-ninth birthday. In Count Saurau's meticulous plans for the event, the high point was to be the emperor's arrival in his box at Vienna's Burgtheater, an occasion that was to be echoed simultaneously throughout the empire. Here, for example, are his instructions to the authorities in Prague:

> Most Noble Count! Your Excellency is doubtless aware of the effect on the populace of the English *Volkslied God Save the King* and of the degree to which it has stirred that people to defend themselves as one man against their external foes.
>
> The hymn, attached, written by Haschka and set to music by the famous Haydn, will be sung by the people on 12 February in every theater in Vienna for the Emperor's birthday, and I am sending a copy herewith, in confidence, to Your Excellency in order that the hymn may also be sung, should you deem it expedient, on the same day in Prague. May that day resound with the voice of the entire population raised for His Majesty's protection.[28]

It goes without saying that the phrase "should you deem it expedient" is mere etiquette. The whole event was the result of careful planning; regional authorities were not only instructed to ensure that the anthem was introduced in every large city but also that it be disseminated in every province so that every local Kapellmeister might see to its performance. To that end, it had to be translated into the principal languages in use in the vast Hapsburg domains: Hungarian, Czechoslovakian, Italian, Polish, Serbian, and Latin. *Gott erhalte* was simultaneously premiered in Vienna, Prague, Graz, Innsbruck, Kraków, Ofen, Pest, Brünn, Judenburg, Loeben, Trieste, and other cities controlled by the dynasty. In most cases, it was sung at the theater during or at the end of the performance. In Innsbruck, it was performed at the conclusion of a concert held at the university; in Prague, it followed the *National Song of Bohemia;* at Trieste, it was performed in the presence of the archduke Ferdinand, Franz II's brother. In Judenburg, it was accompanied by a little religious pageant: "When the curtain rose, to a musical accompaniment, shepherds and shepherdesses came forward to lay their offerings at the altar and then sang the national hymn." [29] In the capital, Vienna, the ceremony was a particularly resplendent one owing to the presence of the emperor himself, who made a triumphal entry into the Burgtheater. *Gott erhalte* was performed in Haydn's own orchestral arrangement. According to one newspaper, "The theater had never been so full, and as some could not see well enough to sing the words, small tapers like those used on Saint John's Day were handed out, thus demonstrating that our Emperor Franz is indeed our own patron saint." [30] Another publication admiringly commented on this novel manner "hitherto unknown in Austria" of paying homage to the emperor, adding that "the public's enthusiasm, on this occasion as on other similar ones, gives us reason to hope that we will have many more opportunities to hear in our theaters the voice of the people united for the Emperor's protection." [31] Only *Der Eipeldauer,* a newspaper with close connections to the Ministry of Police, was to allow itself an ironic comment, recalling the demands of the day and the limitations of such symbolic gestures: "Now the hymn will be sung at every society gathering as well as in public, young misses especially will attack it on the piano. We can but hope that all this singing will not distract us from the question of finances, for these days song alone is not going to do the job." Count Saurau's plan was based on simultaneous celebration, the uniting of all of the emperor's subjects into a single voice, a "we" rallied around its sovereign in song, above and beyond ethnic, national, linguistic, and political differences. Three years after the French *Fête de l'Être Suprême,* a very similar plan was being implemented by the Revolution's foes. However, the choice of theaters or concert halls tends to suggest that the performance was designed not so much to reach the urban and rural population as a whole as it was to impress aristocratic and bourgeois audiences — the bases of Hapsburg power — as well as the critical milieu, an elite whose members, thanks to their daily musical experience, were the only ones capable of deciphering the pages printed with Haydn's notes and Haschka's verses that were handed out at the entrance.[32] With that caveat then, it was indeed "the entire population," as Saurau had hoped, that was to beseech a very Catholic God to protect its sovereign under threat from the French troops.

In passing, the reports praise the authors of what was already being called the *Nazional-Lied* or National Song — especially Haydn, according to the *Wiener Zeitung,* "the most famous composer of our time." There is no record of his being present in the Burgtheater, but a short time before, while correcting the proofs of the score, he was to write to Saurau:

> Excellency! I have never before experienced, in recognition of my feeble talents, such a surprise or mark of favor as this portrait of my revered monarch. I will have the proofs to you at eleven. I am, very respectfully, Your Excellency's most humble and most obedient servant. Jos. Haydn.

Haydn is referring to a small gilt box with a portrait of Franz II that was given him in recognition of his services. According to one of his biographers,[33] he was also given a substantial sum of money. As Saurau was to remark some ten years after the composer's death, Haydn had committed an "unforgivable error" in his 1797 note when he used the verb *überleben,* "survive," instead of *erleben,* "experience";[34] were one to take literally what Haydn actually wrote, his role as the emperor's cantor had been the greatest honor he had ever survived . . . In any event, everything that we know about the composer's personal political feelings would lead us to believe that he fully shared both the spirit and the purpose of his *Kaiserhymne,* which was destined to become one of his most famous works. Indeed, immediately after its premiere, Haydn was to prove his fondness for the tune by using it as a theme in one of his late quartets, one written in what Charles Rosen has described as the "popular style" and one of the most famous pieces in all of chamber music, the Quartet op. 76, no. 3, in C Major, known — for obvious reasons — as the *Emperor* Quartet. The second movement, *poco adagio, cantabile,* opens with the first violin playing the tune of *Gott erhalte,* followed in turn by variations featuring the second violin, viola, and violoncello and finally culminating in a fourth variation that concludes in a *pianissimo* coda. The variations are not of the melody itself, which is played complete, in its original version, five times in a row; what do vary are the instrumentation, harmony, counterpoint, dynamics, and texture of the accompaniment surrounding it. Thanks to this technique of "*cantus-firmus* variation,"[35] the composer preserves the *cantabile* of the political symbol and suggests its permanence above and beyond temporal change, thereby giving a political dimension to the very form of the work. The Quartet op. 76, no. 3, with reference to the 1796 Mass of the same name, could well have been called a *Quartetto in tempore belli,* perhaps even more of a "a war-time symbol . . . than the mass written a few months before."[36] And indeed, the reference to a piece of official music in an instrumental work does make it a "war-time symbol" that was well suited to an elite for whom a taste for chamber music was a sign of cultural identity and moral probity and whose members, for that matter, would most likely not have noticed — as we so vividly do today — the aesthetic hiatus in this passage from public to private. "One cannot imagine the *Marseillaise* or any other anthem serving as the thematic basis of a movement of a string quartet, as here," the critic Cecil Gray was to write. The melody "inhabits all three worlds; the world of religion, the world of national politics, and the world of pure art."[37] In the history of this melody, we witness the convergence, with unequaled force, of the birth of modern political sensibility and the establishment of a canon of classical music. Although Saurau had probably commissioned the imperial anthem from Haydn because of the latter's emblematic rank, the work's prestige has made it one that establishes links between different cultural "worlds."

Yet Haydn, who was sixty-five years old at the time, had not reached the summit of his career. At first, public singing of the anthem was not to outlast the initial burst of enthusiasm; it would not resurface until 1809, and it was not to take hold until a few years after that during the Congress of Vienna [1814–1815]. However, *Gott erhalte* was contemporary with Haydn's oratorio *Die Schöpfung* [The Creation], which was immediately to become the principal musical avatar of Viennese culture. This work — which recounts the story of Genesis from a famous instrumental "original chaos" to the idyll of Adam and Eve in the Terrestrial Paradise — had its origins in Haydn's visit to England. He had arrived in that country bearing letters of introduction and recommendation to Graf Johann von Stadion, the Austrian ambassador — one of which, from Baron van Swieten, expressed his regret at having been unable to accompany the composer "to the great annual commemoration of his idol, Handel."[38] Although they did not alter Haydn's own personal style, the monumental performances of Handel's works in Westminster Abbey did make a profound impression on him. The concerts opened his eyes to the potentialities of a genre to which he had hitherto paid little attention, as well as to the dramatic powers of "musical portraiture" or "tone-painting," the *Tonmalerei* of the baroque period. After his second visit to London, Haydn returned to Vienna with a libretto by an unknown author drawn from the Bible and Milton's *Paradise Lost,* which would become the libretto for *Die Schöpfung.* Baron van Swieten, who was an amateur writer and composer, translated the English text, adapting it to suit Viennese tastes, and saw to organizing the institutional framework and social network that were needed for the work's performances and dissemination. The first performance took place on 29 April 1798 in the palace of Prince Schwarzenberg, under the aegis of the *Gesellschaft der associierten Cavaliers* [Society of Associated Knights]. The considerable impact of that private concert was to be even stronger on 19 March, following the work's first public performance in the Burgtheater, with Emperor Franz II in attendance. From 1802 on, *Die Schöpfung* was to be performed on a regular basis for the benefit of Vienna's *Bürgerspital,* a charity hospital, and two years later, the composer was made an honorary citizen of the city of Vienna.[39] Thus, van Swieten and his group succeeded in crowning the repertory of past masters with a great contemporary oratorio: "An annual performance of the Oratorio continued in Vienna almost without a break from 1798 to the present day; in this respect it occupied the position of *Messiah* in England and America."[40] In addition, the work, which was published and sold by subscription throughout Europe, was immediately performed in other capitals. Its premiere in London took place on 28 March 1800 to general acclaim, apart from a few critics who considered it on the whole a "very charming production," "although . . . not equal in grandeur to the divine compositions of the immortal Handel. . . ."[41] A French version was performed in Paris on Christmas Eve 1800 in the presence of First Consul Bonaparte, who had just emerged unscathed from a bomb attempt. "The performance of this noble Oratorio is as much a triumph for France as for the fatherland of this immortal artist," wrote the French correspondent of the *Allgemeine musikalische Zeitung.* "Great men belong to the nations who know how to appreciate them. . . ." In Germany, where the piece was to be performed in a number of cities, the same newspaper exulted: "Heil to our German fatherland that can count a Haydn among its sons!"[42]

In Austria during Haydn's last years — he was to complete his last instrumental work, a "National Hungarian March," around 1802 — the cult of "great music" was to be an element in the political movement led by Graf Stadion, who became minister for foreign affairs following the first occupation of Vienna in 1805. His goal, which inspired the romantics with new historicist notions, was to strengthen the empire by bringing the different national traditions together in a federation.[43] The *Vaterländischen Blätter* fondly envisaged the empire's various peoples "amicably coming together, like members of the same family, united around *Vater Franz*"; the same newspaper, which had connections to Stadion, was to praise a musical art that enabled its listeners "to forget the lack of class harmony in the harmony of notes."[44] This patriotic musical movement was to find its focal point in Haydn's oratorios. In 1808, "Papa Haydn" made his final public appearance at a concert at the University of Vienna at which *The Creation* was performed in an Italian version by the poet Carpani, who was also to write a biography of the composer — at the time, the Hapsburgs were striving to consolidate their authority over their Italian territories. Nearly unable to walk, the venerable composer was greeted with fanfares and bade a farewell by Beethoven, Salieri, Lobkowitz, and other prominent figures of Vienna's cultural life. "In honoring Haydn as no other Viennese musician had ever been or had ever deserved to be honored, Austria's aristocracy was in a way celebrating itself, for Haydn was the last great living representative of a kind of culture that that aristocracy had done so much to promote."[45] With the same spirit of personal identification with the nation's grandeur, the aged Haydn was also to make *Gott erhalte* into a private ritual. In 1808, the composer Sigismund Neukomm paid him a visit: "He is very weak, and one must take his arm to help him take a few steps in his room; despite that, he plays three or four times each day his ever-beautiful *Gott erhalte Franz den Kaiser*, and sometimes even manages to find a new bass for the tune, although sometimes too he comes up with nothing, which makes him impatient and say that he realizes that nothing works any more."[46] According to his manservant, Haydn played the imperial anthem a final time a few days before his death, "even three times running, with so much expression and taste that even our good Papa himself was surprised and said that he had not played like that for a long while. . . ."[47] He died on 31 May 1809 during the second occupation of Vienna. Two weeks later, in the Schottenkirche,

Mozart's *Requiem* was performed in his memory with a number of French in attendance, among them the museum curator Vivant Denon and, among the military, Henri Beyle (today better known as Stendhal).

After its composer's death, *The Creation* was to maintain its position in the great oratorio tradition that Vienna carried forward after 1814. However, the work was to fall out of favor in the romantic era. Schiller and Beethoven — and later, Schumann and Berlioz — both spoke sarcastically about a work too replete with the candor of *Tonmalerei* and the extinct fires of the aristocratic Enlightenment. Relegated to the role of kindly patriarch, its composer came to be regarded with veiled contempt by a generation that far preferred Beethoven-style pathos. On the other hand, Haydn's instrumental works were to remain one of the pillars of the "pure" music so dear to romantics like Tieck and Wackenroder, who at the turn of the century had launched the notion of a "religion of music" that was soon to be under the aegis of Haydn, Mozart, and Beethoven, the "Viennese trinity." As for *Gott erhalte,* now firmly anchored in ceremonies and men's minds, it was to reaffirm its role as the official symbol of the Austrian state, particularly when a version for military band was adopted in 1826 for performance at great public occasions. This regulation official use did not prevent the dissemination and spread of a new text produced in northern Germany in 1841 by the romantic poet Hoffmann von Fallersleben: this was the *Deutschland über alles* that was to become the German national anthem after having become known and popular within the pan-German nationalist movement. However, Haydn's hagiography, filled as it was with patriotic zeal for the Hapsburg states, added another twist to the legend surrounding the national anthem. In 1847, an article attributing the tune of *Gott erhalte* to an Italian gave Anton Schmid, an official at Vienna's Imperial Library, an opportunity to write a new narrative of its origins:

> In England, Haydn had been introduced to *God Save the King* and come to envy the British nation a hymn in which it would, on solemn occasions, publicly express its respect, love, and devotion for its ruler. When the Father of Harmony returned to his beloved *Kaiserstadt,* he spoke of his feelings to that true friend, connoisseur, defender, and protector of so many great representatives of Art and Science, Graf van Swieten . . . [Haydn added] that he hoped for a similar hymn for Austria, so that it might also attest to the same respect and devotion for its sovereign. In addition, such a hymn would also be a noble means of rekindling the fire in

the hearts of the Austrians in the battles then being waged against the invading foes from across the Rhine and of augmenting and inciting to combat the volunteers then being called up in the general mobilization. Graf van Swieten at once spoke to His Excellency Graf Franz von Saurau, head of the Government of Lower Austria and author of the aforementioned mobilization, and thus was born a hymn that not only counts among Haydn's greatest creations but has earned him the crown of immortality.[48]

This fable, which has no historical basis, has nevertheless been a part of the Haydn legend right to the present time.[49] According to this new version of its origin, the great composer was not only the creator of the national anthem, he had also come up with the idea of creating one. The loyal servant of the aristocratic regime thus became a free patriot, rich in worldly experience. The public powers move into the background and honor comes to have a place within the canon of classical music. Thanks to the musician's sacred aura, the action of the state is transferred to the will of the nation. When the time came to invoke the voice of the people "as a whole," united around the "father of the people," Haydn, the "Father of Harmony" was, for modern times, a figure more respectable than the assistant chief of police.

# 4

# Beethoven and the
# Concert of Europe

On 22 December 1808, in Vienna's Theater an der Wien, Ludwig van Beethoven introduced his Fifth Symphony, Sixth (*Pastorale*) Symphony, the concert aria *Ah! Perfido,* and the Fourth Concerto for piano and orchestra — all of them works hitherto unknown to the public and that showed him to be at the height of his creativity, and works that today are among the most famous of all the classical repertory. To conclude the concert, in which he had displayed all of his talents — as composer, pianist, and conductor — he brought all of the participants together to perform a final apotheosis, the *Choral Fantasy* for piano solo, soloists, chorus, and orchestra, op. 80. This work began with Beethoven at the piano playing an extemporaneous solo introduction — the printed score has a composed cadenza — which, after the orchestra's entrance, leads to a tune in the popular style derived from the *Gegenliebe* of 1795. This is reprised and played with variations throughout the *Choral Fantasy* very like the method the composer would employ more than fifteen years later for the *Ode to Joy*. The vocal variations — first for the female and male soloists, in turn, and then for full chorus — are set to a text by one of Beethoven's friends "following his indications." [1] The poem is a paean to the "music of our lives," to inner and outer peace, and to the union of music and poetry, all coming together like the waves of the ocean in "peace and joy" [*Fried' und Freude*]. The final verses, sung by the chorus, are as follows:

*Nehmt denn hin, ihr schönen Seelen,*    Take then gladly, happy Souls,
*Froh die Gaben schöner Kunst.*    What that noble Art bestows.
*Wenn sich Lieb' und Kraft*    When Love and Strength are
    *vermählen,*        joined together,

*Lohnt dem Menschen Göttergunst.*    Then mankind is blessed by the
Gods.

The union of "Love and Strength" under the aegis of the arts, accompanied by the full orchestra in the finale, is the kernel of this virtual manifesto that Beethoven offered to the public in 1808. Its praise of the experience of art is related to that contained in Schiller's 1795 *Briefe über die ästhetische Erziehung des Menschen* [Letters on the Aesthetic Education of Man]; rooted in the Enlightenment tradition, it reflects the emergence and growth of a particular cultural awareness, a *Bildung* or comprehensive aesthetic outlook, that began in Germany at the time of the Napoleonic wars and that would eventually come to form one of the pillars of the bourgeois universe.

The chaotic progress of the 22 December concert, which was marked by disputes between Beethoven and his musicians, illustrates the gap that then existed between those ideals and actual contemporary musical practice. In the nascent world of commercial music making, such a concert, known as an *Akademie* and put on by a composer for his own benefit, was still an unusual event; Beethoven, thirty-eight years old at the time, was able to take the risk because he was Vienna's leading active musical personality. He had determined to present the concert a short time after receiving a particularly appealing proposal from Jérôme Bonaparte, king of Westphalia and brother to Napoleon, to serve as his Kapellmeister. By showing the Viennese what they would be losing were he to leave to take up this post, Beethoven's initiative was part of a campaign of self-promotion that would shortly enable him to attain "the highest degree of independence and security possible in a semifeudal system of patronage."[2] Indeed, under the terms of a contract drawn up and signed in 1809 by three noblemen willing to free his "powerful genius" from all material cares, Beethoven was to receive a large sum of money on the sole condition that he reside in Vienna or some other city within the Hapsburg Empire. True, given the devaluation of the Austrian currency in 1811 and the deaths of two of his protectors, his tranquility would not be destined to last long. However, it is well known that his career was closely linked to an aristocratic world in which "family ties were accompanied by musical alliances" and that, throughout his life, he managed to be exceptionally well placed vis-à-vis members of the intellectual and political elite.[3]

His privileged status, however, did not make him a favorite of the emperor, even less a "court musician." Indeed, "most of Beethoven's main supporters among the aristocrats were non-Austrian in origin, deriving from Hungary, Bohemia, Russia and Germany."[4] He had no personal relationship with the emperor Franz I, and he was never to dedicate a work to him as he would to Friedrich Wilhelm II and Friedrich III of Prussia, Alexander I of Russia, or Maximilian Joseph of Bavaria. Aside from the casual attention he received from the empress Maria Theresa, Beethoven's only contact with the imperial family was through Archduke Rudolph, the emperor's younger half brother, who was his student, a signatory to the aforementioned 1809 contract, and the dedicatee of more than a dozen of his works. However, since Rudolph played no significant political role, it can be said that Beethoven was never in contact with the inner circles of power of the Austrian Empire.

What we know of his political awareness, which was rooted in his experience as part of the Josephinian elite in Bonn, is in line with this objective distancing from the ideological underpinnings of the Austria of Franz I. Beethoven's biography contains many episodes that, while showing his allegiance to Enlightenment values, illustrate a certain tension in his relationships with those in power. On the other hand, the ambiguous memory of what he once ironically described as his "revolutionary fervor" would appear to have had but little effect on his public attitudes. We have no direct surviving evidence of Beethoven's support for the French Revolution that would allow us to attribute to him any lasting and systematic republican convictions. The "republican" image that some biographers have created for him rests on a handful of ambiguous or questionable episodes — most importantly the dedication of the *Eroica* Symphony to Bonaparte, subsequently torn up following the news of his coronation, or the incident at Teplitz at which Beethoven is said to have refused to bow when the royal family passed by — episodes that, without perhaps being untrue, have been rendered suspect by the manner in which they have been exploited. On the other hand, throughout almost his entire life, Beethoven was to contribute willingly to Hapsburg propaganda and aspire to a position in its institutions. In addition to the 1797 *lieder* to poems by Friedelberg and the numerous military marches, there is his music for August von Kotzebue's dramas *Die Ruinen von Athen* and *König Stephan* [The Ruins of Athens, King Stephen], written for the opening of the Imperial Theater in Pest in 1812. The first of those works recounts the story of a goddess of antiquity who, returning to earth in modern times, discovers a Greece debased at the hands of the Turks; only in the lands of Franz I, a benevolent sovereign and patron of the arts, does she find the noble spirit of antiquity. Both dramas conclude with triumphal choruses in honor of the sovereign, reminiscent of the finale of the cantata for Leopold II: "Heil, unserm König! Heil!"

Furthermore, Beethoven's triumph in elite cultural circles reflects the immediate perception of his exceptional musical talent. Up to the turn of the century, the status of piano virtuoso was a factor essential in the composer's output, which followed in the stylistic footsteps of Mozart or late Haydn. Beethoven's announcement in 1802 of a "new path" in his work, following the earliest symptoms of his deafness and the great crisis described in the famous "Heiligenstadt Testament," marks the onset of what Romain Rolland was to call his "heroic period." Basically, this is embodied in the overtures for *Egmont, Coriolanus,* and *Leonore,* the *Waldstein* and *Appassionata* piano sonatas, the *Emperor* Concerto and lastly — and above all — the Third and Fifth Symphonies — a handful of works that, from their creation to the present day, have been pillars of the classical repertory. Descriptions of this style and its forging often invoke the influence of French revolutionary music, drawing, for example, comparisons between the funeral march in the *Eroica* and Gossec's *Marche lugubre* or calling attention to the similarities between the initial motif of the Fifth Symphony and Cherubini's *Hymne au Panthéon.*[5] The latter comparison does recognize Beethoven's affinities with Cherubini's operas and symphonies, for which he openly expressed admiration; indeed, the libretto for *Fidelio,* which is very much in the "heroic style," is derived from a French play by Jean-Nicolas Bouilly. However, it is less easy to establish any specific link between Beethoven's music and revolutionary anthems. In 1799, a series of articles in Leipzig's *Allgemeine musikalische Zeitung* offered a detailed analysis of such French "national hymns," which, the author noted, had hitherto been regarded as "minor" works; this sign of interest serves to demonstrate that the musical output of the Revolution was known in Germany and that some there, counter to prevailing opinion, were prepared to regard it as a valid artistic expression of political ideas that were not necessarily reprehensible.[6] We can imagine that Beethoven was aware of this discussion and curious about the works in question, and some French influence on his vocal and, especially, his political music cannot be excluded, although it is not easy to distinguish it from the Enlightenment heritage reflected in the Bonn cantatas. And, that being said, there is no documentation to show that he had any direct knowledge of revolutionary anthems nor that they had inspired him to embody his own political ideas in his instrumental works. Further, his "heroic" compositions, which are characterized by a dramatic expansion of the classical sonata form, are in direct contradiction to the basic principles of revolutionary musical aesthetics, which regarded as suspect semantic uncertainty in any music without words and which gave absolute pride of place to sung music as the direct and transparent expression of the nation's voice. Beethoven's possibly defiant attitude toward power should not imply that during his lifetime his compositions were viewed as carrying any critical message: the ripping of the dedicatory page of the *Eroica* Symphony, for example, was an eminently private act that was not discovered until after his death and one that could therefore have had no influence at all on the recognition of the merits of the work, which was premiered in 1805 and published under the title *Sinfonia grande Eroica per festeggiare il sovvenire di un grand Uomo* [Grand Heroic Symphony to Celebrate the Memory of a Great Man].

The unusual scale of these orchestral works, often verbally associated with some mythical content, explains why they were immediately spoken of as kinds of sublime experience. The earliest reactions to the *Eroica*, which mingled praise for its sublimity and colossal character with accusations of excessive length, rules flouted, or outright oddity, reveal a tension with regard to Beethoven and his work that, along with his reputation as a difficult and even wild-eyed genius, was to characterize the perception of his difference.[7] In 1810, an article on the Fifth Symphony by E. T. A. Hoffmann in the *Allgemeine musikalische Zeitung* was to be the first contribution to a type of musical aesthetics whose influence would continue to spread: Beethoven's instrumental music, according to Hoffmann, "inspires fear and trembling, awe, sorrow, and awakens the endless nostalgia that is the very essence of romanticism."[8] Here, Hoffmann is enlarging on a view of music that had first been formulated in the writings of Tieck and Wackenroder, at the heart of the romantic movement in Jena with the group that formed around the Schlegel brothers, Friedrich and August Wilhelm. "For Hoffmann, as for many of his generation, the Fifth Symphony had been the epiphany of a new era in musical history."[9] In a Germany that was experiencing a surge of anti-Napoleonic nationalism, such wholly metaphysical discourse on art could not help but have some political resonance. Recognition of Beethoven's greatness was inseparable from his national acceptance as part of the framework of German culture — a perception that would be more acute, indeed, in northern Germany than it was in Vienna, where the more important concern was Austrian patriotism. For that matter, Beethoven himself was the first to advance the notion that his work had a patriotic value because of its aesthetic importance, invoking in turn both those national identities. In 1807, at the same time that he was threatening to leave Vienna, he explained to officials at the Imperial Theater that "the favor and approval which he has enjoyed from high and low, the wish wholly to fulfill the expectations which he has been fortunate enough to awaken, and, let him venture to say, the *patriotism* of a *German* have made this very *place* more estimable and desirable to him than any other." In 1809, when the aforementioned agreement was being drawn up, he made it known that he felt "so much patriotism for his second fatherland, that he will never cease to count himself among Austrian artists." [10]

The enthusiasm aroused by Napoleon's defeats soon enabled Beethoven to realize what he called "his ardent wish, and one long cherished, to lay at the altar of the fatherland the fruits of my labors." The military situation inspired him to compose a piece of political music in which he deliberately set out to reach a larger audience: "It is certain that we write better when we write for the public and if we write quickly," he confided to his journal. [11] On 21 June 1813, near the Spanish village of Victoria, the Duke of Wellington inflicted a stunning defeat on the troops of Jérôme Bonaparte. Following the disaster of the Russian campaign and this breach in the peninsular front, Napoleon's decline was to accelerate at Leipzig, where Austria joined with Prussia and Russia in a push that was not to stop until it had reached Paris. In an article about the new works of patriotic music, the battle of Leipzig was metaphorically described by one Viennese newspaper as " 'Die Befreiung von der Sklaverei,' eine Kantate von Alexander, die Musik ist von der verbündeten Mächter" ["The Liberation from Slavery," a cantata by Alexander, music by the allied powers]. [12] And if the war could be described as a cantata, and if the sound of war (at least according to Edmund Burke's essay on the subject) was one of man's sublime experiences, then music could in turn be employed to depict war. [13] The genre described as *battaglia* or "battle" music, a Renaissance invention, had been revived at the time of the Seven Years' War [1756–1763] and was to become extremely fashionable on both sides of the Rhine in the Napoleonic era — in France we find many *Batailles d'Austerlitz* and *Batailles d'Iéna*, while works like the *Schlachten bei Leipzig* quickly proliferated in Germany. Such compositions were particularly attractive to those who had not taken part in the actual battles, especially those younger members of the bourgeoisie who were prevented from achieving military glory owing to the aristocratic make-up of the allied armies; also thanks to such compositions, as Zelter was to write to Goethe, "women now can know exactly what a battle really is, even though soon nobody will know what music is."[14] That comment clearly reflects the misuse of a genre that, owing to its descriptive and narrative conventions, necessarily excluded the deployment of autonomous musical discourse, while at the same time opening itself to the moral reproach of mere frivolity. Indeed, E. T. A. Hoffmann, in his article on the Fifth Symphony, had condemned the whole genre as a collection of "ridiculous *faux pas*," little suspecting that his hero Beethoven would soon be making one himself.

However, the incursion of the *Eroica*'s composer into the field at the urging of his friend Johann Nepomuk Maelzel appears to have been taken quite seriously, by him as well as by his public — although there were some who were quick to qualify it as "hack work" that would, with time, drop out of the Beethoven catalogue or be regarded as a mere curiosity.[15] On 8 December 1813, the Viennese flocked to the university's auditorium to attend a benefit concert for the Austrian and Bavarian soldiers wounded in the battle of Hanau on 30 and 31 October. The program included Beethoven's Seventh Symphony, which had not yet been played in public; two marches, which were performed by Maelzel on a mechanical trumpet; and *Wellingtons Sieg, oder die Schlacht bei Vittoria* [Wellington's Victory, or The Battle of Vittoria], op. 91 (often popularly referred to as the "Battle Symphony"), which was dedicated to the English prince regent, the future George IV. The concert's organizers had managed to assemble some of Vienna's most important musicians — including the Imperial Kapellmeister Antonio Salieri, the famous pianist Hummel, the young Meyerbeer, the violinist Schuppanzigh, Spohr, Moscheles, Giuliani, Dragonetti, and other well-known talents, all under Beethoven's direction. The success of the work Beethoven was laying at the altar of the fatherland was to be phenomenal — and from a financial standpoint as well, thanks to two further concerts in January and February of 1814 in the Redoutensaal of the Imperial Palace. Anton Schindler, a witness, friend, secretary, and future biographer of Beethoven, writes of a triumph that "surpassed anything ever yet experienced in a concert hall,"[16] and a newspaper reported applause that "rose to the point of ecstasy,"[17] with the result that "Beethoven suddenly found himself at a level of national popularity he had not experienced before, a level as elevated as that of Haydn after the premieres of his oratorios *The Creation* and *The Seasons*."[18] Following the concert, Beethoven wrote a message of thanks to the participants, "an unusual congregation of admirable artists wherein every individual was inspired by the single thought of contributing something by his art for the benefit of the fatherland." For his own part, he wrote: "To me the direction of the whole was assigned only because the music was of my composition; had it been by another, I should have been as willing as Mr. Hummel to take my place at the big drum, as we were all filled with nothing but the pure love of country and of joyful sacrifice of our powers for those who sacrificed so much for us."[19] This letter, which concludes with a tribute to Maelzel, reflects Beethoven's desire to be recognized as the protagonist of a collective patriotic action. The fact that it was not published, owing to his quarrel with Maelzel over the author's rights to the piece, gives us a glimpse into the private and backstage aspects of this public event.

Such a "supra-individual" performance is, indeed, the very theme of Beethoven's work, which, far from constituting a heroic glorification of a single *grand uomo*, as its title might suggest, is in fact more a collective fable in which the figure of a leader is totally absent. And it is a fable based entirely on national airs. In 1803, Beethoven had composed piano variations on *God Save the King* and *Rule Britannia* (WoO 78 and 79); in 1813, he was to arrange the English anthem for soloist and unison chorus with instrumental trio (WoO 157, no. 1), noting in his journal: "I must give the English some notion of the blessing they have in their *God Save the King*."[20] Those pieces are evidence of his interest in those patriotic works, although it was Maelzel who appears to have suggested that he include them in his *Battle*— a practice quite common at the time, as witness in 1799 the quotations of the *Marseillaise* and *Gott erhalte* in Salieri's cantata *Der Tyroler Landsturm* [The Tyrolese Territorial Reserves].[21] In the *Battle of Vittoria,* the national tunes form the basis of the entire work, serving both as musical themes and political signals. Indeed, the role they play reflects fairly precisely their dual function as public sign and private symbol: whereas in the work's first section, the marches *Rule Britannia* and *Marlbrough s'en va-t-en guerre* depict the British and French armies in a naturalistic way, in the second section, the "symphony of victory," the national anthem *God Save the King* serves what might be described as an emotional purpose. On each occasion, the political and musical elements are differently employed: in the first section, the musical development gives way to descriptive music, with a rhythmic and harmonic interplay using the two tunes; following a fearsome climax, we have a sad and pitiful reprise of *Marlbrough*— the shreds of the French march altered to mock the conquered foe, the tune known to have been Napoleon's favorite now turned against him. In the work's second section, Beethoven combines a fanfare motif with the first part of the English anthem, whose cadence is never played. In this procedure, in which some have seen a touch of irony, the discourse is advanced by the very fact that the symbol is incomplete, its constituent parts being used solely for musical ends. Since we are dealing with a victory and not a defeat, one is not surprised at the total absence of the *Marseillaise,* which was not one of the Napoleonic Empire's symbols — and to which, for that matter, there is no reference whatsoever in either Beethoven's life or in his work.[22]

After this triumph, Beethoven's career was closely linked to subsequent events, with many signs of his allegiance to the regime — at the January and February 1814 concerts, for example, a portrait of the emperor Franz I was unveiled during the finale of *The Ruins of Athens.* On 31 March of the same year, the allied troops marched into Paris, accompanied by Tsar Alexander I and King Friedrich Wilhelm III; news of the fall of the French capital reached Vienna on 10 April, and on the following day, a *Singspiel* by Georg Treitschke, *Die gute Nachricht* [The Good News] was performed to great acclaim at the Kärthnerthor Theater. Hastily written, the piece had been set to music by various composers (Hummel, Weigl, and even, post mortem, Mozart); the final number, for bass soloist and chorus, with orchestra, *Germania, wie stehts du jetzt im Glanze da* [Germany, There You Stand in All Your Glory!], was by Beethoven (WoO 94). It celebrated a young and powerful Germany, in which the nation's glory combines with that of the victorious rulers, and culminated in an apotheosis of Emperor Franz. Shortly thereafter, the latter's triumphal homecoming was to inspire numerous works of "greeting": Hummel and Beith rapidly composed an opera, *Die Rückfahrt des Kaisers* [The Emperor's Return]; Ignaz Sauer composed an oratorio entitled *Der grosse Tag des Vaterlandes* [The Fatherland's Great Day]; and Diabelli quoted *Gott erhalte* in a piano composition. Beethoven himself appears to have considered writing an opera on the subject. With less bombast, but with an acute sense of political occasion, the return of Prince Clemens von Metternich, since 1809 Austria's chancellor, was also celebrated musically: on the evening of 20 July, nearly two hundred musicians gathered beneath his windows to serenade him with a *grosse Nacht-musik,* a tribute that began with Beethoven's overture to *Die Geschöpfe des Prometheus* [The Creatures of Prometheus]. Official music — Beethoven's as well as that of his colleagues — thus had its moment in the limelight; aside from Salieri's patriotic choruses, most of it was even performed without the authorities having taken the initiative. Unlike *Gott erhalte,* which was commissioned at a time of military and political weakness, the works of this period were not designed to create some consensus between the state and society but to be a part of an existing consensus in the euphoria of military victory, and it was precisely that convergence of public spirit and state interests that was to ensure their success. It goes without saying that the government maintained control of all these activities: texts were subject to censorship, and police authorization was required for each concert; the press was obedient, as were the impresarios of the few available concert halls. However, none of Beethoven's works composed between 1813 and 1815 as blatant reflections of official discourse was composed at official behest nor played as a part of any official ceremonial program.

Beethoven's popularity continued to grow throughout the year 1814. On the same day as the premiere of Treitschke's *Singspiel,* he played the piano in a benefit concert for the military that included the first performance of the *Archduke* Trio, op. 97, dedicated to Rudolph. The enthusiasm his music aroused led to a reworking of the opera *Leonore,* whose 1805 and 1806 versions had both been disappointing failures most painful for the composer. In that opera, he had included some material from his cantata for Joseph II, in particular the melody of the aria for soprano and chorus, now associated with Florestan's freedom. In 1814, with Treitschke's assistance, he made important changes in both the music and the libretto: whereas *Leonore* had concluded in the dungeon, the revised version ends in the prison courtyard in the full light of day, where Don Fernando, the state minister, "the brother seeking brothers," arrives in great pomp to liberate the prisoners. In this finale, the chorus celebrates the love of Leonore and Florestan with a paraphrase of the *Ode to Joy:* "Let him who hath the love of a noble wife lend his voice to our song of rejoicing!" The premiere of the opera, now called *Fidelio,* on 23 May 1814 was a further triumph for a composer who, according to the press, had become the "public's favorite," and the piece would remain on the bill for months to come, the central German work in a repertory that was, ironically, dominated by "revolutionaries" like Cherubini and Méhul. Maynard Solomon wrote: "Although in 1805–6 the opera had been regarded as a work about 'rescue,' in the sense of enlightened faith," in 1814 "the new version was directly perceived as a celebration of the victory over the Napoleonic armies, as an allegory for a Europe liberated from the aggressions of the usurping tyrant."[23]

Beethoven's European allegory was soon to find a public worthy of it when, in September 1814, visitors began to pour in to the city for the Congress of Vienna. The most powerful European rulers and diplomatic missions from many smaller states, members of the nobility, leaders of the victorious armies, favorites (both male and female) of the powerful, the curious, chroniclers and adventurers of every hue — all were to make up a public avid for concert music, opera, and other more, or less, artistic entertainments. On 22 September, the king of Wurtemberg arrived in Vienna; on the 23rd the king of Denmark; on the 25th, Alexander of Russia and Friedrich Wilhelm of Prussia both made triumphal entries, welcomed by the emperor of Austria in a repeat of their meeting in Leipzig. The following day, the monarchs assembled at the Kärthnerthor Theater for a performance of *Fidelio*.[24] In coming months, the Englishmen Castlereagh and Wellington; France's Talleyrand, accompanied by the Duc de Dalberg; the Prussians Hardenberg and Humboldt; the tsar's delegates, Stein, Nesselrode, Capo d'Istria, and Razumovsky; the Hapsburg's Gentz and Metternich, together were to negotiate the continent's fate. Indeed, the Congress of Vienna laid the groundwork for a new geopolitical era built on the notion of a European balance of power. The system, which Metternich was to dub the "Concert of Europe," was to determine the fate of the Western world well beyond the institutions and mechanisms set up in 1814–15. Far from limiting themselves to mere resistance to French militarism, republican or Bonapartist, the Congress was to guarantee the hegemony of the victorious dynasties over national, liberal, and democratic movements, all subsumed in the single ghost of Revolution. It is in this context that Metternich's 1824 statement should be read: "For me, Europe has long had the validity of a fatherland" — an enlargement on the earlier boast to the Duc de Dalberg in 1817: "In me, you see Europe's grand minister of police. I am ever vigilant. Nothing escapes me."[25]

The theory behind this policy was set forth by Friedrich von Gentz, the Congress's secretary and an associate of the Austrian chancellor: "By their geographic situation, through their customs, their laws, their needs, their way of life and their culture, the states of this continent, taken as a whole, constitute a great political federation that has — and rightly — been called the European Republic."[26] Notwithstanding their conservative character and their source from the pen of a political romantic, such ideas echo those of the abbé de Saint-Pierre and Emmanuel Kant, the authors of the earliest proposals for a European political federation. Shortly after his return from

Elba, Napoleon too was to call for the creation of a "great federative European system."[27] Following these shared feelings, Europe gradually came to
be conceived as a political entity, to surpass the limitations of mere geogra-
phy or of Voltaire's "Republic of Letters." Even the romantics' rediscovery
of the Middle Ages, insofar as it was not exclusively nationalist, was to bolster the notion of the continent's original cultural unity. Madame de Staël,
influenced by Wilhelm Schlegel, was to find in the spirit of chivalry "a kind
of European patriotism that filled every soul with the same feelings."[28] On
the other hand, the Concert of Europe, hostile in principle to Kant's and
Schiller's theoretical ideal liberty, was to remain a concept that would be
deeply antipathetic to the nineteenth century's bourgeois intelligentsia.

It can be said, too, that the politics of the Congress of Vienna also set the
tone at the worldly level. "Vienna is indeed the center of Europe, and it was
then its capital," wrote the Count de La Garde, a privileged witness to that
exciting time whose book bears as its epigraph a quotation from the Prince
de Ligne: "It is a political fabric heavily embroidered with festive celebrations."[29] The partying that went on enabled the European aristocracy to
reaffirm its shared identity and to reconnect with a prerevolutionary past
that was to a great extent an illusion. On 23 November, for example, a mock
mediaeval tournament was held at which noblemen dressed as knights
jousted to music composed by Moscheles, a pupil of Beethoven; there were
tableaux vivants in which they dressed as antique gods accompanied by a
romance by Queen Hortense, *En partant pour la Syrie,* or by symphonies
by Haydn and Mozart. All of these parties and entertainments, far from af-
fording a break from the serious business at hand, were often occasions at
which the implacable struggles that riddled the "political fabric," barely
held together by the thread of counterrevolution, were actually played out.
We understand, therefore, the zeal of the Hapsburg secret police, led by
Baron von Hager and assisted by a number of informants, some of whom
were prominent men like the poet Carpani, the Italian translator of Haydn's
*Creation.* The composer Sigismund von Neukomm, a protégé of Talleyrand and former pupil of Haydn who had composed a *Requiem* in memory of Louis XVI that was performed on 21 January 1815, was kept under
close surveillance on direct orders from Metternich himself.[30] The organization of these artistico-mondain gatherings was overseen by a Festival
Committee appointed by Franz I, their musical aspects being entrusted to
Salieri. La Garde describes a "monster concert" at the Imperial Palace in
which Salieri led an orchestra of pianists, "an unparalleled racket" that, he

adds, "was more a harmonic *tour de force* than a concert in any tasteful sense of the word."[31] However, music was not associated with frivolous amusements only. On 18 October, a commemoration of the battle of Leipzig was held in the Prater, attended by the sovereigns and their troops. La Garde has given a description of the climax of this "great military festival of peace," which followed an open-air mass:

> Then a chorus performed the hymn to peace, in German. Whereupon the entire army and the mass of spectators mingled their voices with those of the musicians. No, the human ear has never heard anything more imposing than those thousands of voices raised as one to celebrate the benefits of peace and the glory of the Almighty.[32]

The actual contribution of the crowd to that "hymn of peace" remains, of course, a moot point; in any event, the aristocrat did not hesitate to recognize those "voices raised as one" in that apotheosis of the Restoration, describing it as the "great *états généraux* of Europe." So it was that the commemoration by the Concert of Europe of the French defeat was inspired by the earlier French revolutionary celebration, albeit now under the aegis of the church. The record of this type of mass open-air ritual does not end there: the celebrations for the battle of Leipzig — that held at Vienna is but one example — were to be a model for future events that were to become a traditional element in the German nationalist movement.[33]

Having said that, there were other occasions during the Congress of Vienna, apart from the more frivolous ceremonies, at which "great music" was performed, music composed by local luminaries whose names were familiar to even the most uninformed visitor. Indeed, the Duc de Dalberg was reported to have said: "It is a crying shame that Vienna has not yet erected a monument to Haydn. Paris would have done so a long time ago."[34] On 16 October, Handel's oratorio *Samson* was performed in the presence of a number of crowned heads at a concert organized by the *Gesellschaft der Musikfreunde*, Vienna's already prestigious Society of the Friends of Music, which had been founded in 1812. However, more than anyone else, it was Beethoven who was to undertake to combine greatness and festivities in music. Indeed, this required little more than his presence, so well-known had his name become: "At these times the master was an object of general curiosity to all the foreign visitors, for it is the lot of genius to attract the attention of the nobility, particularly when that genius has a touch of the heroic," Schindler was to write, describing Beethoven's visit to the residence of Count Razumovsky. It was Razumovsky, the composer's longtime patron and the tsar's envoy to the Congress, who afforded him entry to the highly placed power figures who frequented his palace, especially the Russians and Prussians; however, Archduke Rudolph also wished "to have a part in the triumph of his exalted teacher by inviting foreign nobles to his own rooms to meet Beethoven." For a man who was deaf and reputed to be misanthropic, the composer appears to have carried off these worldly occasions with a certain virtuosic flair. "In later years," Schindler was to report, "the great master would recall not without emotion those days in the imperial castle and the palace of the Russian prince and would say with a tinge of pride that he himself had been courted by the highest rulers of Europe and had comported himself admirably." [35] Yet Beethoven, obviously able to bank on his prestige, could also refuse to go along with what he viewed as aristocratic frivolities. When Archduke Rudolph asked him to compose music for the "tournament" held on 23 November, his letter of reply dripped with sarcasm:

> I see that Your Imperial Highness is eager further to assess the effects of my music, even on horses. So be it, we shall see whether with it the knights will be able to perform their somersaults — Ha! Your Imperial Highness's manner of thinking of me even on such an occasion does make me laugh. I am, life long,
>     your obedient servant Ludwig van Beethoven.
> P.S. The requested horse-music [*Pferdemusik*] will be arriving at Your Imperial Highness's at full gallop! [36]

However, in the event the composer was to delegate that task to Moscheles. "Beethoven replies with a courtier's laughter, but its sound is a bit strained, and one cannot be sure that he actually found the pleasantry in all that good taste, whereas the archduke was not even aware of having made one," as Jean and Brigitte Massin have noted. For Beethoven saw his role among the powerful in quite another light. As the rulers were assembling, he composed a *Chor auf die verbündeten Fürsten* [Chorus for the Princes Assembled] (WoO 95), a setting of a poem by his friend Joseph Karl Bernard, the future publisher of the establishment newspaper *Wiener Zeitung;* this was a short but weighty work for chorus and orchestra in praise of the *weisen Gründer glückliche Staaten* [the wise founders of happy states]. Notwithstanding the chorus's relative technical facility, there is no trace of its having been performed during the Congress of Vienna. However, it does set the tone for Beethoven's contribution to that historic event, namely, to carve a place for himself in the hearts of men through the medium of art.

This he was to undertake to do in another work of a quite different kind. On 10 September, the censor rejected for the second time Bernard's poem for a cantata entitled *Europa Befreyungstunde* [Europe's Hour of Liberation]. Since the censor was not required to explain his rejection of the text, we can only speculate on his reasons. Michael Ladenburger believes that its francophobic tone may have been the cause.[37] In any event, Beethoven then turned to Alois Weissenbach, the author of several successful patriotic pieces. A physician in Salzburg who had fought in the imperial army against the Turks and the French, and who was described as "very patriotic, the enemy of everything foreign," Weissenbach had come to Vienna for, in his words, "the sole pleasure of contemplating all of those crowned heads who were gathered there."[38] He had attended the performance of *Fidelio* on 26 September and been transported. The composer's visit was the beginning of a somewhat odd relationship, since Weissenbach was as deaf as his famous friend. That, however, did not prevent them from rapidly turning out the cantata known as *The Glorious Moment,* op. 136. Beethoven was soon able to announce a mammoth concert for 29 November in the Redoutensaal of the Imperial Palace, the program to include the Seventh Symphony, *The Glorious Moment,* and *Wellington's Victory.*

The concert was a huge success. Schindler reported nearly six thousand people in the audience and wrote that the cantata was greeted with lengthy applause, even though the text did not emerge without criticism.[39] The triumph was enhanced by the high-ranking personages who were in attendance at Beethoven's personal invitation. "The highest court dignitaries, kings and queens, foreign princes and princesses — all honored the performance of this music with their presence," the *Wiener Zeitung* reported.[40] Tsar Alexander and Tsarina Elisabeth, King Friedrich Wilhelm, Empress Maria Ludovica of Austria, the Prince of Sicily, even members of the English mission, were all there: "The King of Prussia paid an *Extrahonorar* of 10 ducats. He's a lout [*Lump*]! Only the emperor of Russia paid honestly 100 ducats for his ticket," Beethoven was to comment.[41] The emperor Franz was absent, however, as was the archduke Rudolph. The Austrian government was informed of events by one of Baron Hager's secret informants:

> The performance, which was held yesterday, did not result in any increased enthusiasm for the talent of this composer, who has his supporters and his adversaries. In contrast to the former, foremost among whom are Razumovsky, Appony, Kraft, etc., who adore Beethoven, the vast majority of connoisseurs now absolutely refuse ever to listen to Beethoven's works again.[42]

The spy was probably right to refer to the polemics that surrounded Beethoven's person even at the height of his fame. In any event, the political language and the hostility of his tone suggest that the company the composer kept was not always well regarded in certain official Austrian circles. The police report is of an event that was attended by the rulers of Russia and Prussia but not that of Austria — this at the very time when the "Polish question" that would two months later bring the former allies to the brink of war was beginning to surface. However that may be, it must be said that *The Glorious Moment* reveals no personal attitude — and even less an original one — vis-à-vis historic events.

As its title indicates, *The Glorious Moment,* for soloists, chorus, and orchestra, is the musical representation of a moment, that moment when, according to the grandiose opening statement,

| | |
|---|---|
| *Europa steht! Europa steht!* | Europe is risen! Europe is risen! |
| *Und die Zeiten, die ewig shreiten,* | And the times in their headlong rush, |
| *der Völker Chor, und die alten Jahrhundert,* | The chorus of peoples and former centuries, |
| *sie schauen verwundert empor!* | Look on in amazement! |

The dynamic shift between the *fortissimo* "chorus of peoples" and the *pianissimo* "former centuries" indicates the scale of the space in which this vision is rooted; the solo voices — *Der Führer des Volks* [The People's Leader], *Der Genius* [The Guardian Spirit], *Vienna,* and *Die Seherinn* [The Seeress] — all contribute to the uplifting epiphany. It is the dizzying point where History coalesces into Present; awestruck, the people and peoples admire and bless the spectacle of Mankind's liberation. Europe is at peace thanks to the Princes assembled at Vienna, whose majesty outshines that of Ancient Rome. "I am Europe," Vienna sings in an aria with chorus, hailing the five foreign princes present at the Congress, each introduced by fanfares whose order and lengths suggest political rank: first, the Russian tsar, next the king of Prussia, then Denmark, lastly, Wurtemburg and Bavaria; the entrance of the emperor Franz is that of a *primus inter pares.* After Vienna has "hailed all the princes" and "embraced all peoples," the chorus salutes her. This embrace of city, princes, and peoples is emphasized by a thrice-repeated phrase, amplified by a lengthy ornamented vocal passage, which elevates the glorious European moment and gives it a universal dimension: "In the peaceful union of brothers / Liberated mankind itself embraces!"

The invocation of the brotherhood of mankind under the aegis of its rulers is embodied in the voice of the people, represented throughout the work by the chorus. It is the "chorus of peoples," it invites the listener to join in the "great circle of the people," it is the adoring voice of Vienna, the conscience that calls out to the world or praises before God the union of prince and army. In the final number, it is divided into three parts: a choir of women, a choir of children, and a choir of men. Each part announces its entrance and sings a very simple, typically "popular" melody: the women contemplate the "brilliant chorus of princes," giving them, as mothers, their "holy blessing." The children represent the "choir of innocence," and their naive melody is sung in two-part harmony, in thirds. Lastly, the male chorus enters, "a warrior chorus with weapons and flags," and sings a unison march accompanied by a percussion section *alla turca* — triangle, cymbals, and bass drum. The three sections then unite, superposing their voices. Each retains the same text, but the orchestra, performing *tutti,* with the *alla turca* percussion, emphasizes the martial atmosphere that dominates the conclusion of the first section:

Frau - en den glän — zen - den Chor der Für - sten zu schau - en

kom - men, es tre — ten her - vor die Kin - der, di from - men

Hee - re, ein krieg - ri - scher Chor mit Fah - nen und Weh - re

The chorus then becomes one again, an impersonal choir that performs a fugue in which Vienna is invoked as *Vindobona,* its Latin name, while the counter-subject is sung to the words *Welt, dein grosser Augenblick* [World, thy great moment]; city and world, Latin and German, are thus joined in a final synthesis. In the monumental Handelian style, the absence of grammatical subject combines with contrapuntal dexterity to create the traditional image of political power. The fugue's massive grandeur leads to a homophonic apotheosis whose long-held *fortissimo* notes set a seal on the world's glorious moment.

*The Glorious Moment* is the artistic representation of a perfectly closed political universe: no crack appears to threaten this edifice, in which the population, the peoples, the emperor, princes, fatherland, Europe, the world, and mankind all fit together in a coherent structure of equivalences and hierarchies. The system finds reflection in music of an archaistic style whose vocabulary is drawn from the oratorio and cantata tradition, a style that almost totally eschews the recurrent motifs, thematic development, harmonic relationships, and other customary resources of the classical. At the same time, it is a music marked by a concept of dynamic relationships derived from the baroque, and the final climax is arrived at through a cumulative process that Beethoven had earlier employed in works like the *Choral Fantasy* or *Fidelio;* the discourse of the Enlightenment breaks into the exaltation of mankind and universal brotherhood, echoing the 1790 cantatas and the heroic themes of the *Egmont* and *Coriolanus* overtures. The three choirs of the first section of the last movement repeat the dramatic schema in which the people's voice was raised in revolutionary anthems; whether here the composer is drawing directly upon the French repertory (possible, although we have no evidence) or on his reading of Plutarch, we are struck by the historical weight of a model. At the end of the Napoleonic era, whether it be to engage in a revolution or to combat one, musical representations of political power will henceforth include the myth of the fusion of the community into one single voice. However, by the very fact of becoming part of a common political vocabulary, the invocation of that voice does not, in and of itself, create the significance of the work in which it is embodied.

*The Glorious Moment* cantata, through its political message, was to play a part in the ideological shaping of the Concert of Europe; as a project planned to perpetuate that moment in an artistic form, it aspired to monumental status. That is the sole and unique context in which Ludwig van

Beethoven was to join his work to the construction of a "European" political identity. It is because of that ideological origin as much as because of its real or purported aesthetic weaknesses that the work was to be severely judged by posterity; indeed, there has been a tendency to view its artistic failure as a direct result of its ideological moorings. Of course, that judgment is difficult to confute, although it can in no way be called final. However, rather than point out the aesthetic or moral caesura between the works Beethoven composed at the time of the Congress of Vienna and the rest of his oeuvre, what matters to us here is to emphasize continuity, to indicate how those works foreshadow his later style, especially in such large-scale "public" works as the *Missa Solemnis* and the Ninth Symphony. We do not apprehend the presence of politics in Beethoven's work, in the *Choral Fantasy* as much as in *Wellington's Victory,* by dividing his oeuvre into music that is "ideological," and thus bad, and music that embodies the composer's true beliefs and is therefore good. Notwithstanding the obvious differences between them, the political image bank that the *Ode to Joy* draws upon, far from reflecting a world opposed to that of *The Glorious Moment,* as exegetical tradition would have it, is in part a product of Beethoven's experience as a composer of official state music for the Congress of Vienna.

# 5

## The Ninth Symphony

In one of Beethoven's 1812 notebooks, along with sketches for the Eighth Symphony, we find musical ideas for the words *Freude schöner Götterfunken Tochter* together with the words: "Work out the overture!" In the margin is written: "Fragments [of the *Ode*], as in *Fürsten sind Bettler* but not its entirety . . . Make something using fragments of Schiller's *Joy.*" Shortly before the Congress of Vienna, therefore, Beethoven had again been thinking of his old plan to set Schiller's *Ode to Joy* to music. The version now in his thoughts was not, however, the later one of 1803 ("All men will become brothers"), but still the earlier 1785 version, "Beggars will become the brothers of princes," which in his notebook entry has taken a clearly antiaristocratic form: "Princes are beggars."[1]

In 1814, Beethoven again took up the 1812 notes; setting Schiller's text aside, he used the melodic themes he had noted down for an overture, sketches for which appear between those of the *Chor auf die verbündeten Fürsten* [Chorus for the Princes Assembled] and *The Glorious Moment.* The manuscript bears the inscription: "Overture by L. v. Beethoven, on the first of Wine-month (October) 1814 — Evening to the name day of our emperor." The work was to have been performed on the evening of 4 October at the fifteenth performance of *Fidelio,* in honor of Emperor Franz. However, the Grand Overture, op. 115, was not to be have its first performance until Christmas Day 1815; nevertheless, because of its original purpose, it has become known as the *Namensfeier* [Name Day Feast] Overture.

The composition of the Grand *Namensfeier* Overture entailed sawing the 1812 plan in half: Schiller's *Ode* would find its place in the Ninth Symphony, the 1812 music would be used for the emperor. Are we to regard this episode (as do Jean and Brigitte Massin) as evidence that in Beethoven's mind Schiller's *Ode to Joy* expressed a critical, if not revolutionary, attitude?[2] Or should we, with Alexander Thayer, see continuity between his 1814 support for the Concert of Europe and the ideal of brotherhood to which he would give expression in the Ninth Symphony ten years later?[3] One is tempted to answer: Both. Just as his antiaristocratic sentiments did not prevent Beethoven from participating in a glorification of the nobility, traces of his "official" music crept into works that had no connection to the political universe of 1814. What the history of the *Namensfeier* Overture does demonstrate is a certain pragmatic method of developing plans and materials that makes it difficult to make clear-cut distinctions between the composer's "occasional" and "expressive" compositions. Above all, it brings out the musical continuity between the composer of official, "state" music and the composer of the *Ode to Joy*. If the same melody can hymn universal joy and also honor the emperor Francis, we must either believe, with Metternich, that the emperor was the guarantor of universal joy, or we must assume a continuity between the musical rhetoric of the Revolution and that of the Restoration — a continuity that, when added to the nonreferential nature of the actual sounds themselves, sums up all the ideological ambiguities of Beethoven's music.

This is not to underestimate the semantic changes wrought by the evolution in individual and collective expectations that themselves underpin attributions of specific meanings. More than ten years were to elapse between the jottings in the 1812 notebook and the composition of the Ninth Symphony, years during which Beethoven's view of the world was to change markedly, a change brought about both by the course of political events and by events in his own personal life. The concert of 29 November 1814, which saw him at the peak of his popularity, was repeated on 2 December, but at the second one more than half the seats had gone begging; there would not be another benefit concert until 7 May 1824, the date of the premier performance of the Ninth Symphony. The same program was to be performed a third time on 29 December, a benefit concert for the Hospital for the Poor, but it is clear that as public enthusiasm for the Congress waned, Beethoven's career as a composer of patriotic music also began to lose steam. This did not prevent him from producing several more such works in 1815, among them a chorus, *Es ist vollbracht* [It Is Finished] (WoO 97), for a *Singspiel* by Treitschke on the news of the Battle of Waterloo. On 16 November 1815, the musical authorities made Ludwig von (*sic*) Beethoven an honorary citizen of Vienna in recognition of his "humanitarian" efforts on behalf of the hospital. The hospital's board that had backed this honor to an "artistic genius" and "noble philanthropist" had also been the moving force behind the bestowal of the same honor on Haydn eleven years earlier.[4] This official recognition of his artistic and moral merits both crowned and marked the end of Beethoven's public triumph at the time of the Congress of Vienna.

The ensuing years, lived under a regime that hardened its repressive attitude without however halting the nobility's economic decline and the rise of a nationalist and liberal bourgeoisie, were to be marked by a sharp change in the composer's social status, one that began in 1816 with his adoption of his nephew, Karl. "Vital to an understanding of Beethoven's life in Vienna is the certainty that until 11 December 1818 he encouraged, or at least permitted to pass unchallenged, the assumption that he was of noble birth," Maynard Solomon wrote, describing a "nobility pretense" that took advantage of the ambiguity created by "van" — which was Flemish and common — and the German and aristocratic "von."[5] The December 1818 date is the one on which the composer openly admitted his nonaristocratic origins to the Landrecht, the court for nobility before which his suit against Karl's mother, Johanna van Beethoven, was being heard. This episode marks the date after which members of the nobility tend to play less of a part in his daily life while members of the bourgeoisie become more numerous and influential, as can be noted particularly in the "conversation notebooks" upon which Beethoven was increasingly forced to rely owing to his almost-total deafness. The notebooks were replete with critical remarks about Austrian political power, and most were destroyed by Schindler after the composer's death, for, as he would say in justification: "There were extremely rude and unbridled attacks against both the emperor and the prince imperial — now the emperor — and against other high officials in the imperial household. That, unfortunately, was a subject Beethoven greatly enjoyed."[6] Many other contemporary witnesses confirm the openness with which Beethoven criticized the authorities, thanks to the dual impunity afforded him by, on the one hand, his fame and his connections in high places and, on the other, by his reputation as person who was somewhat unbalanced. For example, on one occasion he had burst out against the emperor, saying: "Such a rascal ought to be hanged to the first tree!"[7] According to another witness, he was especially upset by Franz I's attitude with regard to culture: "Music here in decline. The emperor does nothing for it and the rest of the public will put up with anything."[8] Thus, his poor rapport with the world of Austrian politics seeped into the question, which considerably darkened his later years, of his own music's relevance in light of the changes that occurred around 1820, in particular the advent and irresistible rise of Rossini.

Despite such privately expressed criticism, Beethoven's late middle age was not marked by any sharp avoidance of contact with the powerful. Indeed, he was never to find himself closer to becoming an official Hapsburg musician than at the end of 1822. At the urging of his old friend and protector, Graf Moritz Lichnowsky, he personally asked to be a candidate for a post as Kapellmeister whose incumbent had just died. The imperial librarian in charge of musical affairs, Graf Moritz Dietrichstein — a former "knight" in van Swieten's musical group — informed Beethoven, through Lichnowsky, that, to his great regret, the post in question was not going to be refilled; he went on, however, to suggest another way of approaching the court, namely, by producing a musical work, specifically a mass, in the emperor's honor. "Since the post has not been formally abolished but is merely for the moment vacant, after the mass composed for the emperor, it will be . . . ," a notebook entry records Lichnowsky as explaining in February 1823.[9] The composition of such a work entailed fulfilling a number of generic requirements, which Dietrichstein set forth in a letter; from stylistic indications to comments on the liturgy, the letter, which suggests a mass that will be "neither too long nor too difficult," reads like an unwitting but systematic condemnation of the *Missa Solemnis* that Beethoven had recently completed.[10] However, as indicated by a series of sketches for a Mass in C-sharp major that date from 1823, the composer appears to have given serious thought to meeting the official's expectations. A year later, however, he had not made much progress, and, pleading overwork, he put off the emperor's mass *sine die,* to the great disappointment of his protectors, including Archduke Rudolph.

Among the reasons Beethoven gave for his abandonment of the mass was the need to finish an oratorio that had been commissioned — and paid for — in 1819 by the Gesellschaft der Musikfreunde, whose members, after a four-year delay, were growing impatient. In 1823, the composer had finally settled on a poem by his friend Karl Bernard, *Der Sieg des Kreuzes* [The Victory of the Cross]; however, here too, probably little motivated by that text, he found himself unable to settle down to work. The Gesellschaft chose to forget about both the work and the money rather than risk a quarrel with the great composer, on whom, along with other prominent figures, it was to bestow honorary membership in 1825. Thus, the imperial official's hope for a mass for the emperor was never to be realized, nor was the Gesellschaft's commission aimed at carrying forward the great oratorio tradition of Handel and Haydn with a work by Beethoven.

The situation illustrates the divergences between the notion of an "official sublime" rooted in sacred tradition and based on a strict observance of generic rules and the creative path of a Beethoven who at that very moment was at work on his own vision of how to embody the collective aspiration to a monumental style with the *Missa Solemnis* and the Ninth Symphony. Such a gulf may seem paradoxical, since Beethoven's archaistic tendencies since the time of the Congress of Vienna, his decision to study ecclesiastic modes and Palestrina's masses, to take up the baroque *Tonmalerei* techniques, to return to the monumental Handelian style — all of that, in principle, was in keeping with the officially entrenched historicist trend. The cultural and political recognition of this range of older styles and techniques to be employed in the representation of power figures, far from condemning any work produced in such a spirit as being nothing but ideology, was offering artists new opportunities to come up with an inventive symbolic configuration that would be both aesthetically original and politically significant. Thus, without abandoning the prestigious effects of the "official sublime," Beethoven succeeded, in the monumental works of his late period, in turning its potential for assent to the creation and administration of his own political universe — a fantasy empire, perhaps, but no more so than is usual in works of art.

Which helps to explain the complex relationship of the *Missa Solemnis* and Ninth Symphony with tradition and, to some degree, the multiplicity of their interpretations. Indeed, neither of those strongly personal works were, a priori, incompatible with the political world of the Hapsburgs. The *Missa Solemnis,* in particular, is neither heretical nor revolutionary, it is merely unusual and eccentric. Its eccentricity lies not only in its dramatic and subjective presentation of the text of the mass; it is the result of a novel combination of rhetorical and stylistic devices, traditional and sometimes even very old, joined to a classical orchestral language and expanded to a monumental dimension hitherto unknown in music. The most glaring departure from tradition occurs in the passage in the *Dona nobis pacem* section marked *Bitte um innern und äussern Frieden* [Prayer for Inner and Outer Peace], in which an "anguished" [*ängstlich*] recitative is superimposed on *topoi* typical of genre "battle" music; this portrayal of wartime experience, which is reminiscent of Haydn's *Missa in tempore belli,* leads into a *fugato* on a theme from Handel's "Hallelujah" chorus — in other words, we have a linkage of contemporary official music with the monumental Baroque tradition that Beethoven had already drawn upon in *The Glorious Moment.*

As a matter of fact, the *Missa Solemnis* had originally been conceived as a work of official or "state" music. In April 1819, the pope had made Archduke Rudolph a cardinal and soon afterwards appointed him archbishop of the town of Olmütz; his consecration ceremony had been set for 9 March 1820, the feast day of the patron saints of Moravia. Shortly after the announcement, Beethoven wrote to his pupil and protector announcing his wish to "contribute to the glorification of this solemn day" by composing a mass.[11] The composer was thus giving himself less than a year in which to create a work he regarded as an "occasional piece" intended to celebrate the alliance of throne and altar in the person of a member of the imperial family. He set to work at a pace that, aside from the many sketches and the usual reworkings, was also slowed by lengthy consultations of the religious music in the archduke's library. The composer was often to assure the latter of his desire to complete the mass in time for the ceremony, but the work was not to be finished until 1823, three years after the promised date. The delay was probably due to a conflict between the demands of officialdom and Beethoven's creative processes, but it had the effect of separating the work from the official function that had motivated it. However, the mass had already as it were auto-annulled its functionality, for it is far too long for liturgical use — and we can only imagine the dilemma it would have created for the new cardinal-archbishop had it been completed in time. Thus, the work managed to disappoint official expectations by flouting the rules of the genre it set out to follow while still being in a style that was fully in keeping with the culture of the elite who controlled official "state" ceremonies.

This explains why, after having "missed" the consecration at Olmütz, the composer decided to take another approach to the political power structure and proposed that every great European court subscribe to a manuscript version of the mass, which could also — he took care to point out — be performed if need be as a "great oratorio." With this end in mind, he was to address himself directly to various rulers as well as to personalities like Goethe, Zelter and Cherubini. Only the king of England — his lack of response to *Wellington's Victory* will be recalled — was not solicited; on the other hand, the most enthusiastic response came from the king of France.

Thus, Beethoven conceived a plan to "sell" his *Missa Solemnis* to the entire Concert of Europe — the list of subscribers includes most of the sovereigns represented in *The Glorious Moment.* This subscription sale, he hoped, would bring in a large sum of money while not spoiling subsequent publication — which was not to occur until 1827, under the auspices of Schott and Söhne, after many simultaneous negotiations with at least half a dozen other publishers. With Beethoven, economic concerns vied with his ambition to have his work recognized as an unparalleled expression of the great art of his time, in keeping with a Promethean concept of his own role that prompted him to write to Archduke Rudolph: "There is nothing more elevated than to draw closer than other men to the divinity — and from there to cause divinity to irradiate all mankind." [12] It must be said that to his friends Beethoven managed to couch his ambition in less grandiose terms. A note from Schindler signed "Fidelissimus Papageno" makes mention of the fifty ducats paid by Alexander I and gives us a glimpse of the half-serious, half-joking light in which the composer and his entourage viewed the official side of the project: "I take pleasure in reporting to you herewith, that by command of the Emperor of all the Russias, 50 horsemen in armor are arrived here as a Russian contingent to do battle under you for the Fatherland." [13] However that may be, Beethoven's pseudo-patriotic endeavor was to be only half successful, for the *Missa Solemnis,* op. 123, far from leading to the spiritualization of mankind or its creator's imperial triumph, was to remain for decades practically unknown. Following its partial first performance in Vienna and a complete performance in Saint Petersburg in 1824, hearings of it were to be extremely rare, and it was not until the second half of the nineteenth century that it would truly become a part of the repertory as a result of its composer's quasi-canonization.

The fate of the Ninth Symphony in D minor, op. 125, was to be quite different, although at the time of their simultaneous premieres, on 7 May 1824, both works bore the same official political stamp as "new masterpieces" by a personality called upon to perform an important patriotic task. The composition of a symphony in D was an old plan that had resurfaced in November 1822 with a commission from the London Philharmonic Society. The composer accepted the commission, with an enthusiasm that was reinforced by plans to travel to England and by his admiration, reported to us by Schindler, for the British political system. "If God gives me back my health, which at least has improved somewhat, I shall yet be able to comply with all the requests which have come from all parts of Europe, even from

North America," he wrote in reply to the English Society.[14] The last allusion is to a request for an oratorio from the Handel and Haydn Society of Boston; although nothing was to come of it, it does serve to show that in Beethoven's time the frontiers of the classical music world had already extended far beyond Europe.[15] However, notwithstanding the London commission — the Ninth Symphony would be performed there on 21 March 1825 under the baton of Sir George Smart — Beethoven did not intend to forgo premiering his new works personally, although he was hesitant about doing so in Vienna, fearing the fate that might await them there. As he was to say in 1822: "They have been out of fashion for a long time, and fashion is everything."[16] For that reason, he had thought of giving the first performances of the mass and symphony in Germany — not in the Hapsburg domains there but, rather, in Prussia, where the intendant of the Theater Royal in Berlin had shown some interest. "When this plan became known in Vienna, however, a small band of artists and music-lovers who had retained their sobriety and reason united to avert the disgrace that threatened the imperial capital," wrote Schindler.[17] He thereupon produced a letter to the composer, an "Appeal from his Admirers," which read, in part:

> It is the wish of those of our countrymen who reverence art to which we desire more especially to give expression; for though Beethoven's name and creations belong to all contemporaneous humanity and every country which opens a susceptible bosom to art, it is Austria which is best entitled to claim him as her own. Among her inhabitants appreciation for the great and immortal works which Mozart and Haydn created for all time within the lap of their homes still lives, and they are conscious with joyous pride that the sacred triad in which these names and yours glow as the symbol of the highest within the spiritual realm of tones, sprang from the soil of their fatherland. All the more painful must it have been for you to feel that a foreign power had invaded this royal citadel of the noblest, that above the mounds of the dead and around the dwelling-place of the only survivor of the band, phantoms are leading the dance who can boast of no kinship with the princely spirits of those royal houses; that shallowness is abusing the name and insignia of art, and unworthy dalliance with sacred things is beclouding and dissipating appreciation for the pure and eternally beautiful.
>
> For this reason they feel a greater and livelier sense than ever before that the great need of the present moment is a new impulse directed by a

powerful hand, a new advent of the ruler in his domain. It is this need which leads them to you today, and following are the petitions which they lay before you in behalf of all to whom these wishes are dear, and in the name of native art.

Do not withhold longer from the popular enjoyment . . . a performance of the latest masterworks of your hand. We know that a grand sacred composition has been associated with that first one in which you have immortalized the emotions of a soul, penetrated and transfigured by the power of faith and superterrestrial light. We know that a new flower glows in the garland of your glorious, still unequaled symphonies. For years, ever since the thunders of the Victory at Vittoria ceased to reverberate, we have waited and hoped to see you distribute new gifts from the fulness of your riches to the circle of your friends. Do not longer disappoint the general expectations! Heighten the effect of your newest creations by the joy of becoming first acquainted with them through you! Do not allow these, your latest offspring, some day to appear, perhaps, as foreigners in their place of birth, introduced, perhaps, by persons to whom you and your mind are strange! Appear soon among your friends, your admirers, your venerators! This is our nearest and first prayer.[18]

For Beethoven's admiring public, the premiere of the *Missa Solemnis* and the Ninth Symphony was an act of patriotism that carried forward and transcended the period of the Napoleonic wars. Representing the "initiates of art" and the hearts of the multitude, the signatories saw themselves as the spokesmen of a people who regarded great music as a creation of divine origin embodied in the works of the "sacred triad," the symbols of a lost Golden Age. The tacit reference to Rossini and Italian music is obvious, albeit secondary, for even bad music, "fashionable" music, also represents an absolute principle — the figure of sin or even profanation. The present moment is a solemn one, more solemn perhaps even than the period of French aggression, for it is the very sanctuary of the nation that is threatened. An awareness of that threat is what motivated the appeal to Beethoven, as the last survivor of the great triad, to save the fatherland with his works. The hero is summoned from his retirement to return to the world to accomplish his mission; this "second time," when the Ninth Symphony will form a pendant to *Wellington's Victory,* will have the dramatic force of prayer. Clearly, the appeal embodies the notion of a holy war, one in which, given the theological concept of the nation, the foreigner appears as Evil incarnate and the Artist as the Savior designated by God.

The document, which was signed by thirty persons, was published in February 1824 in the *Theater Zeitung* and the *Wiener musikalische allgemeine Zeitung,* both published by friends of the composer. The author of the text has not been identified; the person most active in gathering signatures was Graf Lichnowsky. The list of names gives us some knowledge of Beethoven's supporters in Viennese society at the time of the Ninth's premiere: it includes officials in the imperial bureaucracy, members of the bourgeois musical establishment, among them several publishers and a piano manufacturer, as well as what was left of his longtime protectors in the upper ranks of the nobility. We also find the names of the principal figures in the historicist movement, among them Dietrichstein, Mosel, and Kiesewetter, all three of whom had direct links to the court, as well as the names of Hauschka and Sonnleithner, both members of the Gesellschaft der Musikfreunde, the former in charge of negotiations with regard to the oratorio and the latter of an unsuccessful attempt to have the Ninth first performed under the society's auspices. No one in the composer's intimate circle of friends signed the letter, which was hand delivered by two court officials during the course of a formal call. Schindler, however, clearly states that he had been aware of what was afoot:

> I found him holding the Appeal. He told me what had happened and handed me the page with a restrained emotion that revealed how much it had moved him. While I read the document, which I already knew, he moved to the window and watched the clouds as they passed. I put it down in silence, waiting for him to begin speaking. Finally, he turned to me and said, in a loud voice: "It is very beautiful! — It rejoices me greatly!" That was the signal that enabled me to express to him — in writing, unfortunately! — my own joy. He read it and quickly replied: "Let's go out." Once outside, contrary to his usual habit, he remained sunk in thought; which was further proof of what was going on in his mind.[19]

In reading that account, we get the impression that Beethoven was in agreement, if not with all the contents of the appeal, then at least with its general import. We may even suppose that, having been composed by people who knew him well, it put forth the arguments that were the most likely to persuade him. The fact that the text was produced by the composer's close friends explains the rumor that circulated following its publication according to which Beethoven himself had been its author or at least its instigator. That suspicion was to arouse his indignation: "Now that this thing has taken this turn I can no longer find joy in it. The atrocity of attributing such an act to me sickens me with the whole business," he himself was to write in his conversation notebooks.[20] In any event, the publication of the appeal proved that it had not been intended solely to persuade Beethoven, but that it was also designed to have a certain impact on the Viennese cultural scene. As for the rumor concerning the composer's participation, that reveals that the impact was not precisely the one intended.

The whole episode, which could only strengthen the composer's apprehensions about a public "caught up in fashion," was to contribute to making the organization of the concert more difficult. An additional problem was created by the ban on performing religious works in a theater. Fairly early on, and apparently because of its length and difficulty, it had been decided that the *Missa* would not be performed in its entirety. In a letter to the censor, Beethoven announced "only three church works, which, moreover, are called anthems"[21] — the sole instance of his using the term "anthem" with regard to his late works — in an attempt to downplay their religious character. The censor refused to go along with his argument, and it was only through the intervention of Graf Sedlnitzky, whom Lichnowsky had contacted, that the ban was lifted. Schindler refers to the touch-and-go nature of this maneuver in the notebooks on the day following the concert: "Yesterday, I still feared secretly that the Mass would be prohibited because I heard that the Archbishop had protested against it."[22] On 7 May 1824, the Viennese public was invited to attend the Kärthnerthor Theater to hear a "GREAT MUSICAL CONCERT by Herr L. v. Beethoven," with a *Grand overture* to be followed by *Three grand anthems, with soloist and chorus* and a *Great symphony, with, in the finale, soloists and chorus, to the Schiller Lied to joy.* The overture was the one now known as the *Weihe des Hauses* [The Consecration of the House], op. 124, which had been composed in 1822 for a new version of *The Ruins of Athens*. The *three grand anthems* were the *Kyrie, Credo,* and *Agnus Dei* of the Mass in D. The soprano Henrietta Sontag, the mezzo-soprano Karoline Unger, the tenor Anton Haitzinger, and Seipelt, bass, were the soloists, with the theater's orchestra and chorus, the latter augmented with amateurs, under the leadership of Michael Umlauf. The poster added: "Herr Ludwig van Beethoven himself will take part in conducting the orchestra."[23]

The concert was a success. One of the most famous images of Beethoven is of the moment on 7 May when, as he stood totally deaf and absorbed in the score of the Ninth, Karoline Unger took his arm and turned him around to face the audience that was applauding him. Schindler's almost stenographic entries in the notebooks help us to picture the scene: "Never in my life did I hear such frenetic and yet cordial applause. Once the second movement of the Symphony was completely interrupted by applause, and there was a demand for a repetition. The reception was more than imperial — for the people burst out in a storm four times. At the last there were cries of Vivat! . . . When the parterre broke out in applauding cries the fifth time, the Police Commissioner yelled Silence! — The court only 3 successive times but Beethoven 5 times." [24] In his biography, Schindler was to go into greater detail: "All the seats in the house were filled. Only one box remained empty: the Emperor's, although the master and I had gone in person to present an invitation to all the members of the imperial family, and some had promised to come. The Emperor and Empress were not in residence, and the Archduke Rudolph was still at Olmütz." [25] The first performance of Beethoven's two great works therefore took place in an atmosphere of tension vis-à-vis the power structure: the court was avoiding him, the church was threatening to ban him, the police were attempting to quell a triumph that, apparently, was viewed as a threat to imperial privilege. Schindler's remarks are evidence that in the minds of Beethoven and his friends, the contrast between the public's enthusiasm and the chill emanating from officialdom was one of the more satisfying elements of the triumph: a "more than imperial" reception.

However, the success was overshadowed by the venture's commercial failure, which was exacerbated — despite the inclusion of a Rossini aria! — when the concert was repeated on 23 May in the Redoutensaal as well as by the quarrels that broke out between the composer and his collaborators. These were to be Beethoven's last public concerts, and in 1826, when the Ninth Symphony was published by Schott and Söhne, he would give proof of his withdrawal from all contact with Austria's political world by dedicating the work to Friedrich Wilhelm III, the king of Prussia — the "father of his subjects" and "protector of the arts and sciences," as he was called in the letter written by the man who now described himself a "citizen of Bonn" and, therefore, one of his subjects. [26] The dedication completes the political picture in which the Ninth Symphony first saw the light: the persistence of Josephinian Enlightenment ideals, now projected onto the king of Prus-

sia — one of the sovereigns of *The Glorious Moment,* and one who was soon
to put an end to such anachronistic and unjustified expectations — came
to hinge on the discourse of nationalism, the fruit of the experience of the
Napoleonic wars and clearly evident in the appeal from his admirers.

Here, we have a historic trajectory resembling that of Schiller: his works,
banned in Vienna by the censor in 1783 and not authorized until 1808, were
to become immensely successful after 1813 and remain so for the next ten
years. When, thirty years after first planning to do so, Beethoven finally
came to set *An die Freude* to music, that egalitarian manifesto of 1785 had
been subjected not only to its 1803 revision, which had expurgated all reference to "tyrants," but also had accumulated a hagiographic tradition that
had, through the heat of the wars of liberation, turned the "Weimar classics" into the canonical bases of German literature. Given those differences,
in 1823, Beethoven was finally able to realize his youthful dream: to hymn
the *Ode to Joy*— or, rather, "a whole" made up of "bits and pieces," as he
had said in 1812.[27] This elaboration of the text was an integral part of the
composing process, and it was to have important consequences for the
work's worldwide significance. Of the eight eight-line stanzas, each with a
four-line "chorus," Beethoven was to retain the first three stanzas and the
first, third and fourth chorus; his selection thus omitted two of the poem's
fundamental themes, namely, drinking and suffering. In Schiller, communal drinking was a ritual performed by those who, in the name of "good"
and "blood" [*Gut und Blut*], swore to stand together against falsehood:
"Tighten the holy circle / Swear on this golden wine / To be faithful to this
vow / Swear it by the judge of the stars." The suffering was that of mankind
as a whole: "Suffer with courage, ye millions / Suffer for a better world!"
Beethoven, who had at one time adopted the motto "To Joy through Suffering" [*Durch Leiden Freude*],[28] and whose myth was to be constructed in
large measure on that stoic image, thus removed this compassionate dimension from his Ninth Symphony to hymn the Utopia of a Joy where Sorrow had left no trace. Further, he was to alter the order of the fragments he
did retain in such a way that the original text is completely turned round.
Where the poem is structured as a succession of utterances by a soloist and
choir, the finale of the Ninth Symphony brings in four soloists, a four-part
chorus, and a full symphony orchestra. Whereas, in Schiller, the chorus on
each entry introduces a new text, in Beethoven's *Ode to Joy* the chorus repeats, after the soloists, the second half of the three first stanzas. As for the
choruses in the poem, they appear later in the symphony, with no link to the

alternative principle that originally defined them. This tends to turn Beethoven's text into a kind of communal song in which the chorus takes up the
soloist's melody and repeats it, on the principle of imitation or even apprenticeship.

The collective hymn treats of a Joy of which the world's suffering has
been deprived. That said, we may wonder whether suffering is not in fact
the motif of the preceding instrumental movements. For in fact, the establishment of a narrative thread leading from conflict to its resolution is at the
crux of the transformation in the symphonic form that is one of Beethoven's
principal contributions to musical history. Whereas the center of gravity of
the classical symphony had always been its first movement, Beethoven, beginning with the *Eroica* Symphony, was to make the final movement the
culmination of the musical tensions built up throughout the work, and he
would often do this — as in the Fifth Symphony — via an exhaustive development of the same basic material, in the Fifth through the famous opening
four-note theme. His last symphony is only the final example of this progressive reinforcement of the cathartic role to be fulfilled by the final movement, using materials introduced in the preceding movements — here, by
grafting on a vocal form old in itself, namely, the cantata. From the time of
its first performance, and in very different ways, generations of listeners
have seen this musical journey as a depiction of human existence. The work
has been the subject of countless "mythic" readings: philosophical, religious, literary (especially epic), musical (put forward principally as alterna-
tives to programmatic interpretations), and, most insistently, autobio-
graphical — without any of them being deemed the "right one," and this as
much because of the work's aesthetic creativeness as of the differing political benefits that any interpretation can entail. The only point on which
there is complete agreement concerns the work's "human" dimension. In an
instrumental work with no program and no title, such interpretations of its
content will always veer, more or less, toward a kind of metaphysical aesthetics of music. In the Ninth Symphony, the hearing that turns the *musical*
discourse into a discourse on humanity is inherent in the score itself, both
because of Schiller's poem and because of the manner in which it is introduced. The *Ode to Joy* is the happy denouement of a drama whose literal
meaning will always be unclear or — to put it perhaps a better way — will always be protected by the semantic indeterminacy of the preceding instrumental movements. At the same time, the musical importance of those first
three movements is what makes this "musical chimera" — as Roland

Barthes was to call it[29] — the touchstone for the social significance of music as an art form, to a degree that it would probably never have attained had it been couched in the form of a mere cantata. Whence this dual role: both a symbol of music in political life and a symbol of politics in musical art.

The element that makes the work a "musical chimera" is concentrated in the fate of the melody used as the principal theme of the last movement, which in German literature is known — and rightly — as the *Freudenmelodie* [the Joy melody]. Beyond its verbal significance, the "Joy melody" marks the first appearance of vocal music in a work of instrumental music. That fact, added to the difficulty, even for a German-speaking public, of understanding the words when sung, was to lead many exegetes to overlook the meaning of Schiller's words in favor of a pure metaphysics of the human voice. Here, we have the vocal-music symbol first introduced in the form of an instrumental melody. The fourth movement of the symphony begins with a fanfare and a double-bass recitative whose transitional function between the instrumental and vocal modes is noted in the score by this paradoxical indication: "In the nature of a recitative, but *in tempo*." The phrases of the recitative are linked by musical quotations from the three preceding movements, the last of which, the *Adagio,* leads into the first part of the *Ode to Joy* theme, played by the woodwinds. The theme is then introduced in its totality — one might almost say displayed — by the cellos and double basses, which play its twenty-four bars in unison; the ensuing variations, which shift the tune from its first form to a march-like version, foreshadow the formal development of the finale as a whole, the transformation of an elemental and basic matter into an apotheosis.

The theme has often been praised for the genius of its simplicity and sometimes decried as a trivial tune that owes whatever interest it might have solely to the use to which Beethoven has made of it. Whatever the case, reference is usually made to its *Volkslied* character, and in this respect some commentators have even maintained that it actually is a folksong — that, notwithstanding the fact that their supposition can be disproved by Beethoven's numerous sketches, which have been preserved. Indeed, the sketchbooks demonstrate for us how difficult the composition process was: there was very little about it that was instinctive or even spontaneous. Beethoven very purposefully set out to develop a melody that would be hymn-like and that would fall into the "popular style" favored by Haydn and Mozart, a style that he himself had nearly always eschewed in his major works — indeed, his avoidance of it was to contribute to his reputation as a "composer for connoisseurs."[30] In fact, there are only a very few melodies that might have served as "forebears" of the *Freudenmelodie*. The closest is probably that of the *Gegenliebe*, the song of mutual love that was to become the theme of the *Choral Fantasy*, an idealized reconciliation through music — but it is a bit much to view the theme in the Ninth Symphony as having been based on one single melody present throughout Beethoven's life and leading back to the ideals of his youth. The other possible sources could be found perhaps in the choruses of his official compositions, beginning with the Bonn cantatas, including *Fidelio* and *The Ruins of Athens*, up to *The Glorious Moment* of the Congress of Vienna, all avatars of the communal anthem. However, where Haydn and Mozart freely blended their "popular" melodies into the overall musical fabric of their works, Beethoven, for his part, emphasized the very different character of his *Freudenmelodie* in relation to the rest of the work. The narrative strategies he was to deploy to introduce, set forth, and develop a melody whose very structure makes it a self-contained whole, an independent musical object, were to play a decisive role in the symphony's interpretation, from the viewpoints of both execution and exegesis. The duality between the autonomy of the "joy melody" and its structural role in the fourth movement reflects the differing interpretations which, in the history of the Ninth's reception, have served either to emphasize the theme's role as a communal anthem for the public arena or to view it solely as one integral and concrete element in a total work of pure music.

Some particularly pertinent verbal evidence of Beethoven's creative process can be found in the sketches analyzed by Gustav Nottebohm.[31] The composer's words at times seem to be rough sketches for some sung text and at others merely comments by the composer, it is not always possible to tell which. Thus, Beethoven entered in his notebook an introductory fanfare in C major, followed by a few notes of a recitative, beneath which he wrote the words: "Heute ist ein feierlicher Tag / meine Fru . . . dieser sei gefeiert durchmit Gesang und . . ." [Today is a festive day, my friends . . . let us celebrate it with [or by] song and . . . ].[32] What we have here is a toast in the *Trinklied* tradition, someone raising his glass to a circle of friends, a company now broadened to include all men, made brothers in the joys of wine. Over the first phrase of the recitative, Beethoven wrote: "Nein diese erinnern an unsre Verzweifl" [No, that would remind us of our despair]. In the same manner, he selected the texts for each of the recitatives that follow the quotations of the prior movements, each phrase serving to justify the rejection of the melody quoted. And at the end of the series, we find the "joy" theme, followed by a long melisma and the note: "Ha dieses ist es. Es ist nun gefunden Freu . . ." [Ah! here it is! It's been found . . . ]. Then Beethoven wrote: "Lasst uns das Lied der unsterblichen Schiller singen" — "Let us sing the immortal Schiller's song!" The sequence of sketches narrates a thematic search born of despair, it tells of a series of reasoned rejections of preceding melodies until the *Freudenmelodie* at last appears — rejections that define, a contrario, the characteristics of the latter — pleasant, serious, serene, lively, not overly tender. The search has been accompanied by what we might describe as an incentive, an apprenticeship: the composer/soloist is in search of a melody that the others — the plural "you" of "friends" — can sing, in imitation, after him. The instrumental portion of the symphony is the domain of the possible melodies from which the communal song will emerge — for if the "joy melody" appears to be introduced as the contradiction of the preceding movements, it is at the same time foresounded (as it were) in certain passages of those movements (especially in the Trio of the Scherzo). The "discovery" of the theme, therefore, is the *telos* of a twofold quest, one strictly musical and ongoing throughout the symphony, and the other metadiscursive, in which the symphony itself, through the soloist, announces the "replacement" of those thematic materials by the new melody. The baritone is both the actor in this quest and the master of ceremonies at a "fête" that will consist in a unison singing of the anthem — Schiller's *lied* — that he will bring to the community's attention.

In the final version of the work, the identification between the soloist and composer fades away, the "festive day" loses its temporal significance, Schiller's name disappears. The simple C-major fanfare of the sketches is replaced by the long, dissonant chord that Richard Wagner was to dub a *Schreckensfanfare,* a "fanfare of terror." However, the learning or apprenticeship process remains, as the soloist exhorts his "friends" to abandon the preceding melodies and to sing the melody of joy. The "different" character of the *Freudenmelodie,* as well as its relationships with the symphony's other musical materials, is actually dramatized in the work itself, not only in the opening musical prelude but in the very first entrance of the human voice, when the baritone utters words that are not by Schiller, but by Beethoven himself: "O Freunde! Nicht diese Töne! Sondern lasst uns angenehmere anstimmen und freudenvollere!" [O friends, not those sounds! Rather let us sing a more agreeable and more joyous song!].

The voice makes its entry by denying the effectiveness or validity of the preceding themes to express joy and announcing the search for a "more joy-ous" song, which will be the one taken up by the chorus. The concept of a communal apprenticeship based on imitation is expressed in the passage following the recitative, when the baritone, in two exchanges with the basses of the chorus, sings the word *Freude,* as though establishing a phatic contact with the community of singers prior to launching into the *Ode to Joy* itself. It is a gesture that will be amplified by the manner in which the first stanza of the poem is set to music: after the soloist has sung the melody through in its entirety, it is taken up again by the chorus in unison:

| | |
|---|---|
| *Freude, schöner Götterfunken,* | Joy, lovely divine spark, |
| *Tochter aus Elysium,* | Daughter of Elysium, |
| *Wir betreten feuertrunken* | Drunk with fire, we enter, |
| *Himmlische, dein Heiligtum!* | Heavenly one, your shrine! |
| *Deine Zauber binden wieder,* | Your magic spells reunite |
| *was die Mode streng geteilt;* | What convention has rough sundered; |
| *Alle Menschen werden Brüder,* | All men will become brothers |
| *wo dein sanfter Flügel weilt.* | At the gentle touch of your wing. |

These are the most famous words of the Ninth Symphony; they are the text that is always sung, in German or in translation, when the *Ode to Joy* is performed as a separate entity. However, the symphony's final movement has actually just begun, and the "joy melody" will now be subjected to a lengthy metamorphosis. The rhetorical strategies employed are vital to the work's meaning; the entry of the human voice is a "genre shock," after which " . . . in each case the next genre used provides a clue to the meaning of the passage in the dramatic program of the movement."[33] Thus, Schiller's text is set against various rhetorical-musical backgrounds, now *cantata pro-fana,* now "battle" music, now merely military music or music in the reli-gious tradition. These mutations do not involve any abandonment of the melody's original form, which is reprised several times in what might be de-scribed as a rising spiral of repetitions, every section of which "remains in-complete or heads seamlessly to the next in such a way that no large-scale closure takes place until the end."[34] And, in fact, the second stanza, *Wem der grosse Wurf gelungen* . . . [Let whoever has had the great fortune . . . ], which sets forth the rules for membership in the ideal community, is sung by the four soloists, and the chorus, still in imitative mode, again repeats its second part. The same applies to the third stanza, *Freude trinken alle We-sen* . . . [All creatures will drink Joy], in which joy, as a principle of the natural order, leads the way from the social towards the cosmic. The setting of this stanza ends with an additional repetition of the last line, *Und der Cherub steht vor Gott* [And the cherub stands before God], at which point, reflecting the meaning of the text, the music seems to hang suspended for a long instant. This pivotal moment, intensified by a modulation from D to B-flat, is followed by a variation that is in sharp contrast to those we have heard hitherto, namely, a march *alla turca* in which the successive entrances of wind instruments and percussion produce the effect of an advancing host, a device similar to the one employed in *Wellington's Victory*. In counterpoint to the *Freudenmelodie* played by the winds, the tenor soloist sings four lines, the last two of which will be taken up by a three-part men's chorus:

| | |
|---|---|
| *Froh, wie seine Sonnen fliegen* | Joyful as the suns that soar |
| *Durch des Himmels prächt'gen Plan,* | Across the splendour of Heaven's plain, |
| *Laufet, Brüder, eure Bahn,* | Brothers, run your course, |
| *Freudig, wie ein Held zum Siegen!* | Joyfully, like a hero towards Victory! |

Here we have a repetition of the apprenticeship situation, but this time in the form of a martial exhortation accompanied by military band music and the antique image of the sun. As in *The Glorious Moment,* the men of the community become an army, and the solo voice sings of the transformation of "brother" into hero. The march leads into an instrumental *fugato* that has been interpreted as a battle allegory, which leads to a return to the first stanza, *Freude, schöner Gotterfunken,* now sung *in toto* by the full chorus. This is the culmination of the imitative section, the moment of fulfillment when, for the first and last time in the entire symphony, the entire community, *fortissimo,* intones the *Ode to Joy.*

The anthem over, the movement has reached a crucial point: a new melody in G appears, introduced by the male chorus. The whole of this *Andante maestoso* section is sung by the chorus alone, to the words of Schiller's first "chorus":

| | |
|---|---|
| *Seid umschlungen Millionen!* | Embrace, you millions! |
| *Diesen Kuß der ganzen Welt!* | This kiss is for all the world! |
| *Brüder — überm Sternenzelt* | Brothers, up there in the star-filled vault |
| *muß ein lieber Vater wohnen.* | A loving father surely dwells! |

In this "kiss for all the world," the union in joy of all mankind, which has hitherto been perceived as a collection of individuals, becomes complete. The father creator appears as the synthesizing principle of the communal utopia in the form of a question — or even perhaps wager — as to the existence of an invisible God beyond the limits of the visible. This religious quest in the text is accompanied by an archaistic moment in the music, a veritable "Gregorian fossil" inserted into a "quasi liturgical" structure based on the sequence: first versicle — response — second versicle — response — hymn.[35] This evocation of a tradition of sacred music has the effect of attenuating the interrogative nature of the text when there is mention of prostration, of bowing humbly down:

| | |
|---|---|
| *Ihr stürzt nieder, Millionen?* | Do you bow humbly down, ye millions? |
| Ahnest *du den Schöpfer, Welt?* | World, do you *feel* your Creator? |
| *Such' ihn überm Sternenzelt,* | Seek him up there in the star-filled vault, |
| *über Sternen muß er wohnen.* | He surely dwells among the stars. |

This last image has often been associated with a sentence Beethoven scrawled in his conversation notebooks in February 1820: "das Moralische Gesez in unß u. Der gestirnte Himel über unß. Kant!!!" [The moral law within us and above us the starry sky. Kant!!!][36] The linkage between Beethoven and Kant, of considerable importance in the composer's own career and reputation as well as in the cultural pantheon of the Enlightenment, is rooted in this connection between the cited principle of moral law and the starry sky of the *Ode to Joy*. In addition, the passage on prostration in the Ninth Symphony, a work that in the modern era is regarded as a "paradigm of musical sublimity," has recently been connected to Kant's own remark on the sublime:

> In religion, it seems in general that to prostrate oneself, to bow the head in adoration, to evidence awe and contrition in one's deportment and one's voice, is the only fitting attitude in which to approach the divinity, and it is for that reason that the majority of peoples have adopted and continue to observe such an attitude. However, such an expression of feeling [*Gemütsstimmung*] is not of itself nor necessarily, far from it, linked to the notion of *awe inspiring grandeur* typical of religion and its goal.[37]

*1. Portrait by Joseph Stieler, 1819–1820 (detail).*
*Courtesy of Beethoven-Haus Bonn.*

2. *Title page of the first edition of the Ninth Symphony, 1826.
See page 98. Courtesy of Beethoven-Haus Bonn.*

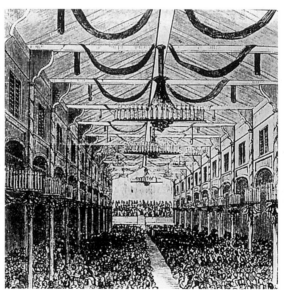

3. *Concert at the Beethovenhalle, Bonn, 1845. See page 141.*

4. Beethovenfries, *by Gustav Klimt, 1902 (detail):*
*"This kiss is for all the world!" See page 172. Österreichische Galerie Belvedere Vienna.*
*Erich Lessing / Art Resource, NY.*

5. *Beethoven, sculpture by Max Klinger, 1902. See page 172.*
*Courtesy of Museum der bildenden Künste, Leipzig.*

6. *"Lenin listening to Beethoven," drawing. Lenin Museum, Moscow.*

*7. Illustration for Kurt Weill's article "Beethoven und die Jungen" [Beethoven and the Young], by Thomas Ring.* Sozialistische Monatshefte, *March 1927.*

*8. Satirical drawing for the 1927 Centenary,* Illustrierte Kronen-Zeitung, *27 March 1927. "Today I don't mind being deaf!"*

Brauner Künstlertraum

"Der Berliner Bildhauer Georg Kolbe erhielt den ehrenhaften Auftrag, ein Denkmal des Generalissimos Franco zu schaffen. Gleichzeitig wurde er mit der Herstellung eines Beethovendenkmals für die Stadt Frankfurt am Main betraut."

Berliner Zeitungsmeldung

Selbstgespräch im Traum: „Franco und Beethoven, wie schaff' ich dies bloß? Am besten mach' ich wohl einen Kentauren, halb Tier, halb Mensch."

9. "Brauner Künstlertraum" [The Artist's Brown Study], photomontage by John Heartfield, circa 1945. "Franco and Beethoven—how on earth can I manage that? Perhaps as centaur, half wild beast, half human." Courtesy of Beethoven-Haus Bonn.

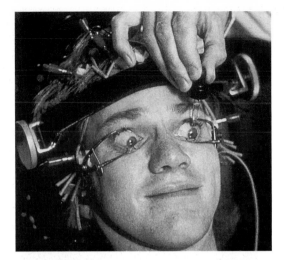

10. The "Ludovico" treatment in Stanley Kubrick's film A Clockwork Orange, 1971. See page 225. Copyright 1971 Warner Bros., Inc., and Polaris Productions, Inc. All Rights Reserved.

11. Publicity poster depicting Beethoven as a blues musician, 1983. Courtesy of Beethoven-Haus Bonn.

*12. Andy Warhol,* Beethoven *(detail), 1987.*
© *2003 Andy Warhol Foundation for the Visual Arts/ARS, New York.*

Even though Beethoven takes pains to illustrate Schiller's interrogation with a sudden drop in dynamics, that criticism of prostration has almost never been mentioned in exegeses of the Ninth Symphony — which may be seen as an effect of the inertia of the traditional Christian world, backed by an archaistic musical rhetoric. Nevertheless, at the conclusion of the *Andante maestoso* section, Beethoven combines the religious "hymn" with the *Hymn to Joy* in a double fugue for chorus that reproduces the baroque Handelian style in all its sumptuosity. This gesture, in which the work takes impetus for its final flight from the traditionally conceived monumental apotheosis, is one of the clearest indications of the stylistic link between the Ninth Symphony and the *Leopold* cantata and *The Glorious Moment*. The non-hierarchical principle that links the two themes of the double fugue programmatically establishes a complementarity between the transcendent and the worldly. In the very last vocal section, the two worlds will once again be brought together in homophonic phrases that create a new text with fragments of what has come before:

*Diesen Kuß der ganzen Welt!*    This kiss is for all the world!
*Freude, schöner Götterfunken.*    Joy, lovely divine spark.

And it is with that "synthetic" hymn, in which the images of rituals both sacred and profane merge, that the narrative process comes to an end with the powerful D-major coda that concludes the Ninth Symphony.

The work's openness to being viewed as a narrative "on" the concept of hymn can serve to explain — without, however, justifying — the process that entails extracting the *Ode to Joy* from its symbolic ritual context and transferring it onto a virtual ritual as a musical symbol for a political community. But that is not the "true program" of the Ninth Symphony, nor is the political use of the *Ode to Joy* the culmination of its career and reputation. It does, however, exist at the very heart of the work's historical role, which is marked by an ideological ambiguity with deep roots in Western history. In the monumental works of his late period, Beethoven called upon all the elements that had ever in one way or another played a part in the creation of his musical language. If that be true of his notions of melody, his harmonic language, his concepts of form, his art of orchestration, it is also true for the rhetorical devices and historical significance attached to them. In the singular finale that contains the *Ode to Joy* we can recognize the trace of pieces written for "enlightened despots," the French-revolutionary ideal of the "unique voice of the nation," a concept of divinity linked to a concept of nature, a tradition linked to a theologico-political concept of society, and, finally, the bourgeois ideal of *Bildung* or "aesthetic education" grafted onto a metaphysics of music, all elements that, at one or another moment in its course, take the form of a collective song of adoration — which, since antiquity, has been the very definition of anthem. In modern times, from the point of view of the power elite, the anthem is the favored genre of official political music, in other words, of state music, and they have made it their principal rhetorical device — independent of the fact that the same rhetoric can also be utilized, as it often has been, to question and even to bring down some real historical state. The presence of the anthem in the musical utopia of Beethoven's late period raises the question of the state's presence in music, both as symbol and as the expression of some abstract organizational principle in man's life. Independent of the political situation in which the invocation may be expressed, independent of the actual concrete or utopian form of state involved, such an "official desire" — a *désir d'État* — has haunted this music ever since its creation, and it continues to do so in our own day.

# Political
# Reception
# of the
# *Ode to Joy*

# 6

# The Romantic Cult

Ludwig van Beethoven died on 26 March 1827, and his funeral was held on the afternoon of Thursday the 29th. In Vienna, it was a major event. According to contemporary reports, the schools were closed and soldiers from the local barracks were called out to ensure public order. A crowd estimated at between ten to thirty thousand people gathered outside his residence, the poetically named Schwarzspanierhaus, the House of the Black-Robed Spaniards. The huge courtyard where the bier had been placed soon became overcrowded, and the gates finally had to be locked. The funeral cortege set out at approximately four thirty in the afternoon; although the distance between the house and the church was a mere two hundred yards, the procession took more than an hour and half to get there.[1] Eight singers bore Beethoven's remains to the Alsergasse church, and the pall covering the casket was carried by eight Kapellmeister, who were in turn escorted and flanked by forty torchbearers, most of them professional musicians. The procession was led by a group of priests carrying the parish crucifix; the coffin was followed by the deceased's relatives, including his brother and sister-in-law, Johann and Johanna van Beethoven, a group of trombone players, a chorus, students from the conservatory, members of public bodies, and other musicians and performers. "No Emperor of Austria ever had a funeral like that of Beethoven," wrote Graf Zmeskall, one of the composer's friends.[2] However, few aristocrats were present, and few representatives of the court, with the exception of Dietrichstein. The funeral was a tribute paid by Vienna's cultural elite to one of their own, and the state was not invited. That the death of a musician could assume the same importance as that of a dynastic political figure, deriving its significance from outside the political arena, reveals the full import of the event, which, Zmeskall was to add, "raised a hitherto unheard of furor in Vienna."

Music was played throughout the proceedings: in the courtyard, a funeral chorale from Anselm Weber's opera based on Schiller's play *Wilhelm Tell* was sung first; for the occasion, a *Miserere* that Beethoven had composed in 1812 in Linz was then performed in an arrangement for a vocal quartet with two of Beethoven's *Equali* for four trombones (WoO 30); during the street procession, the funeral march from his Sonata op. 26 was played in an arrangement for wind band that the composer had made in 1815 to accompany a patriotic drama.[3] Following the mass, during which Ignaz Seyfried's *Libera nos Domine* was sung, many Viennese followed the hearse to the gates of the cemetery at Währing; since graveside speeches had been banned by the church, it was at the cemetery's entrance that the actor Heinrich Anschütz delivered the funeral oration, which had been written, at the request of Anton Schindler, by the poet Franz Grillparzer, Austria's foremost man of letters:

> Standing by the grave of him who has passed away we are in a manner the representatives of an entire nation, of the whole German people, mourning the loss of the one highly acclaimed half of that which was left us of the departed splendor of our native art, of the fatherland's full spiritual bloom. There yet lives — and may his life be long! — the hero of verse in German speech and tongue; but the last master of tuneful song, the organ of soulful concord, the heir and amplifier of Handel and Bach's, of Haydn and Mozart's immortal fame is now no more, and we stand weeping over the riven strings of the harp that is hushed.
>
> The harp that is hushed! Let me call him so! For he was an artist, and all that was his, was his through art alone. The thorns of life had wounded him deeply, and as the cast-away clings to the shore, so did he seek refuge in thine arms, O thou glorious sister and peer of the Good and the True, thou balm of wounded hearts, heaven-born Art! To thee he clung fast, and even when the portal was closed wherethrough thou hadst entered in and spoken to him, when his deaf ear had blinded his vision for thy features, still did he ever carry thine image within his heart, and when he died it still reposed on his breast.
>
> He was an artist — and who shall arise to stand beside him?
>
> As the rushing behemoth spurns the waves, so did he rove to the uttermost bounds of his art. From the cooing of doves to the rolling of

thunder, from the craftiest interweaving of well-weighed expedients of art up to that awful pitch where planful design disappears in the lawless whirl of contending natural forces, he had traversed and grasped it all. He who comes after him will not continue him; he must begin anew, for he who went before left off only where art leaves off. Adelaide and Leonora! Triumph of the heroes of Vittoria — and the humble sacrificial song of the Mass!—Ye children of the voices divided thrice and four times! heaven-soaring harmony: "Freude, schöner Götterfunken," thou swan song! Muse of song and the seven-stringed lyre! Approach his grave and bestrew it with laurel!

He was an artist, but a man as well. A man in every sense — in the highest. Because he withdrew from the world, they called him a man-hater, and because he held aloof from sentimentality, unfeeling. Ah, one who knows himself hard of heart, does not shrink! The finest points are those most easily blunted and bent or broken. An excess of sensitiveness avoids a show of feeling! He fled the world because, in the whole range of his loving nature, he found no weapon to oppose it. He withdrew from mankind after he had given them his all and received nothing in return. He dwelt alone, because he found no second Self. But to the end his heart beat warm for all men, in fatherly affection for his kindred, for the world his all and his heart's blood.

Thus he was, thus he died, thus he will live to the end of time.

You, however, who have followed after us hitherward, let not your hearts be troubled! You have not lost him, you have won him. No living man enters the halls of the immortals. Not until the body has perished, do their portals unclose. He whom you mourn stands from now onward among the great of all ages, inviolate forever. Return homeward, therefore, in sorrow, yet resigned! And should you ever in times to come feel the overpowering might of his creations like an onrushing storm, when your mounting ecstasy overflows in the midst of a generation yet unborn, then remember this hour, and think, We were there, when they buried him, and when he died, we wept.[4]

Thus, after the sublime female figures of Adelaide and Leonore, after the symbols of power embodied in the battle music and the mass, after the "voices divided thrice and four times," the Ninth Symphony is the work that was to crown the legacy of the great composer after his death. This was the dead man's ultimate embrace of the Mankind that had avoided him. The hero, with his Christ-like attributes, is fully present in this last work, which — although it is not defined as such chronologically — else where would the last quartets fit in? — is indeed, because of its pure emblematic force, a true finale. The *Ode to Joy* is the swan song intended for his own veiled hearing. Beethoven was accompanied on the way to the church by his own funeral march, and at the cemetery gates it was again his own music that was sung to honor him. At the moment of his disappearance, his works were invoked for reasons that were not, or at least not only, aesthetic, but that were above all commemorative. Henceforth, listening to those works will be a way of remembering him, of renewing the link with the composer and with those other men assembled at his grave. The labors of the creator of the Ninth Symphony had produced and formed his own *Denkmal,* his own monument. And that monument, raised over the great man's remains, is a memorative sign for the "representatives" of a nation in the presence of its great. Within the Platonic trinity of the Beautiful, the Good and the True, music is at one with its own past, just as it is now with poetry, its sister art. There is a diachrony created in the national spirit by the line of great composers, from Handel to Beethoven; there is a synchrony, uniting Beethoven and Goethe as the two complementary halves of a classical grandeur already fading into history. Thus, in Grillparzer's funeral elegy, what we see taking form is a topography of Germany's national culture.

A highly coded set piece, the oration is neither very original nor very personal. Grillparzer knew the composer and had even planned an opera with him, but their aesthetic differences went deep. It would not be Grillparzer who would portray Beethoven for posterity but, rather, romantic writers like E. T. A. Hoffmann or Bettina von Arnim, the latter of whom was to write: "In everything that concerned his art, [Beethoven] is so true and so sovereign that no artist dares approach him. In the rest of his life, however, he is so naive that you can do anything you like with him."[5] That letter, written to Goethe and published in 1835, depicts the composer as a kind of blind force of nature, and that picture was to prove more influential than the quasi-Apollonian image put forward in Grillparzer's funeral oration. And yet, his text is both elegy and program. In condensing the *topoi* already created during Beethoven's lifetime, and with his collaboration, the poet laid out the commemorative program of a vision of the artist that was to take hold and prevail throughout the nineteenth century, the century to be known as the "*Bildung* century," a century of culture, of ideals, and of cultivated and cultured education.

Indeed, the Beethoven myth was to flourish in a society marked by the very German idea of self-learning or self-education through general culture — *Bildung* — that Thomas Mann was to describe as the "universal ideal of the private man."[6] The image of the "cultivated (*gebildet*) man" achieving personal freedom through a study of the arts and sciences had taken shape in the days of the great Weimar classical writers, beginning with the recognition (by the pietists, among others) of the value of personal religious experience. That model, whose example was provided by Goethe's *Wilhelm Meister* and whose theory was set forth in his *Briefen über die ästhetische Erziehung des Menschen* [Letters on the Aesthetic Education of Man], was to accompany the bourgeoisie's rise to power: it was a corpus of extrareligious values, above political divisions, that were, in principle, accessible to all, but that, in practice, served to define and to demarcate social strata.[7] In this ideology, the art of music has a preponderant role to play. At local concerts and at great festivals, every cultivated man can find within himself the paths to the infinite laid out by the romantic musical aesthetic. Thanks to the customs of singing and performing chamber music, he can participate in a kind of social interaction that is morally superior to the prosaic mores of community life. Through music, which Schopenhauer was to regard as the highest incarnation of an aesthetic experience that Kant had defined as basically "disinterested," the autonomy of the world of art takes on an ethical dimension and contributes to the creation of an individual's inner freedom thus turned toward the commonweal.[8]

Here we have a paradox of which the Ninth Symphony was to be a kind of programmatic expression — a fact that helps to explain the work's central role in what some were to call "the religion of music." In any event, this was the direction some of the earliest critics tended to take in their desire to understand the meaning and significance of the incongruous cantata at the heart of an instrumental work. In 1826, Adolf Bernhard Marx, in an article in the *Berlinische allgemeine Zeitung*, set out to justify "the composition's completely new form": "When instruments and voices sound together, the latter are given pride of place, as was man at the Creation, for song includes words, and the musical power inherent in man represents what is human, in contrast to the instrumental portion, which represents what is above and beyond man" — a dialectic which, Marx adds, in typically Hegelian language, ultimately consecrates man as the "conqueror, through his spiritual power, of the instrumental Proteus."[9] Here we have an interpretation that, emphasizing the relationship between the human and the musical, appears to have little interest in the literal import of Schiller's words — an attitude it shares with the Viennese correspondent of Leipzig's *Allgemeine musikalische Zeitung*, who, in 1824, "heard" (metaphorically) in the final chorus a salute to the "divine art of music" and to Beethoven, its "high priest."[10]

In the nineteenth century, music became a singularly important element in the creation and perception of a specifically German identity. One sign of this change in symbolic coordinates was the 1837 publication of *The Glorious Moment* under a new title, *Der Preis der Tonkunst*, a "Praise of Music" rather than praise for the Concert of Europe. The growing number of publications devoted to music played a central role in this phenomenon by providing a forum for cultural debates that, without getting directly involved in politics, did at least touch upon them. The case of Robert Schumann, who in 1834 founded the influential periodical *Neue Zeitschrift für Musik* in Leipzig, illustrates "the complementary coherence between an individual's ambition to gain public prominence as a musician and a man of letters and a generational politics in which culture served as an instrument of national identity."[11] Schumann was being very serious when he wrote: "Just as Italy has its Naples, France its revolution, England its navy, etc., the Germans have their Beethoven symphonies. With his Beethoven, the German forgets that he has no school of painting; with Beethoven, he imagines that he has turned round the outcomes of the battles lost to Napoleon; he even dares place him on the same level as Shakespeare."[12] The concern for national greatness accompanied the universalism of the more liberal sectors of the bourgeois intelligentsia — men like the writer Robert Griepenkerl, for example, a contributor to the *Neue Zeitschrift für Musik* who held that art was a *weltliche Evangelium*, a "secular Gospel" that embodied the history of the world, and who viewed Beethoven, in retrospect, as the "prophet of the July revolution." The same idea appeared in his 1838 novel, *Das Musikfest oder die Beethovener* [The Feast of Music, or The Beethovenians], which described a ceremony organized to pay homage to the composer in a small German town. "Who knows what whore might have given birth to this disguised *Freude* of Schiller's!" one of the characters exclaims ironically after having heard a performance of the Ninth — a question to which an "editor's footnote" replies: "Es war die Freiheit" [It was Freedom!]. It was in this oblique and almost surreptitious way, in a tragicomic work of fiction, that for the first time Beethoven's image and reputation came to include the idea that in the *Ode to Joy* one was actually hearing an *Ode to Freedom*.[13]

The commemorative ceremony described by Griepenkerl in his novel is an imaginary and parodied account of a project that was actually put forward at Bonn University at the time. The prestige of that institution had grown since Beethoven's time: since 1819, it had been able to boast of having August Wilhelm Schlegel, the great philologist, as a member of its faculty, and, since 1823, it could claim to have the first-ever professor of musicology in Germany, Heinrich Carl Breidenstein. This last novelty was not owing to any exceptional merit on the part of Breidenstein, whose actual scientific contribution, if we are to believe his biographer, was practically nil;[14] he lacked, for example, the reputation of Johann Nikolaus Forkel, the first biographer of Johann Sebastian Bach, who had as early as 1802 hailed that "national classic" in the context of the new *Musikwissenschaft*. However, Breidenstein's appointment was part of a trend that, by recognizing musical studies as a science, was to bring the whole weight of academia to bear on defining and legitimizing the classical musical canon. In 1832, Breidenstein published in a local periodical an article entitled "Erinnerung an Beethoven" [Remembering Beethoven]; in that article, expanding on an idea that he had already expressed in 1828, he suggested the erection of a monument to the composer in his native town, "or, even better, a living memorial, one dedicated to art, *Bildung*, education, etc."[15]

At the time, the notion of erecting a monument to a musician was a novel one. There were as yet no statues of the great German cultural figures, with the exception of one of Luther (not exactly an artist), which had been erected at Wittenberg in 1821.[16] The earliest plans for statues of Goethe and Schiller (often represented together) date from 1819, but none was realized until much later, the first statue of the author of *An die Freude* appearing in Stuttgart in 1839. When Breidenstein's article was written, therefore, no writer or musician had yet appeared in public in a marble or bronze version. And, as an observer remarked in 1835, "it isn't for lack of money, for business is flourishing," adding, "when the railroad can carry us at immense speed from one country to another, we are struck by the feeble efforts our cities are making to attract the traveler."[17] The erection of such monuments was to become a familiar subject of local concern, part and parcel of the modernization brought on by the industrial revolution. The practice soon became widespread, creating a sculpted pantheon for the *Kulturnation* and becoming the principal way in which Germany honored its great prior to the creation of the Reich. The first statue of a musician, which was to be Mozart's in Salzburg, was unveiled in 1842; at the time, a journalist praised the "present-day mania" for erecting monuments to artists, since, he wrote, "it proves that the faddish spirit of our century, while complacently elevating so much that is mediocre, does occasionally have a twinge of conscience."[18] At this same period, princes were dreaming up grandiose projects like the Valhalla created by Ludwig I of Bavaria in 1842, or the "great national church," the Hohenzollern sepulcher, that was conceived in 1840 by Friedrich Wilhelm IV, the new king of Prussia; or even the "monument to the nation" of the Cologne cathedral, which, in 1842, was completed in a frenzy of neo-Gothic enthusiasm. However, whereas all of those monumental plans were in general the projects of rulers obsessed with self-legitimization, things were different when it came to cultural figures. On occasion, a monarch might go along with such an enterprise, or even take advantage of it — foremost in this regard was the young Prussian king with his romantic and conservative cast of mind, enchanted with the Teutonic Middle Ages and "great German art." However, the principal initiative was taken by civil society, and above all by the inhabitants of the cities in which the great men had created their works or spent their childhood.

Such figures were often emphatically presented as "German," but in the first half of the century the illuminist roots of the bourgeois *Bildung* meant that their universal significance, which toward the end of the preceding century had already made tributes to great men into veritable "European rituals," was never forgotten.[19] In 1837, the ceremonies held at the unveiling of the monument to Gutenberg at Mainz drew printers not only from all over Germany but from many other European countries as well. With emphases that varied according to the nature of the person being honored, the historical moment and local circumstances, liberalism and nationalism, Enlightenment and romanticism all came into play in connection with every statue, every work of art that was erected as a symbol of history, which, "like Janus, looks toward both future and past."[20] Unlike political heroes, cultural heroes would appear to fall into a category in which discourse about national identity must take into consideration both the frontiers that create it and the universalist movement that transcends and obliterates it. This is especially true of music, whose nonlinguistic character gives an empirical foundation to Kant's claim that the aesthetic experience is a universal one.

More than any other figure, that of Beethoven embodied this dual identiary dimension, both within and outside Germany. However, whereas in

Germany it created a link between national culture and the spirit of universality, in France the composer's reputation grew out of a relationship with a foreign culture, "German music," to be subsumed in the universal — an attempt that went back to the very first Beethoven critics in Paris, who, as early as 1811, were describing him as a "giant genius," while commenting on his "somewhat harsh *Germanisms.*"[21] A few days after his death, *Le Globe* printed a brief notice:

> The arts have just sustained a great loss. A man of rare genius, the Kant of music, Beethowen [*sic*] died at Vienna on the 26th of last month. Even those not sensible to the abstract and one might say metaphysical beauties of his compositions still admire him as the greatest modern harmonist. Never have the instruments of the orchestra been employed with greater novelty and magic; never have such hitherto-unknown effects been created. Like the logically abstruse works of the Königsberg philosopher, his compositions, apparently so mathematical, contain deep within them an intimate and hidden poetry. His music is little known in France: yet we recall the effect produced last year by one of his symphonies performed at the Concert Spirituel. We would hope that the coming week will enable us to hear that admirable symphony once again: we will applaud it as we would the funeral elegy of a great talent.[22]

Thus, as first reaction to Beethoven's death we find an equation between speculative philosophy and instrumental music, giving the latter a potential for "metaphysical beauty," making it in France a reference to a specifically German cultural sphere. In the article in *Le Globe,* that musical language is to be employed for commemorative ends, as a metaphoric funeral oration, performed — in the absence of the great man's remains — in a concert hall replete with his spirit. The "admirable symphony" referred to was probably the Second Symphony, op. 36, not a particularly funereal piece.[23] The notion that Beethoven's works were able to commemorate their own creator whatever their specific content was not, obviously, unique to Grillparzer — nor to *Le Globe,* for that matter.

On 9 March 1828, the Orchestre de la Société des Concerts du Conservatoire de Paris gave its first concert, under the baton of François-Antoine Habeneck; the program opened with the *Eroica* Symphony and included works by Rossini and Cherubini, the latter of whom was at the time the director of the Conservatoire. That concert marked the beginning of an institutional career that was eventually to make Beethoven, hitherto a marginal figure, central to Parisian musical life, as well as the first appearance of an orchestra that, through its performances of the nine symphonies, was to come to be unanimously recognized as the best in Europe. Two weeks later, the second concert in the series was held, this time offering only works by Beethoven, including, by "general demand," a repetition of the *Eroica.* This was indeed one way of regarding the great symphonist's works as his own funeral oration, for the concert was explicitly "dedicated to the memory of L. V. Beethoven."[24] Thus, in nineteenth-century France, the principal body devoted to symphonic music began its career under the aegis of a commemoration of the classical canon; soon, there were to be performances "in memory of" Mozart and Haydn — which did not prevent Beethoven from dominating the repertory to an overwhelming degree. Thanks to Habeneck, the composer was to transcend the strictly musical sphere and become a presence influencing the whole of the romantic generation, as the works of Balzac, George Sand, or Victor Hugo amply attest. "A revolution has recently occurred in the musical empire," wrote Castil-Blaze in 1828 following the first performance of the *Eroica;* "has anyone ever produced newer effects, more startling original innovations or more elevated forms than are to be heard in Beethoven's work?"[25]

For certain members of the Parisian elite, joined by many famous foreigners, the encounter with the musical genius created a truly international artistic community. In 1829, the young Hector Berlioz published his first piece on Beethoven in *Le Correspondant,* the "unknown biography" of a "volcanic genius," the composer of a "sublime music," which he was presenting "at a time when the works of this great artist are exciting such a high degree of admiration on the part of musical Europe." And he goes on to quote at length from Adolph Bernhard Marx, writing about a "symphony in D minor" that he has never heard but one that he deems "the culminating point of its composer's genius."[26] On 27 March 1831, Habeneck finally conducted the first French performance of the Ninth Symphony. Opinions were divided regarding the *Ode to Joy:* "What was Beethoven thinking in this piece? That is what I cannot understand, notwithstanding my study of it," wrote François-Joseph Fétis in *La Revue Musicale,* where a short while earlier he had noted that owing to Beethoven's deafness, at the end of his life, "composing had been nothing but dreaming."[27] Although Fétis continued to admire Beethoven, his reaction attests to the initial resistance to which the Ninth Symphony gave rise, not only in France but in Germany as well and, most especially, in England. Nevertheless, the romantics were to end up by imposing their version of music history. In 1838, Berlioz described "the alliance between chorus and orchestra" expressed by the baritone's "oath," prior to exalting that "popular, tumultuous joy, which would be like an orgy were it not that in the end every voice again returns in a solemn rhythm to send, in ecstatic exclamation, their final greeting of love and respect to divine Joy." [28] And although Berlioz regarded the whole as expressive of a "purely musical and poetic" intent, the violinist and critic Chrétien Urhan saw it as an expression of the "ardent mysticism" of its composer, that Christ-like "martyr" whose biography he reads throughout the symphony until the final *Ode to Joy*, which he heard as "church music, but music for the church of Heaven." [29]

In Urhan's article, the religious vision contrasts with that of others who found a Masonic message in the Ninth Symphony, where Schiller's lines about "brothers" crown the "trials" depicted in the first three movements. In the 1830s, the author of the "revolution" that Castil-Blaze described in purely musical terms was beginning to take on political significance as well. At the time of France's July revolution, the youthful Franz Liszt was to make sketches for a "Revolutionary Symphony," which, with its quotations from the *Marseillaise* and Luther's chorale *Ein' feste Burg*, was directly inspired by *Wellington's Victory*. The simultaneous — and often contradictory — projection of Beethoven's works into the religious and social spheres was taken up by some of the followers of Saint-Simon, who, addressing those "artists who love the people," were to dream of massive performances of his symphonies or of some "hymn for the future" in which Beethoven would somehow be combined with Rossini. It was this "emotional power exclusive to music" that the composer Félicien David wished to put at the service of Saint-Simonian ideals, claiming that he had never heard "a more sublime composition than the symphony for large chorus." [30] At the time, however, the effect of such political readings was to be relatively limited. The great discovery of the 1830 romantics was to be the expressive power of the art of music on the individual, as well as music's openness to an infinite variety of interpretations. As Balzac was to write in 1839, "everyone interprets music according to his own sorrow or joy, his hopes or his despair." [31]

Agreement on the private and personal nature of aesthetic experience and the "monumental" scope of Beethoven's works, however, did not obviate the desire to pay tribute to the great man in some visible and permanent form, namely, by means of a statue. And when, in Bonn, that desire began to take concrete form, its promoters, aware of the composer's international fame, would turn not only to the rest of Germany but also to what they were to call "the artistic world." On 17 December 1835, the "Bonn Association for the Beethoven Monument" issued an "Announcement to Beethoven Admirers":

> At all times and by all peoples it has been viewed as a sacred duty to honor the memory of great men with lasting monuments, left to future generations as symbols of contemporary admiration. That obligation, so pressing with regard to all outstanding men, is even more imperative when it is a question of a genius whose admirable works are known not only in Europe but even in the most-distant lands; when it is a question of a man whose name comes first to mind whenever there is a question of the most daring and sublime works of the human imagination, of the most prodigious spring of artistic invention, and, above all, of the perfection of music as an independent art; in short, when it is a question of Ludwig van Beethoven! [32]

The committee was presided over by August Wilhelm Schlegel and made up of the elite of Bonn's cultural life — including Breidenstein, the only musician in the group, a professor at the Bonn *Gymnasium,* a geologist, a jurist, and a canon. The document, dated on the composer's birthday, was sent to all of the principal musical publications in Germany, France, and England; the signatories were addressing "all of Beethoven's admirers for their support, either though private subscriptions, concerts or dramatic offerings." In Germany, the appeal proved effective, particularly with Ludwig I of Bavaria and the future Friedrich Wilhelm IV. In Paris, it was printed in the *Revue et gazette musicale* of 24 April 1836, whose editor, the German Maurice Schlesinger, was to be the project's principal Parisian representative. However, the response was neither rapid nor effective. Later, Breidenstein reported that Cherubini, who had written promising to give a benefit concert on behalf of the monument, had later turned a cold shoulder. [33] Whether this reflected jealousy on Cherubini's part or was a sign of some tension between Habeneck and Schlesinger, the fact remains that in Paris, where the Beethoven cult was then at its peak, Bonn's first "Announcement" was received with virtual silence. The same was true for London. In July 1837, the *Musical World* expressed regret at the absence of the fashionable public at the benefit concert given at the Drury Lane Theatre by George Smart and Ignaz Moscheles, who conducted what the journalist described as "the universal Hallelujah" of the *Ode to Joy*. However, he added, "why is the monument to be at Bonn and not at London, in St. Paul's, or Westminster Abbey?" Indeed, the very idea of a statue was itself questioned, for, he went on, "after all, the greatest monument Beethoven can have is the proper performance of his works: the annual repetition of the choral symphony by 1000 or 1500 persons — the grand masonic hymn of Europe upborne by 1000 voices, and supported by an orchestra of 500 instrumentalists, would be the apotheosis which even the composer would have desired for an extension of his thread of life to have witnessed."[34] It is probable that this mention of a "grand masonic hymn of Europe," an opinion shared by enthusiastic French Freemasons, represents the first attempt to make the *Ode to Joy* into an explicitly "European anthem."

That such an idea was put forward as an alternative to the plan for a statue does demonstrate, however, that the 1835 appeal was not merely a way of affirming the Beethoven cult in a public way but also a recognition of its inherent limits and contradictions. For the romantics had found themselves caught in a paradoxical situation. As champions of the *Eroica*'s composer, they had in all good faith to want to see him triumph and to contribute, as musicians and critics, to that triumph. However, at the same time, the idea they had formed of Beethoven's exceptional nature and of the aesthetic experience in general led them to be deeply wary of having their enthusiasm turned into something banal, a phenomenon they attempted to forestall by putting emphasis on the works of the composer's later period, reputedly incomprehensible to the uninitiate, and by distancing themselves from what they regarded as "inauthentic" admirers. Thus, in the same issue of the *Gazette* in which the Bonn committee's announcement was printed, Berlioz railed at the audience at the Conservatoire concerts, "since for such people Beethoven is the fashion, just as Gluck was for the fops at the court of Louis XVI. And it may not be long now before those gentlemen replace the feigned enthusiasm they now display with contempt: then his fame will indeed have come full circle."[35] Here we have a dramatic reversal of the historical course of public recognition: contrary to prevailing fashion (the eternal figure of evil), true glory now rests in the contempt of the ignorant. For Berlioz, this position is made ever more paradoxical because of the massive and large-scale vocation of his own "monumental" music[36] — to use his term — often intended for official ceremonies. But the monumental ideal contained in a work of art does not require the respect of a mob of living

human "statues" steeped in mediocrity. In Berlioz's view, the perfect commemoration would be one in which the most grandiose forces would be at
the service of a single individual sensibility — in other words, himself:

> I would fit out a ship and I would set sail with an orchestra of the follow-
> ing: sixty violins, thirty violas, and thirty violoncellos, all French; twenty
> English double basses, four flutes, four Parisian oboists, four German
> clarinetists, eight German bassoonists, four German trumpets, four
> Parisian horn players and four from Vienna, and two percussionists from
> Paris, and I would set sail for the world of Ancient Troy.
>
> Once arrived in that sublime region, my first concern would be to rid
> it of all its beastly Turks, who know no poetry other than the Koran and
> no music other than that of fifes and cymbals; I would get rid of all the
> Greek pirates or fishermen, all the bored or boring English tourists, all
> of the idle, skeptical, mocking Voltairean French, without imagination or
> nervous fibre, enthusiasm or hearts, and all the Italian dilettanti. In so
> doing, I would achieve near solitude, in which the silence would be bro-
> ken only by the plaints of the sea of Hellas, the murmurs of the Xanthus,
> and the mysterious sounds of the wind amongst the great tombs. I would
> build a temple of sound at the foot of Mount Ida, the interior decorated
> with two statues only, and one evening, as the sun was setting, after hav-
> ing read Homer and strolled the paths immortalized by his genius, I
> would have the king of orchestras recount to me that other poem by the
> king of musicians, the Heroic Symphony of Beethoven. — Ah, you say,
> with your imagination thus inflamed, your soul so uplifted, your heart so
> swelled with poetry, with such great memories, with the imposing as-
> pects of such a landscape, with your entire being penetrated in such cir-
> cumstances by such music, that would be a real Pindaric orgy to die
> for! — I should say it would.
>
> Instead, one has to go to 2, rue Bergère, to a small, dank, dirty hall,
> where a few oily lamps accentuate the shadows, where one finds pale
> women raising their gaze to heaven with carefully studied poses and red-
> faced men either making an effort not to fall asleep or beating time incor-
> rectly with their heads. . . .[37]

Compared to that "Pindaric orgy," a mere statue in a small German town
would inevitably be seen as something of a letdown. Which is probably why
in the early stages the Bonn monument aroused little enthusiasm or comment on Berlioz's part.

On the other hand, his colleague Robert Schumann elected to air his misgivings in public. The banalization of the great tradition disturbed him a great deal: if Beethoven was the symbol of Germany's cultural greatness, he was also in other nations a symbol of a bourgeoisie that appeared to be moved by any purely external demonstration of artistic talent. The combat against the "pedants," who saw only harmonic rules being flouted when they should have been hailing the power of genius, was accompanied by an even more urgent struggle against the "Philistines" — such was the purpose of Schumann's Davidsbund, a league of real or imagined characters who live in his writings and compositions. In an article written in 1835, the character Florestan inveighs against the "Beethovenians listening wide-eyed" to the Ninth Symphony. "Once outside, under the dim street lamps, Eusebius says, as if to himself: 'Beethoven . . . what power the name has! The grave sonority of its syllables vibrates in the soul as if eternally. It seems that there could be no other letters to make up such a name!' 'Eusebius,' I reply calmly, 'are you too going to start praising Beethoven?'"[38] Eusebius's ecstasy over Beethoven's very *name* and Florestan's reproach signal Schumann's own discomfort at the spread of that Biedermeier sensibility, one that was, in fact, very close to his own. Here we have the critic in what we might call his tragic role: since silence on the part of the Davidsbündler members can only lead to the triumph of the Philistines, the one solution, precarious as it may be, is to bring the matter out into the open. In response to the appeal of the Bonn committee, Schumann was to publish an article entitled "A Monument for Beethoven: Four Opinions."[39] Florestan addresses Beethoven ironically, using the familiar "Du": "Your D-minor symphony, all of your sublime paeans to sorrow and joy, are still not great enough to prevent us from raising a monument to you, and there's no way you can get out of it!" Monuments to great men are doomed to failure, for none of them can come close to true greatness; no statue can replace the master's living presence, the presence of Beethoven the man laying his hand on Florestan's fevered brow, his music itself, "the templed pillars of his C-minor symphony." The second character falls in with the skeptical tone: "Börne says: 'We'll end up by erecting a commemorative monument to God Himself.' And I replied that even *one* single monument is a ruin before the fact (just as the ruin is a vanished monument), and that the whole thing is moot; why not two or even three" — for, as Jonathan says, Vienna and Leipzig too have every right to erect a monument to Beethoven. The dilemma does not absolve the men from their responsibility to history. Eusebius breaks in: "Right now, I am addressing hundreds upon hundreds of people; this is a German question; this is the most sublime of German artists; this is the supreme representative of the German language and intellect, not even excepting Jean-Paul; he belongs to *our* art." The affair is at once national and, in a way, even corporative; the musicians are called upon to intervene in the place of the princes. After having suggested various kinds of tribute — a giant statue that foreigners may mistake for that of some German emperor, or an assembly of the "singing German people," or even an academy in which German music would be taught only to "priests" — Eusebius makes the following fervent appeal: "Do not hang back! Think of this monument as your own!" As the character Raro, Schumann then concludes by supporting the plans for the monument and listing a long and varied list of musicians and towns that must now join their efforts. "And then some tall obelisk or pyramid will tell our descendants that the contemporaries of a great man, honoring the fruits of his genius above all others, made an effort to give some extraordinary evidence of it."

That, therefore, is the sense of collective responsibility that made Schumann, notwithstanding his private thoughts on the matter, decide to support the project. His own contribution, however, did not take the form of any collection or concert, but the very individual one of a project for a piece of music. As early as 1832, in fact, he had thought of honoring "this German name" with a composition; the "Announcement to the Admirers" was to furnish him with a pretext to compose a work for piano. This was to be the Fantasy in C Major, op. 17 — a title that was to cause him considerable problems, all closely connected to its oddity as a private monument. In the first sketches, the work was dedicated to someone whose name the composer scratched out — which suggests that it was not Beethoven, although that is not impossible. In any event, between September and December of 1836, Schumann produced a new title page:

*Ruinen, Trophaeen, Palmen,*
*Grosse Sonate*
*für das Pianoforte*
*für Beethovens Monument*
*von Florestan u. Eusebius*
*op. 12*

[Ruins, Trophies, Palms / Grand Sonata for Pianoforte for Beethoven's Monument by Florestan and Eusebius, op. 12]

Accompanied by a letter describing it as a "small contribution to Beethoven's monument," the piece was dispatched to the publisher Kistner, who rejected it. In October 1837, Schumann included the *Sonata f. Beethoven* in a list of his unpublished compositions; thus, Beethoven's monument was still, implicitly, a piano sonata, one of the Beethoven genres par excellence, and its three movements (*Ruins, Trophies, Palms*) laid out a commemorative program that recalls the logic of his article: a monument looks towards its ruin, and vice versa. This tension between memory and decline appears in the music itself, for it is true, as Charles Rosen has said, that the Fantasy, op. 17, "commemorates the death of the classical style."[40] In its first movement, the work appears to adhere to the dramatic development of a sonata, even though its initial harmonic imbalance is already fairly far from the Beethoven style. However, the sudden interruption of the development by the section marked *Im Legenden Ton* [Like a Legend] tells us clearly that this monument includes a ruin; for it was on legend above all that the romantics were to focus their quest for a lost national past, in contrast to Enlightenment yearnings for universal form. Furthermore, in the first movement of opus 17, the break with classicism is reinforced by a return to private, intimate meaning, external to the work itself, in the form of a quotation from Beethoven's opus 98 song cycle, *An die ferne Geliebte* [To the Distant Beloved].

At the time of the work's composition, the composer's relations with Clara Schumann, the *ferne Geliebte,* had reached a dramatic climax: Schumann was soon to bring suit against her father, Friedrich Wieck, whom he was to compare to the character of Pizarro in *Fidelio.* Opus 17 has therefore been described as having a "dual program," namely, that of "a small contribution" to Beethoven's monument as mentioned in Schumann's letter to the publisher Kistner, and a "small contribution" to Clara, a private and even secret program about which Schumann was to write to her on 19 March 1838: "The first movement could well be the most passionate thing I have done — a profound cry for thee."[41] At the time, Clara Wieck was giving concerts in Vienna, poetically hailed by Franz Grillparzer as "a little shepherdess" who alone, in her innocence, had succeeded in freeing Beethoven's captive spirit.[42] Schumann wrote suggesting that she share in a kind of private rite at the latter's tomb: "Twine together two branches of myrtle, lay them on the tomb — then softly say your name and mine — not a word more — you understand me."[43] A few weeks later, he sent his score off again, this time to the publishers Breitkopf and Härtel. The work was now called *Ruinen, Siegerbogen u. Sternbild und Dichtungen* [Ruins, Triumphal Arch and Constellation, and Poems], that is, the same program as the sonata for Beethoven, slightly revised. However, Beethoven's name is not mentioned. In October 1838, Schumann himself was to visit the graves of Beethoven and Schubert and to pick flowers there for Clara, "almost envying the man who rests just between the two of them," as he was later to write.[44] In March of 1839, Breitkopf and Härtel finally published the Fantasy, the title page of which now read:

> *Fantasie*
> *Für das Pianoforte*
> *Hrn. Franz Liszt*
> *zugeeignet*
> *von*
> *Robert Schumann*
> *op. 17*

[Fantasy for Pianoforte, Dedicated to Herr Franz Liszt by Robert Schumann, op. 17]

We are left with this question: How did we move from a "Sonata for Beethoven" to a "Fantasy for Liszt"? The answer is to be found in the nature — problematic because heavy with destructive or sterilizing potential — of the romantics' aesthetic connection to and roots in the founding figure of Beethoven. While in the first half of the nineteenth century the cult was to become dogma in the musical world, as reflected in the academism of many of the composer's epigones and imitators, for the most important artists, those who were actually laying the foundations of the movement, admiration was not untinged with reservations. The dialogue between tradition and progress often took the form of an anxious question: How is one to compose after Beethoven? — the answer to which was partially found by singling out this or that work in which the nobility of the past combined with a pioneering audacity. Thus, great musicians were to be seen appointing each other, in turn, "Beethoven's heirs." However, such an attitude, based on an objective approach to musical form, a keen awareness of historical development, and a political view of cultural identity, especially national cultural identity, drew its strength from a strictly private experience involving an individual discourse with music and life. For the romantic musicians, the Beethoven myth was also a private and personal one. For Schumann, Beethoven — and even his name, which sent Eusebius into ecstasies — was the signifier that formed the hinge between the life of the emotions and that of art, public vocation and religious feeling, multifaceted embodiments all of which were ruled by the dialectic that combined the site of symbolic marriage with that of imaginary burial, that made a sonata a fantasy that flouted and denied the Beethoven sonata form, that made — finally — a monument into a ruin without a trace of the figure it purported to honor. In this sense, the mutation of Schumann's Sonata for Beethoven into a Fantasy dedicated to Franz Liszt may be explained by the fact that its composer had not deemed his monument worthy of its dedicatee;[45] however, far from revealing Schumann's impotence or foretelling his future insanity, it can also be viewed as a sign of life and creative power.

That being said, why Franz Liszt? In 1837, he had praised Schumann in the pages of the *Revue et gazette musicale,* and a short while afterwards he had dedicated his *Grandes études de Paganini* to Clara Wieck. According to Alan Walker, a reciprocal gesture was called for, and Liszt's efforts on behalf of the Beethoven monument made the Fantasy a suitable candidate, since it had been "a work itself intended to raise money for the Beethoven monument and purportedly in the 'spirit of Beethoven.'"[46] However, it was only after the publication of opus 17 that Liszt was to enter into the saga of the monument. If there is really some connection between the two, that connection is far from clear, and we should look for it in the other direction, that is, we should regard the Fantasy as an implicit way of designating Liszt to lead the tribute to Beethoven. In any event, that is exactly what Liszt was to do. Following the 1835 appeal, the project remained more or less stalled for many long years. In Bonn, lack of money was accompanied by disagreements among the committee members: in 1838, the elderly Schlegel had retired, disappointed in his hopes that the statue itself might be the work of one of his friends, the brother of the poet Ludwig Tieck. Breidenstein was to take over from him, although he lacked his predecessor's prestige and was a controversial figure even in Bonn. He attempted to inject some life into the project by issuing a new appeal, but with no real success — although concerts were held in several German towns and although, in Paris, the *Gazette musicale* published a pamphlet on Beethoven's life that included a painfully small list of contributors: "Monsieur Peret, in Moulins, 6 frs.; Madame la Vicomtesse de Sagey-Boussière, 20 frs.; Madame Lesueur, 5 frs.; a subscriber, 5 frs.; Monsieur d'Ortigue, 5 frs. . . ." This only served to exacerbate the tensions in Parisian musical life, the subscribers to the

Société des Concerts du Conservatoire apparently having decided to turn their backs on the whole affair.[47] "How terribly selfish men are! People only seek out genius for their own self interest," commented Schlesinger's publication, perhaps unaware of the double-edged implications of the statement.[48] Such were the circumstances in which, on 3 October 1839, Liszt took it upon himself to write from Pisa to the Bonn committee: "I am offering to make up the entire sum necessary to raise a monument to Beethoven, asking no privilege other than that of naming the artist to whom the work will be entrusted. That artist is Monsieur Bartolini, of Florence, whose works are known to you and whom Italy honors as its greatest sculptor."[49] The *Revue et gazette musicale* published the document straightaway, followed a few days later by a letter from Liszt to Berlioz:

> Beethoven! Is what I have read possible? The subscription for the monument of the greatest musician of our century has raised 424 francs 90 centimes in France. What a shame for you! What an affliction for us all! Such a state of affairs must not be allowed to continue, is that not so? Beethoven's tomb must not depend on such lethargic and parsimonious charity. It should not be, and it shall not be. [. . .] No vast sum is needed for its execution. Three concerts in Vienna, Paris, and London should suffice, more or less. The rest can be obtained, God willing, out of the pocket of the tireless vagabond, as you have called him. Thus, if no obstacle independent of my own determination turns up, the monument will be up within two years.[50]

The course of the monument's history was to be decisively altered by Liszt's intervention, which was hailed by the musical press in France and Germany. Only *La France Musicale,* the journal of the Escudier brothers and a rival to Schlesinger's, found a pretext to inveigh violently against the elitist nature of the project, stating that it might well bring together "the most famous composers," but that nonetheless "the great majority of musicians are completely unaware that there is a subscription open for Beethoven's monument." And the journalist went on to express his reservations: "Famous men in the arts and sciences are today's saints. Fine! The church used not to canonize pious and beneficent men until a hundred years after their deaths. The church used good sense; let us try to do likewise."[51]

Bonn, on the other hand, replied to Liszt by saying that "only the artist admired by all of Europe is capable of such great veneration for his illustrious predecessor, and that artist deserves to see his own name perpetuated alongside the one that it will henceforth be preserved for all time."[52] The response, which canonized the promoter of the tribute as well, is a clear expression of what Liszt's support meant to an obscure local committee even poorer in glory than it was in funds. At the same time, the promise well suited Liszt's legend, which he had been carefully nurturing since childhood. Not that Liszt saw himself as a new Beethoven; at this period, he was still more a pianist than a composer, and his modesty would have prevented him from making any such claim — in other words, it would not have been his style. However, unlike Schumann or Berlioz, his personal Beethoven myth did include an actual meeting with the great man. Even although, in 1823, the composer had given the eleven-year-old virtuoso a somewhat chilly reception, the years had burnished the memory until it had assumed the form, still current in the Lisztian bibliography, of a *Weihekuß*, a kiss of consecration, with the Master embracing the child on the forehead at the conclusion of his concert. This purported kiss condensed the Liszt/Beethoven relationship into a form of devotion that was eventually to lead the former to acquire such relics as Beethoven's piano and his funeral mask. From his Parisian period on, Liszt had been hailed as a kind of ideal interpreter of the great composer's works, since such a critic as Joseph d'Ortigue could state that "Beethoven is for Liszt a God before whom he bows his head"[53] — and Berlioz exclaim ecstatically after hearing him play the *Hammerklavier* Sonata, op. 106: "that sublime poem which, for nearly all pianists, was until today the enigma of the Sphinx. Like a new Oedipus, Liszt solved it, and in such a way that the composer, had he been able to hear him, must have trembled with joy and pride in his tomb."[54]

Thus, Liszt gave "Beethoven concerts" in Vienna, London, and Paris on behalf of the Bonn monument. On 25 April 1841, he joined forces with his friend Berlioz in performing the E-flat piano concerto in the hall of the Paris Conservatoire — an event that afforded Schlesinger's paper a further attack on the Société des Concerts: "We know that proposals were made to it, and that they were coldly received and almost ignored, out of I know not what timid scruples and banal pretexts. . . ."[55] We may suppose that the Franco-German crisis of 1840, which set off an immense poetical and musical outcry on both sides of the Rhine, did little to increase the enthusiasm of the Parisian representatives; in fact, rather than a concert on behalf of Beethoven's statue, Habeneck announced one for that of Cherubini, who had just died. In any event, Liszt was able fairly quickly to collect ten thousand francs, which, out of total of sixty thousand, was by far the largest individual contribution to the undertaking. And thus, the plan for the monument was at last crowned with success. However, Liszt's participation had created mixed feelings among those in Bonn. In January 1840, the committee announced: "The sum available to us at this time amounts to 40,000 francs, and would undoubtedly have been even larger had your generous proposal not been made known so early and so widely." [56] Which was probably true, but quite tactless all the same. In fact, in the very first response to Liszt's offer, the one in which he was assured that his name would be forever linked with that of Beethoven, an objection had been raised to the one prerogative the pianist had claimed, that of giving the commission to the famous Bartolini, a close friend. Diplomatically, the committee had based its rejection of this demand on a technical argument, namely, that the monument had to be in bronze rather than marble. However, as Breidenstein makes clear, the real reason for the refusal was that Bartolini was a foreigner. In keeping with Friedrich Wilhelm IV's desire to "foster young artists," a public competition was announced, theoretically open to all nationalities but in which only Germans were to take part. On 19 February 1842, first prize was awarded the Dresden sculptor Ernst Julius Hähnel. And, after many delays, the Bonn committee was at last able to announce the statue's unveiling for the year that would have marked the composer's seventy-fifth birthday, scheduling the celebrations for the month of August 1845.

# 7

## The 1845 Ceremony at Bonn

The 1845 Bonn festival was a totally new kind of event on the international musical scene, and its historical importance is matched by the painful, and even scandalous, memory of how it unfolded. According to one of the participants, the Englishman Henry Chorley, its two-faceted image was comparable to the sorrow one felt each time Beethoven's personal fate came to mind, contrasted with the pleasure to which his works gave rise, and he wrote: ". . . it is singularly in accordance with a life that produces feelings like these, that the record of one of the most remarkable musical celebrations which the world has ever seen, should be flawed, and specked, and spotted in no uncommon degree by traces of anger, jealousy, and unkindness."[1] It is tempting, and not at all baseless, to imagine the shadow of the great man being commemorated hovering over the events of his commemoration; in the case of Beethoven's commemoration, the shadow is multiform; the very fact that Beethoven is admired by all seems to bring out the differences — indeed, the dissimilarities — among his admirers. Thus, at the foot of his statue the "good burgers" of Bonn were to assemble to celebrate their famous fellow citizen and consolidate shared local memory; there were also the elite of "musical Europe," composers, performers, and critics, all desirous both of honoring their symbolic forebear and of ensuring themselves a place among his descendants; there were members of the European aristocracy, caught up almost despite themselves in a new dynamics of identity in which none of them would be acting as protagonists. And each of these groups had its own motives, each its own ambitions, and the contradictions created by this situation were to play no little part in the course of events.

In 1845, Bonn was a small town in one of remoter provinces of the Prussian kingdom, and its ten thousand inhabitants had rarely witnessed any important event — unlike the rival and neighboring city of Cologne, the largest city in the Rhineland where, three years before, a huge festival had been held to celebrate the beginning of work on a new cathedral. The inauguration of the Beethoven monument, therefore, afforded an opportunity to mobilize the entire community in support of an event that would mark the town forever and make it known the world over as "Beethoven's birthplace." That was the true purpose of locating the statue in the very center of town, on the cathedral square — a bold alteration of the urban space that had apparently not been wholly to the liking of Friedrich Wilhelm IV, who would have preferred seeing the monument erected in a park on the outskirts of town.[2] However, the inhabitants had finally managed to prevail, and from the outset they took pains to see to it that they would be in control of the celebrations by setting up various organizational committees.[3] On 23 July, the statue's arrival from Nuremberg, where Hähnel's model had been cast by Jakob Daniel Burgschmiet, was the occasion for a preliminary celebration that was entirely in the hands of the local population:

> Yesterday evening, Beethoven's statue arrived in our city on a boat escorted by many smaller boats filled with citizens from neighboring towns, all illuminated and decorated with flags and greenery. An immense crowd thronged the banks of the Rhine, and at Bonn the landing stage was filled with the members of the committee for the monument's erection along with many musicians and music lovers and students from the university bearing torches. The statue's arrival was hailed by shouts of Viva! and with an artillery salute. The monument, covered in wrappings, was immediately brought ashore and placed on a flower-bedecked cart which bore it to the cathedral square. The carriage was preceded and followed by youths with torches, who sang national songs throughout. All of the houses in the streets through which the procession passed were lit with candles placed in the windows, and there were flags hanging from nearly every story.[4]

Beethoven's monument was thus a motivating force that strengthened bonds between the local communities and heightened a regional awareness that took the shape during the festivities of a huge chorus made up of citizens from all over the Rhineland, accompanied by an orchestra from Cologne that was also augmented by regional musicians. The emotion was fueled by a romantic nationalism personified by the youth of Bonn's university who now gathered around the monument, torches in hand, their voices raised in "national songs." The river cortege of the great man's bronze statue, surrounded by a flotilla of small boats, powerfully evokes the image of the Rhine as the symbolic axis of German identity.

However, such idyllic scenes at the river's edge did not mean that the small community in Bonn itself was free from rivalries, and the Beethoven affair was to bring them all to the surface. "Just as seven Greek towns, seven wealthy cities, each jealous of its preeminence, vied amongst themselves for the signal honor of having been Homer's birthplace, two houses in the town of Bonn vied for the honor of having harbored, on the quiet and starry night of 17 December 1770, the birth of the child who would grow up to be Beethoven. The debate was a lively one. One of the houses belonged to a Doctor Schilt, the other to a local bookseller who could not have hoped for a better insignia for his shop. In the town, opinions were divided; some plumped for the doctor's house, others for that of the bookseller," Jules Janin wrote upon his arrival from Paris to attend the celebration.[5] The local dispute took on added importance with the arrival of the hordes of curious visitors who, barely descended from their trains, all immediately set out to view the birthplace and even to take some of it away with them in their bags — like the "English tourists" who, according to the *Revue et gazette musicale,* "do not leave without taking away a few fragments of stone, whitewash or plaster from Beethoven's house."[6] And not only the English: Antoine Elwart, the French composer and critic, was to report proudly in *La Presse* how, when visiting the composer's house, he had "indulged in petty thievery of all kinds, and with a success of which any English tourist would have been proud; with a small pocketknife, I cut a piece out of the wooden banister on the stairs, another piece from the keyboard in the workroom, a string from the same instrument, a sliver of the oak casing of his organ, and, lastly, a large piece from the window frame in his workroom."[7] The rush to acquire what Elwart described as "precious relics" did not surprise the inhabitants, who were well aware that the event was beyond their control even if working to their advantage. "There is practically no merchant who does not want to turn a profit from the name *Beethoven.* We have Beethoven cigars, *Beethoven trousers with stripes like bars of music and with pauses, quarter-note rests, and other musical signs,*" wrote the correspondent of *La Revue et gazette musicale,* in an ambiguous tone that does not conceal a touch of salesmanship.[8] At the time, commercial exploitation in the form of souvenirs was something quite new and was widely deplored by men like the critic Léon Kreutzer, who, upon seeing "Beethoven cravats" wound around the necks of English visitors, was quick to cry "sacrilege": "It is sad to say, but Bonn's shopkeepers have proved themselves to be singularly irreverent with regard to the memory of the famous composer, they have acquired a immense love for lucre."[9] The so-called sacrilege, however, was also, in its modest way, a sign of modernity, the harbinger of a whole new industry that was to become inextricably linked with the presumably ascetic cult of great artists and which, although it cannot perhaps be categorized as vandalism per se, has always — and even today — had its elements of "petty thievery" and "relic-mongering."

The sudden focus on the town of Bonn as the center of European musical life was for its citizens both a stroke of good fortune and a source of problems. The gap between the town's somewhat provincial local society and the international scope of the Beethoven festivities was not fully revealed until the latter half of June, when Liszt, upon his arrival, noted that the intended "concert hall" — that is, the hall of the military riding school — was not up to snuff. The committee then had another look around, only to reach the conclusion that there was no other place available. The only solution was to build a new hall, and Zwirner, the architect for the new Cologne cathedral, was called in to help. Work was quickly begun on the Beethoven-Festhalle, a huge, flimsy wooden structure able to hold nearly three thousand spectators, and construction proceeded at a frantic pace, night and day, the musicians being forced to begin rehearsals to the accompaniment of hammering. It was with some justified pride that the inscription above the door announced: "Through the unity and enthusiasm of the Citizens of Bonn, erected in 11 Days, from the 27th of July to the 7th of August 1845." The interior was decorated with a huge portrait of Beethoven flanked by two angels, allegories of his major works, chandeliers and many flowers, and everyone agreed that it was most suitable. Even the acoustics were found to be good. Thus, the festival began by constructing, literally, its own venue in the town, even if it were to be allowed to disappear with the departing visitors: "A hall in which nearly a quarter of Bonn's entire population could assemble was naturally far too large for the town's everyday activities," a melancholy Breidenstein was later to write. The proprietor of the *Goldener Stern,* the hotel that was to become the festival headquarters, was to have the same experience on a somewhat smaller scale, having erected a temporary dining hall to which he too gave the name of Beethoven.

A parade of the famous and the curious attended "this almost totally European *meeting* [English in original] of the sons and friends of the musical art," as Berlioz was to describe it; he himself, as he was to confide to his sister, was there only because Liszt had made him come.[10] Nevertheless, writing in the *Journal des débats,* he was quite prepared to praise "the sincere and pure piety of this vast assembly gathered on the banks of the Rhine with the sole purpose of paying homage to the intellect and to genius."[11] Spohr, Meyerbeer, Fétis, Schindler, Moscheles, Smart, Elwart, Chorley, Pauline Viardot, Camille Pleyel, Jenny Lind, Janin, Schlesinger, Rellstab, Félicien David, Hallé, Fischoff, Chélard, Franco-Mendès, Daussoigne, Oury, Pischek, Sax, Hogarth, Dragonetti, Techlisbek, Lindpainter, Massart, Wolff, Ganz, Davison, Verhulst, and many other well-known musicians and writers, as well as such personal friends of Beethoven as Karl Holz or Franz Ries, adventuresses like Lola Montès, and even, it would appear, a considerable number of pickpockets, were to make the journey from nearly every large city in Prussia and Austria, from Paris and Lyons, London, Brussels and Liège, Amsterdam and The Hague . . . and, Berlioz added, "from everywhere: Franz Liszt, the soul of the festival." Everyone in this elite gathering — according to *Le Ménestrel,* "even those who weren't attending pretended that they were"[12] — felt that they had come together in the belief that they belonged "to nations that were *truly initiates* of the cult of art." Only the Italians were absent, since, as Berlioz reported without batting an eyelid, "musical Italy views Beethoven as an enemy" — a judgment that was probably a bit unfair, since although it was true that at the time, public taste in Italy was "a thousand miles from Beethoven's artistic ideal," it is difficult to view as an enemy someone of whose existence one is largely unaware.[13] In any event, even if the nuance is heavy with implications, the Bonn meeting was indeed *almost* European; Jules Janin was to underline the significance:

> Not enough has been said about the great idea behind this festival: not enough has been said about the high degree of calm and almost religious enthusiasm that has brought all these souls together in one place, and about the dignity with which European patriotism has responded on this occasion to the peaceful appeal of intellectual Germany.[14]

In writing of "European patriotism," Janin employed the formula that *De l'Allemagne* had used to describe the spirit of mediaeval chivalry — and, indeed, he was much touched by the absence in Bonn of the late August Wilhelm Schlegel, "the powerful critic, taught at the school of Madame de Staël." Yet the event he was describing was a wholly modern one; we would look in vain in history for a precedent to such a coming together of "musical Europe," to employ the term of which Berlioz was so fond. And the assembly was, unquestionably, the most illustrious and the largest that the city had ever witnessed within its confines. Nor was the presence of all of these people easy to manage, on either the symbolic or the material levels. However, we shall not dwell on the practical problems with which all of the chronicles of the festival are replete: problems in finding lodgings and meals, problems getting into concerts, and even, it would seem, problems in finding someone to complain to. The true difficulty was to arise out of the juxtaposition of the local community and the visiting cultural elite, and the conflicts within that elite — not to mention the national rivalries that were both to poison and serve to legitimize personal and cultural differences. For while it was all very well to speak of "European patriotism," the climate was heavy with nationalist feelings. According to the English George Smart, "the French, like the Jews, are not popular here."[15] For their parts, the Frenchmen Kreutzer and Elwart were to rack up complaints against the Germans and the English, and there were many English quick to speak badly of the French. Some of this may reflect the 1840 crisis, but such comments actually reveal the widespread existence of what today we would call knee-jerk prejudices, a situation that Berlioz, at a time when the word was still a neologism, was to attempt to ward off by counseling "good self-protection from narrow notions of nationalism."[16] As for anti-Semitism, although not yet as virulent as it would later be in the case of someone like Wagner, it was already latent in the "cultivated" discourse on musical matters. Faced with all of these tensions, it was Franz Liszt, the man "from everywhere," who — in the matter of nationalities as in all the rest — was to be the lightning rod of a dynamic that he had helped to create but that was doomed to veer beyond his control.

His stay in the area, however, had started out auspiciously. When the statue was brought ashore, he had walked through the streets of Bonn at the head of the procession, greeted by cheers on every side; his participation, however, had already begun to stir up resistance among the members of the committee — which, while allowing him the honor of composing a work for the festival, had turned down his offer to perform Berlioz's *Requiem* — as well as having furnished the main argument against Breidenstein, who had perhaps despite himself become identified with a "progressive" trend that was thought to pose a threat to the "authentic" Beethoven tradition. Indeed, the Protestant Breidenstein had found an enemy in a musician with close ties to conservative Catholic circles, a certain Friedrich Heimsoeth, and Heimsoeth had the support of Liszt's enemy, Anton Schindler, the great uninvited guest at a celebration he thought he should himself be leading and at which he would be present like a kind of ghost, having requested the committee to be so kind as to pretend he was not there. Liszt's reputation, as well as his temperament, which, as Mendelssohn said to Schumann, always made it seem as if he were "swinging from scandal to apotheosis,"[17] made it inevitable that he would be at the center of things, for better or for worse. And the most violent attacks against him did not come from Bonn's conservative bourgeoisie. In Paris, Le Ménestrel was already deploring in June the fact that the conductor Habeneck, "that great name amongst Europe's celebrated artists," had not been invited to the festival. "True, the gentlemen on the other side of the Rhine have provided themselves with Franz Liszt as compensation," the journalist added sarcastically, planting the germ of an idea that was to flourish during the festival: "For you will see that Franz Liszt will make sure that, when all is said and done, the Beethoven celebration will be his celebration and that he will have himself carried in triumph through the streets of Bonn."[18]

Where Habeneck was concerned, on 27 July the committee had announced that he had accepted — "with enthusiasm"— its invitation to conduct the festival orchestra. However, at the last minute he pulled out for "unexpected reasons"; whatever they may have been, the result was very much in keeping with the Conservatoire's general attitude throughout. Yet Habeneck was not to be the only important figure to be absent. Felix Mendelssohn, Germany's most reputable conductor, had turned down the same offer because of his busy schedule. Nor were Spontini, Auber, Halévy, or Chopin to be present, and nor was Richard Wagner, who would proceed to hold his own Beethoven festival in Dresden the following year, crowning it with a performance of the Ninth Symphony. As for Robert Schumann, people were so certain that he would appear in Bonn that many thought they had actually seen him there. Davison, dispatched from London's Musical World, reported seeing him sitting tranquilly at table,[19] and Janin described seeing Schumann offering his arm to "a very pretty woman, Clara Wick [sic], whose husband he is." However, although Schumann's spirit could be said to have been present during the events at Bonn, his body was well and truly elsewhere. His absence, added to Mendelssohn's, has been seen as indicating a boycott of Liszt by the Leipzig group.[20] And it is true that ever since the appearance of the Fantasy, op. 17, relations between the two men had begun to cool, and also true that in his final years Schumann was to turn against Wagner and Liszt and crown Johannes Brahms as Beethoven's successor. However, his absence from Bonn was completely in keeping with his general attitude toward the monument itself. At first, although in low spirits, he had planned to make the trip. Had he not written to Liszt, on 1 August, "I should be there for the festivities"? However, his use of the conditional already gave a hint of his indecision. The Schumanns had left Dresden for Leipzig on the previous day; on 2 August, Robert was unwell, and on the 3rd, at Weimar, he awoke feeling "ill and sad." On that day, Bonn suddenly disappeared from the itinerary: instead of heading west, the couple turned south toward Schwarzburg, "very romantic, but *unheimlich* [very eerie]," Saalfeld, Pösneck, Gera, Zwickau, Schneeberg . . . There, Robert felt "a bit better," as he reported in his journal, and, on 10 August — the anniversary of his father's death — "much better." On the 12th, when Beethoven's statue was being unveiled at Bonn, the Schumanns were being met by their children at the railway station in Dresden.[21]

Upon the receipt of Mendelssohn and Habeneck's excuses, Louis Spohr, a well-known composer and conductor, now found himself at the head of the festival orchestra. This brought Liszt face to face with a man of comparable stature at the time, and one with the additional advantages of being older, more traditionalist, and more German than he. The performance of Liszt's cantata for Beethoven, for example, was to create considerable uneasiness among those who considered the young virtuoso as "a non-German below the level of Spohr and the other German celebrities in attendance,"[22] and although no one contested his prowess at the keyboard, by daring to conduct the orchestra despite his lack of experience, Liszt lay himself open to hostility and even sabotage on the part of Spohr's supporters, "an opposition that was fairly formidable," Berlioz was to comment, "based as it was on something real and reasonable."[23] The rivalry between the young Hungarian Liszt and the elderly German Spohr thus marked the gap that existed between the romantics and Beethoven's last contemporaries, men who had become the patriarchs of German music — a gap that was to become clearly evident (and quite ironically, where the festival was concerned) when it came to the *Ode to Joy,* which was idolized by Berlioz and his friends but which Spohr regarded as "monstrous and devoid of taste" and so "trivial" in its treatment of Schiller's poem that, as he was to say a few years later, "I have never been able to understand how a genius like Beethoven managed to sink so low."[24]

Thus it was that, on 10 August 1845, it was Spohr who conducted the festival's inaugural concert, at which the *Missa Solemnis* and the Ninth Symphony were performed in a Beethovenhalle packed with some two thousand people. The Mass was received with respect but without fervor; Kreutzer, his recent journey uppermost in his mind, compared the work to the new cathedral at Cologne, while Janin, who appears to have been bored to tears, was to write: ". . . it was not so much like having a pleasant experience as it was like kneeling for a religious ceremony; it was less a concert than a funeral hymn; it was the supreme farewell being paid by a grateful Germany at the tomb of this illustrious deceased!"[25] It would be difficult to find a clearer expression of the priority of the commemorative duty over aesthetic pleasure. In any event, even Breidenstein was to admit that the Mass had been given a cool reception. On the other hand, the Ninth Symphony aroused the audience's emotions. Specialists were equally enthusiastic: Smart, who had been over the score with Beethoven himself, was to say that he had never heard the work better played. Berlioz, minimally more severe, stressed the moment when the "religious chorus — *Ihr stürzt nieder, Millionen* — had sounded, imposing and strong as the voice of a congregation in a cathedral."[26] The same passage moved the reporter from the *Allgemeine musikalische Zeitung.*[27] Only Elwart, in an open letter to Habeneck that appeared in *La Presse,* missed the absence of the "very French *brio*"[28] provided by the Conservatoire orchestra. Breidenstein was to remember it as a triumph: "One could well say that this concert, with the astonishing and marvelous vista of the *Festhalle,* was in and of itself worth the trip to Bonn."[29]

Thus, the festival got under way most auspiciously. The same was true on the following day, 11 August, which was taken up with an outing on the Rhine to mark the christening of a new steamship, the *Ludwig van Beethoven* — the new national hero was thus incarnate, on the waves of Germany's great river, as a "symbol of a tacit link between technological and musical progress."[30] "This great river, this great people, this great national pride, were sights to behold!" Janin was to exclaim.[31] Yet the pleasure cruise was the result of a change in the original program brought about by the monarchs and members of the aristocracy who were to be present. In the beginning, the date for the statue's unveiling had been set for 11 August, although the sovereigns' presence had yet to be confirmed. Three weeks before the festival, Ludwig I of Bavaria had announced that, although he was "a great admirer of Beethoven, Germany's inspired poet of music," he found himself unable to attend; Friedrich Wilhelm IV then let it be known that his presence depended "on circumstances," in other words, it depended on the visit of Queen Victoria of England and her prince consort, Prince Albert of Saxe-Coburg-Gotha, who had been born in the Rhineland, had been a student at the university of Bonn, and became attached to the Prussian royal house. The Kaiser did not confirm his visit until 2 August; a "royal box" was thereupon added to the Beethovenhalle, in extremis.[32] A few days later, however, it was learned that Queen Victoria was not expected at the castle in Brühl until the evening of 11 August, the day that had been set for the unveiling ceremony. The committee then decided to put off that ceremony by a day in order that Their Majesties might attend. "We did not receive this news until 6 to 8 August, and one can imagine the confusions and complications to which it gave rise," wrote Breidenstein, who was to fall ill in the midst of the preparations. Thus, while the demands put forward by Liszt, who was used to playing in the best halls in Europe, had forced the people in Bonn to improve their infrastructure, the family diplomacy of the King of Prussia now forced them to alter their scheduled program. It would appear that the decision to ensure the royal presence at all costs was based as much on the desire to increase the glamour and political significance of the ceremony as it was on the fact that Friedrich Wilhelm IV had personally sponsored the plan for the monument himself. Nonetheless, it was clear that the royal "summit" was going to upset the schedule of the entire festival; many of the region's nobles, for example, refused to release those of their personal musicians who had been approached to participate. Breidenstein, while taking care to spare the king, cited the "travels of the British queen" as one source of the problems.[33] The English Davison, while not naming Queen Victoria, was to write that the king of Prussia, by refusing to release the tenor who had been scheduled to sing in the Ninth, "deserves a severe reproach for this somewhat unceremonious treatment of the greatest genius Prussia has ever produced."[34] And Kreutzer, the Frenchman, asked:

> First of all, did the presence of the king of Prussia and the queen of England not somewhat alter the character of the festival? Did it not turn a family reunion of artists gathered to honor the memory of a beloved master into an official ceremony? Did the events not forgo their atmosphere of pious devotion only to gain some vain glamour and worldly frivolity? Alas, I do think so.[35]

The disparate commingling of bourgeois, artists, and kings around Beethoven's monument was therefore a delicate matter, although Jules Janin did
manage to praise in the same breath "all those heads crowned with royalty
or glory, those benevolent majesties of fortune or of genius." [36]

The unveiling of Hähnel's statue finally took place on Tuesday, 12 August 1845, as the high point of a day clearly centered on the town of Bonn itself. Accompanied by a chorus and a detachment of troops, the committee
members, prominent local citizens and officials, delegations from Bonn's
schools and institutions, churchmen, indeed, the entire population and the
handful of celebrities who had dared join in, all proceeded to the cathedral
square, which was decked out with the flags of Prussia, England, Bavaria,
and Bonn. High mass was celebrated in the packed church, while Breidenstein conducted Beethoven's Mass in C Major, op. 86. Next, everyone came
out to take their places for what *Musical World* was to describe as the "instant . . . that has been the theme of conversation in musical Europe for
twelve long years.." [37] After a suitable pause, the king and queen of Prussia
and Queen Victoria and Prince Albert, along with their respective en-
tourages, appeared on the balcony of one of the houses overlooking the
square. They were invited to sign a commemorative scroll, a copy of which
was to be enclosed in the statue's base along with scores of the *Missa Solemnis* and Ninth Symphony, which Schott had provided for the occasion.
Then came the time for the unveiling. This was Breidenstein's great moment, and he began by delivering a lengthy speech in German. Unfortunately, even the Germans present were unable to understand what he was
saying, since his voice was blown away by the wind. "The Ceremony began
with a Speech (from a Paper) by Dr. Breidenstein without his hat," [38] was all
that George Smart could find to say on the subject. In fact, the speech
touched on all of the *topoi* of the Beethoven legend, "the most brilliant star
of all of Germany's artistic heroes." [39] He was portrayed, in what was to become the classic mode, as a Prometheus chained by his personal misfortunes but sustained by "friendship, the seed of Joy." At his tomb, absent a
consort or son, "an entire world weeps, all hearts sensitive to sweet
sounds." In his music, Breidenstein declared, we hear "the triumphal
march of heroes and the funereal tones of adversity, the thunder of the heavens and the horrors of battle, the musings of the shepherd by his stream, the
affliction that besets the hermit in his cell, and the divine spark of the gods,
embellished by an inimitable art in the manner ideal for the imagination of
the enraptured listener." He concluded:

Eighteen years have passed since the death of Ludwig van Beethoven, and, like a swift stream ever in search of the highest and most distant places, the glory of his name and works continues to mount and to increase. Those works are and will remain his most beautiful monuments, even if in thousands of hearts other monuments exist in sign of love and gratitude. And, according to age-old custom, it has fallen to the city of his birth to give visible sign to those feelings and to guarantee for the present and for posterity, as an eternal proof of gratitude and reverence, that the young and the priests of the sacred art of music may ever find in the immortal master their great model.

And so the moment is nigh; it is come. Let the veil fall that now conceals his head, crowned as it is in glory, shielding it from our eyes. Let it fall, and reveal to us the master: Ludwig van Beethoven!

And fall it did. The applause and shouts of the crowd were accompanied by drum rolls and salvos of artillery, trumpet fanfares and the ringing of bells, "all that admiring hubbub," as Berlioz was to write, "that is the voice of glory in civilized nations."[40] Chorley described Liszt at that moment: "I believe that I have never seen on any face so noble and serenely radiant an expression."[41] Their Majesties, however, were much let down to find that when the supreme movement arrived, Beethoven was displaying to them what Karl Schorn was to describe as "the posterior portion of his body."[42] In installing the rulers on the balcony of Graf Fürstenberg's dwelling, no one, apparently, had realized that Beethoven's statue, which was still covered, would be facing the opposite direction. Although Breidenstein was to maintain that Friedrich Wilhelm IV himself had chosen the viewing site, the echoes of the monumental (in this case, literally) gaffe would follow him to his grave. Victoria was disappointed, but confined herself to noting in her journal: ". . . unfortunately, when the statue was uncovered, its back was turned to us."[43] The press, on the other hand, fell upon the stunned committee members — although some journalists chose to see the whole thing as politically symbolic. Thus Davison, the *Musical World* correspondent, wrote that the statue, with its back turned "disdainfully" to the monarchs, was "emulating the stern republicanism of the master mind of which it was the effigy."[44]

Those who viewed the statue head on found it imposing enough, well sited on its four-sided base with its classical bas-relief allegories representing Fantasy, the Symphony, Theater Music, and Religious Music. Men like Smart or Moscheles who had known the composer in life were happy to see that the statue resembled the model. On the other hand, those like Kreutzer or Davison, who had never seen him, were among the most disappointed: "People agree in saying that the great composer's features are perfectly exact," Kreutzer wrote. "I could easily agree, but, alas, where are the marks of genius?"[45] Of course, Hähnel's task had not been an easy one. Beethoven had been worshiped by a generation that, while idolizing him as a kind of demigod, had nevertheless preserved a clear memory of his physical appearance. His features were widely familiar through many portraits, but because of the difficult conditions under which those had often been executed, they were, by definition, no more than approximations and differed greatly one from the other. For that matter, the best-known portraits — those by Stieler, Waldmüller, Mähler, Schimon — were not necessarily the most faithful, and their reproductions, whether copies or lithographs, further added to the distortion. Above and beyond the question of likeness, Beethoven's statue found itself caught between contradictory trends: the composer had been a man like any other, but he had been no ordinary man; he had simultaneously represented the rising bourgeois culture and an element of it that had to be transcended. The monument's promoters had set out to harmonize the real and the ideal — the age-old debate where statuary is concerned — by asking Hähnel to modify the first project he had submitted in 1842, which had had an "allzu grosse Realität," or untoward realism.[46] Breidenstein was to sum up the final version in a wonderfully paradoxical phrase, calling it a "total likeness, albeit somewhat idealized."[47] A recent book has described the Bonn statue as a "static hybrid — half-divine, half-pedestrian," clad in simple period garb and wrapped in a voluminous cloak that lends it a classic and timeless quality[48] — whereas Jules Janin, in 1845, faithful to his romantic ideal, saw it as "the antique costume of the old German masters."[49] As for Schindler, he had begun by denouncing Hähnel's project as depicting the "ordinary prose" of a Beethoven "looking like a Philistine" but was among those who found the statue "like" at the time of its unveiling. Fifteen years later, however, he had changed his mind, having come to consider that "there is nothing to be seen . . . that conforms to reality" on the square in Bonn.[50] Rather than merely revealing inconsistent points of view, what we have here is an indication that, at the time when the last men who could have seen Beethoven's actual features were disappearing, the reality that now mattered was an ideal one.

That being said, musical monuments, unlike effigies, did not have to worry about likeness — at least, not stylistically. Since originality was rec-

ognized as essential to the merits of a work of art, pastiche, at least in principle, was not a viable way to pay tribute to Beethoven. On the other hand,
musical tributes were nonetheless subject — and perhaps to an even greater
degree — to the sublime ideal embodied by the genius they were to honor;
they were also required to keep within certain rhetorical limits deemed
suited to the genre. In composing his ceremonial work, Breidenstein had
apparently not paid sufficient attention to this latter aspect. His "Choir for
Men's Voices for the Inauguration of Beethoven's Statue" was given an
open-air performance immediately following the unveiling:

| | |
|---|---|
| *Du Meister bist's, der Töne Hort!* | Thou, master and guardian of music! |
| *Des hohes Bild* | The great image |
| *Vor unsern Augen ward enthüllt,* | Was unveiled before our eyes, |
| *An diesem Ort* | Here in this place |
| *Wo deine Wiege stand,* | Where your cradle stood, |
| *Denn hier bei uns am deutschen* | For here, at home in the German |
| *Rhein* | Rhineland — |
| *Ob jedes Land dich nenne sein* | Though every land proclaim thee theirs — |
| *Gewalt'ger ist dein Vaterland.* | Here, powerful one, is thy Fatherland.[51] |

Although the strong wind ensured that the patriotism of William Smets's
poetry was no more clearly understood than had been the words of Breidenstein's earlier speech, the latter's music was a sitting target for the critics. Kreutzer deplored the fact that Liszt had not managed "to prevent a
ridiculous composer from subjecting Beethoven's statue to the martyrdom
of a music so odious as to have made it wince despite its being made of
bronze."[52] The loathing was not directed solely at the work's composer. At
the time, choral music was severely structured according to social hierarchies that were reflected in musical genres. "Compositions for mixed chorus (with or without orchestra) and for men's chorus (without orchestra)
were felt to be on different artistic levels, despite, or even totally regardless
of, the existence of both bad oratorios and excellent men's choruses."[53]
Breidenstein's work in honor of Beethoven, an anthem with band accompaniment, obviously embodied some masculine, petit-bourgeois ideal — and
the *Allgemeine musikalische Zeitung* did concede that it "did not lack imposing passages."[54] A work combining such forces, however, performed
before the elite of musical Europe, was doomed in advance.

The right to pay a musical homage to Beethoven composed in the properly "elevated" manner was reserved to Franz Liszt, who on the same evening was to conduct the Symphony in C Minor and play the Concerto in E-flat under Spohr's baton at a concert planned to illustrate "the diversity of Beethoven's work," and which also included the overture to *Coriolanus*, the Quartet in E flat, op. 74, selections from the oratorio *Christ on the Mount of Olives*, and two numbers from *Fidelio*. On the following morning, 13 August 1845, there was an "artists' concert" at which compositions by Mendelssohn and Weber were performed along with works by Beethoven that had been requested by Queen Victoria; in the presence of the monarchs, whose arrival was greeted by the singing of *Heil Dir im Siegerkranz,* the Prussian anthem using the tune of *God Save the Queen,* Liszt then conducted his first-ever work for soloists, chorus, and orchestra, the "Cantata for the Inauguration of Beethoven's Monument at Bonn," to a poem by Bernhard Wolff, a writer and professor at Jena.[55] In a letter addressed to Abbé Lamennais, who had been his spiritual guide ever since his stay with the Saint-Simonians, Liszt described Wolff's text as a "sort of Magnificat for human Genius conquered by God in the eternal revelation of time and space — a text that might apply as much to Goethe or Raphael or Columbus as it does to Beethoven."[56] The cantata's four movements represent the search for an answer to the opening question of the text: "Why is this crowd assembled here?" A martial motif that first sounds at the beginning of the work is linked to an ascending melody that is introduced towards the end of the first movement in a *mezza voce religioso*. This is soon triumphantly taken up by the chorus, which announces, in the words of the text, the "day of genius's consecration."

In the second movement, a long, homophonic cantilena over a rapid figure played by the double basses depicts the contrast between the eternity of the celestial vault and the transitory life of "peoples" here below. The third movement, after invoking the historical role played by the princes in the outmoded style of early Italian opera, voices a crucial question in a very Germanic accompanied recitative:

| | |
|---|---|
| *Aber soll der Menschheit Streben,* | Yet should mankind's striving |
| *auch entfluten mit dem Leben?* | Pass away at the same time as life? |
| *Wird den Nichts den fernsten Jahren* | Will nothing preserve his works |
| *was sie wirkten aufbewahren?* | For the years to come? |
| *Wenn sein Volk der Fürst vertritt* | If the Prince represents his people |

| | |
|---|---|
| *in des spätesten Annalen,* | In the annals of posterity, |
| *wer vertritt denn ihre Qualen,* | Who shall represent their sufferings, |
| *wer verkündet was sie litt?* | Who report what they have endured? |

And the chorus murmurs, "Arme Menschheit" [unhappy mankind]. However, the answer is soon vouchsafed: the witness to mankind's sufferings in the "book of universal history" is, of course, "Der Genius!" — a genius who now makes his triumphant — but totally impersonal — entry to the martial theme heard at the work's beginning. The climax subsides with a long *decrescendo* that leads into the fourth and final movement. After a silence, the orchestra plays the theme of the *Andante cantabile* of Beethoven's *Archduke* Trio (op. 97), which Liszt's score marks as *Andante religioso* — a well-known melody that here is like its composer's calling card:

den     nicht     irrt___     des     All - tags     Spott.

We next have an exalted portrait of the man whose name will ring out with a return of the tonality and rhythm of the first "genius theme": *Heil! Heil! Beethoven Heil!* The exclamation rings out in the final climax, in which the chorus, in response to the initial question, proclaims: "This is the festival that has brought us together," and extends the homage into the future, for, as the text has it:

| | |
|---|---|
| *noch sein Bild der Nachwelt sagen* | His image will tell posterity |
| *wie die Mitwelt ihn verehrt.* | How much his contemporaries |
| | venerated him. |

Franz Liszt's "Cantata for the Inauguration of Beethoven's Monument" manages to condense into one work of art the whole of the problem posed by the Bonn statue. The genius Beethoven is portrayed as the universal figure par excellence, as a Promethean spokesman for mankind (*Menschheit*), while the national (*Volk*) significance is laid upon the prince and drained of any human dimension. In offering the composer mankind's total and lasting admiration, the "Magnificat for human genius" is at the opposite pole from a nationalistic vision. In both its universalist program and in the cyclic organization of its apotheosis, Liszt's cantata is an attempt to emulate the sublime Beethoven of the Ninth Symphony, although devoid of symphonic pretensions and very much in the genre of secular cantata established by *The Glorious Moment.* The stylistic distance from Beethoven's cantata, clearly evident from the harmonic point of view, is also brought out by the absence of Handelian references and by the manner in which the "genius theme" is introduced and elaborated, a foretaste of the organic method to be employed in some of Liszt's future compositions. Both in its text and in its musical language, the work consciously participates in the dialogue between tradition and progress so dear to its creator's generation; it has a role in the transmutation of official music into a ritual element of the secular cult of great composers. Its symbolic function is multifaceted: it speaks of Beethoven, of the monument, of the inaugural festival; it reflects, in the dialogue between soloists, chorus, and orchestra, the assembly that is erecting the monument; and, in celebrating genius, it is also celebrating itself. The work is itself a monument which, while expressing its creators' personal homage, makes concrete through its quotation of the *Archduke* Trio the idea that Beethoven's finest monument is to be found in his own works. While in the Ninth Symphony Beethoven introduces the *Freudenmelodie* instrumentally as a prelude to the coming collective anthem, in Liszt's work it is one of Beethoven's own instrumental melodies that is used to herald the identity of the genius being hymned: "Beethoven's *Andante,* which is *cantabile* only in the imagination, becomes in Liszt's hands a melody that is actually sung, a religious hymn." [57] The addition of a text to this last virtual monument dramatizes the passage from *cantabile* to *religioso* in the social sphere; the sign of aesthetic autonomy is where a religion of art finds its anchor. Here, we have a monument to Beethoven that is very different from the one dreamed of by Schumann, trapped in the "romantic but *unheimlich*" landscape of his own personal myth. Independent of its strictly musical qualities, the programmatic optimism of Liszt's cantata, what we might even call its naiveté, completely ignores the problematic aspect of the commemoration, the Schumannesque dialectic of monument and ruin. That, however, was not to prevent the work's nearly instantaneous transformation into a ruin itself: aside from an unfortunate Paris premiere under Janin's auspices, it was not to be heard again until 1987! Nonetheless, Liszt's work remains the most readerly musical expression of the Beethoven cult that the romantic generation was to produce.

On the same day, 13 August, which was also the final day of the Bonn festival, Liszt was to take it upon himself to assume responsibility for another tribute to Beethoven, albeit in a somewhat less artistic fashion. "Upon entering the town, our feelings were vivid and profound; gradually, they were to slacken and become blunted," Kreutzer wrote. "There was unrest and confusion everywhere; the hotels were stifling, the concert halls were stifling, the church was stifling, and it was stifling in the square around the statue." [58] It would seem that on the last day, the "stifling" disintegrated into outright suffocation. Following the "artists' concert," a final banquet was held in the Beethoven Room of the *Goldener Stern* hotel, with Spohr, Liszt, and Breidenstein presiding. Berlioz did not attend — or at least, chose not to mention it — nor did many other chroniclers — and not without reason, for the occasion turned out to be a fairly traumatic one. However, we do have some reports from witnesses that are in agreement on certain essential points. After a meal that included copious amounts of drink, various unto-

ward incidents occurred when it came time to offer the toasts. Regierungs-
präsident von Auerswald first proposed a toast to the health of King
Friedrich Wilhelm, then Breidenstein raised his glass to Beethoven and
Spohr his to Queen Victoria; Wolff rose to propose a toast to Spohr, Liszt,
and Breidenstein, the trio seated at the head table, describing them as, respectively, the tonic, third, and dominant members of a "perfect chord."
Smets paid tribute to the monument's creators, Hähnel and Burgschmiet.
Then came Liszt's turn to take the floor. In somewhat hesitant German —
his habitual language was French — he proposed a toast to "all the nations
assembled to pay homage to the master. Long life and prosperity to those
who have come here as pilgrims: the Dutch, the English, the Viennese." At
that point, Hippolyte Chelard, a French musician resident in Germany,
called out: "You've forgotten the French." According to Elwart, Chelard's
intervention was "a dignified and moderate toast,"[59] but according to
Moscheles' report, Chelard rose to his feet "in a passion" and screamed out
to Liszt.[60] The *Allgemeine musikalische Zeitung* took Liszt's omission to be
a reproach for France's minimal participation in erecting the monument —
which had indeed been the burden of his 1839 letter. In any event, Chelard's
interruption created an enormous brouhaha, during which Liszt vainly
tried to explain that, having lived among the French for fifteen years, it had
hardly been his intention to insult them and that, furthermore, he had also
neglected to mention his own country, Hungary — all of which, according
to Moscheles, only got him "entangled deeper and deeper in a labyrinth of
words." Wolff, the author of the cantata's libretto, vainly tried to speak up
on behalf his colleague, while everyone in the room began to take sides for
or against him. As the pushing and shoving intensified, people also began
to turn against Breidenstein as the man responsible for all of the problems
that had occurred during the course of the festival. "Knots of people are
seen disputing in every part of the great salon, and on the confusion increasing, the cause of dispute is lost sight of," Moscheles reported, describing a terrible uproar in which he was the only person to keep his head
and pronounce "funeral orations over those who had perished in this tem-
pest of words." According to Smart, Moscheles eventually ran from the
room shouting, "I am ashamed of my countrymen!" And Smart adds: "I
conclude he did not like the remarks about the Jews which he must have
heard."[61] Karl Schorn described an inebriated Lola Montès who, "with the
practiced skill of a trained dancer, leapt upon the table amongst the glasses
and bottles and, gesturing wildly, called out to Professor Wolff: 'Say some-

thing, Monsieur Wolff, say something, I beg you.'"[62] Schorn, however, who wrote his account some fifty years after the event, was apparently the only one to have seen the magnificent spectacle of the notorious femme fatale dancing drunkenly at the tribute to Beethoven before a thunderstorm broke and brought the debacle to an end. However, it would appear that things were still far from over: Chorley was to report that Liszt's gaffe led to a second incident in the hotel's corridors, where Elwart was complaining that since Queen Victoria's health had been drunk, the same should have been done for Louis-Philippe. "The slight to the king of France is an insult to the great French nation!" he is said to have shouted, whereupon an Englishman replied: "Then why not a toast to the emperor of China or the Tartar cham?" The description of this scene, which led to another near riot, backs up Elwart's own description of his feelings during the toast to Queen Victoria:

> I would really have liked to combine all of the female toasts in a blanket toast offered to our excellent and venerable Queen Marie-Amélie, whose birthday it happened to be, but I did not want to give the Germans the pleasure of toasting our queen, those Germans whose pompous toasts had omitted any mention of Auber, who fills their opera stages that are so devoid of indigenous works; of Habeneck, who has done more for Beethoven's glory than the whole of Germany put together. Thus, I drank a toast with myself alone, in company with my heart; and the thought of my mother, no longer with us, and the mother of all the French, caused a tear to fall into my silent glass.[63]

"And so ends the Festival doings," Smart noted, "and very bad was the ending."[64] Following the incidents of the final day, the elite attending the festival were to return to the castle at Brühl for a party that included the king and queen of Prussia, the queen and prince consort of England, and the king and queen of the Belgians — thus, an "almost European meeting," and one much more peaceful than that of the "musical Europe" who had assembled around Beethoven's statue. They enjoyed a concert at which Meyerbeer, the Prussian *Generalmusikdirektor,* performed a cantata for Victoria that included the words: "Welcome, O Queen! — the peoples are assembled to bless you as you pass . . ."[65] After having heard the "Cantata for Beethoven," therefore, the artists joined in eagerly applauding a piece of official monarchical music amidst a "glittering assembly" — "the black dinner jackets were, I swear, a sad sight," Berlioz reported.[66] Following the commemorative adventure at the bourgeois level, aristocratic society now offered virtually the same artists a cosmopolitan haven where they could lick and tend their wounds. Indifferent to the barbs against princes and universal history, the king of Prussia congratulated Liszt on his cantata: "You created a beautiful thing, and I know something about that, and so does the Queen of England, and Prince Albert even more than me!" According to Janin, who described the scene, "Liszt then breathed more easily, and calm returned to his worried heart." [67] The next day, back in Bonn, he was to lay the first paving stone of the new Beethovenstrasse and acknowledge the tribute of inaugurating a Lisztstrasse before fleeing to Cologne, where, exhausted and ill, he would be tended by Princess Marie Kalergis. He was never again to return to Beethoven's native town, where the memory of the concluding scandal was to remain an indelible one.

Obviously, better organization would have mitigated many of the festival tensions, but it would probably not have made them disappear entirely. Apart from the more or less incompetent bourgeois, the more or less vain musicians and artists, and the more or less capricious sovereigns in attendance, the problems were also part of a moment of historical transition. The presence of kings, bourgeois, and artists at the unveiling of a single bronze statue bore witness to one simple fact: in 1845, everyone loved Beethoven. However, there was far less agreement as to what that might truly mean. The political situation of the day was fraught with nationalist frictions; despite the visits exchanged by Queen Victoria and King Louis-Philippe two years earlier, the old anti-French coalition seemed to be re-forming. Yet the detail of those various conflicts has less weight than does the image of one man who, independent of his country of origin, found himself alone in the midst of a European assembly toasting privately with his motherland, "in company with my heart." The nationalism that was an integral part of a man's intimate feelings thus prevailed over the intersubjective and international community that had been brought together around the monument, and the explosion at the concluding banquet represents the failure of the hopes that Beethoven's statue might become a kind of focus for a shared European memory.

Yet the Bonn festival was far from having been a total failure. At the festival's end, Berlioz could still write in the *Journal des débats:* "The admiring throng departs in wonderment, dazzled by the blaze of that glory, to report to all of Europe with what great beating of wings and sparkling eyes it lit upon the town of Bonn to crown the figure of the greatest of its sons." [68]

Breidenstein, who was to take immense pains to justify himself, was to write a detailed report in which, replying to "those who see everything through dark glasses," he was to emphasize that, God be praised, and notwith-standing all the unseemliness, "since August 1845, on the cathedral square at Bonn, the monument to the immortal Beethoven still stands."[69] And that, indeed, is a fact, for the statue is still there today. What, however, does that really mean? A melancholy Berlioz also wrote: "The party is over. Beetho-ven's statue stands on the square in Bonn, and already children, quite heed-less of his greatness, are playing around its base; his noble head is battered by the winds and the rain, and his powerful hand, which penned so many masterpieces, is a perch for common birds." That the tribute would be triv-ialized and made banal was confirmed three months later in the *Revue et ga-zette musicale,* which announced that a "portable and convenient" Beetho-ven bust now decorated an allegory at the Société des Concerts: "While a gigantic statue of the great composer was being erected on the public square at Bonn, in Paris a young and very talented artist was modeling with reli-gious care the bust of that same great man, but in modest proportions that make it suitable for any drawing room and even for any boudoir."[70] Yes, Berlioz left Bonn already haunted by "the inevitable moment when every-thing grows cold and dies away, when enthusiasm subsides into tradition," but the Beethoven cult would not live without this tradition of enthusiasm, supported by the mechanical, industrial, and commonplace reproduction of commemorative signs. The "portable and convenient" objects, the peri-odic tributes, loom very small compared to the "extraordinary sign" for which Robert Schumann appealed in 1836. In March 1854, Schumann was committed to the insane asylum at Endenich, near Bonn. His doctor relates that the composer refused to believe that the town to be seen in the distance was really Bonn because, he said, he could not see the statue of Beethoven. We wonder whether that was a symptom of his illness or whether we might instead be hearing the ironic voice of Florestan.[71]

# The Ninth in the Era of
## Nationalist Movements

There was no celebration in Paris on 17 December 1870 to commemorate the centenary of Beethoven's birth. Not that the French had lost interest in the composer; quite the contrary, since the days of Berlioz and Habeneck, his prestige had continued to grow, thanks especially to the Concerts Pasdeloup — at which the German text to the *Ode to Joy* was replaced with French words in 1863 [1] — whose performances had made him known to a much larger public than had been possible in the smaller auditorium of the Conservatoire. The latter, however, became a kind of "musical museum," performing defunct composers ninety percent of the time, with Beethoven always in the lead. The predominance of the composer of the Ninth Symphony was to remain constant throughout the rest of the century, his work becoming a model to be followed by anyone aspiring to official recognition. The year 1876, for example, saw the announcement: "A competition open to all French musicians is to be held by the City of Paris for the composition of a symphony with soloists and chorus."[2] At the time of the centenary, the omission of any recognition was due to other circumstances: at that date in France, owing to the chaotic military and political situation, musical journals had interrupted publication, and when newspapers did manage to appear, they were more concerned with the water supply to the besieged capital. When it began to publish again after the Commune, the *Revue et gazette musicale* bitterly deplored the fact that "only Paris had been silent in that universal concert, that festival of mankind."[3]

Indeed, in December 1870 the composer had been honored in all the large towns of Germany, as well as in London and Milan, Brussels and Madrid, New York and Saint Petersburg, in "every intellectual center of both hemispheres"[4]— but not in Paris. However, there was one tribute to Beethoven on French territory on the centenary day: in the town of Sarcelles, the band of the Prussian regiment played the *Egmont* Overture to remind the troops of "the mood of the day, and their duty." The same spirit prevailed in many of the commemorative ceremonies that were held on German soil: in Dresden, a *Festspiel* entitled *Das Erwachen der Künste* [The Awakening of the Arts] was performed in which the Muse Polyhymnia, kneeling on the field of battle, crowned a bust of the composer with laurels, accompanied by music from *The Ruins of Athens*. The performance concluded with the 1814 chorus *Germania*.[5] As this appropriation of the homage to the Austrian emperor indicates, at the moment of the German Reich's founding, the composer of *The Glorious Moment* was no longer just a composer of official music, he was the very symbol of such music, ready to be borne onto the battlefields — both real and symbolic — of Wilhelm I and Bismarck — and principally because of his own political music, which had so far escaped aesthetic ostracism. In the nationalist era, Beethoven's figure was to become both the focus of and an instrument in the conflicts among nation-states, a political and military struggle that would take the form of a cultural confrontation.

The composer was far from being the only classic to be called upon in this way. Schiller, the universal "poet of liberty," was also to become a hero of official nationalism, which had celebrated his centenary in 1859 with great pomp. The nationalist Friedrich Ludwig Jahn, founder of the German gymnastic-club movement and a historic figure in the *Befreiungskriege*, was to make a modest contribution to this situation when he put forward the notion — holding it to be historical fact — that the ode entitled "To Joy" had originally been called "To Freedom." In an article published in 1849, Jahn maintained that in 1796 a one-armed man named Heubner had told him: "Schiller did not write an *Ode to Joy* but a poem that read *Freiheit schöner Götterfunken* [Freedom, brilliant spark of the Gods]. Since the censor blacked out the word *Freiheit*, they had to replace it with *Freude*. I personally did that, for at the time I was Schiller's copyist."[6] The story, of course, is an appealing one, but its having been first brought to light a good half century after the event makes it difficult to reconcile with historical fact. Apart from the many references to the title *Ode to Joy* by its own author, the anecdote also ignores the fact that no censor had been involved in the poem's 1786 publication and that there is no trace of any copyist named

Heubner in Schiller's employ. Notwithstanding its apocryphal character, however, the tale was to leave an impression, particularly in attitudes towards the Ninth Symphony.

The nationalist recruitment of Schiller and Beethoven was to put the finishing touches on the development of a *Bildung* that was to become an essential element of the conservative class created in Germany by the alliance between *Junker* and bourgeoisie. A remark by Bismarck — "If I were to hear that music often, I would always be very brave" — sums up the *reichdeutsch* version of the legend of a nationalist Beethoven.[7] Indeed, Bismarck's use of the conditional betrays the admission that, in fact, he probably did not hear the music all *that* often — or, rather, that he was not especially eager to enroll the composer in his political combat, whose strictly symbolic aspects interested him very little. The anecdotes handed down to us by his biographers "show that Bismarck and his family enjoyed and admired Beethoven's music, but none indicates that the chancellor interpreted that music in political terms."[8] Which has not prevented his remark from being repeated ad nauseam, often in a more affirmative form: "When I hear that music, I become braver." In 1892, the conductor Hans von Bülow was to take the association a step farther by dedicating a performance of the *Eroica* Symphony to Bismarck, the "Beethoven of German politics,"[9] who had been let go by Wilhelm II two years earlier but who was already on his way to becoming thought of — thanks in part to the street kiosks bearing his name — as the empire's founding father. In his attempt to imply that Beethoven would have admired Bismarck more than he had Bonaparte, Bülow even went so far as to have song sheets passed out in the hall with verses honoring the chancellor, inviting the audience to sing them to the finale of the *Bismarck* Symphony.

In Vienna, the 1870 centenary was celebrated somewhat differently. Faithful to their allegiance to German culture despite their 1866 defeat by Prussia, which had effectively buried the plan for any *grossdeutsch* unification that would include Austria, the leaders of the city's musical institutions planned to bring together the most outstanding figures of German music for a commemorative festival. With this in mind, they invited both Richard Wagner and Franz Liszt, the great names of the *neudeutsch* school, on the one hand, and, on the other, Clara Schumann and Joseph Joachim, friends and supporters of Johannes Brahms — the Hamburg native who in 1862 had, like the Rhinelander Beethoven, moved to Vienna to become its musical establishment's foremost composer. According to the organizing committee's plans, Wagner was to conduct the Ninth Symphony and Liszt the *Missa Solemnis,* while Clara was invited to play the *Emperor* Concerto under Wagner's direction. In the event, both of these factions were to decline the invitation when they learned of the other's presence, and the committee members — which included the famous anti-Wagnerian critic Eduard Hanslick — were obliged to fall back on personalities of the second rank. Ten years were to pass before the Hapsburg capital was to hold a Beethoven festival that fulfilled its expectations, with the unveiling of Kaspar von Zumbusch's monument on the new Ringstrasse.

On 17 December 1870, Liszt celebrated in Pest, where he conducted the Ninth Symphony and his second "Cantata for Beethoven," which had had its premiere a short while before at Weimar as part of another commemorative festival. As for Wagner, who was living near Lucerne with Cosima Liszt-Bülow, his participation in the centenary took the form of an essay, *Beethoven,* the longest of his many pieces devoted to the composer. In his foreword, Wagner wrote: "The form of this labor was suggested to me by the thought that I might be asked to give a speech as part of some ideal ceremony to the glory of the great composer," and he went on to explain that he had decided to express his thoughts in writing because "no other opportunity worthy of the occasion was offered me." [10] The last remark can be read as a reference to the aforementioned Vienna festival, which Wagner had decided to shun just as he had the one in Bonn in 1845. In mentioning some ideal commemoration, he was making clear just what he thought of the real ones — those that had not been organized by himself, at any rate. Yet the myth he was creating around his own persona meant that he could not help but go along with this invitation to conduct the Ninth, a work that had accompanied him throughout his career and sections of which he had even reorchestrated. He had first heard the work in Paris in 1840 thanks to Habeneck's orchestra, and he had made it a "cry of universal human love" at his concerts at Dresden in 1846, a symbol of his participation in the 1849 revolution alongside Bakunin, and had described it as the "human gospel of the art of the future" in his Zurich writings: the appearance of the voice in a symphony, he was to write in 1851, had marked the limit of "absolute music," beyond which there was no possible progress other than with the "universal drama" uniting all of the arts in a *Gesamtkunstwerk,* a total work of art. No one but Wagner would have held himself up as the "heir of Beethoven" sought by the romantics, nor would anyone else have been so bold as to lay claim to the title — although he was to have considerable trouble basing his pretensions on a coherent reading of musical evolution, given what Klaus Kropfinger was to call "the insubordination of history."[11] Indeed, although Wagner managed to carry over into the field of opera an ideal of "great music" that the romantics had built up around Beethoven's symphonic work, he persisted in rejecting the notion that it might be possible to succeed in going further with the genre of the "symphony with chorus." "Might as well say that Columbus discovered America simply to abet the sordid business of the Jews of today!" he was to exclaim in his *Art Work of the Future*,[12] little dreaming that towards the end of the century the Jewish Gustav Mahler, in his Second Symphony, the *Resurrection,* would be the one who would provide Beethoven's Ninth with a true descendant in the heart of the standard repertory.

Although, with Wagner, aesthetic considerations were always to have strong links to politics, with Beethoven, artistic meaning was directly connected to morality, viewed as the sworn enemy of what Schiller had earlier singled out as evil incarnate, namely, "fashion." "We can state with some assurance that the men most enthusiastic about Beethoven's music were more active and energetic citizens than those who were enchanted by Rossini, Bellini and Donizetti, and were a class of rich and noble idlers," Wagner wrote in 1849, citing Parisian society as the "conclusive proof" of the corrupting effects of bad music.[13] With time, the antiaristocratic or "communistic" tone of Wagner's writings during the revolutionary period was to evolve into an antimodernist criticism of a bourgeois culture that he viewed as being dominated by money and frivolity, a situation that his own works were intended to combat — on the condition, as he was to insist, that they be produced outside the traditional operatic framework. In realizing this project, which was to result in the Bayreuth Festival, he relied on the support of the king of Bavaria, Ludwig II, who believed that the future creation of the *Ring* cycle would be a materialization of the *Ode to Joy:* "All men will become brothers where your gentle wings are spread," he wrote Wagner in 1865.[14] At the time of the 1870 commemorations, viewed as a confrontation of that holy German art — *heilige deutsche Kunst* — hymned in *Die Meistersinger* with a French civilization that was viewed as the source of every kind of degeneracy, Cosima Wagner would note in her journal: "The war is Beethoven's jubilee."[15]

However, *Beethoven* is not just some nationalist tract, or, rather, it is not only that. Wagner struggles to combine Schopenhauer's concept of music with an appeal for the regeneration of the German people through art: "As the German armies are victoriously advancing to the very heart of French civilization, there suddenly awakens within us a feeling of shame because we live dependent on that civilization." [16] The exhortation to abandon "Parisian fashions" is formulated on behalf of a particularly German perceptive specificity whose highest expression is to be found in a composer who, because of his own deafness, isolated himself from the phenomenological world and turned completely towards the inner life. Beethoven is the man who, confronted with the prevailing reign of fashion, was to realize the metaphysical potential of music, replacing the experience of pure representation with that of the world's essence or *Ding an sich*. And, since "the same instinct that led Beethoven's mind to conceive of the *good* man also led him to create the *melody* of that good man," the *Freudenmelodie* is a concentration of the moral value of art:

> The highest art never gave birth to anything more artistically simple than this melody, innocent as the voice of a child; the instant we hear this theme, murmured in the most uniform manner, played in unison by the lowest string instruments of the orchestra, we are overcome with a sacred trembling. This theme becomes the *cantus firmus,* the chorale of the new church around which, as in the church chorales of S. Bach, harmonious voices join in counterpoint. There is nothing to equal the sweet intimacy this melody achieves, primitive and so pure, as each new voice joins in, until every ornament, every burst of increased feeling, is united with it and in it, as though the world were breathing, assembled around a dogma of the purest love at last revealed. [17]

For Wagner, this communal fusion occurs completely independent of Schiller's words, whose universal aspiration plays no part in his own concept of universality; instead of the political myth of the nation's voice, he has in mind the Protestant choral tradition and even, perhaps, the "breathing world" of Schopenhauer's Hinduist mysticism. However, he arrives at the principle for a different cult, a "new Church" whose "sacrosanct book" is no longer the Bible, nor any political ideal or mystical experience, but a piece of music, one produced by the very German line extending from Bach to Beethoven. The appeal is addressed to a "German audience," but the author is dreaming of a much broader one, for in the face of the French taste that has become "the only creative ferment of European culture," it is the world itself, no longer in the philosophical but in the political sense, that is, thanks to the *Ode to Joy,* to unite in the communion of the faithful: "It is along this path, which begins in the deepest inner being, that the German spirit must guide its people so that it may bring happiness to other peoples, as its mission dictates."

Wagner's concept is one of the most fully elaborated examples of the romantics' "religion of music," now tinged with the ideology of the "musical nationalism" that was at the time prevalent almost everywhere in Europe. In 1870, such bellicose rhetoric was wholly in keeping with the imperialist aims of Prussian militarism, without however accepting all of its tenets; for, as the conclusion of *Beethoven* was to note, "the world's benefactor still comes before the world's conqueror."[18] On 22 May 1872, Wagner laid the cornerstone of his *Festspieltheater* in Bayreuth and crowned the ceremony by conducting Beethoven's Ninth Symphony and his own 1871 *Kaisermarsch* composed in honor of Wilhelm I. The founding of the Bayreuth Festival was thus sealed by the work regarded as the supreme expression of German music and by music that the heir to that tradition had composed to celebrate the foundation of the German Reich itself. However, that alliance was not to last for long. When the theater opened in 1876 with the *Ring des Nibelungen,* the Kaiser attended the first two days, and even congratulated the composer on the "national" character of his accomplishment — but then, called away by military maneuvers, he failed to show up for the performances of *Siegfried* and *Götterdämmerung.* Wagner was soon to voice his own disappointment with Bismarck's policies, and in 1879 he expressed regret that he had failed to foresee that an "uneducated Pomeranian *Junker* would be incapable of understanding anything that a good German had to say."[19] Henceforth, the Prussian Beethoven and Richard Wagner's Beethoven were to be two different beings.

While the Beethoven-Reich combination was an important part of official rhetoric, a theme echoed, when appropriate, by men like Hans von Bülow, the influence of the Wagnerian vision was felt throughout German society. It was especially prevalent in musicological studies: in his biography of Beethoven, Ludwig Nohl included a long quotation from Wagner's centenary essay, and his next book about the composer was dedicated to the "Master of Masters [*Meister aller Meister*], Richard Wagner at Bayreuth."[20] The Master of Master's followers bent every effort to put forward a version of musical history in which it was not so much a question of recognizing Wagner as Beethoven's heir as it was of hailing Beethoven as Wagner's forerunner. This project went beyond musicology, and many Wagnerites, adopting their hero's mind-set, came to consider his work an antidote to the decadence of German culture and the "decline of Europe." The best-known of these critics was Friedrich Nietzsche, who dedicated to Wagner his 1872 *Birth of Tragedy* (*Die Geburt der Tragödie*) — in which the *Ode to Joy* figures as the epitome of Dionysian intoxication [21] — and whose first "untimely meditation" contains a violent diatribe against the Philistine *Bildung:* "*their* candy-box Beethoven is not *our* Beethoven." [22] Nietzsche was to enlarge on the forerunner premise in *Richard Wagner at Bayreuth:* "Before Wagner, music functioned within fairly narrow limits. It dealt with the permanent conditions of man, what the Greeks called *ethos,* and it was only with Beethoven that it attempted the language of *pathos.*" [23] This vision of history, which Nietzsche himself was soon to abandon, was nevertheless passed on via a broad network that included the numerous Wagner associations and such publications as the *Bayreuther Blätter.* It spread abroad as well, for example to France, where in 1885 the *Revue wagnérienne* was to publish the centenary essay, translated by Théodore de Wyzewa, in its first issue. Shortly thereafter, the review's editor, Édouard Dujardin, set forth the notion of "Beethoven the precursor" in an article on Victor Hugo's demise. [24] In Germany, under the aegis of the Wagner cult presided over by Cosima Wagner following the composer's death in 1883, support for the Beethovenian lineage was to find expression in the language of an extreme nationalism. Wagner's son-in-law, Houston Stewart Chamberlain, in his letters from Bayreuth to Wilhelm II, was to hold Beethoven up as the model the German race was to emulate in its quest for world cultural supremacy. Later, and now out of sympathy with the Wilhelminian regime, Chamberlain would make the composer of the *Eroica* an emblematic figure in the *völkisch,* racist, and antimodernist writings that would earn him a place in the Nazi Pantheon. [25]

Wagner's powerful influence, however, did not obliterate every other approach taken to Beethoven in pre–First World War Germany. As the violinist Joseph Joachim was to write: "Wagner was under the delusion that he was the only man in the world who understood Beethoven, but it so happened that there were other people who could comprehend Beethoven just as well as he." [26] In the field of musicology, the *Neudeutschen* found themselves up against such authorities as Hanslick, Nottebohm, the American Beethoven specialist Alexander Thayer, or, later, Heinrich Schenker, who dedicated his monograph on the Ninth Symphony to Johannes Brahms: "In the beginning was the content," wrote Schenker as exordium to his analysis of the work's "musical content," in which he employed a strictly technical language that was designed to restore to absolute music the honorable place it had lost through the literary divagations of the Wagnerites.[27] Of course, the followers of Brahms, the majority of whom were located in Vienna, were just as convinced of the civilizing mission of German music, as well as of Beethoven's determining role therein, and in the end, with their positivist methodology and formalist aesthetics, they were to be the ones who would prevail in the specialist sphere.

Moreover, Beethoven's incorporation into the Reich Pantheon did not prevent his adoption by its most radical opponents as a figure in the bourgeois *Bildung* whose most "progressive" elements they were eager to retain. In 1841, Friedrich Engels had shared with his sister his admiration for the Fifth Symphony: ". . . the desperate inner strife in the first movement, the elegiac melancholy and soft plaintiveness of love in the Adagio, and the powerful, youthful celebration of freedom by the trombones in the third and fourth movements!"[28] Engels' romantic interpretation, which emphasized the idea of freedom without being overtly political, would often be evoked by Marxists, who later in the century were to make Beethoven a part of the rhetoric and rituals of the social-democratic movement. May Day celebrations were to be the focal point of that tradition, which attained an early high point on 18 March 1905 with a concert given in memory of Schiller and the 1848 revolution. The event was organized by Kurt Eisner, who stated that on that occasion "Beethoven's Ninth Symphony was performed for the first time by members of the proletariat."

> The divine spark of joy beams out to the great proletarian class struggle like a lighthouse to guide the society of poverty and uncertainty towards the art work of the new society.
> The day in which mankind, freed and seasoned by the proletarian class struggle, will be taught to the sound of the world anthem [*Welthymnus*] of the Ninth, the day when it will have become the catechism of the soul, will be the day when Beethoven's art will finally return to the homeland from whence it came: namely, to Life![29]

Hegelian-Marxist dialectic hews to the notion that the world anthem, conceived in the spirit of the "bourgeois" revolution of 1789, will find its true "homeland" thanks to the socialist revolution: the emphasis on the universal scope of Beethoven's work, anchored in the internationalist practices of a proletarian movement that was to adopt the *Internationale* of Eugène Pottier and Pierre Degeyter as its anthem in 1892, was a violent response to and denial of the nationalist readings prevalent in Germany. However, it was still a reading that was basically not all that far removed from a tradition that had always emphasized the work's sublime dimension and moral content, in the framework of an epic view of community life. There is no insurmountable difference between the socialist Eisner's "catechism of the soul" and the "assembled world" of Wagner, the former revolutionary, for in both, music is linked to politics in a kind of civic religion. The contradiction between the political interpretations, which mirror their authors' political stands, is increased by their both being grounded in a work that each regards as the program, symbol, and celebration of a utopia.

This route from the musical to the political was not dissimilar to the one carved out under the Third Republic in France. Republican discourse on Beethoven is also replete with nationalist echoes — but it is a nationalism that presumes the universality of the values upheld by French "humanitarian messianism." While the Germans saw Beethoven's international acceptance and reputation as corollary to his German character, the French, alert to any elements that might assist in the composer's "de-Germanization" (i.e., his Flemish origins and his affinities with Jean-Jacques Rousseau, that other misanthropic genius), attempted to deduce "Frenchness" from the universal values incarnate in his work. The Ninth Symphony was always at the core of this procedure. Paradoxically, however, whereas in Germany Schiller's words often took second place to the music's expressive power, in France, where the language difference got in the way of access to the text, it was the meaning of the words themselves that were to come to be emphasized in political readings. Without oversimplifying, we could sum up the French republican interpretation of the *Ode to Joy* by saying that it consisted in replacing the word "joy" with the word "liberty."

The origin of this decisive act illustrates both the specificity of the French vision and its link to Wagner's German followers — for indeed, the whole history of Beethoven's reception in France at that period is closely connected to that of Wagner. And it is not without a certain irony that the source of this mutation of an *Ode to Joy* into an *Ode to Liberty* should be the same Friedrich Ludwig Jahn for whom "liberty" meant, above all, liberation from the French. The lack of any historical basis for his tale did not prevent it from finding its way into the biography of Beethoven published by Ludwig Nohl in 1877: "We know that Schiller originally wrote '*Freiheit schöner Götterfunken*' but that subsequently he gave his poem the deeper and more transcendent significance of an inner freedom and a search for wholeness."[30] These lines were to make a strong impression on Victor Wilder (or van Wilder), a critic and librettist born in Gand — and a Wagner translator later to be hounded into silence by Chamberlain and the *Revue wagnérienne*— who wrote a serial life of Beethoven for *Le Ménestrel,* later published in book form (in 1883). In the days when 1798's cry of *Liberté, Égalité, Fraternité* was still much in the air, it was Wilder who introduced the *Ode to Liberty* theory into France, while omitting to note Nohl's dismissal, based on Wagner's authority, of the political interpretation of the notion of *Freiheit* as superficial. Wilder was to take the same path by giving prominence to that "revolutionary word of liberty" while at the same time protesting that he was not indulging in "politics" or "sociology." In his view, the substitution had "obviously deprived the lines of their primitive energy, but had made them acceptable to the police," and Beethoven had gone on to retain *Freude* because "censorship had not abated in his day." He then proceeded to reinterpret the work:

> For this word of joy, of indeterminate meaning and vague significance, substitute the one that had been in the poet's thoughts, and you immediately have the key to Schiller's lyricism, the motive for the warlike tones that lead heroes to conquer their independence, and the tune of the chorale expands with religious accents to celebrate the triumph of liberty.[31]

It is significant that Wilder himself was not convinced of his discovery's historical validity: "Is this explanation in keeping with the facts or is it based on some slightly suspect legend? In the end, it makes little difference." Certain that he was expressing "the meaning that Beethoven intended," he went so far as to suggest an "interpretative translation" so that his version might actually be sung in concert. In its "new form," the Ninth Symphony was indeed performed at Paris on 22 and 29 January 1882 under Charles Lamoureux, to whom Wilder's book is dedicated. Writing in *Le Ménestrel,* he reported that "the majority of those present appeared to enjoy the innovation," and that "the meaning of Beethoven's complicated work thereby seemed clearer and more easily grasped."[32]

In reality, that opinion was not shared by all; the experiment was not repeated, and it resulted in numerous critical remarks directed against its author. However, although the literal replacement of *Freude* with *Freiheit* was not to be repeated, things were to be different with regard to the exegesis, where the notion would become firmly anchored in the overtly political meaning of which its inventor had deprived it. Such was the case with Octave Fouque (or Fouqué), author of *Les Révolutionnaires de la musique* [The Revolutionaries of Music], published immediately after Wilder's work, who criticized the famous "translation" as being "too narrow": "The philosophical joy that we have attempted to define cannot exist apart from a deep feeling of freedom for oneself and others. So Schiller in his poetry is also evoking equality and fraternity." The author depicts a Beethoven "whose joy is intermingled with that of his fellows" and who, inspired by the "spectacle of mankind at labor and the hope of unlimited progress," had, at a time when a monarchy inimical to liberty was triumphant, attempted to "celebrate in a great work the magnificent sentiment of our threefold and luminous motto." In short, Fouque adds, after a comparison with the *Eroica,* "in the ninth symphony there is no hero, only the masses on the move." [33]

There is no doubt that in this instance the masses on the move represent all mankind, joined in the republican faith that was to bring the delegates from some twenty countries to come together to sing the *Marseillaise* at the centenary celebrations of the Revolution.[34] However, under the Third Republic, which had just made that republican hymn France's official *national* anthem, Beethoven could also be viewed as a hero of the *French* republic in a strictly patriotic discourse that was part of the same revolutionary heritage — that of Michelet and Quinet, for example, both fervent "Beethovenites." [35] And also, in a conscious and purposeful withdrawal caused by the defeat of 1871: "After such experiences, let us withdraw into ourselves, let us concentrate our hopes: let us direct them solely towards France," Edgar Quinet's wife was to write in 1885 with regard to the music of a man whom she nevertheless readily recognized as having had "all mankind" in mind. Thus, she views the Fifth and Seventh Symphonies as "heroic *Marseillaises*" and, in the finale of the Fifth, "something like the return of Alsace-Lorraine to the motherland." The Ninth Symphony's *Ode to Liberty* is nothing more nor less than a new French national anthem: "Here at last is the anthem of deliverance, of liberty reborn, of France regenerated, the anthem of a Republic made unshakeable by the union of all the French in a vast love of the Fatherland." And in 1893, at the time she published her writings, Madame Quinet was to add a note that reflects the missionary vocation of French republican discourse:

The Republic has no better means of propaganda than the anthem "All men are brothers." What a marvelous chorus that is! It begins in a confused murmuration, a vague perception of the human consciousness;

but it grows, it finally bursts out in this anthem of love and pride! Ah! It is indeed the *Marseillaise* of all mankind.

> *All men are brothers.*
> *Liberty! Liberty!*[36]

Madame Quinet presented her striking formula, "the *Marseillaise* of all mankind," as that of a simple working woman, one who attends her Sunday-afternoon concert as if it were a "divine service" and who sets out to share such a private experience in a purposely naive way. A few years later, however, the musicologist Julien Tiersot was to attempt to find a firm historical footing for the notion of a "republican Beethoven." He was probably the first to have suggested that Beethoven's music had been influenced by Gossec's and Méhul's anthems, linking it to the ideas of Rousseau and Robespierre. For him, the Ninth Symphony fulfils the injunction contained in the *Lettre à d'Alembert:* "Make the spectators the spectacle," and Robespierre's comment regarding national holidays — "Bring closer through charm and friendship and the bonds of virtue men who were put asunder" — are "almost literally Schiller's words: *Deine Zauber binden wieder / Was die Mode streng getheilt*" [Your spells reunite what was so strongly separated by convention]. In keeping with his threefold admiration for revolutionary celebrations, folksongs, and an *Ode to Joy* that he regarded as "the anthem par excellence," Tiersot drew from his analysis a practical recommendation: "We think that it is not being unfaithful to the composer's intention if we transcribe or transpose the *Ode to Joy* anthem to a range more suited to the voice, in order that it can have a place in the repertoire of pieces that can be sung by all."[37] He proceeded to do just that in 1902, publishing in a series entitled "Popular Songs for Schools" his arrangement of the work for chorus, now entitled *Anthem for the Future,* to words by Maurice Bouchor, a book that was to go through successive editions throughout the twentieth century.[38]

Although Beethoven's admirers were to occupy a relatively modest place on the French cultural scene up until the end of the nineteenth century, in 1903 a book appeared that was to reach a much larger public, especially among intellectuals who hoped to "provide French socialism with an ethic and aesthetic dimension it has hitherto lacked."[39] The author was Romain Rolland, at the time engaged in giving lectures on the revolutionary anthems in tandem with Julien Tiersot. His *Life of Beethoven* was the first in a series of volumes that the editors of *Cahiers de la quinzaine* were devoting to "famous men." Echoing Charles Péguy's concern over the consequences of the Dreyfus case, Rolland in his preface praised such men of "justice and liberty" as Colonel Picquart and the Boers. The book opened with a humanist critique of European culture:

> Around us, the air is heavy. Old Europe grows fat in an oppressive and polluted atmosphere. A materialism devoid of grandeur weighs on the mind and hampers the action of governments and individuals. The world is dying of asphyxiation in its base and cautious selfishness. The world is stifling. Let us throw open the windows. Let in the free air. Breathe with the breath of heroes.

The hero, the "strong, pure Beethoven," is a powerful individualist personality who, having managed to give aesthetic shape to his motto *Durch Leiden Freude!* [Joy through Suffering!], arrives at a communal vocation, "the greatest and best friend of those who suffer and those who struggle." In this, Rolland of course is alluding to the republican themes of his predecessors, as well as to the composer's own Flemish origins. However, for him the *Freiheit/Freude* debate is nothing but a "false interpretation," since, he says, "his kingdom was not of this world." Beethoven's message is not expressed on a political level but on an ethical level depicted in religious metaphors, in which Christian imagery does not exclude the vitalist celebration of a "holy orgy" and even "demoniacal passion." The melody of the Ninth's finale is "a veritable god": "Joy descends from the heavens wrapped in a supernatural calm." This is the truly mystical moment in which Beethoven's life and work come together to declare a "war against sorrow," which, rooted in the individual aesthetic experience, is really that of all mankind: "Warlike joy is followed by religious ecstasy; then a holy orgy, a delirium of love. All of mankind, trembling, raises its arms to the skies, utters powerful cries and embraces."[40]

This religious dimension was further emphasized in a pamphlet of 1909, in which, although both Bacchus and Prometheus are evoked, Beethoven's sufferings are linked to a higher example: "Jesus, suffering, mounts Calvary once more," exclaimed the socialist Georges Pioch. "Yes, a musician, but a prophet as well — I am tempted to say, a Messiah." Pioch, for whom Beethoven was purely and simply "divine," was aware of the dangers of such a turn toward religion, for he felt compelled to explain: "'Divine' in this instance means only the ultimate in mind, beauty, and love attainable by man." With regard to the Ninth Symphony, which he deemed "the *Mar-*

*seillaise* for the regenerated and fraternal societies to come," he put his finger on the element that may well have been the ultimate goal of the entire cult surrounding the "great democratic musician": "It is, if I may so express it, music's great social act. It has raised that art, generally viewed as one aimed at pleasure, to the dignity of Gospel, and that Gospel, now shining forth in man, has forever eclipsed all the Gospels produced by the lie of God. . . ."[41] Impossible to put it more clearly: the "religion" of Beethoven had a deeply anticlerical tinge. In the minds of his socialist admirers, the composer was the reincarnation of an old republican divinity, the Supreme Being, the secular messiah or the pagan god, summoned to prevail over the "lie of God" of the Catholic church.

The fact that this divinity, rather than drawing crowds to the Champ-de-Mars or into the churches, was to be found only in books or concert halls, did not prevent the Catholic camp from reacting. The reaction, of course, did not consist in attacking Beethoven — far from it — but merely in defending him from the "political toadying" aimed at turning him into "a kind of apostle of the Revolution." Vincent d'Indy, whose opinion had weight owing to his dual position as a unanimously respected musical figure — even by the political left — and a very active and militant Catholic with connections to the far-right movement of Charles Maurras, was to depict in his own *Beethoven,* published in 1911, a composer inspired above all by his Christian piety and by the love of his "unique German fatherland." In keeping with his criticism of "political toadying," D'Indy was in favor of removing all political content from the Ninth Symphony, replacing the republicans' "liberty" with an indubitably Catholic substitute, namely, "charity":

> Following a repeated exposition of this theme of "mutual love," a first variation describes the soul setting forth to do battle against the army of Hatred, against the mob of the "unloving"; a second variation enables us to witness that battle, and a third returns the soul victorious. Yet this victory does not suffice. Who then has the power to make Love everlasting? It is at this point that a liturgical hymn sounds forth, a psalm composed in the eighth Gregorian mode (with perhaps a bit less subtlety in the use of the tritone than was the case with the composer monks of the Middle Ages). "Look up, ye millions, to beyond the stars! There you will see the dwelling of the Heavenly Father, of Him from whom all Love flows." And the religious melody joins the theme of Charity to conclude in an exuberant outburst of almost-frenzied joy.[42]

Thus, in pre–First World War France, each faction had its own Beethoven — especially since the decline of Wagnerism had left the field open to a new cult around a great composer, Wagner thus becoming, in a way, the precursor of his own precursor. Théodore de Wyzewa, a former Wagnerite and anti-Dreyfusard, was to concentrate on Beethoven's psychology;[43] Ricciotto Canudo regarded the Ninth as a new version of Genesis;[44] and the musicologists Jean-Gabriel Prod'homme and Jean Chantavoine engaged in a scientific discourse of dizzying hermeneutic complexity designed to come up with the best synthesis, namely, the notion that, in one way or another, in the Ninth Symphony modernity was actually *thinking:*

> It has given rise to much commentary and much astonishment, and has raised many discussions; but today, it has nothing but admirers, for it is viewed above all as a deeply human work, one that, while of special importance in its creator's own life, appears to us as one of the great masterpieces of modern music, and appears to us moreover as an expression of modern thought, containing as it does, insofar as a work of art can, aspirations to happiness and universal brotherhood.[45]

Prod'homme's wise commentary well describes the consensus that then existed with regard to the *Ode to Joy.* In 1909, the president of the Republic approved the plan for a Beethoven monument in the Ranelagh park in Paris. This work, by José de Charnoy, was not to be unveiled until after the First World War, but the president's action bears witness, if such were needed, to the composer's conclusive incorporation into the cultural establishment landscape. However, official admiration for the German Beethoven was not to extend to the inclusion of his music in French state ceremonies. In her *Ode triomphale en l'honneur du centenaire de 1789,* the composer Augusta Holmès had indeed featured a children's choir singing "All men are brothers" and even an apotheosis based on a "Hymn of Joy and Victory," but her pouring of revolutionary rhetoric into a Wagner-Franck mold avoided any explicit reference to Beethoven.[46] In the prewar years, with their increase in anti-German feeling, such a gesture would have been even more unlikely. It is principally this absence from civil ceremonies, as well as the few references made to the composer in the strictly political arena, that makes Leo Schrade's thesis difficult to accept: "France can rightly say that it at one time believed in Beethoven with everything that a belief or a faith implies."[47]

Nonetheless, although Beethoven was not God personified, he was undoubtedly "a god enshrined in the Pantheon of the Third Republic."[48] And with a host of idealized and sublime images not devoid of exaggeration and even kitsch — as witness the *Homage à Beethoven* by Jean-Paul Laurens, a republican who, at the height of the impressionist era, set out to resuscitate high-flown historical painting for government purposes. Only the sculpted works of Antoine Bourdelle escape the academism that marked the plastic representations of the composer, and even they do not really break with the traditional iconography. Romain Rolland may well have regarded Beethoven as "the heroic force of modern art," but enlisting him in the republican and anticlerical struggle did not make him an avant-garde idol. As a general rule, in the early years of the century, major artists did not make up the vanguard of Beethoven's admirers. Although in Paris, anti-German nationalism was to exacerbate the modernist reaction against romanticism, the process was not all that different in Germany, even though it was to take longer. On the other hand, one of the last acts of the romantic cult took place at Vienna with a homage by artists who were unquestionably in the front line of stylistic renewal: A 1902 secessionist exhibition in the workshop of the architect Josef Hoffmann brought together Gustav Klimt's vast *Beethoven* fresco and a polychrome statue by Max Klinger, accompanied by a performance of the Ninth Symphony arranged for wind instruments by Gustav Mahler, the opera's principal conductor. In Klimt's fresco, the juxtaposition of the hero, who has Mahler's features, with a gorilla's blank and lubricious gaze, illustrates the ability of the Beethoven myth to reflect the tensions in the bourgeois soul that were then being explored by Freud — even if they were to be relieved in an apotheosis of the *Ode to Joy* in which the celestial and the sensual unite in a joyous embrace. However, as evidenced by Guillaume Apollinaire's contempt for Klinger's statue, even that splendor was part of a vanishing world.[49]

At the same time, in Paris, when bourgeois enthusiasm for the music of "Beethoven's colossal frescoes" was readily being refocused on "an intimist cloud of nuances or arpeggiated chords,"[50] a confirmed Wagnerite like Raymond Bouyer, the declared enemy of musical impressionism, still clung nostalgically to a "god Beethoven" who alone "stood firmly and intact on his pedestal. Everything else is crumbling, and his figure stands above the ebb and flow of novelty."[51] Claude Debussy, however, committed to his nationalist, anti-Wagnerian struggle, spared the composer of the Ninth Symphony only a few ironical remarks, aimed less at his music than at the "metaphysics" that surrounded it:

The choral symphony has been wrapped in a vast fog of words and a great many weighty epithets. We are surprised that it hasn't been buried forever under the mass of prose it has inspired. Wagner set out to augment its orchestration. Others have attempted to explicate its meaning with luminous pictures. If we accept that there is some mystery in the symphony, we might be able to clear it up; but would it really be worthwhile?

Critical of Wagner, critical of program music, critical of critics, Debussy appears to be distancing himself from the era's entire musical *doxa,* even if it meant moving even closer to the elitist and antidemocratic sensibility than he already was. Yet it is noteworthy that when he comments on the Ninth Symphony itself, he takes the same tone as his predecessors, albeit ending on a questioning note:

As for the human outpouring that bursts the habitual symphonic confines, it springs from his soul, drunk on liberty, which by an ironic twist of fate had been badly bruised from flinging itself against the golden bars erected by the uncharitable friendship of the great. Beethoven must have been pierced to the heart and have ardently wanted to bring about the communion of mankind: thus this cry uttered by the thousand voices of his genius to the humblest and poorest of his "brothers." And did they hear him? . . . An unsettling question.[52]

Unsettling question: how does one get out of the impasse into which one is led by denouncing the "fog of words" if one does not accept the "weighty epithets"? For Debussy, the solution was simple: one must, after Wagner, compose both with and contra Wagner — a question that was now far more pressing for a musician than was the old fable of Beethoven's heir. However, as far as Beethoven himself is concerned, the question takes a very different form, since beneath all those "epithets" we are aware not only of the rumblings of the inflamed discourse of the French at that period but also of similar sounds emanating from Germany, Austria, and even England,[53] and indeed from an Italy finally converted to the music of the "classical" repertory — or from even more distant countries like the United States or Argentina . . . in fact, from the entire Western world. Above and beyond all the political differences, Prussian nationalists, German communists, French republicans, Wagnerites of every land, and apostles of love, and even theoreticians of pure music, all came together in unison in a Ninth

Symphony that had become the musical fetish of Western metaphysics — as well as the instrument of its social spread in the form of an ethics of community song. And distancing oneself from such a "mass of prose" was all the more difficult because all of those many readings, far from being capable of being denounced as so many betrayals of the Ninth's mystery, were but variations of the social metaphor inscribed at the heart of that formidable "musical chimera." Are we to believe that at the dawn of the twentieth century the *Ode to Joy* was on the way to becoming itself a kind of weighty epithet? Ought we to conclude that it had to be resisted?

That, in any event, was the conclusion reached by Friedrich Nietzsche following his break with Wagner. In *Menschliches, Allzumenschliches* [Human, All-too Human], that "book for free spirits" published in 1878 under the influence of Voltaire, he had written:

> 153. *Art makes the thinker's heart grow heavy.* — The strength of the metaphysical need and the trouble that nature has in breaking away from it can be deduced from the fact that, even in the free spirit that has freed itself from metaphysics, the highest effects of art touch long-silent and even broken metaphysical chords, as when, for example, a passage of Beethoven's Ninth Symphony makes one feel as though one were soaring above the earth in a great starry dome, the dream of *immortality* in one's heart: the stars seem to shimmer on every side and the earth to swallow one up even more deeply. If one becomes aware of this condition, one may perhaps feel a deep stabbing sensation in the heart and heave a sigh for the man who can lead him back to his lost beloved, whether it be called Religion or Metaphysics. It is at such moments that one's intellectual character is put to the test.[54]

That passage touches us, revealing as it does how keenly the tension created between the aesthetic experience of the Ninth Symphony — rooted in the most intimate subjectivity — and the radical criticism of metaphysics, based on a recusal of the "educator," Schopenhauer, was felt as a virtual deprivation. It is this "overturning of every value" that was to characterize Nietzsche's thinking: "I only attack those things that I know thoroughly — that I have experienced myself, that — to a certain extent — I myself was," he wrote in a scratched-out fragment of the manuscript of *Ecce Homo*.[55] In *Human, All-too Human,* the Ninth Symphony is the vector of a profound nostalgia for that "lost beloved" in which we recognize, within religion and metaphysics, the romantic religion of music. Henceforth, Nietzsche's enthusiasm for the work was to wane at the same pace as his hatred for Wagner increased. And although his rejection of Beethoven was never to be total, the composer did become for him, rather than the source of some aesthetic experience, a *name* embedded in a criticism whose favorite targets were German nationalism and romantic musical ideology; a name which, openly defiant of Wagnerian tradition, he was to link with French culture and particularly to "Rousseauian moralism" which, as we know, he loathed. "Beethoven is the hybrid product of an old, dying soul that will not die, and of a rising and very young soul that will not be *born;* his music is bathed in the half-light of an eternal mourning and an eternal hope that is beginning to spread its wings, the *light* that bathed Europe when it dreamed with Rousseau, danced with the revolution around the tree of liberty, and, finally, almost worshiped Napoleon."[56] In *Beyond Good and Evil,* Beethoven is mentioned among the "Europeans of the future," but the praise is equivocal, that of a "Tantalus of the Will" already struck by the stigmata of nihilism. Indeed, Nietzsche appears to have been the only one to have held Beethoven partly responsible for the "heavy and polluted" atmosphere of European culture that Romain Rolland, for his part, was to set out to combat by invoking the composer's name. In France, the impact of such criticism did not go unnoticed by Pierre Lasserre, who stated in 1907 that Nietzsche had made Beethoven the "official mourner at the funeral of old Europe."[57] Lasserre, the author of *Le Romantisme française,* or "French romanticism," a book aimed at countering it, was at the time acting as the German philosopher's mouthpiece in the far-right-wing publication *L'Action française;* added to the monarchical sympathies of such as Debussy, this situation serves to demonstrate that, in contrast to a Beethoven "ensconced in the Pantheon of the Third Republic," the recusal of the metaphysical aspects of the Ninth Symphony can easily be viewed as part and parcel of the antiromantic tendencies of the nationalist far right and fuel for the reactionary criticism of democracy. This, obviously, is only a minor aspect of the overall problematics inherent in Nietzsche's work; however, the question is relevant to the attempts to deconstruct the "great democratic composer," a process that Nietzsche may be said to have initiated.

That being said, the author of *Human, All-too Human* is not the only one to have taken note of the exhaustion of the Beethoven myth. Others in pre–First World War France were also feeling a kind of disgust at a certain kind of art — and they were to express this not by means of a philosophical critique but by a very subtle and finely focused use of irony. In 1912, Erik

Satie included in his *Mémoires d'un amnésique* [Memoirs of an Amnesiac] an article entitled *Parfait entourage* ["Perfect Company"]: "Living surrounded by glorious works of Art is one of the greatest joys one can experience," he wrote, going on to cite among his treasures "a magnificent fake Rembrandt," a "Portrait attributed to Anon.," and finally an "imitation Téniers." He then says:

> However, what surpasses those masterful works, what crushes them beneath the formidable weight of its genial majesty, what makes them pale in its dazzling light? a fake Beethoven manuscript — a sublime apocryphal symphony by the master — which I think I piously purchased some ten years back.
>
> Of all the great composer's works, this Tenth Symphony, hitherto unknown, is among the most sumptuous. Its proportions are as vast as a palace; its ideas are shady and cool; its development sections are precise and just.
>
> This symphony had to exist: the number 9 cannot be Beethovenian. He loved the decimal system: as he always said, "I have ten fingers."
>
> Some, who have come with filial piety to absorb this masterpiece with their meditative and attentive ears, have unreasonably found it to be one of Beethoven's inferior conceptions, and have said so. They have even gone further.
>
> Beethoven cannot be inferior to himself, never. His technique and form remain augural, even when infinitesimal. Rudimentary is not a word that can be applied to him. He is not to be intimidated by the counterfeit imputed to his artistic self.[58]

From the "sacred relics" that someone like Elwart hammered out of the Beethovenhaus in 1845 to Satie's derisory 1912 "monument to human thought," we can measure a certain historical trajectory in the sacralization of art. Over and against Romain Rolland and his epic incantations, the composer of *Sports et divertissements* "sets out to disenchant the enchanted soul," in the words of Vladimir Jankélévich.[59] However, is it really necessary to dissect this "pointillist" humor that, via Benjamin's theory of aura, will lead us directly to the *Beethoven* of Andy Warhol? It is futile to belabor irony: let us leave the "sublime apocryphal symphony by the master" where Satie has pinned it for us, like a butterfly.

For that matter, in an age of "weighty epithets," neither Erik Satie's humor nor Nietzsche's "European of the future" were to be on the agenda. In

1914, Beethoven set off for the front, just as he had in 1870, now even more imposing in his new steel helmet. However, although in France his works were to disappear from some concert programs and his name be removed from the Pantheon of certain conservatories, the composer of the Ninth was on this occasion to remain in the thoughts of men on both sides of the trenches: "In our muddy knapsacks, between the notebook and the flash-light, we piously kept the *Vie de Beethoven* [by Romain Rolland]," a veteran was to write.[60] The notion of a French Beethoven, strongly put forward by Camille Mauclair, long-time colleague of the prominent right-wing figure Maurice Barrès, was to have its corollary in wartime with the wresting of the Ninth from the Germans: "The *Ode to Joy* is the only Allied anthem, the credo of all our just hopes, and criminal Germany must be forbidden from ever playing a single measure of it."[61] Thus, two nationalist Beethovens found themselves standing face to face on the battlefields of the Great War, in a fatal confrontation of their symmetrical and incompatible messianism. However, the use of the composer as a tool of militarist propaganda ulti-mately awakened the protests of some members of the liberal elite: In 1914, in neutral Switzerland, Hermann Hesse published an article entitled "O Freunde, nicht diese Töne," in which he urged his compatriots not to im-peril "the foundations of Europe's future."[62] And in 1915, Romain Rolland, the high priest of the Beethoven cult, who had kept himself *Au-dessus de la mêlée* [Above the Battle], to quote one of his best-known works, was to mention Hesse's article with sympathy.[63] As the war pursued its course, more and more people were to come to believe that the composer deserved better than to preside over a massacre.

# 9

## The 1927 Centenary

The centenary of Beethoven's death, 26 March 1927, was a world event. Just what that "world" comprised, however, requires some definition. Obviously, it included all of Europe, North and South America, Australia, and the Soviet Union. The Ninth Symphony had been given its first performance at Tokyo in 1924, at which time Romain Rolland's book was also published there, apparently with great success.[1] The attendance of representatives from China, Turkey, and what was then Persia at some of the official 1927 events suggests that Beethoven's appeal extended wherever Western culture was dominant, or at least accepted. And if their admiration for Beethoven served to make people more alike, that same admiration would also bring them closer together. The diplomatic implications of the event were mentioned in an article by Aristide Briand that appeared on the front page of the *Neue freie Presse,* Austria's largest newspaper, on the centenary day itself: "The celebrations for Beethoven summon the civilized world to gather in reverence," the French minister for foreign affairs wrote.[2] The call to "gather in reverence" betrays the concerns prevalent in international life at a time when the problems of the League of Nations centered around the specter of a possible world conflagration and when growing pacifist and internationalist movements were mobilizing to forestall catastrophe. "The celebration is being echoed throughout the entire world, in every cultured land on either side of the Ocean (wherever peace reigns)," stated the official report of the Vienna ceremonies, considering the "sacred bond" created by Beethoven as the guarantee that peace would prevail: "May it last forever!"[3] In the postwar era, the gloomy *Kämpfer* of the preceding generation had become a messenger of peace whose moral influence both nourished and transcended the political sphere. In the front rank of the homage stood a Germany and Austria that had now become republics, a United States that had become one of the great powers, and a Soviet Russia that had not yet become rigidly and wholly totalitarian, all come together to honor the "great democratic musician," the "hero" hailed in the Parisian newspaper *Le Temps:* "If the expression 'universal admiration' has any meaning, we can say that the genius musician, and his work, enjoys it."[4]

If, and only if, the expression "universal admiration" has any real meaning — which is far from evident. For the newspaper, the words were mere rhetoric, but the question remains: what meaning? For it is clear that, notwithstanding the vast spread of Beethoven's music over the past century and the impact of the commemoration itself, the majority of human beings alive in 1927 did *not* admire him; indeed, it is highly likely that they were totally unaware of his existence, and this was true not only in remote countries of Asia or Africa but to some undetermined degree in the Occidental countries as well. Such had probably always been the case, but it had never prevented the composer's reputation from being infused, even in the beginning, with pretensions to universality. In 1827, Franz Grillparzer had regarded Beethoven as giving "for the world his all and his heart's blood"; in 1835, the Bonn committee had called him "a genius whose admirable works are known not only in Europe but even in the most-distant lands"; in 1927, the mayor of Vienna spoke of a homage that was being rendered "wherever music is regarded as a cultural commodity." Each of the statements is false, but each one to a somewhat lesser degree than its predecessor, for from the time of the composer's death to his centenary celebration, the Western concept of intellectual center and cultural commodity had been inexorably broadened. The desire to synthesize and the awareness of nonfulfillment resonate in the juxtaposition of such catch-all terms as "world" or "universe" as well as in the more restrictive phrases that were nonetheless used synonymously, phrases like "the civilized world," "cultured nations," or "music-loving countries." The consensus expressed through the active or passive participation in the commemoration was not in any real sense a "world" consensus, but it aspired to that status in order to support one of the arguments Western culture employed to legitimize its quest for world hegemony, namely, the purportedly universal nature of its cultural heroes. And this at a time in history when imperialist expansion, despite its Leninist or Wilsonian critics, had not yet given rise to any real questioning of cultural Eurocentrism. In short, within the context of the centenary, the true meaning of the word "universe" was simply "those human beings who admire Beethoven."

The spread of Beethoven's influence has often been described in geographical terms: for the protagonists of the various commemorative ceremonies, nothing was more appealing than the image of a man civilizing the earth through his music, a missionary transcending spatial limitations with a message that touched and moved human beings born worlds away from his home and his piano. Such voices cared little about the actual role the "serious music" of the West played in the colonization process, a role that still remains to be examined. While this dissemination in space was perceived as a historical triumph, the great composer's temporal victory had always been viewed as a given; even before his death, Beethoven's works had been deemed immortal, and with his demise he himself became an immortal. It was an enviable status, but as we have seen, it was a fairly static one as well. Immortality, a divine and thus suprahistorical status, had become so obvious an attribute of genius that little attention was paid to its historical significance. Reflection about time itself was a part of the homage: Grillparzer had wanted those attending the funeral to transmit their emotions to posterity, and after him all of the men erecting monuments were desirous not so much of inspiring future generations as of leaving some evidence of their own admiration, so as not to be reproached with ingratitude. Indeed, the concept of concerts was itself designed to keep alive the notion that the works were immortal, pertinent, and unchanging but still, via their interpreters and evolving audiences, relevant to the aesthetic experience of each new generation. Yet at the beginning of the twentieth century, time had begun to pose a perpetual challenge to the business of memory. The last of Beethoven's contemporaries were long gone; what remained to confront eternity were his compositions and the statues, letters, and biographies, as well as "musical tributes" like Franz Liszt's cantatas. While such commemorative pieces had been relegated to the fringes of the repertory, for reasons of aesthetic autonomy, statues had always been, even for those who erected them, questionable objects, intrinsically threatened with decay or insignificance. As for Beethoven's compositions, the complete, "monumental" edition of his oeuvre published by Breitkopf and Härtel in 1884 had done much to protect them from oblivion and adulteration, the inevitable fate of many original works subjected to the vagaries of the modern world. When it came to their interpretation, however, only an unshakeable confidence in the truth of tradition and an almost fanatical obsession with preserving it gave any hope — feeble as it might be! — of retaining some control over the corruption of time.

Owing to the obsolescence of the memory techniques utilized in the nineteenth century, the 1927 centenary was to present an opportunity to pose the question of the victory over time in completely new terms. In that year, the Columbia Phonograph Company announced the publication of series of records with "Centennial versions" of Beethoven's great works to be conducted by the Austrian Felix Weingartner. The announcement explained:

> The phonograph record, by perpetuating the centennial performances of the works of Ludwig van Beethoven, has opened a new path in the commemoration of the great composer. Music has conquered the bounds of time. The celebration of Beethoven's life work from now on is not a mere memory, but an ever-present force making for the music appreciation of the future. The Columbia Phonograph Company, therefore, contributes its centennial recordings as the one lasting memorial to the greatness of Beethoven.[5]

The utopian optimism of the recording firm was to be taken seriously: the invention of sound-reproduction technologies, which reached an industrial level for the first time in the 1920s, was indeed a revolution in music history, allowing the question of commemoration to be couched in hitherto unknown terms. Technology was seen as a way to reverse the tide of forgetfulness and create a musical monument oblivious to the passage of time. Of course there was an element of unreality in all this: today, we are well aware that any recording, any archive, is also threatened by time, that memory is not absolutely intangible. In 1927, however, with the contemporary geographical conquest of what was then the "universe," technology's conquest of time itself was the eschatological summit of the commemoration.

And that was not the only area in which the twentieth-century technological revolution was to contribute to Beethoven's centenary. In March 1927, the Soviet delegate to the international celebration at Vienna, Olga Kameneva, set forth the initiatives that her socialist government was taking, with special emphasis on the role of the radio, which, in her words, would enable the commemorative concerts, speeches, and discussions to be heard in the remotest villages of the USSR. The radio, she stressed, was the basic tool for bringing about revolutionary change in the relationship of the people to Beethoven's works:

> We in the new Russia have set out to combat not only linguistic illiteracy but musical illiteracy as well. In our country, important advances have been made in the spread of music, for whereas in old Russia, Beethoven's works were understood and admired only by musicians and a segment of the intelligentsia, in today's Russia they are available not only to those who live in cities but to peasants as well. Thus, what Beethoven's works represent as revolutionary in the deepest sense of the word is now available to our gifted and music-loving people.[6]

While recordings were to guarantee that the tribute would endure, the radio, which reached every inhabitant, guaranteed that it was simultaneous. In the United States and England, as in the Soviet Union, modern methods of mass communication served to make the tribute to Beethoven limitless in both time and space. Indeed, the two inventions proved to be complementary, if only because radio stations broadcast many recordings; the increased number of gramophones in the home led to a democratization of the access to music, while broadcasting served to increase its dissemination. Each invention was to have a lasting impact on an ever-growing audience of listeners, and that, in turn, could have nothing but a positive effect on individuals and on society as a whole. Such was the view of the commemoration's backers, all of whom, whatever their political beliefs, shared the same faith in the educational power of Beethoven and his music.

Indeed, in the United States, the celebration was organized by a committee that viewed it, above all, as an "educational opportunity," to use its own words. It was presided over by George Eastman, a member of the Columbia board in that country, and included leading figures in economic and cultural life — from Rockefeller to T. S. Eliot, Kellogg to John Dewey. It goes without saying that its task was not limited to recording Beethoven's symphonies for posterity; its principal aim was to promote a wide variety of activities in schools, civic centers, and churches of every denomination, distributing a vast quantity of recordings and pamphlets throughout America and organizing numerous concerts and lectures. In New York, the "civic celebration" culminated with a performance of the Ninth Symphony in Carnegie Hall;[7] at a city hall ceremony, the governor of the state of New York solemnly stated: "That Beethoven was a true democrat with high ethical aspirations makes his message vital for our time."[8] President Coolidge in person lent discreet support to the federal government's backing of the celebration. At the same time in Russia, authorities at the highest levels paid homage to Beethoven. In Leningrad, the composer Aleksandr Glazunov conducted the *Emperor* Concerto and the *Eroica* Symphony[9] for an audience of the cultural elite and foreign diplomats — works that the government representatives, in their speeches, readily connected to Lenin's memory. Festivities were held in many cities in the Soviet Union under the direction of the cultural commissar, Anatoli Lunatcharsky, for whom the composer represented the "democratic intelligentsia" of the Enlightenment, "whose world vision coincides with the principal elements of that of the proletariat," and whose classic works were a model that the socialist revolution owed itself to emulate in creating the "proletarian culture" it was still lacking.[10]

Thus, in New York Beethoven was held up as a democrat and the centenary viewed as an educational opportunity; in Moscow, he was hailed as a revolutionary, and his centenary provided an opportunity to emphasize his role as an educator. In America, the affair took place under the "leadership" of private economic interests; in the Soviet Union, it came about through the centralized action of the socialist government. In both instances, Beethoven's image converged with the official policies and aspirations of a large sector of society, and technology enabled the entire population to participate — or at least to have the possibility of doing so — in the festivities. When it came to universalist exaltation, things were not much different in France, although the lack of emphasis on technology meant that the homage to Beethoven went forward in a more traditional manner: it did afford a propitious moment for reviving José de Charnoy's monument, which was unveiled a few months later in the Bois de Vincennes in Paris. That was part of a series of events got up by private individuals or nonofficial bodies. For example, there was a performance of the *Missa Solemnis* at the church of the Madeleine conducted by Philippe Gaubert accompanied by a mass celebrated by a high church dignitary. One very official tribute was paid in a resolution adopted by the Council of Ministers of the Poincaré government at a commemorative concert given at the Sorbonne. On 22 March, Vincent D'Indy conducted the Ninth Symphony and Henri Rabaud the Fifth, Édouard Risler played the *Emperor* Concerto under Gaubert's baton, and the Capet Quartet played the second *Razumovsky* Quartet. "At the back of the stage, a bust of Beethoven, placed on a column draped in red velvet, seemed, like some god, to be blessing the musical mass celebrated for him by his priests," wrote the *Courrier musical.*[11] Because he was in mourning, President Doumergue was unable to attend, but the government was represented by Édouard Herriot, the minister for public education and fine arts.

At the same time, in a Germany crushed by defeat and the Treaty of Versailles, the tone was in sharp contrast to the euphoria in America and the Soviet Union as well as to France's somewhat uninspired republican events. At the time of Beethoven's centenary, contradictory visions were in conflict in the Weimar Republic, which, while enjoying what was to be perhaps its finest moment, was nonetheless beginning to feel the instability that would bring Hitler to power six years later. Mounting tensions were beginning to be felt in a period that was quick to be denounced as *unbeethovensche;* liberal criticism of the nationalistic Beethoven, which had already been voiced by Hermann Hesse during the war, became more vociferous and vied with the revisionist attitudes toward the romantic heritage that were being adopted by intellectuals whose sympathies were not necessarily always democratic. Cultural criticism was more closely than ever linked to politics, typified by this exaltation of a figure intended to counter cultural "Americanization" — a term that was beginning to be employed both by liberals, who saw it as a challenge to the moral substance of the great idealist tradition,[12] and by nationalists who were eager to defend the composer from the "attacks" suffered since 1918. In his book entitled *Das romantische Beethovenbild* [Beethoven's Romantic Image], which was to be the first modern study of the composer's position and reputation, Arnold Schmitz, influenced by Carl Schmitt, set out to refute a Rousseau-inspired "false image" extending from E. T. A. Hoffmann to Romain Rolland and including Wagner and his "poetic" heroism — replacing it, however, with what he termed the "true" heroism of a Beethoven who used the "real" and "active" effects of French revolutionary music to "combat the French with their own weapons."[13] Adolf Sanderberg, in a speech delivered in the Beethovenhaus at Bonn, described the composer as a "fortress that no Versailles Treaty can destroy." In the face of avant-garde "degeneracy" and communism, Beethoven must, he declared, become the führer of the German people.[14]

Such discussions extended into the political arena itself, where Beethoven was honored by every faction of the ideological spectrum. At both Berlin and Vienna, the composer Hanns Eisler wrote in the Communist Party's official journal that "in reactionary times we must say *Freude* when we want to say *Freiheit,*"[15] thus linking the *Ode to Joy* to the proletarian struggle, Schiller's era to government repression. And indeed, Interior Minister Walther von Keudell, a nationalist member of the coalition led by Gustav Stresemann, the minister for foreign affairs, banned a Beethoven commemorative concert to be given by the choruses of the German labor movements on the ceremonial staircase of the Reichstag. The episode illustrates the tensions that existed in a country in which cultural identity had always been at the core of any definition of national identity and in which cultural debates were now being exacerbated by the increasingly fraught political climate. The ban, however, did not prevent the left from celebrating Beethoven in many other places with public demonstrations, providing the right with a pretext for describing the republican system itself as an "anti-Beethoven State."[16] And it was at this time that Alfred Rosenberg, the ideologist of National Socialism, began to announce in his *Völkischer Beobachter* the dawn of a "new world" to be created by the Aryan race on the "ruins of a decaying world," comparing the impetus of the Hitler movement to the tenor march in the Ninth Symphony, "Joyful, like a hero to victory!"[17]

However, the rumblings on the far right did not prevent the Weimar government from giving Beethoven a fitting and proper celebration in the bourgeois tradition. The principal official commemoration was held at Bonn in May and organized by Carl Becker, the Prussian minister of culture, who managed to persuade both the German and Austrian authorities to join forces for his *Deutsche Beethovenfest* [German Beethoven Festival] — the emphasis on the musician's German significance only slightly mitigated by the presence of Romain Rolland. The events included a series of concerts in the Beethovenhalle, including the Ninth Symphony conducted by Fritz Busch, and a performance of the *Missa Solemnis* in the cathedral, and they concluded with the *Ode to Joy* sung at an open-air concert in the square containing the statue that had been unveiled in 1845. Speaking in Beethoven's native city, *Reichspräsident* and Marshal von Hindenburg hailed the man who had "expressed the German soul in music," while the president of the Austrian Republic, Michael Hainisch, declared the composer to be proof of "the intimate cultural union of Germany and Austria."[18] Yet a few weeks earlier, in Vienna, Hainisch had preferred to put emphasis on Beethoven's sensitivity to the sounds of the natural world around him, to "what we Germans call *Stimmung*," and to conclude that the artist belonged to the land in which he had produced his works — in other words, to Austria.[19] However, since the Allied powers had forbidden any Anschluss, all of these maneuvers on the mined field of pan-Germanism were modulated by the peaceful image of a composer firmly concentrated on the inner life. The sorrow felt by officialdom, whether German or Austrian, was assuaged by the consolation of Beethoven. As Minister von Keudell stated during the Vienna festivities, speaking on behalf of President von Hindenburg: "Today, as a hundred years ago, tears are shed by all German families. Open wounds still bleed. The days of German sorrow are with us. But Beethoven has taught us that he who is receptive to his music cannot be unhappy. He consoles our suffering, he guides us through life's trials and despair."

The trial was equally severe for the former Hapsburg empire, also conquered and now dismembered in keeping with the Wilsonian principle of national self-determination. Of all the ceremonies that took place throughout the world, those at Vienna were undoubtedly the most imposing, inspired by Austria's desire to retain a certain international role for itself in the wake of the drastic reduction in its political, economic, and military status. The importance the event held for domestic politics was made clear in the words of Richard Schmitz, the minister of education, at the opening ceremony on 26 March 1927:

> A cruel fate has inflicted deep wounds on my country, depriving it of its former wealth. We have lost material possessions, but the possessions of the spirit remain. This wealth has been our good fortune and our joy in the most difficult of times, and so it shall remain always. Yet wealth creates obligations. It is for that reason, on this occasion of Beethoven's Centenary, that we have felt ourselves in duty bound to invite all of the great cultivated nations. In so doing, we have desired to give public expression to our recognition of all mankind's right to our Beethoven. Thus, these days have been organized so that the origin, the content, and the goal of the festivities is not the country, but the man; not Austria, but Beethoven. And I see that we have understood each other.[20]

The minister may well have noted that it was not the country but the composer that was being celebrated, yet his remark was also an admission of the importance such festivities represented for a country that he described as simultaneously rich and poor. In that city of the central-European heartland, so rich in both geopolitical importance and the pleasures of high culture, the homage to Beethoven, organized at the highest government levels, took place under an explicitly international aegis. The Vienna centenary was a huge international reunion attended by representatives from thirty-six nations, including ministers and high officials from the thirteen countries of Europe and America, as well as by many cultural figures, most of them musicians and musicologists — an elite that the French *Courrier musical* was to describe as "a public made up of the highest musical authorities and most cultivated minds assembled from throughout the universe."[21] In this spirit, the trip to Vienna was — in the words of the city's mayor, Karl Seitz — a "pilgrimage" to the "holy land." It was, in any event, the most cosmopolitan tribute paid the composer since the inauguration of the Bonn monument in 1845, and the first, following the nationalist apogee, publicly to put on display an international appreciation of Beethoven.

Although the musical heritage inspired the image of national unity that was spread abroad by the many journalists in attendance at Vienna for the commemoration, it was also a point of conjuncture for various Austrian political movements in a country where only a few months later bloody confrontations were to take place in what could be described, without exaggeration, as a civil war. In that tense climate, the Beethoven festivities meant that the members of the conservative government led by Chancellor Ignaz Seipel, leader of the Christian Social Party, found themselves cheek by jowl with members of the opposition represented by Otto Bauer's Social Democratic Party, the "Austro-Marxists," who controlled Vienna in the person of Seitz, its mayor, making it a "red fortress" in a "black Austria." And although both the red and the black loved Beethoven with an equal fervor, they did not necessarily share the same ideas as to how to pay him tribute. The domestic situation obviously took second place when it came to extending the celebrations beyond the country's borders, but it was of primary importance when it came to their organization. During that week of Beethoven fever, all of the symphonies and string quartets were performed at various sites in Vienna's working-class neighborhoods and the Mass in C was performed in a number of churches; the Ninth Symphony was to be heard on several occasions in different parts of the capital. Left-wing newspapers hailed the power of the radio, whose broadcasts of concerts and lectures made the composer "a purveyor of art for the people." "The radio and cultural policies of the Social Democratic government have brought Beethoven to the masses," wrote the *Arbeiter-Zeitung*.[22] Yet all these ceremonies organized or supported by the municipal government were not really part of the centenary program per se but annexed to it as "extra-official activities" to demonstrate that the festivities were indeed reaching "every circle — aristocratic, bourgeois, and working class."[23] At the same time, the organizing committee led by the musicologist Guido Adler, along with the conductors Felix Weingartner and Franz Schalk, had set quite a different goal, namely, a prestigious music festival that was to stress scholarly musicological tradition over and above such more popular works as the Ninth Symphony, and an important musicological congress that was to lead to the creation of an International Musicology Confederation and a group of sacred-music specialists under the patronage of the pope.[24] The musical program opened on Saturday, 26 March, with a performance of *The Ruins of Athens* in a version reworked by Richard Strauss and Hugo von Hofmannsthal; on the following day, after a morning visit to Beethoven's tomb, Goethe's *Egmont* was performed with Beethoven's incidental music conducted by Weingartner. Subsequent days saw performances of the *Eroica* and Eighth Symphonies and the Fourth Piano Concerto in G, as well as chamber works played by the Rosé Quartet and by Pablo Casals, Ignaz Friedman, and Bronislaw Huberman; on 31 March, the festival's conclusion was marked by a gala evening at the Opera and a performance of *Fidelio*. These musical events were interspersed with a whole series of others devoted to music composed prior to Beethoven, ranging from the medieval to the classical periods — including, alongside Mozart and C. P. E. Bach, such obscure and now-forgotten masters as Johann Josef Fux, Johann Georg Albrechtsberger, or Christian Gottlob Neefe. The programs had an undeniable historical and musical interest, although the majority of the population must surely have found them somewhat esoteric. Even in the international press, there were grumblings about the performance of the unfamiliar "Cantata on the Death of Kaiser Joseph II" at the opening ceremony, an interpretation that the reporter for the *New York Times* described as "a proper expression of official grief without the personal note."[25]

It is likely that the choice of the cantata was as much an attempt to bring something new to the program as it was a reference to the spirit of the Enlightenment, which in fact presided over all of the official celebrations at Vienna in 1927. The inclusion of works by the English Henry Purcell, the Italian Pergolesi, and the French Rameau, in addition to Gluck, the cosmopolitan composer par excellence, demonstrate the desire to situate Beethoven's artistic personality firmly within the tradition of the European Enlightenment while at the same time creating a discreet but pervasive aura of nostalgia for the bygone empire. This was the doing of Guido Adler, a true professional when it came to cultural heritage. The successor to Eduard Hanslick at the university, Adler was well-known known for exhuming

compositions written in the eighteenth century by members of the Hapsburg family and describing them as representative of a Vienna School that
had existed prior to that of Haydn, Mozart, and Beethoven; in addition, under the direct patronage of Emperor Franz-Joseph, he had edited a series of
publications entitled *Denkmäler der Tonkunst in Österreich* [Monuments of
Austrian Musical Art]. An exhibition, *Beethoven and the Viennese Culture
of His Time,*[26] completed Professor Adler's historicist endeavors; at the
opening ceremony in the great hall of the Gesellschaft der Musikfreunde, he
used the following language to describe the connection between present
and past:

> At Beethoven's open grave, Franz Grillparzer said: "We here are in a way
> representatives of an entire nation, of the German people as a whole,"
> and now, a hundred years after his death, we are come together here as
> representatives of almost every nation of culture that loves music and
> cultivates it as an art.

The extension of the German nation to the *Kulturnationen* as a whole
assembled around Beethoven's tomb was certainly one way of recounting
the social history of Western music. The official visitors who then spoke on
behalf of their countries were certainly not about to contradict the fraternal
ideal put forward by their hosts; on the contrary, each speaker added to the
consensus about a man who, both in his works and in his life, embodied the
best and most universal aspects of mankind. Although the lengthy series
of eighteen speeches may well have been a trifle boring, one recognizes in
their almost incantatory drone the truly ritual character of the official tribute that the states in the interwar period were paying "the great democratic
composer."

The speakers, all of whom quoted the Ninth Symphony in praising the
composer's universal scope, did not neglect to set the tribute in which they
were joined in the historical realities of their time. "For perhaps the first
time since the war, wounded and half-ruined Europe is affirming, in honoring the memory of a great man, one of the greatest men of all time, the fundamental unity of its culture,"[27] proclaimed — in French — the socialist
Émile Vandervelde, the Belgian Minister of Foreign Affairs, evoking the
Amphictyonic League of ancient Greece. Ambassador Van Beresteyn, the
representative of the Netherlands — speaking in German — hailed the international brotherhood symbolized in an *Ode to Joy* composed at a time
when, he said (somewhat inaccurately), "the European nations were on the

brink of confrontation."[28] Vandervelde viewed the composer as embodying the unity of European culture, but he nevertheless praised a "hymn to joy" that was "addressed to all men, to all free men, to millions of human beings." He probably appreciated the statement of the Swiss representative, the composer Gustave Doret: "In our smallest hamlets, on our highest mountains, I have heard his name spoken with veneration by simple peasants and rough mountain folk"[29] — for in those days Switzerland was often regarded as a model for an eventual European federal-type organization. However, that continental dimension was only brought forward as a synonym for a particular moment in a universal brotherhood that included and transcended it: there was no great difference between the statement of Vandervelde and that of the United States representative, Ambassador Albert Washburn, who was the only person to speak on behalf of a non-European country: "In Beethoven's day, the countries of the New World were busily forging their own destiny, and his powerful spirit was present among them. He was an apostle of liberty, in the best philosophical meaning of the term."[30]

In keeping with the French republican tradition, Édouard Herriot was to draw conclusions from the present entente, urging that Beethoven's works be regarded as the "anthems" of a future universal community:

> The tombs of great men are the hearts of the living. As Frenchmen, we are fond of finding in certain of his works the accent of the ardent passion that gripped our country in the times when we dreamed of giving happiness in liberty to the whole of mankind. Today, as then, aware of our duties to humanity, we cherish in this creature of genius the poet who made music a means of persuasion and action more effective than the word; the man who, despite all, crucified by life, retained only tenderness and pity in his work. And if we have come here as pilgrims, it is to affirm our hope that one day his prophetic anthems will become the hymns of love of a fraternal and reconciled mankind.[31]

Uttered by a former prime minister, the leader of the Radical-Socialist Party and minister for education and fine arts, a man whom his biographer called "the Republic personified," and who, upon his return from Vienna, was himself to write a *Vie de Beethoven,* those words perfectly embody the intellectual tradition and political culture of the Third Republic.[32] Nevertheless, here the classical interpretation linking Beethoven with the Revolution has been diplomatically put in a somewhat different perspective —

"as Frenchmen, we are fond . . ."— and used to praise a man in whom, to quote Herriot once more, "the science of tradition is tempered by the daring of the innovator"; a tempering that distinguished this "revolutionary" reading from that of the Marxists but which was not to prevent German right-wing circles from harshly criticizing the French minister for having attributed to Beethoven "a Franco-Napoleonic vision of a united Europe."[33]

Although that accusation was off the mark, the nationalist reference was indeed present, even if for the French speaker his nation's contribution was the fact of internationalism itself. For at Vienna the Austrians and Germans were not the only ones concerned over the question of Beethoven's national "affiliation." For example, Vandervelde was to state: "Little Belgium gave Beethoven to the larger Germany, and Germany gave him to Mankind!" However, the composer's grandfather having been born in Flanders, the Dutch representative was also able to tie him to the "southern Netherlands," going on to add that the composer, German born and Austrian by adoption, belonged to the "world's culture."[34] The Hungarian representative, Minister Josef Vass, noted that Beethoven had enjoyed spending his holidays on Hungarian territory, where he had conceived unforgettable works; the British delegate, Viscount Chilston, pointed out that the Ninth Symphony had been composed for the London Philharmonic Society, while the Italian Pietro Mascagni drew attention to the importance of the meeting between Beethoven and Rossini. The Polish and Romanian delegates were almost the only ones to bow before historical evidence and forgo any claims on the man who was the center of attention. Such determined efforts may well be evidence of the terrors that internationalist talk raised in a world that was then totally defined by the nationalist paradigm. "Mankind is experiencing a struggle between nationalism and internationalism," observed the Czech Milan Houdza, the minister of education of a state created by the dismemberment of the Hapsburg Empire, before going on to add: "Is there any more perfect harmony than that in which Beethoven has brought together the elements of spiritual nationalism in the broadest cultural solidarity of mankind? No, nationalism must not become the foe of internationalism, nor internationalism that of nationalism."[35]

No one at Vienna had any wish to contradict the equation. And yet, it was to be overshadowed by the brilliance of a figure who, in the words of the Belgian representative, was "above all politics, above any nationality." The political dimension of the *Ode to Joy* was destined to be subsumed into a moral and religious ideal, the "hymns of love of a fraternal and reconciled mankind," which Herriot was to link with the Christian image of a man "crucified by life." In fact, the centenary speeches provide a summary inventory of the religious metaphors that had always filled the exegeses of Beethoven: the Polish minister Julius von Twardowski spoke emotionally of an "Olympic deity" uniting all nations in his "tragic" art, a dithyramb that concluded with the very Catholic invocation: "Praised be his name."[36] And Pietro Mascagni's speech — which had been given Mussolini's personal approval — was replete with references to Jesus Christ himself:[37]

> *Morto come Gesù! . . . Ma, come Gesù, redento! Risorto nella luce abbegliante dell'Arte sua! Risorto per il bene dell'Umanità! Immortale nella Storia, Immortale nell'Arte, Immortale del nostro cuore, che per Lui, per la Sua Gloria avrà palpiti per omnia saecula saeculorum.*

> Dead like Jesus! . . . But, like Jesus, redeemed! Resurrected in the dazzling light of his Art! Resurrected for the good of Mankind! Immortal in History, Immortal in Art, Immortal in our hearts, which beat for him and for his Glory *per omnia saecula saeculorum* — world without end, Amen!

Yet this blatant identification of Beethoven with Christ, which Mascagni had prefaced with praise for Il Duce's "magnifica educazione musicale," was not what laid the foundation for a Christian interpretation of his works. During the opening ceremony, Ignaz Seipel, the Austrian chancellor as well as a Catholic priest and specialist in moral theology, managed — without even having to mention God by name — to establish a truly religious reading. Seipel described post–First World War mankind as being in search of those elements by which it could achieve "true unity":

> One of those elements is music, and especially the music of Beethoven, which leads us to the highest levels of a universal Ethos. Mankind is fervently seeking a renewal of idealism. It is here that Beethoven becomes our guide [*Führer*], he who at the summit of his work, through sovereign and sublime sounds, was able to transmit to the entire world, even to non-musicians, the meaning of Schiller's two phrases: "Embrace, you millions!" and "World, do you sense your creator?"

> Through a sea of tribulations and adversities, though a forest of all kinds of difficulties, Beethoven cleared a path to the heights, providing us with a trusted guide and consolatory example. At the end of his suffering, at the end of the struggle, in individual hearts and in the life of the

community, the sovereign hymn of liberation and joy will ring out for us if only we cleave to the straight path.

May all men follow the true path! Then will these words truly become reality: "All men will be brothers." [38]

Schiller's words finished off the discussion, but, interpreted politically, what we have is a negative argument in which praise for "true unity" is defined by individual and collective *conditions* or statuses summed up in the eminently Christian image of the "truth path." Beethoven is not a god, he is a guide, a guide whose exemplary journey was determined not so much by his art as by his person; his work is a "hymn" containing the sense of an ideal in which all human divisions, political as well as aesthetic, are absorbed into a universal *ethos.* Art is the symbol of the ethical experience; thus, what we have is a notion of a religion of music per se, based on a sacralization of the aesthetic experience, which is the meaning implicit in the speaker's words. At the same time as he uttered them, the chancellor was also to recall the pope's support for the ceremonies, which obviously had considerable significance for a man who was currently governing in close relationship with Vienna's cardinal archbishop Friedrich Piffl—the only nonpolitical figure among the twelve honorary chairmen of the centenary. Under the Vatican's aegis, the theologian Seipel was thus engaging in a delicate hermeneutic exercise designed to make Beethoven a part of Christian tradition while keeping his distance both with regard to any directly political reading and to any so-called Beethovenian "religion," which could only be tainted with heresy in the eyes of the church. From this point of view, putting both music and politics on a back burner was the ultimate step toward raising Beethoven as a moral symbol of Europe's "true unity" in the interwar period, and it was made by a man who was soon, in the name of "true democracy" and "true peace," to ally himself firmly with the far right. [39]

That being said, such theological fine points did not stop the Austrian head of government from joining his colleagues in finding in the *Ode to Joy* an image of that international order that everyone was then trying to establish together. Like Leo Schrade, we can view it as evidence that "the French image of Beethoven dominated the imposing centenary in Vienna" [40]— which the correspondent for the *Courrier musical* proudly boasted in reporting the selection of the French delegate to speak on behalf of all the foreign delegations at the festival's conclusion: "Monsieur Herriot was unanimously chosen for this honor because everyone felt that in representing France he also represented more than France."[41] However, the image of Beethoven as the symbol of international brotherhood was, at the time, an image shared by every European and American democrat, and it did not differ in its discursive logic from the Marxist interpretation, while the now-republican Catholic held it up as a moral exemplum of universal import. Even a faction of the nationalistic German far right diplomatically recognized mankind's right to the Beethoven inheritance, defining it as the legacy of German idealism. In short, during that week in 1927, Beethoven was loved by the entire world, and Beethoven gave generously to all; bathed in his music, *Alle Menschen werden Brüder* indeed — at least for the moment.

For this cosmopolitan and right-thinking elite, the Vienna centenary provided an opportunity to rekindle the best Enlightenment traditions and effect a return to the equally classic charms of the old Viennese lifestyle — as the critic Karl Kraus did not fail to point out in his satirical magazine, *Die Fackel* [The Torch], when he ironically commented on the visitors who, after the moving experience of *Fidelio,* then rushed to the cafés for "a really special evening's fun," not even bothering to complain about being overcharged.[42] The festival agenda included visits to Vienna's cultural landmarks and excursions into the countryside to the places where the Master had been inspired or had spent his holidays, where the "pilgrims" could mingle or meditate as they chose. Finally, in contrast to the 1845 Bonn festival with its attendant scandal, and despite right-wing grumblings in the newspapers or the social democrats' irritation over Mascagni's praise of Mussolini, the celebrations at Vienna in 1927 passed without incident. After a century of Beethoven commemorations, the contrast between the two events could be viewed both as the sign of a certain improvement in political comportment and as proof of the fact that — from Professor Breidenstein to Professor Adler — the "know-how" demanded to arrange and carry off such affairs had increased considerably.

However, for some, the chorus of praise did not quite drown out a certain feeling of uneasiness — that uneasiness often caused by any praise showered on a loved one. Foremost among the skeptics was Karl Kraus, who published a short comment — almost an aphorism — in *Die Fackel,* which he entitled "Desperanto": Beethoven will be deafened by all the words being hurled at him.[43] True, Karl Kraus had the best aim of anyone in Vienna's intellectual circles. However, doubts were also felt by the one man above all who should have been gladdened by the festivities, namely, Romain Rolland, the guest of honor; in delivering his speech, "Actions de graces à Beethoven," before the assembly of the Congress of Vienna, he could not refrain from warning: "His is never an art intended for utilitarian purposes, an art fabricated or adapted *ad usum* of the democrats — what today we call a 'social' art. No, for Beethoven, art is an end in itself." Passing shadows, obviously, for the man who, like Herriot, could still conclude: "In him we are as one, we, all the peoples of the earth. He is the radiant symbol of European Reconciliation, of human brotherhood . . ."[44] Others, however, had a great deal more trouble joining the fraternal chorus, while still not condemning it. Such was the situation of the author Franz Werfel, writing in the *Neue freie Presse:*

> The thousand speeches of recent days have failed to note his rebellious side. They praise the official god who has already for a century been enthroned in glory on Olympus. And let no word be said against the festival! It is already something when, in times like ours, despite the unrest that prevails in business and politics, despite the boards of directors and specialized foundations, despite the most serious concerns like power and money — it is already something when we can find the time to pay a generous tribute to genius! Yet one thing must be borne in mind: Beethoven was the genius of Revolution! Before him, music had served noble and refined pleasures. He gave it a new meaning, he expressed social and ethical upheavals in sound. He was the first to render life's doubts and difficulties in music. And he did so not only though his music's message [*Gesinnung*] but also through its form [*Form*].[45]

So: better an official deity than no deity at all. However, it is that final sentence, written by a man who was to be both Alma Mahler's husband and a friend of Alban Berg, that truly focuses on the problem: faced with the political interpretation of the revolutionary "message," the (real or purported) failure to recognize what was revolutionary in the musical *form* indicates a failure to recognize the revolutionary attitude in the music itself — and thus the role of the musical avant-garde whose participation in the Vienna centenary, as has been noted, was nil. This in a city where, sixteen years after the death of that great Beethovenian, Gustav Mahler, the Second School of Vienna, the school of Arnold Schönberg, Alban Berg, and Anton Webern, had already achieved the essential part of its work: indeed, it was in 1927 that the twelve-tone technique achieved its first great success with the Viennese premiere of Berg's *Lyric Suite.*

That group declared itself to be Beethoven's heirs both in the matter of musical language, as Schönberg did not fail to explain in technical terms, and because of his standing as a historical figure, one who had inspired, in Berg, total veneration. Sanctifying enthusiasm and analytical rigor went hand in hand for those who, in Schönberg's famous phrase, firmly believed that they were ensuring the supremacy of German music for the next hundred years. And they could count on the support of men like Beethoven's biographer, Paul Bekker, who considered the Viennese avant-garde composers to be the direct descendants of the composer of the Ninth Symphony — a work which, by the way, Bekker would have preferred to have seen concluded with a large-scale fugue, a form more favored in contemporary discussions of musical structure.[46] In an article attacking the composer Hans Pfitzner, Berg had denounced the banalization of serious music by noting the "impotence" of emotional aesthetics, and at the time of the centenary he would doubtless have smiled upon reading the "Desperanto" of his much-admired Karl Kraus.[47] Schönberg, for his part, who had been living in Berlin since 1925, when asked to contribute (at fifty years of age) to a survey on "Beethoven in the eyes of the young composers," wrote a piece of which only a fragment, unfortunately, has been preserved:

> The very fact that I have been asked a question about my position vis-à-vis Beethoven, that such a question can be put, seems to me already to spoil the idea of a Beethoven festival. The question would only be a pertinent one if it were to serve to measure the distance that separates Beethoven from those who are asking it. A festival for Beethoven should not celebrate those who take part in it, but only him to whom homage is to be paid. For that, we need to do something special to honor him rather than merely perform his works as usual, without taking any more trouble than usual. To pay tribute to Beethoven, we ought to take the following tack: for instance, an interpretation of the Ninth Symphony in which . . .[48]

The manuscript breaks off at that critical point, and we do not know what Schönberg might have considered a "good" celebration of the centenary. In any case, the denunciation of the distance separating Beethoven and his admirers would appear to disqualify any concrete tribute and is indicative of the gap that had opened between the avant-garde and the public since the advent of atonalism. Schönberg did not send in his contribution, and his silence, joined to the unease that the manuscript fragment reveals, marks his break with the official cult of the great composer. Having said that, by favoring "Beethoven as he really was" over the hermeneutic subject "Beethoven and us," the leader of the twelve-tone school was demonstrating a devotion to the traditional view stronger than that of the festival's organizers. Indeed, in digging up pre-Beethoven compositions, Guido Adler was not necessarily being reactionary; on the contrary, faced with the standardization of the canon established by the romantics — all those "heirs" not one note of whose music was to be played during the festival — his attitude was in keeping with a reform movement that presaged the future rediscoveries of Baroque and Renaissance music. Perhaps Adler viewed this latter task as of greater political importance than the recognition and acceptance of the avant-garde, which at the time would have been an undertaking little likely to meet with consensus — an avant-garde toward which, however, as a close friend of Mahler and, when the occasion arose, even a supporter of Schönberg and his group, Adler was far from hostile. The end result of his decisions, however, was that contemporary works of music were officially excluded from the discussion of Beethoven's significance to the twentieth century. And it was not only the Vienna School, a small and still-controversial elite, that was absent from the commemoration, it was nearly all contemporary composers — aside from such minor figures as Mascagni or Doret, sent by their respective countries, or a Richard Strauss already on his way to becoming the conservative totem the Nazis would soon exploit . . . and whose musical contribution to *The Ruins of Athens*, for that matter, was to be respectfully insignificant.[49]

In fact, the situation was typical of a time in which Beethoven's image was being seriously questioned by circles within the cultural elite. Following precursors like Nietzsche, this attitude had been expressed in 1920 by Ferruccio Busoni during the composer's 150th birthday celebrations. From then on, criticism had not been confined to deploring, with Debussy, solely the speeches devoted to the "Titan." His music too, on occasion, had been pulled from its pedestal. "When he starts in developing, Beethoven is boring," Jean Cocteau had written as early as 1918, preferring the "static" music of Erik Satie, who had himself been one of the very first skeptics.[50] The members of the Dada movement, for their part, amused themselves by depicting Beethoven with his eyes crossed.[51] The antiromantic reaction was only made stronger with the advent of neoclassicism: In 1927, Kurt Weill, Ernst Krenek, Georges Auric, and many other composers were to distance themselves from Beethoven and his cult; in France, it was obvious that "neither the school of Debussy, nor that of Ravel, nor the restless group looking for ever-different effects has any identification with Beethoven."[52] In the Soviet Union too, the futurist avant-garde composers showed little enthusiasm. In 1927, Leningrad's Contemporary Music Association published a pamphlet entitled *October and the New Music,* in which it noted, apropos a concert given to celebrate the tenth anniversary of the Revolution:

> What is closer to the proletariat, the pessimism of Tchaikovsky and the false heroics of Beethoven, a century out of date, or the precise rhythms and excitement of Deshevov's *Rails?* During the playing of Beethoven, the workers were utterly bored, and patiently, with polite endurance, waited for the music to end. But contemporary Soviet compositions aroused contagious emotions among the audience. Proletarian masses, for whom machine oil is mother's milk, have a right to demand music consonant with our era, not the music of the bourgeois salon which belongs to the time of Stephenson's early locomotive.[53]

Of course that passage tells us less about the true feelings of the workers than about those of the futurists, who were soon to be wiped out by Stalin. And indeed, from the point of view of the 1920s avant-garde, driven by the need for constant formal renewal and the desire to achieve close contact with the age, it was difficult not to regard Beethoven as an anachronism. At times, a "modern" approach was indeed found, as was the case with the production of *Fidelio* with constructivist scenery that Otto Klemperer produced and conducted at Berlin's Kroll Opera in 1927, which one enthusiastic critic described as "a *Fidelio* without theatrical pathos, without bombastic sobs, without Philistine banality, without embarrassing naturalism. One felt one was hearing a new work."[54] This kind of theatrical innovation, which was harshly criticized by the right wing, was obviously one solution. Beethoven, however, had written only one opera, and it was difficult to subject the remainder of his work to the same treatment. In fact, performances of the classical repertory were marked by aesthetic fashion: Leon Trotsky, for example, found that on his visit to Moscow in 1925, Klemperer had conducted the Ninth Symphony in "German expressionist" style.[55] Yet the interpreter could not change the work itself, which remained the all-too-evident testimony to its own obsolescence. "Must we acknowledge that the master is, like the other masters of the period, 'stupid,' an over-inflated glory that a perspicacious critic should set out to deflate or at least view his fall from favor as part of the normal aging process of any deity?" Lionel Landry asked when examining the "Beethoven decline" in the *Revue musicale*.[56]

It could be said that Landry's question poses a false alternative, since "over-inflated glory" is indeed a normal part of a deity's aging process. In any event, the image illustrates the crucial historical moment in which the great romantic paradigm was being confronted with the new aesthetic sensibility of a world that was changing at a dizzying speed. And the violence with which conservatives reacted to any questioning of tradition was only one evidence of the change. As Vincent D'Indy wrote at the time of the centenary: "I know that in one particular circle fashion demands that we systematically disparage the composer of the Mass in D. Let us, however, leave that opinion to the imbeciles and the impotent."[57] For his part, Adolf Sandberger, in a speech delivered at the Beethovenhaus, contrasted Beethoven with "those who are turning to new gods," and pronounced a blanket malediction covering the music of Mahler and Stravinsky, the "degeneracy" of Schönberg and his followers, the works of Paul Hindemith and Ernst Krenek, jazz and the futurists, and, lastly, the "revolutionary and democratic" interpretation of Kurt Eisner and the Bolsheviks. America was not to be outdone: one speaker expressed the hope that the commemoration might induce the "musical modernists" "to indulge in less daring inharmonies and less venturesome dissonances,"[58] while the composer Daniel Gregory Mason praised "genius's conservative power."[59]

A century after Beethoven's death, the phrase "genius's conservative power" neatly sums up the spectacular reversal of his position that had occurred in the cultural arena. Yet it would be a mistake to view it solely as the grousings of an elderly academic reactionary. Felix Weingartner, who had good reasons to rejoice at the prestige of the Beethoven cult in 1927 — he was not only the musical director of the Vienna centenary but was also the principal conductor hired by the Columbia Phonograph Company to prove that music had now "conquered time" — was prey to equally serious misgivings. For Weingartner, an assiduous reader of Nietzsche, the moment also, in a way, marked the end of history. Far from rejoicing, however, he could only see it as a twilight:

I cannot avoid feeling anxiety at the thought that Beethoven's centenary — which is being honored wherever music as we know it is performed — is a commemoration of death, or, rather, a festival for the
dead. I cannot think that Beethoven might be dead to the world, for his
works have their own eternal life, but perhaps, one day, the world will be
dead to Beethoven, no longer able to comprehend his greatness and no
longer capable of feeling what he transmits.[60]

One can understand Weingartner's fears: what was at stake was nothing
less than the survival of the great tradition of German classical music, of
which he was an eminent representative. The image that emerged during
the centenary of a fabled world, the great world of the nineteenth century
swallowed up by technology and speed, was rich with Wagnerian overtones. However, the conductor's vision was macabre in other ways: the
"festival of the dead" was not being celebrated by a new race gathered
around the ruins of Valhalla but by a band of ghosts which, lively as they
might seem in the presence of the true face of the living god, had nevertheless already begun to crumble into dust. Weingartner would have been
heartened to know that today, at the dawn of the third millennium, the
world is still not dead — at least not to Beethoven. However, as soon as
there is no memory save that of the past, all who, like Weingartner in com-
memorating the hero's death, also wished to exorcize the world of anti-Beethoven feelings, must turn, rightly or wrongly, back to that past. And of
course a return to the past can, at times, by awakening an awareness of history, lay the foundations for the future. In 1927, however, those who were
paying homage to Beethoven were refusing, in the very act of commemo-
rating him, to recognize in the present the musical symbols of their own
generation's historical experience. From then on, Western music would live
under the weight of that anachronism: allegiance to and support of the romantic paradigm of great classical music, and the divorce between society
and contemporary creation.

# 10

## Beethoven as Führer

At the time of the 1927 centenary, the *Ode to Joy* was regarded primarily as a symbol of universal brotherhood and was closely connected to a yearning for peace — in other words, it was very close to being the world anthem that the French delegates Édouard Herriot and Romain Rolland had envisaged at Vienna. The feeling was not limited to the solemn, and admittedly somewhat limited, framework of the Beethoven festivities. In Paris, for example, there were pacifists who were thinking of a *Supranational Anthem* — a *Himno Supranacia,* to use their preferred language, Esperanto.[1] Herriot evoked Beethoven when speaking of the League of Nations: "I try to imagine the celebration that would have ensued if, after all the nations had signed the Geneva Protocol [in 1924], the Ninth Symphony had then sounded in our midst, as a reality and not merely as a hope."[2] At this period, the pacifist and universalist ideal was closely linked to the coming together of all Europeans and especially with Franco-German reconciliation, which had been sealed in 1925 with the Locarno Pact; the dream of an international anthem did not prevent Herriot from enlisting Beethoven in the plan for a "European union all-too-often torn apart,"[3] nor did it stop Romain Rolland from evoking the influence of Beethoven's music on "the souls of thousands of young Europeans."[4] It is in that context that, during the 1920s, the composer's name was to be associated with the political ideal of a united Europe for the first time since the composer himself, in 1814, had dedicated his works to the service of the "concert of Europe."

Of course, the relationship between Beethoven and Europe had always existed, but it had been couched in cultural rather than political terms. In the romantic era, Berlioz had regarded him as the most eminent representative of "musical Europe," and in 1845 there had been fleeting talk of

"Europe's great Masonic anthem." Later, nationalist movements did not exclude geopolitical thinking on a continental scale, a special sphere in which the universal redeeming mission of national genius played a role. In that connection, the idea of a "European Beethoven" was a corollary to the whole nexus of thinking about Europe and the West in general, about Christianity, Western civilization, and indeed the world as a whole, an amalgam inherited from the Enlightenment that was to perfuse all Western ideology in the nineteenth century. As that century neared its end, thinking began to shift, veering toward a reflection on the "decline of Europe" — but the "future European" that Nietzsche had found in Beethoven still bore the same stigmata that touched all of Western civilization. Nevertheless, owing largely to English and French imperialism, that civilization had promulgated the worldwide notion that a "European" was, above all, a member of the Caucasian race. At the time of the centenary, the universalist formulation making it a tribute paid by "all cultured nations" was therefore very susceptible of creating a restrictive and potentially even racist concept of the very notion of culture itself. In 1927, for example, Raoul-Raymond Lambert — a veteran of 1914–1918 who had set off to war with Romain Rolland's book in his knapsack and who was now Édouard Herriot's personal private secretary — expressed regret — "with no further comment" — that during the occupation of the Rhineland, the road to Beethoven's house had been guarded by "a black with childish demeanor or a Moroccan with an astonished look on his face" rather than by "a chasseur from Lorraine or hussar from Normandy." [5]

Thus, "cultured nations" meant something less than all of mankind but something more than merely Europe. With the increased power of capitalist America and socialist Russia following a war that had affected regions to which Western tradition was totally foreign, the term "Europe" underwent a profound semantic transformation and became an eminently political concept. The Europeanism of the 1920s utilized a variety of often very different kinds of discourse in which democratic, economic, or technocratic ideals coexisted. [6] For some, however, and they were not the least prominent, Europeanism was a political solution to the general problem of decline and needed to be grounded in a cultural identity whose definition was directly inspired by national identities. In Germany, above all, but also in the instance of a French writer like Julien Benda, it was this tradition that fed the notion of a "European nation" defined in cultural terms and projected onto the political sphere in a discourse that closely echoed the epic and mystical appeals of nationalism. It was in this way that the notion of

European political symbols began to take on meaning, and from this perspective, the "universal Beethoven" and "European Beethoven" are no longer at all the same thing.

The man who was to bring it all together was named Richard Coudenhove-Kalergi, an aristocrat devoted to Schopenhauer and Nietzsche who, in 1923, founded in Vienna the most widespread European organization of the interwar period, which he baptized Pan Europa.[7] The son of an Austrian diplomat and a Japanese woman, he heralded his entrance onto the international stage by creating a flag with a blue background and a red cross within a golden sun: "The *Sonnenkreuz* [Sun Cross] joins the two basic symbols of European culture, Christian ethics and pagan beauty; international humanitarianism and modern Enlightenment; heart and mind; man and the cosmos."[8] Coudenhove set out to replace the nationalist German myth of racial community with that of a "European nation" based on a communality of culture and whose "geniuses" were the "great Europeans" — the abbé de Saint-Pierre, Kant, Napoleon, Mazzini, Victor Hugo, and Nietzsche. Beethoven did not, in principle, figure in that Pantheon. Indeed, in Coudenhove's writings, music is mentioned only with regard to the relationship between Richard Wagner and Coudenhove's grandmother Maria Kalergis, to whom the former's *Judaism in Music* is dedicated — a dubious honor that Coudenhove-Kalergi mentions despite his own aversion to anti-Semitism. Beethoven was not to make his appearance in the Pan Europa movement until 1929. In October of that year, Coudenhove set off with Édouard Herriot — who, along with Briand, Seipel and Beneš, was one of his principal supporters — on a lecture tour to Vienna, Prague, and Berlin. In November 1929, at the tour's conclusion, he announced in his magazine that Pan Europa had now found itself a sonic symbol:

> The Pan Europa movement has become a mass movement. To go with its flag, it requires a musical symbol, an anthem.
>
> Only the greatest European composer is worthy to provide the anthem of Pan Europa.
>
> The great European Ludwig van Beethoven composed the melody that supremely expresses the will and desire of the masses for joy, union, and brotherhood:
>
> "The Ode to Joy of the Ninth Symphony."[9]

Although we have no documentary evidence for it, there is every reason to believe that the announcement was inspired by Herriot. Thus, the Pan

Europa anthem is the result of a coming together of the French "republican Beethoven" and the German philosophical tradition, particularly Nietzsche's European-centered philosophy. However, the very phrasing of the announcement reveals the unstable nature of such a doctrinaire alliance: Coudenhove's "will to joy" is considerably different from the more or less Christian "hymns of love" so dear to Herriot or Romain Rolland — indeed, in 1924 the latter, speaking for the union of the "free spirits of the entire world," had even rejected Coudenhove's anti-communist ideas.[10] In 1929, the statement that Pan Europa had become a "mass movement" marked a change of course in its leader's political strategy; having always frequented elite circles, he was now, owing to the rise of fascism, to set out to win over a mass popular audience. True, Mussolini was to agree to receive him as late as 1933, but the Nazis were never to deal gently with the "half-oriental" founder of Pan Europa, the prophet of "miscegenation" [*Rassenmischung*], and eventually banned his activities.[11] In this sense, the notion that an antifascist and anticommunist movement "requires" an anthem was probably a response to Italy's *Giovinezza* and Germany's *Horst Wessel Lied,* as well as to the *Internationale,* the Soviet Union's official anthem.

The response, if such it can be called, proved to be as feeble as was the "mass movement" that had engendered it. Without some musical arrangement that could be sung or played in a ceremonial situation, the life of the Pan Europa anthem was doomed to be a short one; it made but one fleeting appearance, on 17 May 1931, which had been proclaimed "Europe Day" to mark the first anniversary of the Briand Memorandum, the principal Europeanist document of the interwar years. Whereas at the "European Congress" held at Basel in October of the following year — at which Coudenhove's youthful followers appeared dressed in blue shirts and wearing *Sonnenkreuz* armbands on their left arms — Felix Weingartner conducted the *Eroica* Symphony, but not the Ninth. At the time, the leader of the Pan Europa movement had just published *Kampf um Europa* [The Struggle to Unite Europe], clearly a reply to *Mein Kampf,* whose antiparliamentarian and anti-Bolshevik language it imitated. The disagreement between Coudenhove and Herriot that then emerged over the question of the "equal rights" that were contrary to the Versailles Treaty may have played a part in the symbol's failure.[12] In any event, in the early 1930s the leader of Pan Europa began to drift towards an authoritarianism that led him to ally himself with the dictatorial government of the Austrian chancellor Engelbert Dollfuss and alienated him from those supporters for whom "European activism still preserved a democratic dimension."[13] His personal dream was to sink in the general shipwreck of internationalist ideals, which inevitably took down with it the centenary's universal image of Beethoven as well. In 1933, Georges Duhamel was to write: "A vast, a fearful silence, has fallen over the European spirit."[14]

In Germany at this same period, with the Nazi's accession to power and their strict control over the nation's cultural life, the great musical hero was now the composer of *Die Meistersinger*. Winifred Wagner's Bayreuth was for the Führer a private shrine as well as a centerpiece of his cultural policy; echoing the events of the foundation year 1872, the first Bayreuth Festival of the Nazi era was opened with a performance of the Ninth Symphony conducted by Richard Strauss.[15] As early as June 1933, the magazine *Die Musik*—which was soon to become an official organ of the NS-Kulturgemeinde, Alfred Rosenberg's organization for cultural affairs — trumpeted the "nationalization of German music," and an enthusiast wrote that Beethoven and Wagner were the two poles of *urdeutsche* music, now happily united in the personality of Adolf Hitler.[16] Moreover, the act by which the chancellor of the Third Reich set himself up in Potsdam as the virtual heir to the Prussian crown was hailed at Rostock by a performance of *The Glorious Moment* with words especially written for the occasion.[17] In 1934, during the Nazi Party congress at Nuremberg, the Führer's entrance was to be accompanied by the *Egmont* Overture.[18] In 1938, Hitler dipped into his special funds to contribute to the new Beethoven monument in Bonn, already planned in 1927, and when war finally broke out, he was to announce to the party faithful in Munich's famous beer hall: "One single German, Beethoven, has done more for music than all the English put together."[19] On Joseph Goebbels's initiative, Hitler's birthday in 1937 was celebrated with a performance of the Ninth Symphony conducted by Wilhelm Furtwängler with the Berlin Philharmonic; the gesture was repeated in 1942 when the Führer assumed direct command over the Wehrmacht on the Eastern front.

Yet, apart from those isolated episodes, the Nazi leader does not appear to have been especially interested in Beethoven. In general, indeed, Hitler's name is rarely directly linked with Beethoven's, and most writers at the time were content merely to elaborate a nationalist discourse in which Beethoven was already regarded as a kind of führer. However, even that reference was unusual: in 1934, the official radio, which was the basic tool of the propaganda machine, began its important broadcasts of German music with a

Beethoven cycle. The Berlin Philharmonic, which had been brought under direct government control, was the figurehead in a progressively "Aryanized" musical life and worked to make concrete the myth of the inherently "musical soul" of the German people. In addition to the traditional great orchestras, the National-Socialist Party (NSDAP), the Hitlerjugend, the Wehrmacht, and even the elite SS all had bands and orchestras that played Beethoven nonstop. Efforts were made to eschew the universalist or heterodox interpretations that had had their heyday at the time of the 1927 centenary — particularly by getting rid of members of the avant-garde like Paul Bekker, who was soon to die in exile in New York, or Otto Klemperer, who announced, upon his arrival in the United States: "Wagner wanted the world to believe that he and Beethoven were members of the same musical family. But that is not true. At the musical level, Beethoven was Mozart's son, and that line came to an end with Beethoven."[20] Klemperer's words were in sharp contrast to the Wagnerite fervor of the government of the Third Reich, but not to the myth of great German music, to which Germany's Jews were just as devoted as were their countrymen. In August 1934, the German-Jewish *Kulturbund* — a cultural league created by Goebbels that brought together many musicians who had been removed from their public positions — paid tribute to the deceased President von Hindenburg with a performance of the *Eroica* Symphony.[21]

On the other hand, in that same year Berlin's Nazi Party forbade the *Kulturbund* from performing *Fidelio;* at that time, as we know, the regime's repression was in its early days. However, terror aside, the Nazis were hardly innovative in their approach to the classics. The obsession with the "German" character of German music had no need for new ideas or new men to give it the terrorist form that was to make it the crux of the Reich's musical policy. One outcome was to be the remarkable continuity of the musicological establishment, which, not content with merely pursuing its usual course under the aegis of the "New Germany," was also to provide Goebbels with many officials — inter alii, Peter Raabe, the Liszt specialist, who in 1935 took over from Richard Strauss as president of the *Reichsmusikkammer,* the organization set up by Goebbels as a means of exercising control over German musical life; or Hans Joachim Moser and Joseph Müller-Blattau, who collaborated openly with the Propaganda Ministry; or the militant anti-Semite Herbert Gerigk, author of a *Lexikon der Juden in der Musik* that was to serve as an index to assist the persecution of Jewish musicians and their works. In 1936, Gerigk was to relate Beethoven's life through the perspective of his patriotic works, from the early Friedelberg anthems to *The Glorious Moment,* making him again into that militaristic and francophobic First World War figure in the hopes that he would have even more success during the Second.[22] At the same time, other specialists, perhaps less inclined to militancy or more mindful of their scholarly reputations, turned — like Arnold Schmitz — to erudite attempts to qualify a prelogical Beethoven *Weltanschauung* apart from any *Bildung* and expressing the values of nature, the person, family, *Volk,* state.[23] Or they examined the composer's reception since Wagner's time, via Nietzsche and Stefan George, creating an "aesthetic theology" founded on Beethoven, the "Nordic hero" — a hero whose scope, according to the author, should dissuade young musicians from attempting "to show off" by criticizing him.[24]

Given the increasing chauvinism demonstrated by the conservative elite, the only truly original Nazi contribution to the manner in which Beethoven was received (and perceived) was made on the fringes of musicology and musical institutions with the introduction of the so-called racial "science" employed to legitimize the tenets of National Socialism. The protagonist of "racial musicology" was a man named Richard Eichenauer, the author of a book entitled *Musik und Rasse* [Music and Race] published in 1932; others were to follow his lead in exalting Beethoven and his oeuvre based on the shady anthropological categories so dear to believers in social Darwinism. It was in that very area, however, that (aside from the fairly simple refutation of the composer's "Flemish origins") the results turned out to be most disappointing for the Rosenberg-style ideologists. Indeed, because the man Beethoven had been dark, short, and fairly unattractive, it was difficult to hold him up as embodying the purity of the Aryan race. True, Beethoven's physical qualities meant that he was not all that much different from the principal Nazi leaders; in this process, however, which was a bit more abstract than the mere exercise of power, the aim was to base the cultural patrimony of the *Volk* firmly on the concept of biological heredity. One great obstacle was Beethoven's father, whose obvious mediocrity contradicted genealogical theories about genius: try as one might to salvage him by drawing attention to his dream of a creating a "German theater," the image of Johann van Beethoven was that of a drunkard who had exploited his son's talents. As for Beethoven himself, there were some attempts to maintain that, for example, his eyes had been blue, whereas every portrait and witness attested to the fact that they had been very dark. The verdict was unavoidable: the specialists were compelled to determine "Rasse: gemischt" [Race:

mixed] and forced to report a distressing mixture of *fälisch-nordisch-ostisch-westisch*—which, curiously enough, still did not prevent his music—and particularly the heroic style of the Third, Fifth, and Ninth symphonies—from being perfect musical incarnations of the Nordic spirit. At this juncture, "we may ask: how is it that a man so little Nordic in appearance should have had such a wholly Nordic soul?"[25] Indeed, it required only a minimum of logic to demonstrate that such a question destroyed both the pretense that Beethoven was a racial model and the very bases of the "science" being employed. The conceit was so flagrant that even in Nazi Germany there were musicologists who contested the validity of such lucubrations—which, incidentally, served to preserve the reputation of their own science.

The latter exercise is illustrated on quite another level by the scandal caused in 1936 by a book by Arnold Schering, a professor at the University of Berlin, which claimed to link Beethoven's works to literary models, notably Shakespeare and Schiller. Despite his nationalist beliefs—the book is dedicated "to German youth"—Schering drew down the wrath of some Nazi partisans of absolute music, even though he had the support of the dean of musicologists, Adolf Sanderberg, because of the respect owed his reputation and position.[26] The totalitarian nature of the Nazi state did not prevent it from producing a "polycratic" system, rife with ferocious internal struggles and disputes. The sole Hitler decree to touch directly on music dealt with the *tempi* of the national anthem and the *Horst Wessel Lied;* aside from that—and apart from his infatuation with Wagner, which was far from being universally shared even though no one dared admit it—Hitler did not play any real leadership role in musical matters.[27] On the other hand, Goebbels, Rosenberg, Göring, Schirach, Rust, and other figures all vied to bring their influence to bear on musical life, especially on those responsible for musical exegesis and the choice of repertory. For that reason, it is not possible to say that there was a "Nazi image" of Beethoven that reflected a monolithic expression of some official orthodoxy—and the same holds true for other cultural figures glorified by the regime, particularly Schiller and Nietzsche. In November 1934, the 175th anniversary of Schiller's birth was celebrated with great pomp, hailing him as a "precursor of national-socialism," and Hitler's visit to the house in which he had died led the *Völkischer Beobachter* to report that "the twentieth-century German genius pays his respects to the eighteenth-century genius." During the Weimar festivities, following a speech by Goebbels, the composer Hans

Pfitzner conducted the Ninth Symphony.[28] This, however, did not prevent some from attacking the poet's *Bildung-Kosmopolitismus* [cosmopolitan cultural outlook] or from deploring the fact that he had written a play about Joan of Arc. In 1941, Hitler himself had banned all performances of *Wilhelm Tell*, probably uneasy at its justification of tyrannicide.[29] In fact, although the Ninth Symphony was widely performed throughout the Nazi era — figures for 1941–42 show it to have been the most frequently played work in the entire symphonic repertoire[30] — the text of the *Ode to Joy* did pose a problem for some purists. Claiming the work for antifascism, Hanns Eisler in 1938 told the Nazis: "All men become brothers, with the exception of all the peoples whose lands we want to annex, with the exception of the Jews, the Blacks, and a great many others to boot."[31] Almost the same words, minus the irony, were employed by the Nazi musicologist Hans Joachim Moser: the "kiss for the entire world," he wrote in 1941, does not mean a desire to fraternize with just anyone [*mit Hinz und Kunz*], as one was supposed to believe during the "red years," but rather expresses the idea of a mankind that is "the most German imaginable."[32] True, praise of mankind per se did not conflict with National Socialist ideology, which was actually aimed at preserving mankind by excluding the "subhuman," who were by definition not a part of it. The difficulty of being totally consistent with that principle did nevertheless emerge during the war in Poland, where the systematic destruction of a cultural elite did not prevent the governor, Hans Frank, from assembling German occupiers and Polish collaborators in one orchestra; SS officials in Berlin, however, viewed the singing of the *Ode to Joy* by a mixed German-Polish chorus with certain misgivings, and the work was withdrawn from the program when the group toured within the Reich, while in Cracow it had to be performed twice, once for the German occupying forces and again for the local population.[33]

Nazi propaganda abroad also provided a way to gauge the ideologists' flexibility, whether before the war, when it influenced cultural events designed to show the world the benefits of the regime, or during the conflict itself, when it employed culture to establish the "new European order" in the occupied territories. On 1 August 1936, at the opening ceremony of the Olympic Games in Berlin, the NSDAP orchestra played the *Ode to Joy* in the Olympia-Stadion to accompany the choreographed movements of thousands of young gymnasts; the scene made a vivid impression on Baron Pierre de Coubertin, the Olympic chairman, who invoked Schiller's lines in praising "the physical harmony stronger than death itself" that was being forged under the aegis of the five-ringed Olympic flag, and he warmly thanked the German people and their leader.[34] Yet for the games' organizers, the music was simply intended as a proclamation of Nazi *Volksgemeinschaft* and in no way as a manifesto of any kind of international solidarity, even in Olympic athleticism.[35] This comparative latitude in interpretation served to strengthen the Nazi's use of the work so long as it did not imply political opposition — a position not taken by the French deputy Jean Longuet, who urged a boycott of the games in the Assemblée Nationale as a way to "support the Germany of Goethe and Schiller, Beethoven and Kant, Karl Marx and Liebknecht."[36] At the height of the war, the Nazi pianist Elly Ney was prepared to help emphasize the fact that Beethoven was understood "the world over"[37] — but the example she chose was Japan, where, according to her, German composers were favored over "Slavic music" and where in fact some students readily set out to do battle after having heard the Ninth Symphony as a "symbol of the fatherland."[38] In 1943, a close collaborator of Goebbels — who had established a special bureau to promote German music abroad — was to explain music's role in the "community of fate" made up of "Europe's millions": In upholding the nationalist dogma and to counteract the iniquitous internationalism of the Weimar period, the key word to be used in describing the great German composers was now "supranational."[39] In this sense, the international scope of the country's musical patrimony directly served the plan for a "new Europe" under German hegemony, which Nazi propaganda made every effort to put forward as a "European crusade" against bolshevism.

The spread of German music, with all of its discursive possibilities, was integral to the Reich's expansionist policy, while still remaining more or less a part of the international tradition of "cultural relations." Leading the finest German orchestras, conductors like Wilhelm Furtwängler, Willem Mengelberg, Clemens Krauss, Hans Knappertsbusch, Hermann Abendroth, and other well-known musicians toured throughout the allied or conquered countries, in which Beethoven's works were often played for the greater glory of the Third Reich; the effect was especially marked in Austria, where, after the Anschluss, *Fidelio* came to be viewed as a "prophetic" work.[40] And there is nothing to indicate that the war introduced any essential changes where musical rituals themselves were concerned. True, the first concert given after the German entrance into Paris was performed on the Place de la Concorde by the Wehrmacht military band on 9 July 1940; at Strasbourg, the annexation of Alsace led to a rigorous "Germanization" of the Opera's repertoire. In December 1940, the establishment of the German Institute — a major factor in Ambassador Otto Abetz's overall political strategy — was celebrated at the Trocadéro in Paris with performances of the *Horst Wessel Lied* and Bach's B-Minor Mass conducted by Herbert von Karajan, a member of the Nazi Party since 1933. In France in general, however, the many concerts organized by the German Embassy, controlled by Ribbentrop, or by the Propaganda Staffel, which was controlled by Goebbels, were part of a policy of collaboration in which there was no need to link Beethoven and Hitler to serve the latter's designs. Here, one might quote Lucien Rebatet, a notorious pro-Nazi and the music critic on the rabidly collaborationist newspaper *Je suis partout,* who stated in 1941, with regard to the concerts to be given to celebrate the 150th anniversary of Mozart's death: "There is no need, I hope, to dwell in this newspaper on the profound political meaning of these performances, from those at the Berlin Staatsoper to the ones at our own Opéra, of all of the reconciliations which they have already more than symbolized."[41] Thus, francophile Germans and germanophile Frenchmen came together at these high-cultural events that were, in fact, merely reinforcing the path already opened before the war by certain institutions devoted to bilateral "cultural exchanges." As early as December 1937, Paul Valayer, speaking at the Deutsche-Französische Gesellschaft [German-French Society] in Berlin, had stated that it was simply "ridiculous" to attempt to dress Beethoven in "international garb."[42]

Perhaps he was being overzealous. But even in Paris, some visitors did not disdain on occasion to display their universalism: Willem Mengelberg, who conducted the Ninth with the orchestra of Radio-Paris in 1943, explained in the review *Comœdia* that its composer "knows more than any other how to speak to the human heart, all human hearts," adding that his music "must not be the preserve solely of the favored few."[43] And when Hermann Abendroth arrived a few days later to conduct the same work at the Palais de Chaillot with the Leipzig Gewandhaus orchestra, Arthur Hoérée was to exclaim: "Beethoven's powers! It is evident that a festival devoted to the composer of the Ninth Symphony draws an exceptional crowd. That is a fact. And it can be explained only by the universality of a mind in which mankind finds all the feelings that go to make a sentient being, all of the soul's aspirations to the beautiful made sound."[44] Given all these "feelings that go to make a sentient being" it is quite possible that for some, even those who attended the concerts at the German Institute, Beethoven's music, far from expressing the spirit of collaboration, was merely a haven for aesthetic pleasure where it was possible to retreat from the cruel outside world; and it is quite possible that for still others his music may even have slaked their thirst for liberty or caused them to forget their hatred of their oppressor. However, without evidence of some action resulting from such feelings, their possible political significance must remain walled up in the minds of those who may have experienced them. What is made clear is music's semantic ambiguity: the notion of a consolatory or "comforting music," which at the time of the centenary was to salve the wounds of the German and Austrian nationalists, would come to be as precious to a collaborator of *Je suis partout* as it would be to Georges Duhamel, who waited until the liberation before allowing himself to admit the comfort that German music had afforded him during the war.[45] The novels written during and about the resistance might well recount how music, more than any other art, had been used to serve the ends of the occupier,[46] but rare were those who — like Vladimir Jankélévich — refused to listen to it at all.

In any event, whether they listened for consolation or rejoicing, the French did not need to rely on the Germans when they wanted to play and/or hear Beethoven during the Occupation. Quite the contrary, the composer was central to the repertory from the moment the armistice was signed and musical life returned — more or less — to normal. In December 1940, the Ninth Symphony was performed on no less than three occasions in Paris, at the Concerts Pasdeloup and the Concerts Gabriel-Pierné, and at the Concerts Lamoureux, which also programmed some of the other symphonies. There were to be numerous performances of the *Ode to Joy* throughout the war, and although its composer, unlike Mozart, did not have the misfortune to have an anniversary celebration to inspire an avalanche of exegeses and later compromise the musicians who joined Goebbels to pay him homage in Vienna, he did enjoy an especially prominent place in the repertoire.[47] It goes without saying that, just as in normal times, musical life did not a priori aspire to reflect politics. However, the press was quick to seize upon its ideological function. In June 1941, the Orchestre de la Société des Concerts du Conservatoire, with the support of the recording company La Voix de son Maître (Pathé-Marconi, the French avatar of His Master's Voice), organized a large-scale festival at the Palais de Chaillot in which, following concerts of music by Debussy and Ravel, its conductor, Charles Munch, conducted the Ninth Symphony. Such events "figure today in the front rank of the most exalted expressions of cultural collaboration," stated the review *Musique et Radio,* the house organ of the recorded-music industry, which hailed it as the harbinger of the "new European era" in which, "under a sky from which the clouds have already been half swept away one can discern, like a new sun victoriously rising, the round shape symbolized by the recorded disc shedding life and light over the musical world."[48] Thus, in the grooves of Pathé-Marconi's recordings, Beethoven became a "European" symbol, albeit obviously not with the same meaning the expression had had in the internationalist dreams of the 1920s.

Indeed, Beethoven's presence in Parisian concert halls was such that, as early as January 1941, the composer Marcel Delannoy was complaining about "a risk of indigestion."[49] Others were to deplore that he was being played much too frequently, to the detriment of less well-known German composers or even of works of French music — which, however, were also very much present on programs, as was fitting in the ideological context in which "nation," along with "Europe," was a key word in political discourse. The remark about "indigestion" appeared in *Les Nouveaux Temps,* a publication that was free from any hint of Gaullist or other "questionable" allegiances. Far from denoting some form of resistance, however, this is more an indication that musical life retained a certain autonomy under the Occupation, modernists vying with traditionalists, partisans of French music with those of German music. There is nothing to show that the Germans paid much attention — although in June 1941 Robert Bernard, the editor of *Information musicale,* whose position was "resolutely nationalist," did boast to the Vichy authorities that he was continuing to put up a "systematic resistance" to the circulars sent out by the Propaganda Staffel, while also emphasizing that he maintained "extremely pleasant" relations with the Germans.[50] In fact, the latter's real interest appears to have been the censure of Jewish musicians, with the assistance of the Vichy legislation and local anti-Semites.[51] At the same time, Arthur Honegger, who contributed what he called "propaganda for contemporary music" to the review *Comœdia,* was able to express avant-garde reservations about the *Ode to Joy* and even to write that the passage of Turkish music, by its very weakness, showed that "Beethoven had loathed anything military."[52]

In any event, these innocent deviations — what Honegger jokingly called "blasphemies" — remained as rare as they had been prior to the war. There was, of course, no longer any mention of the "republican Beethoven," excepting on occasion to distance oneself from him, but admiration generally continued to be expressed as before. In 1943, Romain Rolland's book on the Ninth Symphony was given a favorable and respectful reception — the dedication to Paul Claudel offered him "this last book of the secrets shared with me by our Beethoven, the light of our youth and still aglow amidst the shadows and storms of the West . . ."![53] There were even some who regarded this unexpected musical flowering as an affirmation of the "true cult" foreshadowed during the Beethoven centenary celebrations at Vienna. Such was the opinion of René Duhamel, the founder in 1931 of the Comité National de Propagande pour la Musique, which was to come to full flower in 1942.[54] This burgeoning musical awareness was abetted by Maréchal Pétain's "national revolution." The Orchestre de la Société des Concerts du Conservatoire traveled to Vichy to pay homage to the head of state, where it programmed French works along with Beethoven's C-minor concerto, played by Marguerite Long under the baton of Charles Munch, in the presence of what *L'Information musicale* was to describe as "the most eminent members of the diplomatic world from every European country."[55] In addition, the success of three Beethoven symphonic cycles given in June 1943 enabled the same publication to rejoice that "a public, made up in large part of young people, had in three years been won away from the mind-destroying vogue for football and the accordion and brought — and with immense enthusiasm — to the sensitive and intellectual world of classical music." For the prophets of this new moral order, the "sudden and magnificent renaissance of musical sensitivity in French youth" was a true "antidote" to the deleterious influence of jazz.[56] This was in keeping with the goals set in 1942 by the Jeunesses Musicales de France, an organization created to popularize classical music, a "phalanx," according to the critic Émile Vuillermoz, which, "having begun as a modest squad . . . quickly became first a battalion, then a regiment, and is now an entire army corps."[57] In short, the Occupation is credited with having provided new generations with the opportunity to establish a true moral rapport with serious music. In April 1944, Vuillermoz was still engaged in praising to French youth "the universal Brotherhood in the *Choral Symphony*."[58]

Two months later, in *Je suis partout*, the same critic published a glowing review of a performance of the Fifth Symphony by the Romanian conductor Georges Georgesco: "He is not one to overemphasize the more or less arbitrary philosophical or emotional intentions behind the famous 'fate knocking at the door' theme. He sees no need to complicate matters. And it is precisely because he does not indulge in meaningless baton waving that he arrives at the truth, the simple and consoling truth." Respect for the score, rejection of subjectivity, clarity of line, all inspired Vuillermoz to exclaim: "What a great and daring novelty!"[59] However, four days before the Normandy landing, his antiromantic, modernist, and "purely musical" credo sounded somewhat strained — which is not difficult to understand, since at the time and for the past several years, for the French, the famous rhythm of "fate knocking at the door" had been the theme of Radio London. Indeed, in January 1941, the Belgian section of the BBC had launched its "V Campaign," the famous "V for Victory," the V whose Morse-code rhythm was an exact duplication of that of the Fifth Symphony's opening theme. The idea had been adopted by Jacques Duchesne for the radio program "Les Français parlent aux Français" [French Speak to the French], and the association with Beethoven had been made explicit on the following 28 June thanks to the musical motif itself, used as the theme music and illustrated during the course of the program by these words by Maurice Van Moppès:

| | |
|---|---|
| *Il ne faut pas Déséspérer On les aura* | Do not despair, We will prevail |
| *Il ne faut pas Vous arrêter De résister* | You must not cease to resist |
| *N'oubliez pas La lettre V* | Do not forget the letter V |
| *Écrivez-la Chantonnez-la VVVV.* | Write it, Sing it: VVVV.[60] |

Goebbels did all that he could to keep a hold on the Victory signal, but the Fifth Symphony's theme, taken up by the Resistance throughout France, was to be firmly linked to the Allied cause — and it is difficult to tell just how much this "pretentious deformation" differed from the "wishes and indications of the German composer" Vuillermoz had hailed at the June 1944 concert. In any event, the anti-Nazis had always heard in Beethoven's music the expression of their own yearnings for freedom. In 1938, at the same time that the communist Hanns Eisler was launching *Freiheit, schöner Götterfunken* as an antifascist rallying cry, the conductor Walter Damrosch was organizing a spectacular performance of the *Ode to Joy* in New York as a "hymn for World peace and joy" designed to muzzle the "European dogs of war."[61] In England and America, Beethoven continued to be played throughout the duration of the war, often by groups of émigré musicians determined not to allow Hitler to be the sole master of the German cultural patrimony. True, under the Luftwaffe's bombs one London critic, mentioning in passing the lack of proof to back up the *An die Freiheit* theory, did wonder whether Beethoven could still "be valid in a world gone mad,"[62] but the response to his rhetorical question was in the affirmative.

"My Beethoven is not your Beethoven," Nietzsche had said, and Gustav

Mahler had repeated his words. The most dramatic illustration of the consensus regarding the Beethoven oeuvre during the Second World War, and of the absolute incompatibility of the different moral and political messages attributed to it, is perhaps the testimony of a survivor of the Nazi extermination camps. The singer Fania Fénelon, deported from Drancy in France to Auschwitz in April 1943, arranged Beethoven's music for the camp's female orchestra conducted by Alma Rosé, daughter of Mahler's brother-in-law, the founder of the Rosé Quartet.

> DA-DA-DA DAAAAAA! This is not London. It is our orchestra rehearsing the first movement of Beethoven's Fifth Symphony, all of which I had written out from memory. That DA-DA-DA DAAAAAA had given me enormous pleasure. [. . .] Alma wanted Beethoven, and I claimed that all I could remember was the first movement of the Fifth and suggested that she put it on her program. For me, it was a rare treat. She did not suspect that I meant anything by it, nor did the SS. They failed to link it to the theme music for the BBC's "France Libre." For them, it was Beethoven, a God, a monument to German music to which they listened with respect, with ecstatic faces.[63]

However, Fania Fénelon goes on to add that the Auschwitz orchestra, when playing Beethoven's Fifth, reminded her not only of Radio London but of "The Berlin Symphonic orchestra" [sic] as well. Her testimony comes in a controversial book in which, for example, Alma Rosé—who died in captivity in 1944 — is depicted as an unfeeling *Kapo* who did everything to win the good graces of Heinrich Himmler and Joseph Mengele in the name of great German music. This does not detract from its pertinence in illustrating the ambiguity inherent in performing music under extreme concentration-camp conditions. The musicians in Theresienstadt's "model" ghetto, for example, carried on their activities in full awareness of the goals of Nazi propaganda, notably during the 1944 visit by the Red Cross; material problems aside, the only real obstacle to musical life in Theresienstadt came from the continuing deportations to Auschwitz.[64] In the extermination camps, music sometimes went hand in hand with terror: in Claude Lanzmann's film *Shoah,* a former SS-man sings a *Treblinka March* that the prisoners had been forced to learn, adding that his rendition is "unique" because "now there aren't any Jews left to remember it." In Auschwitz-Birkenau, the orchestras — which played light music for the most part — were formed and supported on the direct orders of the camp

directors. Some survivors have almost positive recollections of musical activities, associating them with a spirit of resistance or, at the least, thinking
of them as encouragements to survival. "Music and Song as Factors in Mental Self-Defense among Prisoners in Nazi Concentration Camps" was the
title of an article published by a Polish Jew in 1977, a notion that Simon
Laks, a former member of one of the orchestras, has described as "totally
outrageous." In his book *Auschwitz Melodies,* he says that the role of music
was reduced to "ensuring the perfect functioning of camp discipline and,
on occasion, to producing a bit of entertainment and relaxation for our
guardian angels." As for resistance, it was never anything but a "legend"
that surfaced after the war.[65] Primo Levi has said the same thing, evoking
music as "the voice of the Lager, the auditory expression of its geometric
madness, of the determination with which men set out to exterminate us, to
destroy us as men before slowly putting us to death."[66] For Simon Laks, it
is music itself that must be subject to caution: "It is not a book *about music.*
It is a book *about music in a Nazi concentration camp.* I could even say:
*about music in a distorting mirror.*"[67]

The distorting mirror may be nothing other than the moral problem that
colors the whole question of Beethoven and Nazism. For example, one
might ponder exactly what Wilhelm Furtwängler — who publicly defended
Jewish musicians and avant-garde composers but who nevertheless became
one of the principal actors in Nazi cultural policy — meant when he wrote
in 1942, the period of his closest collaboration with the regime: "In the soul
of Beethoven the musician lives something akin to the soul of an innocent
child."[68] Indeed, in the last analysis, the massacre of innocent children, for
example that of the Jewish children in Auschwitz, is precisely what
Furtwängler's Beethoven was to be called upon to legitimize. At Auschwitz
there was even someone who, in his own way and perhaps without realizing
it, was to bear witness to that fact. In the autumn of 1943, five thousand
Jews, including 285 children under the age of fourteen, were deported from
Theresienstadt. In the extermination camp they were kept alive for six
months, during which they were even allowed to engage in some cultural
activities, one of those being a children's choir. Along with folksongs, the
choir also sang the *Ode to Joy,* in Czech, in the Auschwitz latrines. The
group was preparing for a concert that was never to take place, since on
7 March 1944 its members were all murdered along with their elders; already assembled in the gas chamber, the entire group sang the Czech national anthem and the Jewish song *Hatikva.* One of the members of the

children's choir, however, managed to survive. He has said that at the time, having been only ten years of age, he had been unaware of the origin and meaning of the melody; one day after the war someone told him that it was Beethoven's Ninth Symphony. He goes on to say that, fifty years later, he is still trying to understand the choice of that music, in such surroundings:

> Sometimes I think of it as a magnificent demonstration of the spirit of universal values that can survive even the most inhuman deeds ever performed by the hand of man. That it was a protest and a resistance of the spirit in the face of crime and mass violence.
>
> But sometimes I have doubts about that interpretation. Perhaps the choice was the expression of an extreme sarcasm, an almost satanic gesture.
>
> Mass criminality is unequivocal. It is utter evil at its highest degree. But it is also an evil to make use of such innocent children and of such solemn words and music, regarded as the highest expression of the spirit. Perhaps in such a situation the only way that adults were able to confront utter evil was through a radical distortion of values, through sarcasm. [. . .]
>
> It is difficult, and yet I cannot come up with any other interpretation. Both are part of the horrible ambivalence felt by Auschwitz survivors, of the children who retain such memories, things they did not understand at the time but which they still strive to understand as a reflection on history and memory, as well as on the world in which Auschwitz did for a time exist, and then was wiped out.[69]

The problem of the significance to be attached to such an act is an extremely thorny one, perhaps insoluble. On the other hand, we might note that the leader of the Auschwitz choir and the survivor who recalls him, and men like Eisler and Furtwängler, all wanted to uphold the exemplary value of Beethoven's message; in the last analysis, everyone believes in his own kind of "innocence." Almost everyone, that is: on 21 October 1944, Herbert Gerigk, Goebbels's collaborator, raised the "important question" of whether Beethoven, in the light of certain turns of phrase in his correspondence, might not perchance have been a Freemason; in an internal memorandum entirely typical of the Gestapo mentality, he suggested that the authorities carry out investigations in Vienna to clarify the point.[70] Thus, at the time when the Final Solution was in full swing and the Third Reich about to collapse, for the Nazi musicologist even Beethoven had finally come under suspicion. From the historical point of view, we may be right to regard his action as a symptom of Nazism's self-destructive logic, of its desire to bring down with it all of Germany, its population and its culture. To regard it as a symbol falls to the realm of literature. That was Thomas Mann's goal in *Doktor Faustus,* his novel written in exile during the war as a metaphor of the German spirit brought low by Nazism. In a famous passage, the novel's hero, the composer Adrian Leverkühn, expressed his desire to "take back" the Ninth Symphony; a few pages later, the accursed composer's final work, a symphonic cantata entitled *The Lamentation of Dr. Faustus,* is described as "negatively related to" the finale of the Ninth.[71] Despite the remarkable fact that Thomas Mann himself had "no affection" for the Ninth Symphony's finale,[72] and thus independent of his own personal feelings, he stated that for the entire world the work stood for "the good and the noble, what we call human," and he chose its "annihilation" by his novel's hero to represent the moral collapse of Nazism. From this viewpoint, Auschwitz, utter evil, becomes the radical negation of the *Ode to Joy.* The Nazi Beethoven was nothing but a delusion, just another lie. In a way, this is a reassuring, a comforting conclusion. And yet, we are obliged to recognize that it is not historically correct. Notwithstanding Gerigk's paranoia, the Nazis remained devoted to Beethoven up until the very end. On 20 April 1945, the Berlin radio celebrated Adolf Hitler's birthday with a broadcast of the Seventh Symphony; ten days later, it announced his suicide with the funeral march from the *Eroica.*[73] From lowest to highest, the motives of those who have invoked Beethoven's music cover the entire gamut of human feelings, and there are no distinctions in the love that they all bore him. The question of music's ambivalence is always a disturbing one; the question of Beethoven in Auschwitz is terrifying.

# 11

## From Year Zero to the European Anthem

In July 1945, a Frenchman wandering through the still-smoking ruins of the capital of the Third Reich heard Beethoven's *Spring* Sonata coming from a Soviet loudspeaker set up on the Brandenburg Gate. For Edgar Morin, the music heralded "the advent of an age of tenderness" for Germany and for Europe.[1] Nevertheless, once the war was over, and beyond this retrospective hearing, the impulse to link Beethoven and politics was quick to reemerge — in particular within the Commission of the European Union, the precursor to the Council of Europe and the first step toward a European parliament. Speaking at Strasbourg in 1949, the president of France's National Assembly had extended an invitation to the Federal Republic of Germany in which he urged the former foe to abandon its nationalist tradition, which had gone down with the defeat of Nazism. In his speech in that city, which had been a prize target in three Franco-German conflicts, Édouard Herriot expressed the wish that Germany, "faithful to the spirit of Kant, Goethe, and Beethoven, might act in a spirit of sincere cooperation."[2]

The Council of Europe, primary among the postwar European bodies, was created on 5 May 1949. The following year, its secretary general submitted a report on "the practical steps which might be taken to make public opinion directly aware of the reality of European union . . ." and proposed the adoption of a European flag, adding: "The day that a European hymn salutes the European flag, as today the national hymn salutes the national flag in various countries, a great step will have been made along the road towards this essential union."[3] In fact, the "response" to the idea of union was first to take the form of the European Coal and Steel Community, an economic union initiated on 9 May 1950 by Robert Schuman, the French minister of foreign affairs. The question of symbols was of equal interest to many other partisans of a European union that would be politically rather than economically oriented, and foremost among them was Richard Coudenhove-Kalergi, who proposed the adoption of his *Sonnenkreuz* as the European emblem at Strasbourg in 1951 and, four years later, the adoption of "the anthem of the Ninth Symphony as the European anthem."[4] It must be said that the proposal to impose Pan Europa's symbols on the builders of the new Europe failed to meet with the expected welcome. The Council of Europe decided to choose the twelve-star flag against "the blue background of the Western sky" over the *Sonnenkreuz*—Turkey had been most unwilling to be included under the aegis of the Cross.[5] As for the anthem, Coudenhove had to be content with a response that was as respectful as it was evasive with the mere proposal that performances of the Ninth Symphony's "Anthem to Joy" be "promoted" at all European events.[6]

The speech given by Édouard Herriot at the Council's headquarters in Strasbourg was evidence of the impetus to insert the *Ode to Joy* into international political life, an impetus that had begun in the heat of the 1927 centenary and that was now, thanks in part to the same actors, to be channeled into the discreet corridors of European bureaucracy. It was the same thinking that would eventually, in the cold war context, make the melody a weapon in the Western arsenal: the North Atlantic Treaty Organization (NATO) caused it to be played at the opening of its new headquarters in Brussels in 1967 — a preemption that does not, however, appear to have had any "official" sanction,[7] although it was very succinctly stated: "NATO likes this music"— the only comment that the German magazine *Der Spiegel* was able to elicit; its journalist went on to report that the American general presiding over the ceremony was said to have been under the impression that they were playing the Belgian national anthem.[8]

Devotion to "the spirit of Kant, Goethe, and Beethoven" was not, however, solely the province of the state that was to choose the city of Beethoven's birth as its capital in 1949, nor was it confined to the West that claimed to be imbued with it. Beethoven was to become common property on both sides of the iron curtain. His music was performed at official ceremonies in both the German Republics, Federal and Democratic. During the period when the two states were jointly sending teams to sporting competitions — for example to the Olympic Games between 1952 and 1966 — the *Ode to Joy* was utilized as the national anthem. Things were not, however, completely evenhanded, for in the postwar period it was in the East, above all, that the "heroic Beethoven" was to be draped in official splendor. In contrast to the few and often desultory statements by West German authorities, in the East the official discourse was far more systematic and tradition based. The hegemony of Marxist ideology was reflected in the authoritarian imposition of a "revolutionary" Beethoven whose "classical realism" was viewed as a direct precursor of socialist realism, a concept overtly promulgated by the East German government, for the internationalism long associated with the composer served both to increase the cohesion of the communist bloc and support polemics against Western imperialism. In 1970, the chairman of the Council of Ministers of the German Democratic Republic stated: "The creative work of Beethoven belongs to the socialist culture of the German nation, to the democrats and progressives throughout the world."[9]

Whether in the name of Marxism or Western liberalism, such appropriations of Beethoven were designed both to point up the differences between the two Germanies and to distinguish them from the former Nazi reign. From this viewpoint, 1945 can be said to represent a real break, marking as it did the disappearance of "Führer Beethoven" and, in a more general way, the end of all nationalist discourse concerning German music. Yet the use of Beethoven by the Nazis never appears to have been the subject of much criticism. The relative discretion observed in this regard was wholly in keeping with the reappearance in democratic guise of a number of other figures or institutions with links to the Third Reich. In December 1947, two months after the lifting of the Allied-imposed ban on his public performances, Herbert von Karajan conducted the Ninth Symphony in Vienna. "Because of Karajan, this musical drama of mankind has been turned into a military parade," wrote one journalist at the time, adding that in his interpretation "the spirit and taste of the Reich are involuntarily given renewed expression."[10] Unable to express any real technical caveat, the Austrian critic's bitter reaction reveals the price that the musical establishment had to pay in restoring and preserving its links with the great German tradition, which was embodied as much by those conductors who had remained in the country during the war as it was by those returning from exile. In 1951, the aging Wilhelm Furtwängler conducted the Ninth Symphony at the reopening of the Bayreuth Festival, where the composer's grandson Wieland was radically to subvert the nationalist patrimony with a series of productions that would eventually lead to what one might describe as the rout of political Wagnerism. However, comments about Beethoven himself rarely reflected such changes. The eclipse of national discourse occurred almost imperceptibly, indeed, it occurred in silence. That, of course, left the door open to considerable continuity and nostalgia, but the change turned out to be much more profound than the one that had taken place following the First World War, when the composer's image had reemerged purged of its military taint but with its status as a political symbol strengthened.

It can be said that only the Marxist tradition, both official and unofficial, whether voiced by politicians or by intellectuals, continued to claim political significance for Beethoven's music. In France, exegesis strongly imbued with Marxist thought replaced Romain Rolland's humanism: "One thing is certain: in his own [Beethoven's] eyes, *the social and economic factor,* even when it is not the most immediately important, *is always the one that makes it possible to cohere with the whole that he terms Fate and that stands against his liberty,*" wrote Jean and Brigitte Massin in 1954.[11] Indeed, the discovery of social significance in the musical material at its most technical level was to form the crux of the undertakings of Theodore Adorno and the School of Frankfurt — a line of thought that, born in exile as a critique of fascism, was in the postwar years to turn its sights on "late capitalism" and one of its ideological pillars, the culture industry. In Adorno's work, Beethoven occupies a place as crucial as it is complex: according to the philosopher, the great historical break that had caused revolutionary individualism to become the false consciousness of bourgeois society could be found expressed at the core of Beethoven's oeuvre, precisely in the break between his classical period and his late style; and, in keeping with the avant-garde tradition of such as Paul Bekker, Adorno's own preferences were for the late quartets, seen as a rejection of a classical art that had become mere ideology or "affirmative culture."[12] Now, that is an interpretation that must condemn the *Ode to Joy,* to the highest degree "affirmative" music and doomed to use as propaganda — under Hitler, for example, as Adorno remarks in passing. Indeed, the only moment in the Ninth's last movement that interests him would appear to be the negation of the bass's first utterance: "*O Freunde, nicht diese Töne.*"[13] Yet he does consider the work to be *the* representative of "great art," whose vocation it was — like Mahler, Schönberg, or Berg — to express a truth that capitalism attempts to gloss over, namely, the truth of a suffering.

On the other hand, wherever revolutionary universalism breaks with the humanist tradition, Beethoven becomes the artistic embodiment of a bourgeois culture that must be destroyed root and branch. Such was the case in communist China during the 1960s, where the rejection of Western values included a ban on classical music owing to statements like "I was poisoned by Western bourgeois music." That particular erstwhile music lover came to realize that the ideology of universal brotherhood expressed in the Ninth Symphony was a fake beacon, giving an illusion of progress without conflict that obscured the reality of the class struggle. As for symphonic music in general, Chairman Mao's wife, Jiang Qing, described it as a "formalist" invention incapable of being understood by the Chinese, not even by the many bourgeois who listened to it only to give themselves "civilized" airs. "In short, symphonic music reflects the spiritual decadence of the bourgeoisie, it supports bourgeois domination and oppression, private property and individualism"— such was the line taken during the Cultural Revolution in a China in which Beethoven had to bide his time until 1973 before resurfacing.[14] Such a radical rejection remains a very rare event in the composer's history, but it is nevertheless evidence of a deep conviction with regard to his music's political significance.

Where Marxism has not been the basic theoretical referent, however, there has been a general disengagement from politics, and even from history — an attitude summed up in Igor Stravinsky's descriptive formulation of 1947 of "a Beethoven without *Weltanschauung*."[15] In the musicological arena, this has taken the form of a renewed interest in the formal aspects of his music and the psychological facets of his personality. Of course, such positivist or subjectivist points of view are not totally devoid of political import, if only because of what they leave implicit; and, from this angle, it is interesting that such implications are more clearly evident outside Germany and the ambit of traditional musicology. In fact, the book that went the farthest in criticizing the Beethoven myth at that period appeared in the United States in 1954; it was the work of two Viennese psychoanalysts who had emigrated in 1938, at the same time as Sigmund Freud, who directly inspired them. In *Beethoven and His Nephew,* Richard and Edith Sterba went after the romantic hero with hammer and tongs, diagnosing him with pathological conditions that had led to a veritable breakdown of his "moral personality" during his crises with his nephew Karl. There is reference to latent homosexuality and misogyny, greed and narcissism, and even mention of a "torturer" who "abused" his young nephew — all traits in sharp contradiction with the composer's humanist image, all of which explains the scandal that erupted in Germany in 1964 when the book appeared there in German translation. But it was obviously the description of a "Führer-type personality" that had the most impact in the political sphere, that concept, created by Freud in the 1920s, having become a key element in various psychoanalytical critiques of fascism.[16] It should be said that at no time did the Sterbas draw a parallel with that other führer, whose memory all of Germany was busily exorcizing at the time. Nevertheless, their book, which expressed "the painful need to sacrifice more than one illusion to truth," remains almost the only one to have raised the question—without involving the music of the man they still describe as an "immortal composer," language against which, they note, the psychoanalytic method is forced to give way.

On the other hand, music is at the heart of another work which in some ways addresses the same questions raised by the Sterbas while occupying a universe even farther removed from the one traditional to Beethoven. This is Anthony Burgess's novel *A Clockwork Orange*, published in 1962 and brought to the screen by Stanley Kubrick in 1971. Its protagonist, Alex, is a young criminal for whom violence — especially sexual violence — and classical music — particularly that of "Ludwig van" — are the two principal sources of physical pleasure. Intelligent and cruel, indifferent to any kind of moral considerations, Alex is the antisocial being par excellence; at the same time, however, he loves Beethoven, and it is this that enables his reinsertion into the human community. Apprehended at the scene of a murder, Alex is sent to prison but is soon thereafter selected to undergo a special form of treatment, following which, he is promised, he will be released. The treatment, which is known as *Ludovico,* consists of forcing him to view "ultraviolent" films under the influence of drugs that make him physically sick and while he is prisoner of a device that prevents him from either closing or averting his eyes. One of the films is of Nazi extermination camps with Beethoven's Ninth on the soundtrack; after the treatment, Alex can no longer hear the music without experiencing the same feelings of nausea now caused by sex or violence. It is when he realizes what has been done to him that, for the first and last time, he makes any kind of moral statement: "It's a sin!" he cries, horrified. All Beethoven did was to compose music. Thus, the sin resides in having made the Ninth an instrument to change a human being into a clockwork orange — a fruit which, beneath its colorful and savory appearance, Burgess describes as being "only a clockwork toy to be wound up by God or the Devil or (since this is increasingly replacing both) the Almighty State." [17] In Kubrick's film, the moral statement itself is a joke, since it is quickly seen to be merely a tactic, and a fruitless one, to escape from the torture. In the film, Beethoven's music is played in an electronic arrangement by Walter Carlos that makes it intentionally artificial, the sign of a totally alienated universe — an *Ode to Joy* that has itself been turned into a clockwork orange. [18]

Thus, at the height of the cold war, there was a novel in which Beethoven's music served both the pleasures of a criminal and state terrorism. It is in the latter that Burgess's principal originality lies, for the idea of a killer inspired by Beethoven had already been used by Tolstoy in his novella *The Kreutzer Sonata*. The criticism is aimed at totalitarian society, but many people, particularly in the McCarthy era, saw such a specter haunting Western bourgeois societies as well. Yet it must be said that among the latter, Beethoven's social presence seemed in principle fairly far removed from such a sinister image. Its absence from politics following the decline of the nationalist movements served to strengthen the autonomy of the musical establishment, and economic prosperity, along with the ever-increasing gap between the public and works of contemporary music, worked in favor of the orchestras, festivals, and institutions that were continuing to devote themselves to the traditional repertory. In addition, this renewed prestige of classical music was achieved, not under the aegis of some political discourse or state apparatus, but in the diffuse glow created by the culture industry. The growth in the amount and distribution of recorded music and of television made Beethoven a presence in daily life that advertising was quick to seize on, associating the composer with any product that was thought to require a touch of nobility and feeling. At the same time, it abetted such various kinds of simplified popularization as the pop version of the *Ode to Joy* by the Spanish singer Miguel Ríos, arranged by the Argentinian Waldo de los Ríos, which was released in 1970 and of which millions of copies were sold worldwide — in Germany and France, but also in Chile, in Hong Kong, and even in a Rhodesia somewhat isolated owing to its policy of apartheid.[19] The saccharine harmonies of *Song of Joy* did as much to bring Beethoven's melody to millions of men of goodwill as it outraged thousands of scrupulous music lovers. The classic admirers of the classical Beethoven were surprisingly not as outraged by Chuck Berry's *Roll Over Beethoven*, which was taken up by the Beatles in 1963. However, although the rock 'n' roll raucousness of that piece made it a potential weapon against the cultural establishment, it was not a direct quotation of the original involving a sentimental debasement of Beethoven's artistic legacy. The same was not true of the large-scale banalization of a classic such as *Song of Joy*, Waldo de los Ríos's symphonic pastiche, or, later, the romantic pianist Richard Clayderman's fancied-up version of the piano work *Für Elise*.

Despite their *soft* or anodyne character, such appropriations were subject to judgments that were as anguished as they were contradictory. For a conservative elite, such phenomena evidenced the threat hanging over traditional "cultural values"; in 1970, a group of highly orthodox musicologists attempted to respond to the commercialization of Beethoven with a scientific colloquium whose aim was to eschew "heroization."[20] On the other hand, those who blamed the culture industry could see it as the symptom of an alienation as radical as the one depicted in *A Clockwork Orange*. In 1950, Adorno had used the title "Bach protected from his admirers"; following him, many avant-garde artists and intellectuals in the 1960s were to denounce the "neutralization" of the revolutionary content of serious music, which was being turned into a mere item of merchandise to serve to oppress the masses. Since that touched in passing on the "state capitalism of the Soviet Union," it is not surprising that such opinions were viewed with suspicion by establishment circles within the German Democratic Republic.[21] However, instead of focusing on epiphenomena like *Song of Joy*, left-wing critics took aim at the bourgeois classical-music establishment as a whole, and especially certain highly visible interpreters whom Heinz Klaus Metzger was to accuse of "dulling the critical point" of the symphonic repertoire.[22] In denouncing departures from the musical score, his attitude presaged the renewal movement that was shortly to be initiated — minus the Marxist ideology — by conductors like Roger Norrington, John Eliot Gardiner, or Nikolaus Harnoncourt. Pending the "correct" interpretations that would reveal Beethoven as the "negation of the dominant culture," only the recordings of Arturo Toscanini found favor with the critics, whose preferred target for criticism was the man who in 1970 recorded the nine symphonies for the great Deutsche Grammophon bicentenary edition, namely, Herbert von Karajan, conductor of the Berlin Philharmonic, who was at the time widely referred to as the "*Generalmusikdirektor* of Europe."

This whole debate was to culminate with the bicentenary, which set off an explosion of celebration worldwide, including a new wave of commentary on the theme "Beethoven and our era" or "Beethoven and us." Adorno's influence was evident in the work of those who set out to wed aesthetic modernity to Marxist criticism: in France, André Boucourechliev, who composed a "homage to Beethoven" inspired by the late quartets — *Ombres,* for thirteen string instruments, given its first performance by Pierre Boulez — also edited a special number of the magazine *L'Arc,* in which his own vision of a Beethovenian work closely related to contemporary music appeared alongside the historical connection Jean and Brigitte Massin attempted to draw between the *Ode to Joy* and the *Marseillaise.*

Here, criticism by the musical establishment, less frontal, perhaps, than in Germany, tended toward the same end: Roland Barthes, in the language of structural semiotics, postulated a utopian listening related to a "praxis *without rest*" freed from the romantic myth of the "soul," while the pianist Claude Helffer, comparing the interpretation of the sonatas of Beethoven and Boulez, criticized the "abuses committed in the name of 'tradition.'"[23] Boucourechliev also called upon Stravinsky, Pousseur, and Stockhausen to make a connection between Beethoven's legacy and contemporary compositions — particularly those of a generation of serialists who, more than any other avant-garde in history, had serious doubts cast on its status within the classical tradition. Here, however, there was no consensus regarding the way to interact or deal with "the most indisputable, most accepted, most recognized symbol of *our* musical culture," aside from Pierre Boulez's ironic allusion: "Your/my B. is not mine/yours."[24] For the man who in 1951 had written "Schönberg is dead," and who had dedicated a work "in praise of amnesia" to Stravinsky in 1971, the revolutionary era that had linked Beethoven with Rousseau and the French Revolution of 1789 was "closed," and his music a landscape where "dreams of the future will never have a part." The chant of "Genius, Genius, Genius," wrote Boulez, in a poem entitled "Tell Me" published in the German newspaper *Die Welt,* heralded "a moment when, as in Ionesco's play, death invades the entire apartment, ignominiously driving out the living." True, "*deaf* to all pleas," the "Beethoven river" continues in its course, but

> Who does not feel relief in knowing that
> Death —*that death*— is unpredictable?
> Albeit so ineluctable.

Boulez's epitaph is not ill-tempered, but nor is it compassionate. The feeling is rather one of indifference — although an indifference that must be uttered, in face of "ineluctable" death. Boulez is more skeptical than some of his colleagues, who would like to keep Beethoven alive through their own compositions: "Then this music will not be over, dead, but a creator of life," said Karlheinz Stockhausen when introducing his work *Kurzwellen mit Beethoven* [Shortwaves with Beethoven], in which musical fragments and passages of the Heiligenstadt Testament were recorded on six tape recorders and organized by the composer in real time.[25] The experiment was one of a series of electro-acoustical works on the theme "world musics"— including *Hymnen,* 1967, for four national anthems, and *Kurzwellen mit sechs Spielern* [Shortwaves with Six Players], 1968, in which the fragments are emitted by six shortwave radios. "It is certainly in keeping with the spirit of Beethoven — a universal spirit, beyond time — to be able to utilize all of his music (and not only some 'theme') as material for direct development," said Stockhausen, who wants to make this music "the direct go-between for the new and unknown." His work was to be recorded by Deutsche Grammophon on LPs labeled *Stockhoven-Beethausen*—which, albeit immodest, perfectly expressed the programmatic aim of "eliminating the artificial barrier between past and present." This linkage with a Beethoven represented both by his musical compositions and by his most famous literary work takes account of his composite nature, made up of both myth and technique, cultural object and musical idiom; and although collage is obviously an effective way of dealing with such raw material, it remains relatively neutral from an ideological viewpoint — as evidenced three years later by another electrical-acoustic concoction by the Frenchman Pierre Henry entitled *La Dixième* [The Tenth], performed under the usual guise of a "homage to Beethoven."

On the other side of the coin, collage also constitutes the musical high-point of Mauricio Kagel's film *Ludwig van;* its title, however, "Hommage von Beethoven," states its inversion of the traditional terms. The Argentinian Kagel, who moved to Germany in 1957, produced a work that can be seen as a kind of inverted reply to the cantata composed by the Hungarian Franz Liszt, which in 1845 had been intended as an artistic reflection on the social significance of the homage to Beethoven. Where Liszt had been one of a number of well-known creators of the Beethoven myth, the film *Ludwig van* depicts the deliquescence of the romantic *ethos*— excepting the fact that the abundant locks of hair seen tossing over the piano while the *Waldstein* Sonata fades into the *Sacre du printemps* are not those of Liszt himself but of the Nazi virtuoso Elly Ney, dead in 1968 and played onscreen by a man. Allusions to Nazism systematically appear throughout the film, along with ironic references to the fetish of technique and the exploitation of the patrimony, phenomena that are closely associated throughout: the *Fremdenführer* who guides visitors through an imagined Beethovenhaus — in which each room is an installation entrusted to different artists, inter alia Joseph Beuys — has the features of Hitler, but a Hitler who has arrived at a tranquil old age to guard a classical treasure that has become as decomposed as the bodies in any concentration camp. When, at the end, the *Ode to Joy* swells up on the soundtrack, the screen shows us, not men becoming brothers, but animals in a zoo. The moral distortion to which the music has been subjected is thus topped off by voiding the work of the "great humanist" of all trace of humanity, justifying the emergence of the lied *In questa tomba oscura lasciami riposar.*

That being said, it has been noted that notwithstanding all of its macabre connotations, nothing prevents us from seeing and hearing the good-natured message that "all animals will be brothers" in Kagel's zoo.[26] The film does include a clip from a colloquium in which Metzger repeats his charge against Karajan, but, of course, the film is about much more than that. Even the explicit and basic intent to recover the composer's "revolutionary" dimension finds no clear reflection on the screen.[27] True, *Ludwig van* begins with a subjective shot of a Beethoven returning, two hundred years after his birth, to the town where he was born only to discover the souvenir industry that has taken over his house and to listen to the scherzo of the Ninth Symphony in a record shop. However, there is nothing to indicate that the character, who is not shown on the screen, needs to be "protected from his admirers." This ambiguity may explain the attacks on the film waged by the German right wing, only too happy to denounce an "anti-Beethoven film": "The film will divide minds and generations," the influential *Frankfurter allgemeine Zeitung* calmly announced, before going on to perform a critical roasting inspired, as the journalist noted, not by aesthetics but by morality. The attack on Elly Ney, for example, was aimed at the elderly in general, and the zoo sequence inserted solely to demonstrate the inhumanity of the entire project, which could equally have been aimed at Aristotle, Erasmus, or Kant, in other words at two or three thousand years of civilization of which Beethoven constitutes the supreme musical expression. In short, Kagel may well ask that Beethoven be allowed to rest in his darkened tomb; it is he more than anyone else who has set out to disturb his sleep.[28] The violent tone of the article was obviously inspired *a contrario* by the pertinence of Kagel's criticism of a sector of the Federal Republic's establishment, but it must be noted that the latter, far from closing ranks to defend itself against the "outsider," displayed a variety of reactions that seriously damaged the notion of a monolithic culture industry: after all, *Ludwig van* was the result of a commission for television — that oft-disparaged medium — in this instance the Westdeutsches Fernsehen, and several prestigious publications gave it a warm welcome. The fact is that for a generation haunted by the Nazi past, there were many who wanted a rest from the great national cultural figures — for example the journalist for *Der Spiegel* who, with Kagel and the Sterbas, hailed "the end of the myth."[29]

However, the political content of works like *Ludwig van* was only part of the polemics, for aesthetic modernism is a target for many critics who have often associated it with the very thing that the avant-garde had purportedly set out to denounce. The irritation was most intense in the Democratic Republic, where it was said that in the West "Beethoven's music is a by-product of the capitalist leisure industry, disfigured or made the subject of the most outrageous modernistic projects. At the same time, attempts are made to paper this over by giving concerts and sending exhibitions abroad in an attempt to hide a state of affairs that is in violent contradiction to Beethoven's own humanism." Such was the burden of a "Statement by the Central Committee of the United Socialist Party of Germany, the State Council of the German Democratic Republic, the Council of Ministers of the G.D.R., the Council of the National Front for Democratic Germany, and the Confederated Committee of the Federation of Free German Trade Unions"[30]— a verdict that Ernst Hermann Meyer, doyen of East German composers, was to cap by describing Kagel's film as "pornographic."[31] A few choice anti-avant-garde epithets were also employed in France, where the magazine *Europe* published a special issue "in the great tutelary shadow of Romain Rolland." "Fashions change, and Beethoven's genius does not," Jean de Solliers wrote. "Not long ago, certain circles found it chic to look down on him; it was not really clear just why. It was categorically stated that he was passé, that he was behind the times, that it was no longer possible to find him interesting. And then a new generation of snobs came along. It discovered that Beethoven was a daring musician, one of the avant-garde, that he had flouted the generally accepted rules of composition. And one began to treat Beethoven familiarly, to regard him as a man prepared to experiment, to praise him for the supposed faults for which he had formerly been reproached because his procedures had not been understood, and today the same things are praised for reasons that are little better. The sad price of glory!"[32]

Some of the contributors to *Europe,* however, did not join in the attack on the "new generation of snobs": "I am not one of those people who are scandalized when Stockhausen decides to use Beethoven's music as 'material.' Quite the contrary. The aerolite continues its course to other planets," wrote Yves Florenne and Béatrice Didier.[33] And the astronomical metaphor was not a bad choice to illustrate the dilemma the exegetes were facing. Is Beethoven, in fact, like an aerolite, perpetually moving across the sky of history, or is he, since "fashions change, and Beethoven's genius does not," more like an immobile and fixed sun? In the shadow cast by that sun, in any event, we find conservatives of every stripe. Invective worthy of Stalin jostles familiarly with statements by Austrians supporting Beethoven's brand of *Aufklärungskatholizismus* [Enlightenment Catholicism] against "all the petty provocateurs, hippies, and Maoists" out to change the world, against the escapism offered by "drugs, pop music, and sex," which mock Beethoven's message of "responsibility to mankind and moral duty."[34] Unfortunately, those who admire the aerolite often take what they think are original paths but which are actually only some weak echo of a vanished past: for one French Beethoven lover of 1970, the Ninth Symphony's "modernity" was that of a "*Marseillaise* for all of mankind."[35] The "Beethoven and us" formula is always thought to be new by those who utter it, but the terms employed are often drawn from an accepted repertory of admirative or rejective terms in which only the odd period name recalls the passions of yesteryear.

At the time of the bicentenary, it was that imperturbable procession of trite expressions that led Hans Heinrich Eggebrecht to return to the task Arnold Schmitz had begun during the 1927 centenary celebrations and set out to produce a revisionist history of the composer's career. Unlike Schmitz, however, Eggebrecht was not interested in denouncing some "false image" of Beethoven, romantic or otherwise; on the contrary, he took note of its continuities and concluded that all such *topoi* express nothing other than the truth of the work itself, since any exegesis is restricted to the limits that it has set for itself.[36] Here is a real hermeneutic problem, one whose importance is more obvious than its corollary, which is, that once tradition speaks the truth, one need but heed its voice. In reality, that conclusion is not much different from the one that Jean and Brigitte Massin had reached earlier: "One of the great problems faced by any study of Beethoven is that whenever one sets down a judgment that appears to apply very exactly to the precise case of Beethoven, one also has the impression that one has written something that is grossly banal. The problem is that Beethoven is the ideal example of the man-of-genius. . . ."[37] However, the real problem may be that of having dreamed up a particular kind of man-of-genius and then making Beethoven fit into it, even if we brush aside heterodox attempts — for example by describing Richard and Edith Sterba's book as a "total failure," without further commentary.[38] And if such heterodox readings can be described as baseless, or as being themselves guilty of the very thing they are denouncing, must we not conclude that clichés may well be expressing the truth, but that the truth itself has become trivial?

Now, it is just at this critical juncture, at a time when the truth of received ideas was being seriously questioned, that European organizations finally made the decision to make the *Ode to Joy* an official anthem. That decision, taken at the time of the bicentenary, also takes us back to the 1920s, when, after a period of exacerbated nationalism, the work once again emerged as the emblem of rapprochement between peoples. Yet times had changed. Passions had cooled, the hero's "inflated glory" had become even more worrisome. While critics like Boulez and Kagel enjoy more prestige than did their critical predecessors, contemporary admirers no longer have the clout of a Romain Rolland or Édouard Herriot. And the figure of Europe, which was marginal in the 1927 commemorations, was even more absent in 1970. Indeed, in the interwar years Beethoven's image had been the focus of a dispute between nationalism and internationalism, with the decision going provisionally to the latter. Following the Second World War, it was caught between two contradictory universalist notions, that of the Free World and that of the World Revolution. However, if in the 1920s many intellectuals had actively supported Europeanist movements, in 1970 the European idea was viewed with indifference and even hostility by the many who regarded it as "morally unacceptable, to be condemnable and condemned" because of its identification with imperialism and colonialism and even racism. "The text we had in mind was the preface Jean-Paul Sartre had written for Frantz Fanon's *The Wretched of the Earth,* in which he said that every time a European was killed in a third-world country it was like killing two birds with one stone: an oppressor died and an oppressed person disappeared," Maria Antonietta Macciocchi wrote, looking back.[39] People like Claude Lévi-Strauss also undertook to criticize Eurocentrism, albeit less violently. Yet, just as the anthem for Pan Europa had been a result of the 1927 centenary, the 1970 celebrations were to lead to the official adoption of the *Ode to Joy* as the European anthem.

The decision profited from the interest the commemoration had created as well as from an already established consensus within several European organizations, towards which Coudenhove's 1955 letter had been merely the first step. In fact, the history of the European anthem goes back to August 1949, when Jehane-Louis Gaudet, "a mother who had suffered all kinds of trouble during the last war, including internment (by the Germans)," had sent to Strasbourg an anthem of her own composition that she sought to have chosen as the "hymn of the United States of Europe": "It would give an honest woman an opportunity to make herself known. Such an extraordinary thing does not happen all that often," she added in her letter to Paul-Henri Spaak, the "First President of Europe"[40] — a feminist plea that the anonymous bureaucrat entrusted with thanking her (no further action was taken) rather cruelly failed to grasp when he addressed his replies to *Monsieur le Professeur J. L. Gaudet.*[41] Even though it did little more than imitate traditional political compositions, the first postwar proposal for a European anthem did attempt some novelty, its content being based on recent historical experience. Following Jehane-Louis Gaudet, many amateur composers dispatched their European hymns to Strasbourg, each demonstrating a tendency to reproduce their own country's anthem — solemn anthems, triumphal marches, with titles like *The March of United Europe, Europa vocata, Europa!, Hymnus europaeus, Vereintes Europa, Europe, lève-toi!, An Europa, La Marseillaise de la paix, Paneuropa, Inno all'Europa,* or the following *Européenne:*[42]

When the *Ode to Joy* was finally adopted at Strasbourg, a tribute was paid all the above-mentioned precursors: "Proposals and pleas for such an anthem have come from the peoples of Europe in still larger numbers, perhaps, then for the European flag."[43] Yet throughout the 1950s as the scores had piled up in the Council of Europe's archives, no one there had seriously thought that any of the aspiring composers would be successful. The bureaucrats found themselves faced with a dilemma: "There are some pieces that aren't bad and others that would make a bald man's hair stand on end!" wrote one of them in 1962.[44] However, given the similarity of all of the works' aesthetics and purposes, their individual technical shortcomings were not the reason for their systematic rejection; and indeed, the European ideal had also inspired some professional musicians, among them Michel

Roverti, whose *Anthem for the United States of Europe* would be recorded by the band of the French Garde Républicaine.[45] The real reasons behind the mass rejection were to be found elsewhere and were set forth in the aforementioned letter: "It is my opinion that we should avoid settling on some new, anodyne, and simple little tune, and I should be very much in favor of adopting a section of some well-known work, Beethoven's *Anthem to Joy*, for example, or something from Handel's *Royal Fireworks*. Words could be set to it, words that should be extremely simple and avoid some of the complexities that our European institutional creators have managed to come up with." That remark goes to the heart of the matter: the fact that the "proposals from the peoples of Europe in still larger numbers" had, alas, been only "simple little tunes." They were all typical examples of political music but without roots in history, and all of them set out to express a notion of a new identity in an old way. Rather than revealing the hypocrisy of this or that bureaucrat, the dual discourse that entailed praising in public what the "institutional creators" denigrated in private reveals the truly delicate nature of the question of an anthem: the contradiction between the democratic ideology of popular artistic expression and the desire to construct a collective identity by rising above the inertia of political tradition to seek excellence in an elite cultural product.

The way out of that impasse meant turning towards the classical canon of "well-known works" — and the mention of Handel was not haphazard, since he had already been called upon to provide the theme music for the Council of Europe's radio broadcasting station. Eurovision also went to the classical repertory by using the music of Marc Antoine Charpentier. The same thought had occurred to Alfred Max and Jacques Porte in 1957, shortly after the signature of the Treaties of Rome, for their *Cantata of Europe*. The program notes for that work's premiere at Paris's Théâtre des Champs-Elysées in May of that year were written by Denis de Rougemont: "Language divides: it is music that must serve as the profound expression of Europe's creative genius." The first part of the program consisted of a performance with choir of Beethoven's *The Glorious Moment,* conducted by Hermann Scherchen. "The great difference between Beethoven's cantata and that of Alfred Max and Jacques Porte is that the first was composed for a 'practical' Europe, the second for a Europe with a heart," *France-Soir* commented.[46] Pierre Dervaux then conducted the new *Cantata for Europe,* which was scored for the voices of children to represent those orphaned in the various war-torn European countries. André Maurois, writing in *Le Figaro,* praised it: "And one seems to hear intermingled, ushering in the united Europe, the 'Anthem to Joy' of Beethoven's Ninth Symphony and Victor Hugo's noble call, that voice which, during the darkest days of a war, spoke with the courage that we, today, having again found peace, must emulate."[47] For Maurois, no contemporary work — successful as it might be and indeed to the extent that it was even successful — could approach what had already been accomplished in the Ninth Symphony. Beethoven emerged from this concert as the one composer destined to "usher in the united Europe," so long as the work chosen was not the "practical Europe" of *The Glorious Moment* but, rather, the "Europe with a heart" of the Ninth Symphony.

The *Ode to Joy* was performed at Strasbourg on 20 April 1959 on the occasion of the tenth anniversary of the Council of Europe's founding. In 1962, the Belgian National Section of the Council of European Municipalities proposed a *European Communal Anthem* that would be a "'European song' based on Beethoven's music," adding that "the numerous pairing ceremonies . . . had shown the need for a European anthem which could be performed together with the various national anthems."[48] Two years later, the proposal was resubmitted at Rome at a meeting of the Council of European Municipalities, and the "wish was expressed that a European anthem . . . be adopted by the Council of Europe and the European Communities," a proposal that expressed a will to unification that was to become even more pressing with time. Until the end of the 1960s, however, the plan hung in abeyance, although on occasion the Consultative Assembly would issue an assurance that the assembly "has been occupied with it for some time."[49] The final push occurred following the bicentenary celebrations during a roundtable discussion to consider relaunching Europe Day, at which the proposals of the Consultative Assembly Committee on Regional Planning and Local Authorities were considered. "In this time of calculated self-interest, when discussion on the subject of Europe is dominated by figures, tariffs, and contribution levels, it is more than ever necessary that the Assembly should try to raise the debate to its high level of twenty-five years ago," wrote René Radius, the French chairman of the committee.[50] The need to separate the Europe of the heart from the Europe of "contribution levels" was thus used to forestall any future reticence, especially the fear of awakening "European chauvinism," as though, facing technocratic suspicions, concern for the symbolic could ensure the human character of European construction. The Consultative Assembly of the Council of Europe received the report at a meeting that was held from 7 to 8 July 1971 in West

Berlin, over the protests of the government of the GDR. Thus, one might say that it was in the shadow of the Berlin Wall that the Council finally adopted resolution 492 (1971), which made Beethoven's music the European anthem.[51]

The resolution proposed "the acceptance by member countries as a European anthem of the *Prelude to the Ode to Joy in the fourth movement of Beethoven's Ninth Symphony*," and recommended "its use on all European occasions, if desired in conjunction with the national anthem." The text of the resolution was concise, with only that single mention of Beethoven and none at all of Schiller, whose name does not appear. The Council of Europe gave evidence of great exegetic sobriety; indeed it was quite mute, with the exception of one meaningful preambular paragraph: "Being of the opinion that it would be preferable to select a musical work representative of European genius and whose use on European occasions is already becoming something of a tradition." The formula is as vague as it is indisputable, but it does serve to reveal that the adoption of the European anthem had continued to arouse feelings of cultural nationalism that the very notion of Europe was supposed to rise above. Further, it implies that there are other pieces that might have been equally representative and that the difference is to be found in the "something of a tradition," a term that might be considered somewhat ambitious for describing a few isolated instances but that also puts its finger on what is really at stake, namely, that the essential and basic identity of the cultural patrimony is to make up for the tradition-based delays and shortcomings in the process of building a European political identity and that the preference for the classical repertory over purely political music was made to affirm the moral value of that patrimony. In short, on the one hand, Europe was being forged and things were "becoming something of a tradition," and, on the other hand, that forging process was taking place because Europe was already there.

The paradox of the whole proceeding resided in the fact that in building the new, men were turning toward the old; its weakness was that the old could not be used in its actual state. The Consultative Assembly did not adopt either Beethoven's Ninth Symphony nor its fourth movement nor the *Ode to Joy*, but rather what it described as "the Prelude" to the Ode to Joy. Schiller's poem *An die Freude* played no part in the resolution because the Council of Europe was not prepared to adopt its words as its own, as had become clear in the course of the committee's discussions: "As regards the words for an anthem, some doubt was felt, mainly with regard to the words of the Ode to Joy, which were in the nature of a universal expression of faith rather than specifically European."[52]

This is a crucial point: at the very time that the *Ode to Joy* was being adopted as the European anthem there was an awareness of its inadequacy for the role it was to perform. The twisting of the universalist exegesis of the Ninth Symphony into a "European" one totally absent in Beethoven's work and subsequent career was accomplished by passing over in silence the very text that had made it the symbol of the democratic values that the Council of Europe was now desirous of upholding.

With the disappearance of the text went that of the human voice. The parliamentarians themselves were somewhat uncomfortable with a wordless hymn and considered replacing "the profession of universal faith" with a "profession of European faith." That, however, raised other problems directly linked to the nature of European construction: "Members also wondered whether any words acknowledged as 'European' could ever be translated into another language and accepted as such by the other linguistic groups of the European family."[53] The European anthem, therefore, was not a piece of vocal or instrumental music but rather a song without a text, an incomplete symbol. That being the case, romantic doctrine and democratic ideal were in agreement that cultural traditions were the concern of peoples, not states. Thus, the responsibility for overcoming the anthem's defects was to be borne by the collectivity created by "Europeans," a kind of wager on the future that René Radius expressed as follows in his report:

> The committee therefore preferred, for the time being, to propose only the tune for a European anthem, without words, and to allow some time to pass. One day perhaps some words will be adopted by the citizens of Europe with the same spontaneity as Beethoven's eternal melody has been.[54]

And, in fact, the "Europeans" were quick to react. Not that they were asked to do so: the notion of a contest to come up with a text was abandoned, and it was only in schools that any such exercise was ever to be carried out.[55] However, the lack of words was a matter of regret even prior to the adoption of the anthem, and many saw it as an opportunity to lend a hand. As had happened earlier with the music, texts rained down on Strasbourg, only to meet with a similar fate. One of the poets did merit a considered response from the secretary general: "I deeply regret that I cannot follow up with your proposal. On the one hand, we already have the well-known German text ('Freude holder Götterfunke . . . ,' by Elysius) [*sic*], and, on the other hand, I cannot envision the use of a French text without there being at the same time one in all the other Council of Europe languages, which would be extremely difficult to achieve at this juncture."[56] We might wonder why Schiller's poem was brought into the argument against a new text when there was no question of its being used. Perhaps the secretary general, Lujo Toncic-Serinj, might not have expressed it quite this way, but his letter gives the impression that he was well aware that the work's symbolic import, which had been the very reason for its adoption as the European anthem, marked the limits of the operation, beyond which politics, in all their arbitrary nature, must inevitably take over. Having reached this dead end, the hymn was condemned to silence, a state of affairs that continues to prevail today.

Although resolution 492 (1971) of the Consultative Assembly of the Council of Europe is the decisive element in the adoption of the European anthem, the final step was its official adoption by the Committee of Ministers, announced at Strasbourg on 19 January 1972. On that occasion, there was also a decision to take action. Yet when it came to bureaucratic organization, the Europe of the heart had necessarily to become the subject of a commission. The official communiqué concluded with the sentence: "The musical realization of the anthem has been entrusted to Mr. Herbert von Karajan."[57] In fact, during the meeting at Strasbourg delegates had learned that the secretary general himself had asked Karajan to "prepare an official score and to conduct the recording"; the archives contain no trace of that initiative, which was probably the fruit of a personal friendship between the Salzburg conductor and Toncic-Serinj, who was a former Austrian foreign minister. In the course of February and March 1972, Karajan recorded with the Berlin Philharmonic his arrangement of Beethoven's tune, which was issued by Deutsche Grammophon on a record that included the anthems of the other members of the Council of Europe and the whole of the Ninth Symphony's final movement. The score was published by Schott and Söhne in versions for symphony orchestra, wind band, and piano.[58] On 5 May 1972, on Europe Day, Eurovision TV introduced the European anthem with a message in thirteen languages superposed on images of Karajan and his orchestra and dissolves on the European flag. The same day, the anthem was also broadcast by fifty radio stations.[59] As a media event, it was an obvious success. Karajan's prestige lent cachet to the anthem chosen by the Council of Europe; the twelve-star flag also served to enhance the Austrian conductor's European reputation. The same reciprocity was evidenced when it came to the question of royalties, which were to be retained by the arranger but not paid as a direct salary. The artistic status of his arrangement can be weighed in its dual status as a product of a shared patrimony and as the symbol of a governing body, but from a legal standpoint — and unlike national anthems or the Ninth Symphony itself, which are works in the public domain — the European anthem is a work by Herbert von Karajan.[60]

Of what exactly does the score consist? What *is* the European anthem? It is Beethoven's melody, of course, one that has throughout its long life been subjected to countless arrangements — including one by Laurent Dalbecq for wind band, entitled *Le Drapeau de l'Europe* [The European Flag] and published in France in 1968.[61] Given the raw material, Karajan did not need to use a great deal of imagination. His score, like Beethoven's, is in D major, and its approximate duration is two minutes and fifteen seconds. It begins with four bars of introduction which, without being precisely like the original, are reminiscent of the first appearance of the *Freudenmelodie* in the wind instruments. "The European anthem per se" consists of bars 140 – 187 of the symphony's fourth movement; it comprises the whole of the melody that Beethoven had scored to be played in unison prior to subjecting it to variations with a coda leading back to the movement's opening *Schreckensfanfare*. Karajan was to retain the last two elements, that is, the melody played by the violins and its modification into a solemn march; his fragment ends with the cadence that concludes each verse of the text in the Ninth, used here as a conclusion emphasized by a marking of *ritenuto molto*.

Thus, in essence, Beethoven's music is used, as it were, verbatim. Yet the arrangement is rife with implications. The tempo is markedly slower: where Beethoven has marked *Allegro assai* with a metronome marking of half note/minim = 80, Karajan has quarter note/crotchet = 120. Of course, Beethoven's marking has not prevented the performance of many slow versions, but that practice has become more rare with the move toward increased respect for the score and "authentic" performing practice in recent years. As for the new instrumentation, the changes create a uniform sonority that destroys the rich texture and timbre of the original. Given the tradition of the work as pure music, the alterations serve to give it a more ceremonial rhetoric. Framed by the linear introduction and conclusion accompanied by a progressive augmentation of all the musical parameters, the *Freudenmelodie* is brought to a single apotheosis that also marks its disappearance. It is no exaggeration to say that the entire process creates a radical alteration of meaning which, in fact, goes far beyond the Austrian conductor's particular response to the Council's commission. Given the fact that a two-minute segment has been wrenched out of a symphony to become an element in political events that have never been presumed to provide any aesthetic experience per se, the reductive effect is obvious and inevitable. In short, the Council of Europe asked for an anthem without words, and that is what it got. When Karajan described his work, he stated: "The portions sung by the chorus are present in the Anthem's orchestral version."[62] But what does that mean? We may understand it as a way of re-assuring laymen that what we have is indeed the *Ode to Joy*, and its very ba-nality means that it requires "translation" by the musician for the func-tionaries. However, we can also imagine that Karajan conceived his work not as a reworking of the instrumental portion of the Ninth Symphony but as an orchestral transcription of the choral section. And the fact that in or-der to achieve that he merely copied an instrumental passage by Beethoven himself changes nothing — we are reminded of Jorge Luis Borges's Pierre Ménard, who claimed to have written a new *Don Quixote* by reproducing the same text in different circumstances. Thanks to this sleight of hand, the European anthem becomes a translation of the *Ode to Joy* into the universal language of absolute music, the voice of European genius.

"In 1972 the Council of Europe gave Europeans a means of expressing their faith beyond the particularities of language," announced Secretary General Lujo Toncic-Serinj in his annual report.[63] That those means had been the work of a former Nazi was apparently a secondary consideration, given the prestige enjoyed by Europe's *Generalmusikdirektor*. But the mute fate of this expression of faith reminds us that, once we forgo metaphysics, beyond language there lies only silence.

# 12

## From Apartheid's Anthem to the Dismantling of the Berlin Wall

On 28 August 1974, the London *Times* published an editorial entitled "Schiller's Shadow in Salisbury":

> If you hear someone coming towards you down an alleyway at night whistling, in an assertive manner, the choral theme of Beethoven's ninth symphony, you need not necessarily panic. The tune was, of course, made famous by that influential film *A Clockwork Orange,* and one still occasionally hears lads in big boots humming it under their breath along with snatches of Purcell as they knock about the street furniture. But the man in the dark may equally well be that comparatively rare and inoffensive character, the European patriot, buoying up spirits understandably dampened by the current state of the Community by whistling the tune lately adopted by an affirmative resolution of quorate delegates as the international anthem of the EEC. Alternatively, the man may simply be a musician, although the fact that he is whistling at all argues against that. There is a fourth possibility: he may be a Rhodesian.
>
> Mr. Smith's government, after five years' search for something catchy, has settled for Beethoven as a replacement for "God Save the Queen" (which, some time after UDI [Unilateral Declaration of Independence], they came to feel brought a faintly ironic tone on state occasions). From now on the president will open parliament to the strains of that labyrinthine final movement, the initial bars of which should test the resources of the Salisbury brass to the uttermost.[1]

From this collection of characters whistling the *Ode to Joy* in deserted streets, only the musician escapes sarcasm, spared from condemnation by the commonplace notion that whistling a tune is incompatible with a true appreciation of its value; his rapport with Beethoven is serious and subjective, peaceful and independent of any state. The three other characters are not so fortunate. The booted youth of *The Clockwork Orange* who combines personal pleasure and personal violence is the only one who actually frightens the *Times'* editorialist; the "European patriot" and "sentimental Rhodesian" are merely amusing. In both examples, the association of Beethoven with politics is held up to ridicule, and above all the idea that the *Ode to Joy* could become an anthem as dear to the hearts of "patriots" as any classic national anthem.

However, British "Euroskepticism" aside, what really lay behind such a comparison? Is there not a striking difference between the arbitrary act of a racist state and the "expression of European genius"? In fact, the connection is less forced than it might appear, and the newspaper even says so. It chose to take a derisive tone, but its obviously serious purpose was to express a political and moral condemnation of Ian Smith's regime. At the time, what is now Zimbabwe still bore the name of the English adventurer who, in 1890, had conquered large sections of the northern regions of South Africa, true to a desire that Hannah Arendt presented as the motto of imperialism: "I would annex the planets if I could."[2] After a crisis with London that had led to a unilateral declaration of independence in 1965, Rhodesia's white minority — 4 percent of the population amidst six million black Africans — remained faithful to the racist ideology that, in an era of decolonization, had been abandoned by the majority of the Western world. The Rhodesian whites referred to themselves as "Europeans" wherever they may have been born, and they were recognized as such by everyone, their critics included. European was the term employed, for all practical purposes, to describe what was a political and social hegemony based on skin color. The anthem of the Rhodesian Europeans, too, was in a way a "European anthem." And it was in that form that, for the first time since the Third Reich, the *Ode to Joy* became the tool of a state founded on the systematic rejection of the ideal of universal brotherhood.

The Rhodesian anthem was to bring into sharp relief the consequences of the Council of Europe's renunciation of the "universal profession of faith." A few days after Salisbury's announcement, the secretary general received a letter from the French headquarters of the European Veteran's Federation protesting "the fact that the European anthem has become the anthem of apartheid."[3] Rhodesia had been unanimously condemned by the international community, in particular at the United Nations, which had declared a total embargo against the regime in 1966. There was thus every reason to expect that the Council of Europe, the body entrusted with enforcing the European Convention on Human Rights, would deal with the moral problem created by the use of the European anthem, not merely by some random state, but by apartheid itself.[4] At Strasbourg, however, the focus of attention was not on the question of human rights. "If Rhodesia has selected the 'Prelude to the Ode to Joy' in its original version, Rhodesia cannot be subject to reproach since that is a version that is in the public domain. If, on the other hand, Rhodesia has adopted the official score of the Council of Europe, no steps can be taken without the agreement of the person holding the copyright to that score, namely, Mr. Von Karajan" — a quotation from an internal memorandum of the Office of Legal Affairs. However, the document went on, even if Karajan were to transfer his rights so as to allow Strasbourg to institute legal proceedings against Rhodesia, there would be little chance of those proceedings being successful because "that country does not protect within its own territory copyrights held by foreigners."[5] The secretary general therefore replied to the veterans in the following terms: "I understand your feelings, but I am afraid that in this matter no international recourse is available."[6] And he added that "even the United Nations has discussed the possibility of adopting the 'Anthem to Joy' as the universal anthem" — a statement that in this instance only served to support Rhodesia's appropriation of a work "in the public domain and part of the universal cultural heritage," since in 1971 the United Nations had adopted an official anthem, the work of W. H. Auden and Pablo Casals. In short, the Council of Europe treated the problem as though it were a simple case of plagiarism and concluded that, since the *Ode to Joy* belonged to everyone, anyone could do what he wanted with it — including use it as racist propaganda.

This weird twisting of the universality of Beethoven's work was obviously less flagrant than the way in which it was distorted by Ian Smith's government. It was also less naive. In fact, the adoption of the *Ode to Joy* as Rhodesia's national anthem, far from being an attempt to appropriate the composer's symbolic value, seems to have been more the result of utter ignorance. It was not done by a music-loving elite somehow blinded by its aesthetic ideal of a perfect republic, nor was it the hypocritical act of a racist regime attempting to pass itself off as a defender of universal brotherhood. It was, in fact, the act of a group that saw itself as the last bulwark of Western and Christian civilization — but that conceived that role not in terms of an artistic heritage but rather as a battle against atheistic Marxism, embodied both by Zimbabwe's black population, whose most radical faction was waging a guerilla war in the northeastern part of the country, and by the whites in the British government at London, suspected of acting in the interests of Moscow. In standing up to such enemies, preference should have in principle been given to some "original Rhodesian melody," and the Smith government had indeed tried in vain to discover one after abandoning *God Save the Queen* in 1968. It was only in the end, when international pressure and the guerillas had begun to overpower the regime, that on 16 January 1974 the cabinet — as reported in the *Rhodesian Herald*—"listened to a tape recording of the theme from the last movement of Beethoven's Symphony No. 9 in D."[7] Philip Smith, the minister of education, was finally able to put forward an anthem that could "reflect the spirit and determination of the people of Rhodesia and indeed the characteristics which pertain to our national attitude and outlook on life":

> It had to be serious but not heavy, dignified but not pretentious, and at the same time have appeal. Most important of all, it had to inspire and to contain the seed of national pride.
>
> Government has been conscious ever since independence of this void in our national life, but when we became engaged in a war on our northeast border, an anthem was more than ever necessary to reflect the unity of the country and to inspire our fighting men.

Thus, the *Ode to Joy* was to inspire and arouse not only a population in need of moral support but also an army that was engaged in violating all kinds of human rights, torturing prisoners, murdering civilians, razing villages. Given the lack of other sources,[8] there is nothing to suggest that for the Rhodesian government, Beethoven's Ninth Symphony was anything more than a piece of music heard once, in a meeting, after six years of futile search and — under the pressure of many pending matters — seized on in its eagerness to settle once and for all the question of a national anthem. In short, the stigma borne by the apartheid anthem is not its cynicism, but its banality.

The Rhodesian national anthem was played for the first time on 27 August 1974 at the opening of the fiftieth sitting of the Salisbury parliament; thus it was associated with a democratic tradition that the white majority was obviously convinced it was upholding, at least within its own ranks. Beethoven's melody was played by the band of the British South Africa Police, a "well-trained paramilitary organization" (including some blacks deemed useful for infiltrating the African population[9]), and by the band of the Rhodesian African Rifles, a black battalion commanded by white officers, whose leader, Ken MacDonald, had written the official sixteen-bar arrangement — no connection with the one by Karajan. The *Rhodesian Herald* reported a few of the enthusiastic reactions, including one by a sergeant musician of mixed race who warmly observed that "it's just like *God Save Our Gracious Queen.*" However, the newspaper was not merely being formulaic when it invited Rhodesians to "assess the suitability" of Beethoven's melody; most of them were familiar with it only from Miguel Ríos's pop version. Instead of announcing a triumph, the journalist was obliged to note that "opinions as to the choice of anthem are divided."[10] There were many, for example, who deplored the fact that no one had come up with an original melody — a view that the newspaper went so far as to attribute to Beethoven himself, who, as a musician, would have been "flattered that a tune he wrote would be considered versatile enough and virile enough for such a purpose 150 years later," but who, as a man, "would probably be disappointed" since "he had spent his life working out his own solutions, both musical and personal, and . . . would expect other people to do the same."[11] Another contributor to the *Rhodesian Herald,* the music critic Rhys Lewis, went much farther, writing that he was "stupefied" by the "plagiarism" for "local nationalistic ends" of a melody with "supra-national associations" and "indissolubly linked with ideas on the brotherhood of mankind" — an argument that, by concluding that the initiative invited "ridicule," reveals that a part of the Rhodesian elite was not unaware of the moral reproaches being directed against its nation's activities.[12]

As days went by, a growing number of objections appeared in the same newspaper, which, unlike the government-controlled radio and television stations, afforded the country's liberal faction a platform from which to criticize the government. The comment by the principal of one of Salisbury's schools was clearly political: "*Ode to Joy* could be the swansong for any immediate hopes of uniting Rhodesians. It is a choice that reveals once again an incredible lack of awareness that there are six million Africans in this country."[13] Finally, the newspaper even went so far as to seek the opinion of a black, Phinias Sithole, president of the Congress of the African Trade Union, who issued a lapidary judgment: "National anthems arranged by European Rhodesians will have very little meaning for the African worker so long as the latter is not allowed to play a more important role in Rhodesia's life. African workers are excluded from the system of government. This is a government affair. We cannot feel any particular allegiance to the anthem." [14] For the white liberal as well as the black leader, the anthem was symbolic of the abyss between whites and blacks — the *Ode to Joy* turned into a radical negation of brotherhood. However, the harshest blow to the "joyous" symbol of the "rebel" cabinet may have been the one dealt by the *Times* in its editorial:

> It is not so much the bits about intoxication and millions of people embracing that might cause embarrassment, but the remarks about all men becoming brothers and the breaking down of the barriers erected by stern society. The poem was pretty near the knuckle, politically, when it was written (it is said that it was originally an Ode to freedom, *Freiheit*, not joy, *Freude*) and these days it would be found objectionable in many parts of the world. But one may hope that the winning entry will preserve a phrase or two —*Hail Rhodesia, fair and sun-drenched / Daughter of Elysium* . . .
>
> And once the choice is made, it should have a chance of enduring whatever political vicissitudes might be in store, for by a happy coincidence "Hail Zimbabwe . . ." would also scan.

Thus, a further swansong in Beethoven's career, but also, on this occasion, a swansong for the Salisbury regime, which was to find that its new anthem, far from being viewed as the expression of the Rhodesians' proud determination, had on the contrary laid bare their internal divisions, summed up their moral vacuity, and made them the butt of international sarcasm. It was, however, too late to back down. There were many responses to the contest that the government organized to come up with a suitable text. The happy winner was a woman named Mary Bloom.

> Rise, O voices of Rhodesia, God may we Thy bounty share,
> Give us strength to face all danger and where challenge is, to dare.
> Guide us, Lord, to wise decision, ever of Thy grace aware.
> Oh, let our hearts beat bravely always, for this land within your care.

As Peter Goodwin and Ian Hancock point out, although "Mrs. Bloom's banalities had debased one of Beethoven's greatest triumphs," it was not her fault "that an anthem which was meant to express and inspire a sense of national identity was produced just before the nation itself was about to disappear." [15] *Voices of Rhodesia* was stillborn, and it sank without a trace in the shipwreck of the white state of Rhodesia. In March 1980, the country's very first election by universal suffrage was won by Robert Mugabe, the guerilla leader who had only recently laid down his arms. On 18 April 1980, Zimbabwe became an independent country as a former British colony, London having refused to the end to recognize its 1965 declaration of independence. The event was welcomed with huge celebrations attended by many prominent persons, including the Prince of Wales, who was saluted with *God Save the Queen,* and Bob Marley, who, with his band, the Wailers, performed his song *Zimbabwe.*[16] However, that tune was not destined to become the new national anthem either; that honor fell to a religious hymn that had been composed in South Africa early in the century by a black man, Mankayi Enoch Sontonga, and which had already been adopted by both Tanzania and Zambia as their national anthems.

The anthem *Voices of Rhodesia* is obviously a minor chapter in the career of the Ninth Symphony, and not even the most shocking one — the Nazis' use of Beethoven was far more outrageous morally as well as a great deal more sophisticated in its approach to historical logic. However, the case of Rhodesia remains the sole instance in which the *Ode to Joy* itself was officially used as a national anthem, and by a state that — apart from any argument over its political and moral legitimacy — was in fact a legally constituted parliamentary republic. From that perspective, it marks a unique moment of convergence between official music and the classical music canon. The act of making a classical work the symbol of a state is not devoid of aesthetic effects, which was pointed out by the music critic of the *Rhodesian Herald:*

> Affirmative though Beethoven's theme is, the impact he obtains with it derives from the ornamental variation, modulatory treatment and massive choral harmonies that he builds up into a blaze of glory.
>
> To ears familiar with these unforgettable sounds, the 16-bar version of the theme itself will seem inconclusive and poverty stricken. When forcibly wedded to jingoistic words other than Schiller's *Ode to Joy* the outrage to one's sensibilities will be complete, to say nothing of our response to Beethoven's vision being irretrievably damaged by association.

The critic is denouncing the fact that, in the arrangement of the symphonic theme, aesthetic experience has been replaced by a memorative sign which, not content to broadcast in the public sphere a political discourse at odds with the work's original message, also invades the private sphere through its unconscious and uncontrollable logic of "association" — which, as he notes, "irretrievably" damages the individual. Indeed, it is easy to believe that for the rest of his life Rhys Lewis may never have been able to hear Beethoven's Ninth Symphony without recalling the pitiable sounds of the Salisbury bands. It is clear that the scope of his argument extends beyond the question of Rhodesia's anthem and that it is directly applicable to the European anthem as well — aside from the absence of "jingoistic words," which attenuates the involuntary associations but does not dispel them. Were the *Ode to Joy* truly to win acceptance as the symbol of the "European ideal," which is precisely the original purpose of the European anthem, how could anyone listen to the Ninth without thinking of Europe? And in that case, would one not be right in viewing such conditioning as a violation by the state of individual privacy in such a secret and inviolable a sphere as aesthetic pleasure — in short, as a violation of human rights? And that being so, would not a "European" — or even for that matter a "non-European" — have the right on behalf of the European Convention on Human Rights to bring suit to redress the "irretrievable damage" done his enjoyment of Beethoven's music?

Absurd, no doubt. But it is an absurdity that is a direct result of the old Rousseau-inspired plan of creating a "memorative sign" in a public sphere conceived in accordance with a unitary model for the identification of subjective experience with community belonging, and not according to what modern societies in fact are — namely, multiple and fragmented spaces in which the circulation of signs and their association with subjective experiences are victim to ever-larger and contradictory forces, in which, for example, the European anthem is only one more object, drowned in the myriad signifiers that constantly assail the mind of every individual. Everyone enjoys the Ninth Symphony, as he wishes and insofar as he is able, in keeping with a dialectic of memory and perception that relies upon his experience as much as on his sensitivity, associating it with or linking it to an infinity of possible objects, or nothing. Such associations and perceptions, of course, are themselves affected by shared expectations and cannot be described other than by using a vocabulary already informed by the work's past reputation and the musical *doxa* in general, and this sets up a hermeneutic process that is at once individual and collective. Whether the critics of the "cultural state"[17] like it or not, that state can indeed play a role in providing egalitarian access to this aesthetic experience. But when it comes to the hermeneutic process to which the aesthetic experience gives rise, the state, unless it is a totalitarian one, has neither an interest in exercising nor even the ability to exercise control. In short, when one lives in a modern democratic environment, official music is harmless and inoffensive only if it remains discreet — and that (to put it mildly) is exactly what the European anthem is.

That having been said, it had not been the intent of the Council of Europe to furnish the social image bank with that sort of weak and fragmentary datum. The European anthem was not conceived merely as a distinctive sign for European institutions, events or movements, but as the sign of the "European idea" itself, that is, as an ideological draft that was to establish and lend legitimacy to a certain specific political community representative of the European continent as a whole. Such an aim demands an attempt to create effective symbols, but care must be taken to avoid any suggestion of totalitarianism and its avatars. This dilemma, which is perhaps inevitable whenever a democratic regime sets out to create symbols for itself, inevitably led to considerable hesitation and reservations throughout the process of creating a European entity. A part of that procedure involved the creation of unifying symbols, a question that arose as far back as 1953, when Strasbourg began to consider a flag to serve as a "common denominator" on which all of the European entities might inscribe their own emblem [18] — a concern to achieve unification that in the event was often to be accompanied by an opposing concern to preserve certain institutional insignia. As for the anthem, in 1972 the Committee of Ministers of the Council of Europe had prudently announced that it had "chosen an anthem to be proposed to Europeans," a formulation carefully chosen to take into account the reaction of the peoples of other communitarian organizations. Among the latter, however, the question of symbols was not to take on the same urgency, apart from a handful of European deputies who, ignoring the anthem's real status, were from time to time to regret the lack of an official translation of the lines *Freude schöner Götterfunken* [19] — a text which the functionaries at Brussels who got up a chorus of the European communities were regularly to employ whenever they raised their voices to sing the European anthem. In 1979, the first European parliament elected by universal suffrage adopted the twelve-star flag, "resolved to provide the European Community with a symbol with which the peoples of Europe can identify." [20] On the other hand, years would pass before the European Community turned to the question of an anthem.

The sluggishness of its adoption, which was matched by the weakness of the link between Beethoven's melody and Europe, emerged clearly in an episode that did however illustrate Beethoven's link with the French Republic, a link that persisted long after the days of Édouard Herriot and Romain Rolland. On 21 May 1981, the day on which François Mitterrand assumed the presidency, the *Ode to Joy* was performed by the Orchestre de Paris and a chorus of 150 under the baton of Daniel Barenboim as the new French president proceeded up Paris's Rue Soufflot to the Panthéon; along with the *Marseillaise* in Berlioz's orchestration, it was the only piece of music included in the day's official program. The music does not appear to have particularly drawn the attention of those in attendance: "One sensed that in the distance somewhere, beyond the wall of backs each holding aloft a dazed child, something was going on. Was it the Ninth Symphony? Nearly inaudible, *La Marseillaise* completely so," wrote *Le Monde*.[21] And although the sound was better on television, there too the Ninth was no more than a kind of background music meriting no particular comment. In this totally unemphatic way, however, Beethoven's work was being directly linked to the cult of "great men" of which the Panthéon in Paris is the sanctum sanctorum; it was made another element of the symbolic construction surrounding the consecration of the Fifth Republic's first socialist president. In fact, in France the Ninth had never before had the status of official music that was given it in the ceremony that had been conceived by Jack Lang, the future minister of culture.[22] It seems fairly evident that in that context the role of the *Ode to Joy* had nothing to do with Europe, although that was soon to become a crucial element in the program of the new French head of state, working in tandem with Jacques Delors, the president of the European Commission.[23]

Before that program began to have an effect at the symbolic level, in January 1985 the realization that no common anthem had yet been adopted by the Community's bodies led a member of the European parliament to attempt to reopen the debate on the choice of Beethoven's melody, expressing his doubts "that the 'Hymn to Joy,' an orchestral work without words to transmit a specifically European message, was suitable to the development of European cooperation." Deputy Tummers then proposed that it be replaced by a "contemporary European anthem" to be sung in the languages of all of the member states, and that, to promote "contemporary music," a "young composer" be commissioned for the work.[24] The proposal was to remain a dead letter — although the incident does resemble that of the film *Bleu* by the Polish director Krzysztof Kieslowski, in which the character played by Juliette Binoche composes a *Concerto pour l'Europe* officially commissioned from her deceased husband, a famous composer of contemporary music. When the film was released in 1993, a critic for *Les Cahiers du Cinéma* wrote: "Julie's musician-husband is a composer described to us as a star, at least as well-known as Jean-Michel Jarre. His music is in a very pompous neoclassical style and resembles nothing at all, not even today's turned-off contemporary music."[25] Notwithstanding its severity, the remark is pertinent, for the notion of a European musical symbol that can connect and combine public image, communal political goals, and contemporary music would require bridging the gap that exists between contemporary avant-garde language and the tastes of the majority of the population — whence the composer's unbelievability in the film and the hybrid nature of Zbigniew Preisner's music representing the imaginary work. In any event, as the *Cantata of Europe* had already demonstrated in 1957, a contemporary composition on Europe is not inconceivable, even though there is every chance that it will be rife with neoromantic or neoclassical rhetoric; on the other hand, the notion of a "contemporary European anthem" risks coming up against the incompatibility between late twentieth-century musical language and a piece of occasional music whose genre is rooted in the late eighteenth.

There was thus no follow-up to Deputy Tummers's proposal, even though it was put forward at a time when Brussels had finally begun to take a real interest in the anthem question. In June 1984, the heads of state and government meeting in Fontainebleau as the European Council appointed representatives to consider the promotion of the Community's identity and image. This was to become the "Europe of Citizens," known by the name of its chairman, Pietro Adonnino, representing Bettino Craxi, and which included, inter alii, the journalist Max Gallo on behalf of François Mitterrand, Hans Neusel for Helmut Kohl, and David Williamson for Margaret Thatcher, as well as Carlo Ripo di Meana representing Jacques Delors. The members of the Adonnino Committee, in considering ways to make the European Community "a more tangible reality for its citizens," sought to ensure the latter's rights and encourage their participation in the political process. In addition, mindful of the need to reach coming generations who, unlike those who had assisted at the birth of the European bodies, would not have known "the horrors and ravages of war," they dealt with subjects like youth, education, culture, and sport. Among their many proposals, they were to urge the official adoption of the twelve-star flag and the institution of a Europe Day on 9 May, the date of the statement outlining the 1950 Schuman plan. The report also stated:

> The music of the "Anthem to Joy" extracted from the fourth movement of Beethoven's Ninth Symphony is in fact utilized at European events. The Council of Europe has also recognized this anthem as representative of the European ideal.
>
> The Committee recommends that the European Council advocate the playing of this anthem at the appropriate events and ceremonies.[26]

In May 1985, a new European Council meeting at Milan adopted the Adonnino report. Thus, fourteen years after adoption of resolution 492 (1971) by the Consultative Assembly of the Council of Europe, the *Ode to Joy* became the anthem of the European Community. As on that earlier occasion, the decision concerned the music, not the words. In addition, the declaration increased the silence surrounding Beethoven himself, for it did not mention him at all. It attributed recognition of his representative nature to Strasbourg alone, but now linked it with the "European ideal" and no longer with "European genius." The new discourse employed to legitimize the European anthem thus abandoned the 1971 formula with its nationalist inspiration; on the other hand, when mentioning its use as an element of European construction, it implied that what was formerly "something of a tradition" has now become an accepted one, a veritable tradition in its own right.

The discussions of the Adonnino Committee were aimed at "the achievement of an ever-closer union between the peoples of Europe"—a formula employed over the course of European construction to assert the goal of political union without going into the form in which it would be embodied. At the same time, the discussions attested to the desire to make up for "democratic shortcomings," which in February 1992 led to the introduction and inclusion of the entity "European citizen" in the Maastricht Treaty. Indeed, the question of symbols is closely bound up with that of citizenship and thereby with the vast and delicate question of knowing whether, and to what extent, Europe can truly be conceived of as a state — a state that, formally excluding the notion of any specific European nationality, has moved away from the nation-state model on which it had originally been based. The European anthem is part of the European Union's process of "state-building," which is rooted in a concept of symbols that, although differentiating itself at the level of discourse from national anthems, as in its choice of the *Ode to Joy*, still draws its inspiration from the symbols of the nation-states. In this connection, we might mention that although the defenders of European identity have always in principle stood aloof from any kind of European "neonationalism," [27] the fact that Europe is not a nation-state has not in and of itself been any guarantee against its creating various kinds of exclusionary devices based on identity or even against the development of a certain "European racism," particularly with regard to the immigration phenomenon. It was such a concern that led René Girault to wonder: "More than the realization of internal solidarities created by a civilization with common origins, comparable economic development, and assimilable social characteristics, *might European identity, in these troubled times, not be in the process of becoming entrenched in a kind of solidarity that is turned against the outside world?*" [28]

The new symbols of the European Community were officially introduced in Brussels on 29 May 1986 in front of Commission headquarters. The ceremony began with the raising of the flags of the twelve nation members and a speech by Jacques Delors, who saluted "the founding fathers of Europe" before saying: "May this blue and gold flag be for its citizens the symbol of a hope forever nourished by our ideals and our combat." [29] After the speeches, children from the European School raised the new European flag on the esplanade's thirteenth pole, assisted by Carlo Ripo de Meana. The official program for the ceremony noted: "During the raising of the European colors, an arrangement of the 'Anthem to Joy' will be played. Following performance of the arrangement, the chorus will sing the original version of the 'Anthem to Joy' (in German)." [30] The ceremony concluded with the release of balloons at the Schuman memorial. In the span of twenty minutes, it had managed to make a mythical survey of European construction, from its foundations in the life of its member nations to a tribute to its founding father. However, although the heart of the occasion was the raising of the European flag, the role of the anthem, which was not once mentioned in any of the speeches, was relatively secondary. In the program, which was planned to the minute, Karajan's score was referred to merely as an "arrangement" of the "original version," which remained that of Schiller. Perhaps this was just a minor ritual slip betraying some bureaucrat's yearning for the disavowed text. Unlike the printed program, the press release was careful to make the distinction: "During the ceremony, the orchestra will play the Beethoven's 'Anthem to Joy,' which is the European anthem. The chorus of the European Communities will also sing the 'Anthem to Joy' in its German version."

In any event, both symbols were officially introduced and were to go on to make their way in the world. After a somewhat sluggish start,[31] authorities began to note with satisfaction that the flag was becoming quite popular, and it even became necessary to take steps to protect it from being exploited for advertising purposes. The success of the anthem was somewhat less striking. It became a part of the protocol at official proceedings, in keeping with national traditions; it was played at town-pairing ceremonies[32] or on Europe Day; it was heard on the radio and television on the occasion of European elections or at special events. In addition, many artists were to come up with various arrangements of Beethoven's melody, all called *European Anthem*, from the Chorus of the European Communities and Laurent Grzybowski's very Catholic choir to the Fanas accordions and Jean-Pierre Gautier's musical saw.[33] In France, it was to be performed by military bands — often using Dalbecq's version rather than Karajan's — which included it in the repertory of French official music and even made it a part of the "French military patrimony."[34] Along with these unofficial recordings, in 1995 the European Commission and the Council of Europe issued a recording intended to respond to "the long-felt need to offer a definitive performance of the European Anthem."[35] Thus the European anthem enjoyed a favorable reception as a piece of popular music in the broad sense of the term — a reception that was in sharp contrast, however, to its absence from high cultural events, musical or otherwise, perhaps betraying a certain disdain for it by those elite circles more aware of the traditional artistic status of Beethoven's work. In any event, as far as the general public is concerned, there is evidence that, beyond the "definitive recording," intended as an act of closure, recognition of the *Ode to Joy* as a symbol of Europe remains fairly tepid, even in those circles most sympathetic to the European idea.

The problem of the text was to come up year after year, regularly brought before the Commission by various European deputies. "At the present time, the Commission is examining the method by which an appropriate solution might be found," was the fairly standard reply.[36] The curt response may reflect the irritation at seeing raised a question to which no answer was possible. In 1989, a new parliamentary request received a reply that did not alter its gist but that did add one positive statement touching on the fact that the anthem was so far wordless: "Of course, that music is the universal language par excellence."[37] In that highly bureaucratic wording, the ancient *topos* of "universal language," at the heart of the classical music *doxa*, served

to categorize the semiological status of the European anthem in an attempt
to find a way out of an impasse that had its roots in the very nature of European construction. That was the acknowledgment that pure music is a totally unique and separate language that allows man to rise above the "linguistic and literary" problem posed by any question of text. And, in fact,
because of the universality of absolute music — an eminently "European"
tradition — why not an anthem that would not only be wordless, but one
that would be frankly and purely instrumental? The solution would appear
to be logical enough, and it is somewhat surprising that it did not have more
supporters. True, it would have to be applied to a melody that owed its
unique historical importance precisely to the fact that it was *not* instrumental. In any event, at the time, the Commission was not really interested in
settling the problem, and its response, which was not really a response at all,
continued to be: The question will remain under consideration. One can
say that the failure to take a stand was in itself a stand, and one that had not
changed in the quarter of a century since René Radius had appealed to Europeans to make a "spontaneous" gesture. Throughout that time, experience had shown that when it came to an anthem, men — including bureaucrats and deputies — had obstinately refused to accept the sole "universal"
message of music. However, Radius's hopes risked remaining vain ones if
the impasse, instead of being caused by bureaucratic lethargy, turned out to
be indissolubly and actually caused by the choice of Beethoven's Ninth
Symphony as the European anthem, as well as by the nature of any symbol
held up as a counterpart to national anthems when in fact it was nothing of
the sort. In this last sense, no one better summed up what was at stake than
Marcello Burattini, the European Commission's chief of protocol:

> Yes, the European anthem is not one that can be sung, first, because I
> don't really see what words could be set to it — either inanities or frag-
> ments of the treaties. We don't have any history . . . As a general rule, na-
> tional anthems always tell of great deeds, they evoke great historical acts.
> We don't have any of those things, in the first place; and, secondly, some-
> thing that seems insignificant but is really most important, there are the
> languages, and if we have a text then the text must correspond and be
> singable, from the point of view of rhyme and rhythm, et cetera, in all of
> our many languages, and that would open a real can of worms. So for the
> moment, until there is some linguistic reduction to one or two languages,

and perhaps until there is some big wonderful historical event that might be voiced in the anthem, I don't really know what one could use, the verbatim record of a summit meeting, or. . . .[38]

His words have a certain undeniable nostalgia. The lack of some "big wonderful historical event" in the process of Europeanization has sometimes been described as its "mythological deficiency":[39] there is no epic tale comparable to those that have generally underpinned national histories, and which national anthems not only reflect lyrically but often express programmatically. It is a deficiency that the efforts of Denis de Rougemont and others who have supported the European idea have not managed to make up for by creating a kind of retrospective historiographic myth in which the construction of the community would be seen as the culmination of a long historical process going back to antiquity[40] — no more than has the European anthem itself, whose history is marked with the same dull bureaucratic hues as are the fragmented treaties and verbatim records that emerge from the meetings of heads of state.

On the other hand, the great tale is obviously one whose protagonist is not Europe per se but rather the whole of the "free world," one that was at the core of Western ideology throughout the cold-war period and even the prophecies of history's end inspired by the collapse of the Soviet system. Indeed, the impact of the latter event was to find expression in a proposal to change the European anthem with the aim of placing the peoples of Europe at the center of the historical future — a Europe that would now include the former communist bloc and not be confined to Western Europe alone, which the term "Europe" had so often been employed to mean. In March 1990, the European deputy Lyndon Harrison submitted a written question to the Brussels Commission:

> Is the Commission aware that in the text of Schiller's poem that inspired Beethoven to compose his Ninth Symphony, the original text read "Freiheit Schöner Götterfunken," but that at the time the censor had replaced those words with "Freude Schöner Götterfunken"?
>
> Does the Commission not feel that the time has come to lift this two-century-old ban and to reestablish Schiller within his rights?
>
> Considering the enormous steps that the peoples of Europe have taken towards freedom, especially over the past few months, would it not be fitting to give Europeans an anthem which, from its beginnings, was seen as a hymn of denunciation of all forms of despotism or dictatorship?

Need the Commission be reminded that, at his Christmas concert in Berlin, Bernstein used the original words of Schiller's work in annotating Beethoven's Ninth? [41]

The European Commission was thus being asked to rectify the damage done by another official body — the censorship authority of Schiller's day — to the rights of the creative artist by reestablishing an "original" meaning that, retrospectively, was deemed to be the best wording for the present historical moment. The distance between Beethoven's era and the late twentieth century, from Metternich's Concert of Europe to Jacques Delors's new European concert, is revealed in the attitude taken by official organs toward both the freedom of various kinds of artistic expression and the expressions of freedom. From this viewpoint, a European anthem made into an *Ode to Freedom* would be a veritable lyric expression of the fall of communism as well as the promise of a united and democratic Greater Europe. No need to dwell on the theory's lack of foundation: Deputy Harrison accepted as true what the conductor Bernstein knew very well to be a falsehood. Yet his proposal still failed to meet with a response, not because of historical truth but because of the long-standing shortcomings of the European anthem. "The Commission took note with great interest of the honorable member's comments regarding Schiller's 'Ode to Joy,'" Brussels replied, only to conclude, as was its wont: "The Commission is studying the question of the text, but has not taken a position in this regard." [42]

*Freiheit schöner Götterfunken,* European anthem: the notion may perhaps still have a future, either literally or as a metaphor of the *Ode to Joy* — that "profane chorus" which, as was recently stated in a program of the Orchestre de Paris, "serves as the European anthem, restoring Beethoven to his role as freedom's apologist." [43] That being said, the deputy's initiative was directly inspired by the fall of the Berlin Wall, in which event Beethoven did not really have any actual "European" significance. In 1989, the *Ode to Joy* rang out in Berlin as a universal anthem, a revolutionary anthem, a German anthem, or even — possibly — a NATO anthem, but at no time was it performed as *the* European anthem, a role that has so far not much affected the composer's reputation, other than within the European institutions themselves. On the other hand, the events surrounding reunification did serve to reactivate, albeit fleetingly, the link between Beethoven and the German national ideal, but no undue weight should be given this. Indeed, whereas the collapse of the Wall was celebrated by many spontaneous festivities and events involving popular music, the principal invocations of Beethoven were primarily the affair of a few international musical personalities, none of whom were German — with the exception of the staff of Südwestfunk television, who were to accompany the handshake between Helmut Kohl and Hans Modrow under the Brandenburg Gate with a performance of Miguel Ríos's *Song of Joy*.[44] Only three days after the events of 9 November 1989, many East Berliners poured into the Philharmonie to hear the Berlin Philharmonic perform the First Piano Concerto and Seventh Symphony under Daniel Barenboim's baton, a concert that several of them were to describe as marking "the reconciliation of the German people," while expressing regret that the Ninth had not been on the program.[45] On December 18th, Yehudi Menuhin conducted the *Egmont* Overture and the Fourth Symphony to benefit the reconstruction of Berlin's historic central district. And on 23 and 25 December, Leonard Bernstein conducted the Ninth Symphony with an orchestra that included musicians from both Germanies and the four Allied powers. The concerts were performed at both West Berlin's Philharmonie and in East Berlin's Schauspielhaus and were televised live on screens set up across from the Gedächtniskirche and in the Akademieplatz, as well as by satellite transmission to thirty-six countries. Of all of the Beethoven events connected with the destruction of the Wall, Bernstein's concerts were clearly the most prominent, a fact that Deutsche Grammophon was quick to take advantage of by putting on sale a CD of that "historic version" of the *Ode to Freedom*, whose packaging included a piece of the original Berlin Wall.[46]

For the occasion, Bernstein had replaced *Freude* with *Freiheit*. Coming from an American Jew of the same generation as Karajan — who had died only shortly before — the gesture did perhaps make the Ninth Symphony a symbol of German unity, but it was also (and probably more importantly) a symbol of the West's triumph over totalitarianism — for although the emphasis on freedom had a direct connection to the ideological aspect of the event, the Germans' getting back on friendly terms was more reflective of the ideal of brotherhood already present in Schiller's original. This emphasis on the event's political significance was coupled with the conductor's noticeably slower tempo, which brought the *Freudenmelodie* more firmly into the ceremonial atmosphere of the European anthem. However, the impact of the interpretation, under such exceptional circumstances, was of course created by the fact that the performance was of the Ninth Symphony as a whole; it was a Ninth that was performed to "sound" in the political arena without abandoning its status as a great piece of concert music, as though to lay stress on the historic link between aesthetic and political freedom, in keeping with a purpose and logic quite unlike that of an anthem, in which the work of art is constricted to the demands of a genre marked by its political functionality. The two concerts were well received by the international press, with the exception of one journalist from the German Democratic Republic who viewed the "propaganda" operation by the American sponsors as the "falsification of Beethoven's humanist intentions." [47] The enthusiasm aroused in the West by the political implications of Bernstein's gesture did not, however, prevent some experts from leveling severe criticisms against its musical results: "As a symbolic media event, it is a triumph," wrote David Levy. "As a performance of the Ninth Symphony, it is sadly wanting." [48] However, the American critic Richard Taruskin was probably the most violent opponent of having Beethoven and classical music dragged onto the historical stage: "The true musical emblems of that glorious moment were the guitar-strumming kids in jeans atop the wall playing a music that would have landed them in jail the day before. They were the ones who symbolized *Freiheit*. What did Beethoven symbolize? Just packaged greatness, I'm afraid, and all that that implies of smugness and dullness and ritualism. Just what the revolutions of 89 were revolting against." [49] Taruskin went so far as to compare the classical canon to the Soviet system, saying that the praises heaped on the "great Ludwig" resembled the equally outmoded veneration for the great Lenin. His call for a "subversive interpretation" of Beethoven's works and his praise for the tasty oranges of the counterculture, echoing the critics of the bicentenary, however, hinged on the principle of autonomy that had always been accepted by a segment of the musical elite — but hardly by all of them, as was well demonstrated by the participation in the Berlin festivities of such personalities as Barenboim, Menuhin, and Bernstein.

And it must be said that even for those latter, the political gesture symbolized by the substitution of *Freude* with *Freiheit* required some justification, as evidenced by the fact that Bernstein's called upon Beethoven himself to support it; in a program note written especially for the concert and handed out in the hall, he wrote:

There is apparently conjecture that Schiller may have produced a second sketch of his poem, "Ode to Joy," which carried the title "Ode to Freedom." Most researchers today are of the opinion, however, that this rumor is a fraud originated by Friedrich Ludwig Jahn. Whether true or not, I believe that this is a heavensent moment when we should sing the word "Freedom" wherever the score reads "Joy." If there ever were a historical moment in which one can neglect the theoretical discussions of academics in the name of human freedom — this is it. And I believe that Beethoven would have given us his blessing. Let freedom live![50]

Thus, a century after the *Ode à la liberté* of the French Third Republic, the theory of *Freiheit schöner Götterfunken* led to an actual alteration in the Ninth Symphony, in support of the same argument, namely, that the anecdote's authenticity was less important than its moral and political significance — or, as the Italians say, *se non è vero, è ben trovato*. And the composer himself was called upon to bless the event, a Beethoven who, like some deus ex machina, was summoned to descend from the skies on the cloud of his great reputation to give his blessing to a hoax that was held to be truer than the truth. The desire, obviously, was stronger than any claims of autonomy for philosophies of art or affirmations of historical science, to be relegated when necessary to the status of "theoretical discussions of academics." And although such liberties with the facts cannot be justified or passed over in silence, we cannot fail to recognize, in the persistence of this legend throughout the long career of the *Ode to Joy*, a myth that has earned the right, on its own terms, to be viewed as an historic truth. The nationalist Jahn against the French, the liberal Griepenkerl against the Concert of Europe, the Belgian Wilder for the French Republic, the communist Eisler against the Nazis, the London *Times* against apartheid, Leonard Bernstein at the fall of the Berlin Wall, Deputy Harrison for a democratic Europe — all are historical contexts in which it has been felt — Schiller, Beethoven, and historical fact notwithstanding — that the *Ode to Joy*, in order to justify its status as a political symbol, *ought to have been* an *Ode to Freedom*. The conditional, nevertheless, retains its significance. Perhaps it alone illustrates the narrow distance that still, even today, separates the Ninth Symphony from a simple clockwork orange.

# conclusion

## Criticism and Future of a Dream

Everyone agrees that joy is a good thing, and yet the reasons for feeling joyous can be nearly infinite. Everyone loves Beethoven's Ninth Symphony as well, but everyone has different reasons for esteeming it as a thing of value and beauty. And this is hardly surprising, for a work of art is something that is always open, almost it might be said by definition, to varying and contradictory interpretations. Music, more than any other art, involves semantic ambiguities. We readily accept the idea that it is a language, but rare are the occasions on which we can all agree on what it is trying to say. And it is no easier to isolate its meaning when it is accompanied by a poem, like some excess of light, to trick us into a literal understanding without, however, limiting the proliferation of possible exegeses. In the heart of sound, Schiller's text utters a simple and categorical sentence: "All men will become brothers." And yet, men have various motives for calling themselves brothers, motives that often inspire them to do what is best and most noble, but motives that can sometimes lead them into hatred, violence, murder. For that matter, the same is true of other great ideas, such as those of life, or liberty.

From this viewpoint, the *Ode to Joy*'s career as political music is bound up with that of the other ideals that underlie the history of the modern Western world. And there is a temptation to regard it as exemplary, or to draw some moral from it. Yet making the history of a symbol into a symbol of history is a delicate operation. And that is precisely the operation that this volume has attempted to deconstruct by focusing on those moments that have been instrumental in creating that symbol's societal image bank. Indeed, the aesthetic evolution that has occurred since the romantic era has tended to make works of art a special domain in which the history of a people, a nation, a culture, or any other collective incarnation is played out or brought to fruition. This is particularly obvious in the case of works that are regarded as explicit political symbols. As Richard Wagner wrote, "A national anthem is the mirror of a people's character."[1] By extension, therefore, he who creates that mirror's history also creates that of the people that sees itself in it. Aware as one might be of the optical laws governing reflections — we could replace mirror with, say, film — it is difficult to escape completely the image's enchantment. And it is indeed a bit disquieting to realize the extent to which debates about political symbols seem to insist on becoming syntheses of what they symbolize — so that, for example, when analyzing *God Save the King*, we get the feeling that we are talking about the British system itself, or, to take another example, when describing the speeches about Beethoven delivered during his centenary we feel that we are describing the Western world of the day. Ought we to refuse to find any such generalizations pertinent and continue to repeat stories that always, no matter how we relate them, seem to be speaking about something other than themselves?

In fact, if the history of symbols is as much the history of what they symbolize as it is a history of their methods of symbolization, it is not — as the romantic tradition would have it — that some metaphysical essence of the collective mind finds its expression in such special works but, rather, that the public role of such works is defined by methods of discourse and practices that strive to present an overall view of history and of the society. In passing, that is what sets the boundaries of a study like the present one, for such constructs concentrate the views of the various actors into their most schematic (or ideological) form — or bring out the inconsistencies that reveal their most basic limitations. Thus, the commemoration of the Beethoven centenary in America and in the Soviet Union revealed the nature of the two political cultures that were to define the twentieth century; however, it would be difficult for an analysis of those commemorations to reveal anything that one did not already know about those cultures.

Once methodological precautions have been taken, the mirror image can have a certain pertinence. The legitimacy of the European anthem, for example, should be debated above all in terms of its own history, as a product of all of the acts and facts that contributed to its special legitimization, independent of what Europe may or may not be in other areas. Even so, nothing prevents us from believing that such avatars reflect the difficulties and even the dead ends that have marked the history of European construction from the beginning. The mute anthem of the Europeans suits the fragility or ambitiousness of their collective undertaking, their timorous clinging to nationality, their unrealized dream of universality. And on this subject we can even for a moment play the symbol game ourselves to express a viewpoint on the present or future of Europe. At a time when the creation of the single currency, widely hailed as the concrete realization of old "dreams of brotherhood,"[2] is leading some to cherish great-power fantasies in which can be heard the echoes of a lost world hegemony; at a time when, on the other hand, voices on the far right would like to extend their "national preference" into an equally iniquitous "European preference," the European anthem, if it is to have any significance at all — which, in truth, is far from certain — could serve to recall the democratic, egalitarian, and universalist ideal that the European countries hold up as their intellectual and political banner. The legitimacy of the European anthem thus rests on Europe's fidelity to the values that the Ninth Symphony represents in the eyes of history: the more that the European Union becomes a state devoted to guaranteeing its "solidarity turned against the outside world," the more it will become separated from the "profession of universal faith" of Beethoven's and Schiller's work. In addition, its symbol will in the end be but a pathetic and cynical one. Conversely, any effort that Europe can make to see that throughout the world "all men will become brothers" may perhaps contribute to make up for the lack of legitimacy represented by the particularizing appropriation of a cultural patrimony that belongs to all of mankind, if those words have any meaning at all.

In any event, the ideological implications of Beethoven's work go far beyond the question of Europe. The career of the *Ode to Joy* is a tale that, in a way, can be read as a fable on the moral value of Western art. All who have invoked the Ninth Symphony have begun by experiencing its beauty and ended with the need for its morality; because they revered the Beautiful and because they believed that they knew the Good, they have made that Beautiful the symbol of the Good. The problem is the insistence with which the syllogism has been employed by men who could never in any circumstances have been regarded as representatives of the Good — the first to come to mind, of course, are the Nazis, whom we continue to regard as the principal historical incarnations of Evil. Given the realization, notably expressed by André Boucourechliev, that Beethoven's work constitutes "the musical symbol of a community of mankind, of its aspirations, its revolutions — no less, alas, than it does the weapon of its tyrants,"[3] its use by history's evildoers must always arouse some indignant denunciation. Indeed, such indignation is even a kind of duty. However, it still leaves wide open the question of what leads such clearly immoral persons to lay claim to the moral validity of the same aesthetic experience. In short, on what can the moral content of Beethoven's music be based? And how can one speak about him other than by repeating virtuous clichés?

In the course of the present volume it may have become evident that such a moral value cannot reasonably be based on the musical language itself. The musical rhetoric employed in the Ninth Symphony is one derived from the Platonic Sophists; in other words, it is separate from the truth that it in the end serves to communicate. Put another way, musical language is either amoral or it expresses a notion of morality that includes tyrants — which is the same thing. If such were not the case, tyrants would simply be unable to utter it, it would have no meaning for them. There remains the possibility of deriving such moral content from tradition itself, which, after all, is the tradition of the Enlightenment in which the speech of totalitarianism and racism was regarded as deviant or unfitting. In this direction, however, we risk finding ourselves in the situation in which Felix Weingartner was to find himself in 1927, tormented by the thought of a world being made deaf to the past by the rising cacophony of modernity. What true joy can the fact of repeating the speech of tradition, worn out by a musical *doxa* constructed on the kitsch future of romanticism, bring? If tradition is truly the only source of appeal for a moral truth in music, must one not conclude that tradition may well speak the truth, but that that truth is now become banal?

And yet today the Ninth Symphony remains the prime musical symbol of the moral value of art. Its performance at Sarajevo in 1996 under the baton of Yehudi Menuhin is but one example among many, which include its execution at the Mauthausen concentration camp site in 2000 by Sir Simon Rattle and the Vienna Philharmonic in memory of the victims of the Holocaust. But, in the final analysis, what is the importance of such gestures? In 1977, Maynard Solomon wrote: "If we lose awareness of the transcendent realm of performance, beauty, and brotherhood afforded us by the great affirmative works of our culture, if we lose the 'dream' of the Ninth Symphony, we will have nothing left to balance against the crushing terrors of modern civilization, nothing left to set against Auschwitz and the Vietnam War as a paradigm of human potentialities."[4] We can accept that argument, and perhaps we should. It does not, however, prevent us from remarking on its odd logic, for, "in referring to the Ninth Symphony as a 'dream,' Solomon comes dangerously close to saying that we need something to believe in, even if we don't believe in it."[5] In other words, he is forced to recognize, perhaps despite himself, that the moral content of the Ninth Symphony can only be affirmed pragmatically.

That may still be necessary. But it cannot halt the continuing critical impetus. Must we really accept the principle that art is the ultimate guarantee of the morality of the human endeavor? And if so, must we always call upon Beethoven to attest to that fact? Beethoven against Auschwitz, against the Vietnam War, against the Berlin Wall, against the war in the former Yugoslavia, against massacres to come, yes; but only while we get on with that criticism of tradition that remains the primordial task if we are to continue to maintain that the Ninth Symphony, the vestige of an ever-more-distant world, can still speak to us in any significant way — or if we are prepared to accept the idea that one day (why not?) it may well fall silent without that necessarily being a catastrophe.

# acknowledgments

This book is the result of a seven-year labor that began in 1990 when I arrived in Paris from Bariloche, the small town in Argentinian Patagonia where I had spent my childhood and early school years. At the École des Hautes Études en Sciences Sociales, under the supervision of Jacques Leenhardt, my first research project was concerned with the Argentine national anthem. Mme. Françoise Escal supervised my studies of Alban Berg's *Lyric Suite* and then my doctoral thesis on Beethoven's Ninth Symphony and the construction of a European identity, which resulted in this book. I should like to extend to her my warmest thanks for her counsel and for her constant support during the years I spent researching the subject. I should also like especially to thank Pierre Nora, who encouraged me from the time of my arrival in France when I attended his seminar and who, as a member of the jury for my thesis, afforded me the opportunity to transform it into a book.

The assistance of such very diverse organizations as the Archives of the Council of Europe, the European Union, NATO, and the Republic of Zimbabwe, as well as the New York Public Library and the Bibliothèque Nationale de France, in Paris, allowed me access to a vast bibliography, both musical and historical. My thesis, which was accepted in June 1997, would not have been possible without the financial assistance of the Fundación Antorchas de Buenos Aires and the Fondation de Montcheuil, Paris.

I owe a special debt to Rémy Stricker, whose musicological knowledge and sense of style have made him the ideal reader. Other specialists — who are, needless to say, in no way responsible for any of the work's shortcomings — have played a large part in helping to minimize them: Myriam Chimènes, Georges Liébert, Ivan Alexandre, and Pascal Ory. I am also most grateful to Agnès Heller, Jean-Pierre Lefebvre, Philippe Morin, Leo Treitler, and Charles Rosen, who — without having read the work — have been most generous in sharing their thoughts with me.

I should also like to thank those friends whose support, both intellectual and material, has been most warmly appreciated: Sofia Fischer, Miriam Crivelli, Betina Zolkower, Houda Remita, Maristella Svampa, Martine

Burgos, Céline Gaillot, Marisa Pineau, Miguel Vatter, Francesco Forlani, and Claudio Guthmann.

Lastly — but, indeed, foremost — I should like to express my gratitude to my parents, Lilián Canova and Tomás Buch, whose support has been vital throughout my education. I am especially happy to mention this debt because the history of their emigrant families and of our own "Argentine" family (including my Chilean sister and brother) is also, in a way, a part of the European and Western history with which these pages treat.

ESTEBAN BUCH
*Bariloche and Paris, January 1999*

# notes

**INTRODUCTION**

1. Rolland, Romain, *Beethoven: Les grandes époques créatrices (1966)* (Paris: Albin Michel, 1980), 1327.

2. Bernhard, Thomas, *Maitres anciens* (Paris: Gallimard/Folio, 1985), 102.

3. Richard Wagner to Franz Liszt, 7 June 1955, in *Correspondance de Richard Wagner et de Franz Liszt (1841–1882)* (Paris: Gallimard, 1943), 322.

4. Personal communication from Madame Agnes Heller.

**CHAPTER ONE**

1. Ruth Smith, *Handel's Oratorios and Eighteenth-Century Thought* (Cambridge: Cambridge University Press, 1995), 72.

2. 1 Kings, 1:39–40

3. Daniel Defoe, "Augusta Triumphans" (1728), quoted in Robert James Merrett, "England's Orpheus: Praise of Handel in Eighteenth-Century Poetry," in *Mosaic* 20, no. 2 (Winnipeg, MB: University of Manitoba, 1986), 100.

4. James Miller, 1731 and 1735, quoted respectively in Christopher Hogwood, *Haendel,* trans. D. Collins (Paris: J.-C. Lattès, 1985), 101, and Smith, *Handel's Oratorios,* 72.

5. *Common Sense, or the Englishman's Journal* (London), 10 December 1737.

6. Mr. Dennis, quoted in Smith, *Handel's Oratorios,* 74.

7. Ibid., 108 et seq.

8. Ibid., 210.

9. "A Discourse on the Fall of the Operas," *Common Sense, or the Englishman's Journal,* 14 October 1738, quoted in Otto Deutsch, *Handel: A Documentary Biography* (London: Charles and Adam Black, 1955), 469.

10. H. Diack Jonstone, "Maurice Greene," in *New Grove Dictionary of Music and Musicians,* ed. Stanley Sadie (London: Macmillan Publishers, 1980), 684.

11. Deutsch, *Handel,* 469.

12. Thurston Dart, "Maurice Greene and the National Anthem," *Music and Letters* 37, no. 3 (July 1956), 209.

13. Linda Colley, *Britons: Forging the Nations, 1707–1837* (New Haven and London: Yale University Press, 1992), 81 and 286.

14. The larger part of documentation on this subject consists of debates about the tune's origin. Where the words are concerned, the scriptural source of some lines are evident, but that of the poem itself in its present form is also unknown.

15. Colley, *Britons,* 48.

16. *The Daily Advertiser,* September 1745; reproduced in Percy Scholes, *God Save the Queen! The History and Romance of the World's First National Anthem* (Oxford: Oxford University Press, 1956), ill. 3.

17. See, inter alia, Watkins Shaw, "Church Music in England from the Reformation to the Present Day," in F. Blume, ed., *Protestant Church Music. A History,* (London: Victor Gollancz, 1975).

18. Colley, *Britons,* 44.

19. Official indications for its use were not to be issued until 1933, although these were never sedulously followed.

20. Percy Scholes, *God Save the King! Its History and Its Romance* (Oxford: Oxford University Press, 1942), 16.

21. Haydn's Notebooks, CCLN 276; quoted in H. C. Robbins Landon, *Haydn: Chronicle and Works,* 5 vols. (Bloomington: Indiana University Press, 1976–1980), vol. 3, p. 135. Haydn's transcription of *God Save the King,* which is often referred to as an arrangement, is mentioned in the inventory of his papers but has not been preserved. See, ibid., 317–18.

22. Colley, *Britons,* 216 and 227.

23. Richard Clark, *An Account of the National Anthem Entitled God Save the King* (London, 1822).

24. Oscar Sonneck, *Report on "The Star-Spangled Banner," "Hail Columbia," "America," "Yankee Doodle"* (New York: Dover Publications, 1972); also Scholes, *God Save the Queen,* 190 et seq.

25. Scholes, *God Save the King,* 183.

26. Hans Jürgen Hansen, *Heil Dir im Siegerkranz: Die Hymnen der Deutschen* (Oldenburg: Stalling, 1978), 7–11.

27. Paul Nettl, *National Anthems* (New York: Frederick Ungar, 1967), 44.

28. Colley, *Britons,* 145.

29. Anna Seward, "Remonstrance," 1788, quoted in Merrett, "England's Orpheus," 108.

30. James Beattie (1780), quoted in Deutsch, *Handel,* 855.

31. William Cowper, "The Task," quoted in Merrett, "England's Orpheus," 107.

32. William Weber, *The Rise of Musical Classics in Eighteenth-Century England: A Study in Canon, Ritual, and Ideology* (Oxford: Oxford University Press, 1992), 229.

33. Ibid., 236 and 224.

34. Charles Burney, *An Account of the Musical Performances in Westminster-Abbey and the Pantheon, May 26th, 27th, 29th; and June the 3rd and 5th, 1784, in Commemoration of Handel* (London, 1785).

35. David Cannadine, "The Context, Performance and Meaning of Ritual: The British Monarchy and the 'Invention of Tradition,' c. 1820–1977," in Eric J. Hobsbawn and Terence Ranger, eds., *The Invention of Tradition* (Cambridge: Cambridge University Press, 1983).

36. *London Magazine,* March 1820, quoted in Percy M. Young, "The Indispens-

able Mr. Handel: Changing Perception of a National Composer, *Studia musicologica norvegica,* no. 12 (Universitetsforlaget, 1986), 215.

## CHAPTER TWO

1. Jean-Jacques Rousseau, *Essai sur l'origine des langues,* in *Oeuvres complètes* (Paris: Gallimard-Pléiade, 1995), vol. 5, p. 425.

2. *Dictionnaire de musique,* s.v. "Hymne," 855.

3. J.-J. Rousseau, *Lettre à d'Alembert, OC* (1995), 123, 124.

4. *Dictionnaire de musique,* s.v. "Unisson," 1143.

5. Ibid., s.v. "Musique," 924.

6. J.-J. Rousseau, *Considérations sur le gouvernement de la Pologne,* in *Oeuvres complètes,* ed. P. R. Auguis (Paris: Dalibon, 1825), ch. 4, pp. 219 and 237.

7. Julien Tiersot, *Les Fêtes et les Chants de la Révolution française,* (Paris: Hachette, 1908), xxxiv.

8. Marcel Gauchet, *La Révolution des pouvoirs: La souveraineté, le peuple et la représentation, 1789–1799* (Paris: Gallimard, 1995), 30.

9. Herbert Schneider, "Der Formen- und Funktionswandel in den Chansons und Hymnen der französischen Revolution," in R. Koselleck and R. Reichardt, eds., *Die französische Revolution als Bruch der gesellschaftlichen Bewußtseins* (Munich: Oldenbourg Verlag, 1988).

10. *Journal de la municipalité,* quoted in Constant Pierre, *Les Hymnes et les chansons de la Révolution* (Paris: Imprimerie Nationale, 1904), 199.

11. *Chronique de Paris,* 8 July 1790, 753, 754.

12. Mona Ozouf, *La Fête révolutionnaire, 1789–1799* (Paris: Gallimard-Folio, 1976), 470. See also Jean Starobinski, "Le Serment: David," in *Les Emblèmes de la raison* (Paris: Flammarion, 1979).

13. *Chronique de Paris,* 12 July 1790, 769.

14. *Révolutions de Paris,* quoted in Tiersot, *Les Fêtes et les Chants,* 43 (see also p. 44 n. 17).

15. *Gazette nationale ou le Moniteur universel,* 16 July 1790; taken from *Réimpression de l'ancien Moniteur* (Paris: Plon, 1847).

16. André-Modeste Grétry, *Mémoires, ou Essais sur la musique* (Paris: Imprimerie de la République, Year V), vol. 3, p. 13.

17. *Révolutions de Paris dédiées à la Nation et au District des Petits-Augustins,* no. 145 (14/21 April 1792).

18. Quoted in Julien Tiersot, *Histoire de la Marseillaise* (Paris: Delagrave, 1915), 37.

19. Ibid., 46.

20. Jean-Louis Jam, "Fonction des hymnes révolutionnaires," in *Les Fêtes de la Révolution: Colloque de Clermont-Ferrand* (Paris: Société des études robespierristes, 1977), 440.

21. M. Elizabeth C. Bartlet, "L'Offrande à la Liberté et l'histoire de la Marseil-

laise," in J. R. Julien and J. Mongrédien, eds., *Le Tambour et la harpe: Oeuvres, pratiques et manifestations musicales sous la Révolution, 1788–1800* (Paris: Éd. du May, 1991), 127.

22. *Feuille villageoise,* October 1792, quoted by Frédéric Robert, *La Marseillaise* (Paris: Imprimerie Nationale, 1989), 27.

23. *Moniteur,* 17 October 1792.

24. Paul Nettl, *National Anthems* (New York: Frederick Ungar, 1967), 70.

25. Louis Fiaux, *La Marseillaise* (Paris: Fasquelle, 1918), 339.

26. Norbert Cornelissen, 6 Pluviôse, Year IV (26 January 1796), quoted by Fiaux, *La Marseillaise,* 367.

27. *Journal de Paris national,* 10 August 1793.

28. *Moniteur,* 12 August 1793.

29. *Journal de Paris,* 21 Brumaire, Year II.

30. Danton, *Moniteur,* session of 26 Nivôse, Year II, quoted in Tiersot, *Les Fêtes et les Chants,* 100.

31. Jacques-Louis David, *Plan de la Fête à l'Être suprême qui doit être célébrée le 20 prairial, proposé par David, et décrété par la Convention nationale* (Paris, 1794).

32. Michel Vovelle, *Théodore Desorgues ou la désorganisation: Aix-Paris, 1763–1808* (Paris: Éd. du Seuil, 1985), 105.

33. Letter from the Institut de Musique to the Comité de Salut Public, quoted in Tiersot, *Les Fêtes et les Chants,* 151.

34. Quoted in Jules Michelet, *Histoire de la Révolution française* (Paris: Gallimard-Pléiade, 1952), vol. 2, p. 555.

35. Boissy d'Anglas, quoted by Albert Mathiez, "Robespierre et le culte de l'Être suprême," in *Études sur Robespierre* (Paris: Editions Sociales, 1958), 177.

36. Chénier's stanzas appeared, inter alia, in the *Journal de Paris,* no. 527, 23 Prairial, Year II (11 June 1794), pp. 2129–30.

37. Speech of Deputy Veau before the Convention, *Moniteur,* 23 Prairial, Year II.

38. Mona Ouzouf, "Religion révolutionnaire," in Fr. Furet and J. Ouzouf, eds., *Dictionnaire critique de la Révolution française* (Paris: Flammarion, 1988), 609.

39. Speech of M. J. Chénier before the Convention, 1 Nivôse, Year II, quoted by Tiersot, *Les Fêtes et les Chants,* 205.

40. Report to the Convention, 10 Therminor, Year II, quoted by Constant Pierre, in *Le Conservatoire nationale de musique et de déclamation* (Paris: Imprimerie Nationale, 1900), 121.

41. Letter from Minister Turguet to the Conservatoire de Musique, Pluviôse, Year IV, quoted in Constant Pierre, *Le Magasin de musique à l'usage des fêtes nationales et du Conservatoire* (Paris: Fischbacher, 1895; Geneva: Minkoff Reprint, 1974), 81.

42. Jean-Baptiste Leclerc, *Essai sur la propagation de la musique en France, sa conservation et ses rapports avec le gouvernement* (Paris: Imprimerie Nationale, Year IV [1795]), 36 and 40.

43. La Révellière-Lépeaux, *Essai sur les moyens de faire participer l'universalité*

*des spectateurs à tout ce qui se pratique dans les fêtes nationales (1797),* quoted by Jean Mongrédien, in *La Musique en France des Lumières au Romantisme, 1789–1830* (Paris: Flammarion, 1986), 40.

44. See, Mathiez, Albert, *La Théophilanthropie et la culte décadaire 1796–1801,* Paris, 1904, pp. 144 and 449.

## CHAPTER THREE

1. Schiller to Gottfried Körner, 11 July 1785, quoted in Edmond Eggli, *Schiller et le Romantisme français* (Paris, 1927; reprint, Geneva: Slatkine, 1970), 37.

2. Rousseau to Count Gregory Grigorievitch Orlof, at Wooton, 28 February 1767; published in July 1767 at The Hague in *Mercure historique et politique: Correspondance complète de Jean-Jacques Rousseau,* letter 5673 (Oxford: The Voltaire Foundation at the Taylor Institution, 1978), vol. 32, pp. 45–46.

3. See Franz Schultz, "Die Göttin Freude: Zur Geistes- und Stilgeschichte des 18. Jahrhunderts," *Jahrbuch des Freien Deutschen Hochstifts* (1926), 31.

4. See Uwe Martin, "Freude Freiheit Götterfunken: Über Schillers Schwierigkeiten beim Schreiben von Freiheit," *Cahiers d'études germaniques,* no. 8 (1990), 9–18.

5. Friedrich Schiller, *Don Carlos, Infant d'Espagne,* act 3, scene 8.

6. Wieland, "Über Schillers Lied An die Freude, Eine Vorlesung im Zirkel einiger Freunde aus den Jahr 1793," in *Neuen Teutschen Merkur* (1793), vol. 2, pp. 21 et seq. From *Monatshefte des Comenius-Gesellschaft,* N.F.B. 5 H. 5 (1913), 179–88.

7. Recollection of the poet Magenau, quoted by P. Berteaux and G. Stieg, in "Beethoven et Schiller," in "Aspects de la littérature autrichienne au XXè siècle," *Austriaca, Cahiers universitaires d'information sur l'Autriche,* no. 23 (December 1896), 15.

8. Quoted by Rudolph Dau, "Friedrich Schillers Hymne 'An die Freude,' Zu einigen Problemen ihrer Interpretation und aktuellen Rezeption," in *Weimarer Beiträge: Zeitschrift für Literaturwissenschaft, Äesthetik und Kulturtheorie,* no. 24:10 (Weimar, 1978), 39.

9. Ibid.

10. Schiller, tenth of the *Lettres sur Don Carlos,* in *Oeuvres,* vol. 3 (Paris: Hachette, 1859), 243.

11. Bartolomäus Ludwig Fischenich to Charlotte von Schiller, 26 January 1793, quoted by A. W. Thayer and E. Forbes, *Thayer's Life of Beethoven,* 2 vols. (Princeton: Princeton University Press, 1967), 121.

12. *Berlinische musikalische Zeitung* 2, no. 12 (Spring 1806), quoted by Max Friedlander, in *Das deutsche Lied im 18. Jahrhundert* (Stuttgart, 1902), vol. 2, p. 394. See also Joseph Müller-Blattau, "Das Finale der Neunten Sinfonie (Von Formen und Entwicklungsgeschichte)," in *Von der Vielfalt der Musik* (Freiburg-im-Breisgau: Verlag Rombach, 1966).

13. Charles Rosen, *The Classical Style* (New York: W. W. Norton, 1972), 332.

14. Schiller, "Des poésies de Bürger" (1971), in *Oeuvres,* vol. 7, p. 367.

15. Jean Philippon, "Patriotes et patriotisme d'après Joseph von Sonnenfels," in *Les Prémices de la Révolution française en Autriche* (Nice: Faculté des Lettres et Science Humaines, 1990), 122.

16. Swieten, *Allgemeine musikalische Zeitung* (1799); quoted in Tia DeNora, *Beethoven and the Construction of Genius: Musical Politics in Vienna, 1792–1803* (Berkeley, Los Angeles, and London: University of California Press, 1995), 26.

17. Burney, *Monthly Review,* October 1791, quoted in H. C. Robbins Landon, *Haydn: Chronicle and Works,* 5 vols. (Bloomington: Indiana University Press, 1976–1980), vol. 3, p. 103.

18. *Österreichische Monatschrift,* quoted in Landon, *Haydn,* 226.

19. Charles Ingrao, *The Habsburg Monarchy, 1618–1815* (Cambridge: Cambridge University Press, 1994), 225.

20. Ernst Wangermann, *From Joseph II to the Jacobine Trials* (Oxford: Oxford University Press, 1959), 112.

21. Eduard Hanslick, *Geschichte des Concertwesens in Wien* (Vienna, 1969; facsimile, London: Gregg International Publishers, 1971), 172.

22. Haydn to his biographer Griesinger, quoted in Marc Vignal, *Joseph Haydn* (Paris: Fayard, 1988), 1329.

23. Karl Roider, *Baron Thugut and Austria's Response to the French Revolution* (Princeton: Princeton University Press, 1987), 223.

24. Thugut to Colloredo, quoted in the original French in Wangermann, *From Joseph II . . . ,* 185.

25. For the background of *Gott erhalte,* the primary source is Franz Grasberger, *Die Hymnen Österreichs* (Tutzing: H. Schneider, 1968); all of the documents with reference to *Gott erhalte* utilized in the present work appear there.

26. Otto Deutsch, "Haydn's Hymn and Burney's Translation," *Music Review* 8 (London, 1943), 158.

27. Herbert Schneider, "Der Formen- und Funktionswandel in den Chansons und Hymnen der französischen Revolution," in R. Koselleck and R. Reichardt, eds., *Die französische Revolution als Bruch der gesellschaftlichen Bewußtseins* (Munich: Oldenburg Verlag, 1988), 446.

28. Saurau to the Prague authorities, 30 January 1797, quoted in Grasberger, *Die Hymnen Österreichs,* by Vignal, *Joseph Haydn,* 526.

29. *Wiener Zeitung,* 22 February 1797, quoted in Vignal, *Joseph Haydn,* 525.

30. *Der Eipeldauer,* quoted (undated) by Vignal, *Joseph Haydn,* 525.

31. *Magazin der Kunst und Literatur,* quoted (undated) by Grasberger, *Die Hymnen Österreichs,* 31.

32. Otto Biba, *Gott erhalte! Joseph Haydns Kaiserhymne,* facsimile of the first edition (1797) (Vienna: Doblinger, 1982).

33. C. F. Pohl, quoted in Grasberger, *Die Hymnen Österreichs,* 29.

34. Saurau to Dietrichtstein, 28 February 1820, quoted in Grasberger, *Die Hymnen Österreichs,* 36.

35. See Elaine Sismon, *Haydn and the Classical Variation* (Cambridge and London: Harvard University Press, 1993), 178.

36. Laszlo Somfai, "'Learned Style' in Two Late String Quartet Movements by Haydn," *Studia Musicologica* 28 (Budapest, 1986), 325-49.

37. Cecil Gray, *The Haydn String Quartet Society,* vol. 4 (London: Haydn String Quartet Society, 1935), 15.

38. Quoted in Vignal, *Joseph Haydn,* 337; original in French.

39. Hanns Jäger-Sunstenau, "Beethoven als Bürger der Stadt Wien," in S. Kross and H. Schmidt, eds., *Colloquium Amicorum: Festschrift Joseph Schmidt-Görg zum 70. Geburtstag* (Bonn: Beethovenhaus, 1967), 34.

40. Landon, *Haydn,* vol. 4, p. 344.

41. *Morning Herald,* 29 March 1800, quoted in ibid., 574.

42. *Allgemeine musikalische Zeitung,* quoted in ibid., 580 and 586.

43. Theophil Antonicek, "'Vergangenheit muss unsre Zukunft bilden': Die patriotische Musikbewegung in Wien und ihr Vorkämpfer Ignaz von Mosel," *Revue Belge de musicologie* 26-27 (Brussels, 1972-1973).

44. *Vaterlandischen Blätter,* quoted in ibid., 31, and in Mary Sue Morrow, *Concert Life in Haydn's Vienna: Aspects of a Developing Musical and Social Institution* (Stuyvesant, NY: Pendragon Press, 1989), 22.

45. Vignal, *Joseph Haydn,* 705.

46. Neukomm, *Bemerkungen,* quoted in ibid., 717.

47. Ibid., 728.

48. Anton Schmid, *Jopseh Haydn et Niccolo Zingarelli* (1847), quoted in ibid., 517.

49. See the refutation of Schmid in Grasberger, *Die Hymnen Österreichs,* 26. Landon, who did acknowledge the lack of historical bases for this anecdote in his authoritative five-volume work, gives Schmid's text only in his condensed version for the "general public"; see, respectively, *Haydn,* vol. 4, p. 244, and *Haydn: A Documentary Study* (New York: Rizzoli, 1981), 177-78.

**CHAPTER FOUR**

1. The text of the *Choral Fantasy* is usually attributed to Beethoven's friend, the poet Christoph Kuffner; this has been questioned by Gustav Nottebohm. See A. W. Thayer and E. Forbes, *Thayer's Life of Beethoven,* 2 vols. (Princeton: Princeton University Press, 1967), 451.

2. Maynard Solomon, *Beethoven* (Paris: J.-C. Lattès, 1985), 175.

3. Tia DeNora, *Beethoven and the Construction of Genius: Musical Politics in Vienna, 1792-1803* (Berkeley, Los Angeles, and London: University of California Press, 1995), 60.

4. Maynard Solomon, "The Nobility Pretense," in *Beethoven Essays* (Cambridge and London: Harvard University Press, 1988), 313 n. 48.

5. See, inter alia, J. Tiersot, "Beethoven, musicien de la Révolution française," *Revue de Paris* 17 (Paris, 1910); Arnold Schmitz, *Das romantische Beethovenbild: Darstellung und Kritik* (Berlin and Bonn: F. Dümmlers Verlag, 1927); Claude Palisca, "French Revolutionary Models for Beethoven's Eroica Funeral March," in *Music and Context: Essays for John M. Ward* (Cambridge: Harvard University Press, 1985); and Ulrich Schmitt, *Revolution im Konzertsaal* (Mainz: Schott, 1990).

6. Pfarrer Christmann, "Einige Ideen über den Geist der französischen Nation-allieder," in *Allgemeine musikalische Zeitung,* nos. 15–16–17 (16–23 January 1799).

7. See contemporary criticism in Stefan Kunze, ed., *Ludwig van Beethoven: Die Werke im Spiegel seiner Zeit* (Laaber: Laaber-Verlag, 1987), 50–68.

8. E. T. A. Hoffmann, *Écrits sur la musique* (Lausanne: L'Âge d'homme, 1985), 40.

9. Robin Wallace, *Beethoven's Critics. Aesthetic Dilemmas and Resolutions During the Composer's Lifetime* (Cambridge: Cambridge University Press, 1986), 24.

10. Thayer and Forbes, *Thayer's Life of Beethoven,* vol. 1, p. 456.

11. Quoted by J. and B. Massin, *Ludwig van Beethoven* (Paris: Le Club français du livre, 1967), 270.

12. "Concert Anzeige," Vienna (Autumn 1813), quoted by Michael Ladenburger, "Der Wiener Kongress im Spiegel der Musik," in H. Lühning and S. Brandenburg, eds., *Beethoven zwischen Revolution und Restauration* (Bonn: Beethoven-Haus, 1989), 276.

13. Thomas Röder, "Beethovens Sieg über die Schlachtenmusik: Op. 91 und die Tradition der Battaglia," in Lühning and Brandenburg, *Beethoven zwischen Revolution und Restauration,* 241 et seq.

14. Zelter to Goethe, quoted in Eduard Hanslick, *Geschichte des Concertwesens in Wien* (Vienna, 1969; facsimile, London: Gregg International Publishers, 1971), 74.

15. See criticisms of Opus 91 in Kunze, *Ludwig van Beethoven,* 267–88.

16. Anton Schindler, *Beethoven as I Knew Him* (1860), ed. Donald MacArdle, trans. Constance Jolly (Chapel Hill: University of North Carolina Press; London: Faber and Faber, 1966), 170.

17. Quoted in Thayer and Forbes, *Thayer's Life of Beethoven,* vol. 1, p. 566.

18. Solomon, *Beethoven,* 250.

19. Thayer and Forbes, *Thayer's Life of Beethoven,* vol. 1, pp. 566, 567.

20. Quoted in Massin, *Ludwig van Beethoven,* 270.

21. Erich Schenk, "Salieris *Landsturm*-Kantate von 1799 in ihren Beziehungen zu Beethovens *Fidelio*," in S. Kross and H. Schmidt, eds., *Colloquium Amicorum: Festschrift Joseph Schmidt-Görg zum 70. Geburtstag* (Bonn: Beethovenhaus, 1967).

22. Although Romain Rolland merely expressed surprise at the lack of any reference to the *Marseillaise* in Beethoven's work, Jean and Brigitte Massin find that its

absence from Opus 91 is a proof, a contrario, of the composer's republican sympathies. For Röder, on the other hand, the absence can be explained by the piece's non-official status under the empire, and by the fact that the Viennese had received it with "ambivalence." See, Romain Rolland, *Beethoven: Les grandes époques créatrices (1966)* (Paris: Albin Michel, 1980), 417; Massin, *Ludwig van Beethoven,* 270–71; Röder, "Beethovens Sieg," 247.

23. Solomon, *Beethoven,* 251–52.

24. See Thayer and Forbes, *Thayer's Life of Beethoven,* 594; Ladenburger, "Der Wiener Kongress," 288.

25. Quoted by G. de Bertier de Sauvigny, "Metternich et l'Europe," in *Le Congrès de Vienne et l'Europe — The Congress of Vienna and Europe* (Brussels and Paris: Brepols, Commission internationale pour l'enseignement de l'histoire, 1966), 11 and 14.

26. Ibid., 15.

27. G. A. Chevallaz, "Le traité de Vienne et la construction de l'Europe," in *Le Congrès de Vienne et l'Europe,* 110.

28. Germaine de Staël, *De l'Allemagne* (Paris: Garnier-Flammarion, 1968), vol. 1, p. 70.

29. Antoine de la Garde, *Fêtes et souvenirs du Congrès de Vienne,* 2 vols. (Paris: Appert, 1843), vol. 1, p. 15.

30. Maurice-Henri Weil, *Les Dessous du Congrès de Vienne,* 2 vols. (Paris: Payot, 1917), 114 and 372.

31. De la Garde, *Fêtes et souvenirs,* vol. 1, pp. 122–23.

32. Ibid., 55.

33. See George L. Mosse, *The Nationalization of the Masses: Political Symbolism and Mass Movements in Germany from the Napoleonic Wars through the Third Reich* (Ithaca and London: Cornell University Press, 1975).

34. Quoted in Hilde Spiel, ed., *The Congress of Vienna: An Eyewitness Account* (Philadelphia, New York, and London: Chilton Book Co., 1969), 129.

35. Schindler, *Beethoven,* 205.

36. Beethoven to Archduke Rudolph, undated, quoted in Massin, *Ludwig van Beethoven,* 280.

37. Ladenburger, "Der Wiener Kongress," 295. For J. K. Bernard's text, see Wilhelm Virneseil, "Kleine Beethoveniana," in Dagmar Weise, ed., *Festschrift Joseph Schmidt-Görg zum 60. Geburtstag* (Bonn: Beethovenhaus, 1957), 366.

38. Gustav Nottebohm, "Beethoven und Weissenbach," *Beethoveniana: Aufsätze und Mittheilungen* (Leipzig and Winterthur: J. Rieter-Biedermann, 1872), 145 and 147.

39. See Thayer and Forbes, *Thayer's Life of Beethoven,* vol. 1, p. 599, and Journal of Carl Bertuch, quoted by Spiel, *The Congress of Vienna,* 123.

40. *Wiener Zeitung,* 30 November 1814, quoted in Ladenburger, "Der Wiener Kongress," 304.

41. Memoirs of Karl von Bursy (1854), quoted by Massin, *Ludwig van Beethoven,* 306.

42. Report 938, X to Hager, in Weil, *Les Dessous du Congrès de Vienne,* vol. 1, p. 619.

### CHAPTER FIVE

1. See Gustav Nottebohm, "Skizzen zur neunten Symphonie," *Zweite Beethoveniana* (Leipzig: Rieter-Biedermann, 1876), 156 et seq.

2. J. and B. Massin, *Ludwig van Beethoven* (Paris: Le Club français du livre, 1967), 249.

3. "The poetic idea of the work was not changed — the joy of liberated Europe simply taking the place of the joy of Schiller's poem." A. W. Thayer and E. Forbes, *Thayer's Life of Beethoven,* 2 vols. (Princeton: Princeton University Press, 1967), 597.

4. Haydn was an "honorary citizen" (*Ehrenbürger*), whereas Beethoven only enjoyed "citizen's rights" (*Bürgerrecht*) and an exemption from taxes. Other contemporary musicians were given honorific titles for the same reason. See Hanns Jäger-Sunstenau, "Beethoven als Bürger der Stadt Wien," in S. Kross and H. Schmidt, eds., *Colloquium Amicorum: Festschrift Joseph Schmidt-Görg zum 70. Geburtstag* (Bonn: Beethovenhaus, 1967).

5. Maynard Solomon, "The Nobility Pretense," in *Beethoven Essays* (Cambridge and London: Harvard University Press, 1988), 43.

6. Letter from Schindler to Dehn, 10 March 1846, quoted in Massin, *Ludwig van Beethoven,* 352.

7. Thayer and Forbes, *Thayer's Life of Beethoven,* vol. 2, p. 647.

8. Bursy, quoted in Massin, *Ludwig van Beethoven,* 306.

9. *Cahiers de conversation de Beethoven,* translated and presented by J.-G. Prod'homme (Paris: Corrêa, 1946), 224.

10. Quoted in Thayer and Forbes, *Thayer's Life of Beethoven,* vol. 2, p. 840.

11. Beethoven to Archduke Rudolph, June 1819, quoted in ibid., 719.

12. Beethoven to Archduke Rudolph, quoted in Massin, *Ludwig van Beethoven,* 412.

13. Schindler to Beethoven, 9 July 1823, quoted in Thayer and Forbes, *Thayer's Life of Beethoven,* vol. 2, p. 830.

14. Thayer and Forbes, *Thayer's Life of Beethoven,* vol. 2, p. 834.

15. Ibid.

16. According to Rochlitz, quoted in Massin, *Ludwig van Beethoven,* 387.

17. Anton Schindler, *Beethoven as I Knew Him* (1860), ed. Donald MacArdle, trans. Constance Jolly (Chapel Hill: University of North Carolina Press; London: Faber and Faber, 1966), 273.

18. Thayer and Forbes, *Thayer's Life of Beethoven,* vol. 2, p. 897 et seq.

19. Schindler, *Beethoven*, 275.

20. Thayer and Forbes, *Thayer's Life of Beethoven*, vol. 2, p. 899.

21. Beethoven to the censor von Sartorius, April 1924, in *The Letters of Beethoven*, trans. and ed. E. Anderson (New York: St. Martin's Press, 1961), letter 1278, vol. 3, p. 1120.

22. Thayer and Forbes, *Thayer's Life of Beethoven*, vol. 2, p. 910.

23. Quoted in Massin, *Ludwig van Beethoven*, 421.

24. Thayer and Forbes, *Thayer's Life of Beethoven*, vol. 2, pp. 909–10.

25. Schindler, *Beethoven*, 279.

26. Beethoven to Friedrich Wilhelm III, quoted in Thayer and Forbes, *Thayer's Life of Beethoven*, vol. 2, p.1002.

27. It is possible that Beethoven may have set *An die Freude* to music at least once prior to the Ninth Symphony. A sketchbook dated 1798–1799 contains a melody for the verse *Muss ein lieber Vater wohnen;* in a letter of 1803, Ferdinand Ries referred to a *lied* to Schiller's poem that Beethoven had composed "in the four previous years." No other trace of this work, if it ever indeed existed, has been found.

28. Beethoven to Gräfin Marie Erdödy, 19 October 1815, in *Beethoven's Letters*, ed. A. Eaglefield-Hull (New York: Dover Publications, 1972), 180.

29. Roland Barthes, "Musica Practica," in *Beethoven*, a special issue of *L'Arc*, no. 40 (1970).

30. Robert Winter, "The Sketches for the 'Ode to Joy,'" in R. Winter and B. Carr, eds., *Beethoven: Performers and Critics* (Detroit: Wayne State University Press, 1980), 192.

31. Nottebohm, "Skizzen zur neunten Symphonie."

32. Romain Rolland, *Beethoven: Les grandes époques créatrices (1966)* (Paris: Albin Michel, 1980), 935.

33. Leo Treitler, "History, Criticism, and Beethoven's Ninth Symphony," in *Music and the Historical Imagination* (Cambridge: Harvard University Press, 1989), 26.

34. James Webster, "The Form of the Finale of Beethoven's Ninth Symphony," in *Beethoven Forum*, vol. 1, ed. L. Lockwood and J. Webster (Lincoln: University of Nebraska Press, 1992), 28.

35. Martin Cooper, *Beethoven: The Last Decade, 1817–1827* (London: Oxford University Press, 1985), 337–38.

36. *Cahiers de conversation de Beethoven,* 107. The quotation is a paraphrase of a passage in Kant's *Critique of Pure Reason* that Beethoven would have read in an article by Joseph Littrow entitled "Kosmologische Betrachtungen," which appeared in the *Wiener Zeitung* in January–February 1820.

37. Kant, Emmanuel, *Critique of the Power of Judgment.* Quoted in Andreas Eichhorn, *Beethovens Neunte Symphonie: Die Geschichte ihrer Aufführung und Rezeption* (Kassel, Basel, and London: Bärenreiter, 1993), 226.

## CHAPTER SIX

1. See "The Funeral," in O. G. Sonneck, ed., *Beethoven: Impressions by His Contemporaries* (New York: Dover Publications, 1967), 227; archives of the Vienna Supreme Court and the article *Der Sammler,* quoted in A. W. Thayer and E. Forbes, *Thayer's Life of Beethoven,* 2 vols. (Princeton: Princeton University Press, 1967), vol. 2, pp. 1052–55; see also Gerhard von Breuning, *Memories of Beethoven: From the House of the Black-Robed Spaniards,* ed. M. Solomon (Cambridge: Cambridge University Press, 1992), 107–13.

2. Letter from Zmeskall to Thérèse von Brunsvik, quoted in Romain Rolland, *Beethoven: Les grandes époques créatrices (1966)* (Paris: Albin Michel, 1980),1324, n.

3. This had been part of the incidental music for *Leonore Prohaska,* a never-performed play written by a secretary to the king of Prussia; it was the story of a woman who had fought in the Napoleonic wars disguised as a man. See Thayer and Forbes, *Thayer's Life of Beethoven,* 619.

4. The German text, by Grillparzer, can be found in *Almanach der deutschen Musikbücherei* (Regensburg: Gustav Bosse Verlag, 1927); the present English translation is from Thayer and Forbes, *Thayer's Life of Beethoven,* vol. 2, appendix A, pp. 1057 et seq.

5. Quoted in Rolland, *Beethoven,* 286.

6. Quoted in Aleida Assmann, *Construction de la mémoire nationale: Une brève histoire de l'idée allemande de Bildung* (Paris: Éditions de la Maison des sciences de l'homme, 1994), 24.

7. Reinhardt Koselleck, "Einleitung: Zur anthropologischen und semantischen Struktur der Bildung," in R. Koselleck, ed., *Bildungsbürgertum im 19. Jahrhunderts* (Stuttgart: Klett-Cotte, 1990), 29.

8. Carl Dahlhaus, "Das deutsche Bildungsbürgertum und die Musik," in ibid., 228.

9. Adolf Bernhard Marx, "Symphonie avec choeur final sur l'*Ode à la joie* de Schiller," *Revue musicale* (Paris, 1827), vol. 1, pp. 134–35. The article had originally appeared in the *Berlinische musikalische Zeitung,* vol. 3, no. 47 (1826).

10. *Allgemeine musikalische Zeitung,* vol. 26, no. 26 (1 July 1824), 441.

11. Leon Botstein, "History, Rhetoric, and the Self: Robert Schumann and Music Making in German-Speaking Europe, 1800–1860," in L. Todd, ed., *Schumann and His World* (Princeton: Princeton University Press, 1994), 19.

12. Robert Schumann, in *Music and Musicians: Essays and Criticisms,* trans. Fanny Raymond Ritter (New York: Edward Schuberth and Co., 1881), 61.

13. Robert Griepenkerl, *Das Musikfest oder die Beethovener* (Leipzig, 1838), 206; quoted in Andreas Eichhorn, *Beethovens Neunte Symphonie: Die Geschichte ihrer Aufführung und Rezeption* (Kassel, Basel, and London: Bärenreiter, 1993), 302 et seq. and Ulrich Schmitt, *Revolution im Konzertsaal* (Mainz: Schott, 1990), 242 et seq.

14. Siegfried Kross, "Heinrich Carl Breidenstein," in *Bonner Gelehrte: Beiträge*

*zur Geschichte der Wissenschaften in Bonn,* vol. 6 (Bonn: Bouvier-Röhrscheid, 1968).

15. "Erinnerung an Beethoven," *Bonner Wochenblatt,* 5 July 1832; quoted in Willi Kahl, "Zur Geschichte des Bonner Beethovendenkmals," *Beethoven-Jahrbuch,* new series 2, no. 14 (Bonn: Beethovenhaus, 1953–1954), 69.

16. Thomas Nipperdey, "Nationalidee und Nationaldenkmal in Deutschland im 19. Jahrhundert," *Historische Zeitschrift,* vol. 206, no. 3 (June 1968) (Munich: Oldenbourg Verlag), 557.

17. Translated from German in *Revue et gazette musicale de Paris,* 3rd year, no. 19 (8 May 1836), 149.

18. Ibid., 9th year, no. 42 (16 October 1842), 413.

19. Jean-Claude Bonnet, "Naissance du Panthéon," *Poétique,* no. 33, Seuil (February 1978), 59.

20. Assman, *Construction de la mémoire nationale,* 51.

21. *Les Tablettes de Polymnie,* 2nd year, no. 24 (10 May 1811), 371.

22. *Le Globe,* Paris, 5 April 1827, 10.

23. According to a chronology established by A. Jauffret, quoted in Danièle Pistone, "Beethoven et Paris: Repères historiques et évocations contemporaines," *Beethoven à Paris,* special issue of *Revue internationale de musique française,* no. 22 (Paris and Geneva: Champion/Slatkine, 1987), 10.

24. Antoine-Élie Elwart, *Histoire de la Société des concerts du Conservatoire impérial de musique* (Paris: Castel, 1860), 131.

25. Castil-Blaze, "Chronique musicale: Concerts du Conservatoire," *Le Journal des débats,* 19 March 1828, quoted in J.-G. Prod'homme, *Les Symphonies de Beethoven* (1906; Paris: Charles Delagrave, 1909; reprint, New York: Da Capo Press, 1977), 124.

26. *Le Correspondant,* Paris, 4 and 11 August, 8 October 1829. The majority of Berlioz's articles on Beethoven have been collected by J.-G. Prod'homme in *Beethoven, by Hector Berlioz* (Paris: Buchet-Chastel, 1979). The articles from *Le Correspondant,* however, are not included in that volume.

27. François-Joseph Fétis, *Revue musicale,* 2 April 1831, vol. 11, p. 70, and 1829, vol. 5, p. 130.

28. Berlioz, *Beethoven,* 70.

29. Chrétien Urhan, *Le Temps,* 25 January 1838; quoted by Prod'homme, *Les Symphonies de Beethoven,* 462.

30. Ralph Locke, *Les Saint-simoniens et la musique* (Paris: Mardaga, 1992), 94–95 and 129.

31. Honoré de Balzac, *Massimilla Doni, La Comédie humaine,* vol. 9, p. 355. Quoted in Françoise Escal, *Contrepoints: Musique et littérature* (Paris: Méridiens-Klincksieck, 1990), 41.

32. "Avis aux admirateurs de Beethoven," *Revue et gazette musicale de Paris,* 3rd year, no. 17 (24 April 1836), 135.

33. Heinrich Karl Breidenstein, *Zur Jahresfeier der Inauguration des Beethoven-Monuments: Eine achtenmässige Darstellung dieses Ereignisses, der Wahrheit zur Ehre und den Festgenossen zur Erinnerung* (Bonn, 1846), 6.

34. "The Beethoven Commemoration," *Musical World,* vol. 6, no. 71 (21 July 1837), 91.

35. Hector Berlioz, "Deuxième concert du Conservatoire," *Revue et gazette musicale de Paris,* 24 April 1836, 134.

36. Hector Berlioz, *Mémoires* (Paris, 1870; facsimile, Westmead: Gregg International Publishers, 1969), 461.

37. Berlioz, "Deuxième concert du Conservatoire," *Revue et gazette musicale de Paris,* 28 January 1841, 60-61.

38. Robert Schumann, "Discours de Carnaval de Florestan débité à la suite d'une exécution de la dernière symphonie de Beethoven" (1835), in *Sur les musiciens* (Paris: Stock, Musique, 1979), 291.

39. Robert Schumann, "Monument à la gloire de Beethoven (Quatre opinions)," ibid., p. 37 et. seq.; original in *Neue Zeitschrift für Musik,* 24 June 1836.

40. Charles Rosen, *The Classical Style* (New York: W. W. Norton, 1972), 451.

41. Schumann to Clara Wieck, 19 March 1838, quoted by Bodo Bischoff, *Monument für Beethoven: Die Entwicklung der Beethoven-Rezeption Robert Schumanns* (Cologne: C. Dohr, 1994), 201.

42. Grillparzer, "Klara Wieck und Beethoven," in "Beethoveniana," *Almanach der deutschen Musikbücherei,* 64.

43. Schumann to Clara Wieck, February 1838, *Briefwechsel,* vol. 1, p. 94, quoted by Bischoff, *Monument für Beethoven,* 239.

44. Schumann, "Symphonie en ut majeur" (1840), in *Sur les musiciens,* 101.

45. Bischoff, *Monument für Beethoven,* 201.

46. Alan Walker, *Franz Liszt* (Ithaca: Cornell University Press, 1988).

47. Note the almost total lack of coincidence between the names included in the subscribers' lists printed by the *Revue et gazette musicale de Paris* (here 11 April 1839, p. 117) and the subscribers listed by Élisabeth Bernard in "Les abonnés à la Société des concerts du Conservatoire en 1837," in P. Bloom, ed., *Music in Paris in the Eighteen-Thirties / La Musique à Paris dans les années mil huit cent trente* (Stuyvesant, NY: Pendragon Press, 1987).

48. *Revue et gazette musicale de Paris,* 6th year, no. 12 (24 March 1839), 89.

49. Ibid., 6th year, no. 52 (20 October 1839), 415.

50. Franz Liszt, "Lettre d'un bachelier ès musique à M. Hector Berlioz," *Revue et gazette musicale de Paris,* 6th year, no. 53 (24 October 1839), 419.

51. Jules Maurel, "Les 424 francs de la souscription pour le monument de Beethoven," *La France musicale,* 2nd year, no. 60 (27 October 1839), 559-60.

52. Quoted in Walker, *Franz Liszt,* 280.

53. Jopseh d'Ortigue, "Études biographiques: I. Frantz Litz (*sic*)," *Revue et gazette musicale de Paris,* 2nd year, no. 24 (14 June 1835), 202.

54. Hector Berlioz, "Listz (*sic*)," ibid., 3rd year, no. 24 (12 June 1836), 200.

55. *Revue et gazette . . .* , 8th year, no. 31 (2 May 1841).

56. Ibid., 7th year, no. 1 (2 January 1840), 10.

**CHAPTER SEVEN**

1. Henry Fothergill Chorley, "The Beethoven-Festival at Bonn, 1845," *Modern German Music,* vol. 2 (London, 1854); reprinted in *Liszt Saeculum,* no. 25 (Centre international Liszt pour la musique du XIXe siècle, 1979), 112.

2. See Willi Kahl, "Zur Geschichte des Bonner Beethovendenkmals," *Beethoven-Jahrbuch,* new series 2, no. 14 (Bonn: Beethovenhaus, 1953–1954), 72.

3. *Revue et gazette musicale de Paris,* 12th year, no. 26 (29 June 1845), 216.

4. Ibid., 12th year, no. 31 (3 August 1845), 256.

5. Jules Janin, "Fêtes en l'honneur de Beethoven," *Le Journal des débats,* Paris, 13 and 18 August 1845.

6. *Revue et gazette musicale de Paris,* 12th year, no. 31 (3 August 1845), 256.

7. Antoine-Élie Elwart, letters to *La Presse* (1845), reprinted in *Histoire de la Société des concerts du Conservatoire impérial de musique* (Paris: Castel, 1860), 370.

8. *Revue et gazette musicale de Paris,* 12th year, no. 30 (27 July 1845), 247; italics in original.

9. Léon Kreutzer, "Grands festivals de Bonn à l'occasion de l'inauguration de la statue de Beethoven," ibid., 12th year, no. 33 (17 August 1845), 266.

10. Berlioz to his sister Adèle Suat, 6 June 1845, *Correspondance générale,* vol. 3, 1842–1850 (Paris: Flammarion, 1978), 254.

11. Hector Berlioz, "Fêtes en l'honneur de Beethoven," *Le Journal des débats,* 22 August and 3 September 1845; reprinted in *Les Soirées de l'orchestre* (1852) (Paris: Gründ, 1968), and in *Beethoven* (Paris: Buchet-Chastel, 1979).

12. *Le Ménestrel,* 12th year, no. 36 (5 August 1845).

13. Guido Pannain, "La cultura di Beethoven in Italia," *Neues Beethoven-Jahrbuch,* vol. 1 (Augsburg: B. Filser, 1924), 186.

14. J. Janin, "Fêtes en l'honneur de Beethoven."

15. Quoted in Percy M. Young, *Beethoven, a Victorian Tribute: Based on the Papers of Sir George Smart* (London: Dennis Dobson, 1976), 82.

16. See Raoul Girardet, *Le Nationalisme français: Anthologie, 1871–1914* (Paris: Seuil/Points, 1983), 8. *Le Dictionnaire universel* de Pierre Larousse (1874) utilized the Berlioz quotation to illustrate the pejorative sense of the term.

17. Quoted in W. M. A. Little, "Mendelssohn and Liszt," in *Mendelssohn Studies,* R. L. Todd, ed. (Cambridge: Cambridge University Press, 1992), 125.

18. *Le Ménestrel,* 12th year, no. 31 (29 June 1845).

19. J. W. Davison, "Letters on the Bonn Festival," *Musical World,* vol. 20, no. 35 (28 August 1845), and no. 40 (2 October 1845).

20. See Alan Walker, *Franz Liszt* (Ithaca: Cornell University Press, 1988), 441.

21. Robert Schumann, *Tagebücher,* vol. 2, 1836–1854, ed. G. Nauhaus (Leipzig:

Strömfeld/Roter Stern, Deutscher Verlag für Musik, 1987), 393–96; letter from Schumann to Liszt of 1 August 1845, ibid., note. 699.

22. Karl Schorn, "Das Beethovenfest in Bonn," in *Lebenserrinerungen: Ein Beitrag zur Geschichte des Rheinlands im neunzehnten Jahrhundert* (Bonn: Hanstein Verlag, 1898), 207.

23. Berlioz to his sister Nanci Pal, 26 June 1845, *Correspondance générale,* vol. 3, p. 277.

24. Louis Spohr, *Lebenserrinerungen* (Tutzing: Hans Schneider Verlag, 1968), 180.

25. Janin, "Fêtes en l'honneur de Beethoven."

26. Berlioz, *Beethoven,* 163.

27. P. B., "Die Enthüllung des Denkmals für Beethoven zu Bonn," *Allgemeine musikalische Zeitung,* no. 34 (20 August 1845).

28. Elwart, letters to *La Presse,* 347.

29. Heinrich Karl Breidenstein, *Zur Jahresfeier der Inauguration des Beethoven-Monuments: Eine achtenmässige Darstellung dieses Ereignisses, der Wahrheit zur Ehre und den Festgenossen zur Erinnerung* (Bonn, 1846), 13.

30. Ulrich Schmitt, *Revolution im Konzertsaal* (Mainz: Schott, 1990), 130.

31. Janin, "Fêtes en l'honneur de Beethoven."

32. Breidenstein, *Zur Jahresfeier,* 9.

33. Ibid., 10.

34. Davison, "Letters on the Bonn Festival," 470.

35. Kreutzer, "Grands festivals de Bonn."

36. Janin, "Fêtes en l'honneur de Beethoven."

37. Davison, "Letters on the Bonn Festival," 458.

38. Young, *Beethoven, a Victorian Tribute,* 70.

39. Breidenstein, *Zur Jahresfeier,* 16–19.

40. Berlioz, *Beethoven,* 171.

41. Chorley, "The Beethoven-Festival at Bonn," 111.

42. Schorn, "Das Beethovenfest in Bonn," 204.

43. Quoted in Young, *Beethoven, a Victorian Tribute,* 71.

44. Davison, "Letters on the Bonn Festival," 458.

45. Kreutzer, "Grands festivals de Bonn."

46. Kahl, "Zur Geschichte des Bonner Beethovendenkmals," 71.

47. Breidenstein, *Zur Jahresfeier.*

48. Alessandra Comini, *The Changing Image of Beethoven: A Study in Myth-making* (New York: Rizzoli, 1987), 332.

49. Janin, "Fêtes en l'honneur de Beethoven."

50. Anton Schindler, in *Illustrierte Zeitung,* Leipzig, 10 September 1845, and letter of 22 November 1844; quoted by Kahl, "Zur Geschichte des Bonner Beethoven-denkmals," 72 and 67; and in Schindler, *Beethoven as I Knew Him* (1860), ed. Don-

ald MacArdle, trans. Constance Jolly (Chapel Hill: University of North Carolina Press; London: Faber and Faber, 1966), 457.

51. "Männerchor zur Inauguration der Bildsäule Beethovens," in H. K. Breidenstein, *Festgabe zum der am 12 ten 1845 stattfindenen Inauguration des Beethoven-Monuments," Liszt Saeculum,* no. 25 (1979), 31–32.

52. Kreutzer, "Grands festivals de Bonn."

53. Carl Dahlhaus, *Nineteenth-Century Music* (Berkeley: University of California Press, 1989), 161.

54. P. B., "Die Enthüllung des Denkmals," 590.

55. *Bonner Beethoven-Kantate (Kantate zur Inauguration des Beethoven-Monuments zu Bonn für Soli, Chor und Orchester),* text by Bernhard Wolff, introduced and edited by Günther Massenkeil (Frankfurt, New York, and London: C.F. Peter, 1989).

56. Liszt to Lamennais, 18 April 1845, quoted in Comini, *The Changing Image of Beethoven,* 319.

57. Günther Massenkeil, "Die Bonner Beethoven-Kantate (1845) von Franz Liszt," in J. P. Fricke, ed., *Die Sprache der Musik: Festschrift Klaus Wolfgang Niemöller zum 60. Geburtstag* (Regensburg: Gustav Bosse Verlag, 1989), 396.

58. Kreutzer, "Grands festivals de Bonn."

59. Elwart, letters to *La Presse,* 365.

60. Ignaz Moscheles, *Recent Music and Musicians,* trans. A. D. Coleridge (New York: Henry Holt and Co., 1873; New York: Da Capo Press, 1970), 317.

61. See Young, *Beethoven, a Victorian Tribute,* 85.

62. The words attributed to Lola Montès are quoted, in French, in Schorn, "Das Beethovenfest in Bonn," 210.

63. Elwart, letters to *La Presse,* 365.

64. Young, *Beethoven, a Victorian Tribute,* 86.

65. Quoted in Janin, "Fêtes en l'honneur de Beethoven."

66. Berlioz, *Beethoven,* 179.

67. Janin, "Fêtes en l'honneur de Beethoven."

68. Berlioz, *Beethoven,* 152.

69. Breidenstein, *Zur Jahresfeier,* 43.

70. *Revue et gazette musicale de Paris,* 30 November 1845, 393.

71. Eduard Hanslick, "Robert Schumann in Endenich" (1899), in L. Todd, ed., *Schumann and His World* (Princeton: Princeton University Press, 1994); and Bodo Bischoff, *Monument für Beethoven: Die Entwicklung der Beethoven-Rezeption Robert Schumanns* (Cologne: C. Dohr, 1994), 414.

## CHAPTER EIGHT

1. Score published in 1863 by Éditions des Concerts populaires, French text by Jules Ruelle.

2. Quoted in Danièle Pistone, "Beethoven et Paris: Repères historiques et évoca-

tions contemporaines," *Beethoven à Paris,* special issue of *Revue internationale de musique française,* no. 22 (Paris and Geneva: Champion/Slatkine, 1987), 14.

3. *Revue et gazette musicale de Paris,* 38th year, no. 37 (8 October 1870–1871), 278.

4. Ibid.

5. David Dennis, *Beethoven in German Politics, 1870–1989* (New Haven and London: Yale University Press, 1996), 33.

6. Friedrich Ludwig Jahn, in *Bremer Sontagsblatt* (1849), quoted in Uwe Martin, "Freude Freiheit Götterfunken: Über Schillers Schwierigkeiten beim Schreiben von Freiheit," *Cahiers d'études germaniques,* no. 8 (1990), 9–10.

7. Quoted in Ulrich Schmitt, *Revolution im Konzertsaal* (Mainz: Schott, 1990), 257.

8. Dennis, *Beethoven in German Politics,* 37.

9. See Helmut Loos, "Zur Textierung Beethovenscher Instrumentalwerke: Ein Kapitel der Beethoven-Deutung," in H. Loos, ed., *Beethoven und die Nachwelt: Materialien zur Wirkungsgeschichte Beethovens* (Bonn: Beethovenhaus, 1986), facsimile, p. 134.

10. Richard Wagner, *Beethoven* (1870).

11. Klaus Kropfinger, *Wagner and Beethoven: Richard Wagner's Reception of Beethoven* (Cambridge: Cambridge University Press, 1995), 252.

12. Richard Wagner, *Art Work of the Future* (1851).

13. Richard Wagner, *Plan for the Organization of a National German Theater for the Kingdom of Saxony* (1849).

14. Ludwig II of Bavaria to Wagner, 16 September 1865, quoted by Frederic Spotts, *Bayreuth: A History of the Wagner Festival* (New Haven and London: Yale University Press, 1994), 37.

15. Cosima Wagner, *Diaries,* ed. and annotated by Martin Gregor-Dellin and Dietrich Mack, trans. Geoffrey Shelton (New York: Harcourt Brace Jovanovich, 1977), vol. 1, p. 246.

16. Wagner, *Beethoven.*

17. Ibid.

18. Ibid.

19. Cosima Wagner, *Diaries,* vol. 2, p. 253. Quoted in Georges Liébert, *Nietzsche et la musique* (Paris: P.U.F., 1995), 190.

20. Ludwig Nohl, *Beethovens Leben,* 3 vols. (Leipzig: E. J. Günther, 1877), and *Beethoven: Nach den Schilderungen seiner Zeitgenossen* (Stuttgart, 1877).

21. Friedrich Nietzsche, *The Birth of Tragedy* [translation by R. M.].

22. Friedrich Nietzsche, *David Strauss, Apostle and Writer,* in *Untimely Meditations* [translation by R. M.].

23. Friedrich Nietzsche, *Richard Wagner in Bayreuth,* in *Untimely Meditations* [translation by R. M.].

24. *Revue wagnérienne,* 8 May 1885, 104 et seq., and 8 June 1885, 131.

25. See Dennis, *Beethoven in German Politics*, 52.

26. Letter from Joseph Joachim (1873), quoted in Scott Messing, "The Vienna Centennial Festival of 1870," *The Beethoven Newsletter*, vol. 6, no. 3 (San Jose State University, 1991), 62.

27. Heinrich Schenker, *Beethoven: Neunte Symphonie* (1912; Vienna: Universal Edition, 1969).

28. Friedrich Engels to his sister, 11 March 1841, quoted in Dennis, *Beethoven in German Politics*, 41.

29. Kurt Eisner, "Die Heimat der Neunte," *Die Neue Gesellschaft*, no. 1 (1905), quoted in Andreas Eichhorn, *Beethovens Neunte Symphonie: Die Geschichte ihrer Aufführung und Rezeption* (Kassel, Basel, and London: Bärenreiter, 1993), 326.

30. Nohl, *Beethovens Leben*, vol. 3, p. 903.

31. Victor Wilder, *Beethoven: Sa vie et son oeuvre* (Paris: Charpentier et Cie, 1883), 458–59.

32. *Le Ménestrel*, 29 January 1882, 70.

33. Octave Fouque, *Les Révolutionnaires de la musique* (Paris: Calmann-Lévy, 1882), 271–73 and 281.

34. See Pascal Ory, "Le centenaire de la Révolution française," in P. Nora, ed., *Les Lieux de mémoire*, vol. 1, *La République* (Paris: Gallimard, 1984), 548.

35. See, inter alia, Jules Michelet, *Histoire de la Révolution française* (Paris: Gallimard-Pléiade, 1952), vol. 1, p. 122.

36. Mme. Edgar Quinet, "Symphonie avec choeurs, de Beethoven" (1885), in *Ce que dit la musique* (Paris: Calmann-Lévy, 1893), 11 and 403.

37. Julien Tiersot, "Beethoven, musicien de la Révolution française," *Revue de Paris* 17 (1910), 733 et seq.

38. *Hymne des temps futurs: Chant de l'ode à la joie* (Hachette, 1902; reprinted in 1935, 1943 and 1985).

39. Christophe Prochasson, *Les Intellectuels, le socialisme et la guerre, 1900–1938* (Paris: Seuil, 1993), 71.

40. Romain Rolland, *Beethoven* (1903) (Paris: Édouard Pelleton, 1909), 71–72.

41. Georges Pioch, *Beethoven, Portraits d'hier*, no. 3 (Paris, 1909), 70, 68, 79, 95.

42. Vincent d'Indy, *Beethoven* (Paris: Henri Laurens, 1911), 134.

43. Théodore de Wyzewa, *Beethoven et Wagner: Essais d'histoire et de critique musicales* (Paris: Perrin, 1898).

44. Ricciotto Canudo, *Le Livre de la Genèse: La IXe Symphonie de Beethoven* (Paris, 1905).

45. J.-G. Prod'homme, *Les Symphonies de Beethoven*, (1906; Paris: Charles Delagrave, 1909; reprint, New York: Da Capo Press, 1977), 471. See also Jean Chantavoine, *Les Symphonies de Beethoven* (1906), introduction by Antoine Goléa (Paris: Belfond, 1970).

46. Augusta Holmès, *Ode triomphale pour le centenaire de 1789*, voice and piano score (Paris, 1889).

47. Leo Schrade, *Beethoven in France: History of an Idea* (New Haven: Yale University Press, 1942), 143.

48. Stéphane Huchet, "Beethoven et l'iconographie française," *Beethoven à Paris* (see note 2 above), 51 and 68.

49. Guillaume Apollinaire, "L'exposition de Düsseldorf" (1902), *Chronique d'Art* (Paris: Gallimard, 1993), 25.

50. Michel Faure, *Musique et société du second Empire aux années vingt: Autour de Saint-Saëns, Fauré, Debussy et Ravel* (Paris: Flammarion, 1985), 74.

51. Raymond Bouyer, *Le Secret de Beethoven* (Paris: Fischbacher, 1905), 10.

52. Claude Debussy, *Monsieur Croche, antidilettante* (Paris: Gallimard, 1926), 42 and 44.

53. George Grove, *Beethoven and His Nine Symphonies* (3rd edition, 1898; New York: Dover Publications, 1962). Bernard Shaw, *Shaw's Music*, The Bodley Head Bernard Shaw, 3 vols., ed. Dan H. Laurence (London: Max Reinhardt, The Bodley Head, 1981).

54. Friedrich Nietzsche, *Human, All-too Human* [translation by R. M.]. See also pars. 155 and 173.

55. Friedrich Nietzsche, crossed-out passage from par. 7 of *Ecce Homo*, quoted by Liébert, *Nietzsche et la musique*, 67.

56. Friedrich Nietzsche, *Beyond Good and Evil*, pars. 245 and 256 [translation by R. M.].

57. Pierre Lasserre, *Les Idées de Nietzsche sur la musique* (Paris: Mercure de France, 1907), 9.

58. Erik Satie, "Parfait entourage," *Revue musicale S.I.M.*, 8th year, nos. 7–8 (July–August 1912), 83; reproduced in *Écrits*, collected, edited, and with an introduction by Ornella Volta (Paris: Éditions Champ-Libre, 1981), 20; also see pp. 294 and 304.

59. Vladimir Jankélévitch, "Satie et le matin," *La Musique et les heures* (Paris: Seuil, 1888), 9.

60. Raymond-Raoul Lambert, *Beethoven rhénan (Reconnaissance à Jean-Christophe)* (Paris: Les Presses françaises, 1928), 67.

61. Camille Mauclair, "Le bienfait de Beethoven," *La Semaine littéraire* 35, Geneva (19 March 1927). The passage is included in the 1927 article as a quotation from a text written during the First World War. Mauclair expressed the same idea circa 1916 in *L'Art indépendant français sous la IIIe République* (Paris: La Renaissance du livre, 1919), 155; see also "La Musique et la douleur" (1915), in *La Religion de la musique* (Paris, 1928).

62. Hermann Hesse, "O Freunde, nicht diese Töne," *Neue Züricher Zeitung*, 3 November 1914, and *Journal de Genève*, 16 November 1914; quoted in Eichhorn, *Beethovens Neunte Symphonie*, 330.

63. Romain Rolland, *Au-dessus de la mêlée* (Paris: Paul Ollendorf, 1915), 58.

## CHAPTER NINE

1. Yano Jun'ichi, "Why Is Beethoven's Ninth So Well Loved in Japan?" *Japanese Quarterly* 29 (1982), 475–78.

2. Aristide Briand, "Frankreich und Beethoven," *Neue freie Presse,* 26 March 1927, morning edition.

3. *Festbericht vorgelegt vom Exekutivkommittee der Feier: Beethoven-Zentenarfeier,* Vienna, 26 to 31 March 1927 (Vienna: Universal Edition, 1927), 83.

4. *Le Temps,* 25 March 1927.

5. *The Life and Works of Ludwig van Beethoven: Beethoven Centennial, 1827–1927* (Columbia Phonograph Co., 1927).

6. Olga Kameneva, "Beethoven als Erzieher in Sowjetrussland, *Neue freie Presse,* 29 March 1927.

7. *New York Times,* 27 March 1927.

8. Message from Governor Albert Smith, *New York Times,* 26 March 1927.

9. *Neue freie Presse,* 29 March 1927.

10. Anatoli Lunatcharsky, "Was ist aktuell an Beethoven?" in *Musik und Revolution, Schriften zur Musik,* G. Bimberg, ed. (Leipzig, 1985), 204.

11. *Le Courrier musical,* 29th year, no. 7 (1 April 1927), 194.

12. See speech by Hermann Abert, printed in *Internationaler Musikhistorischer Kongress: Beethoven-Zentenarfeier,* (Vienna, 1927), 66; see also, by the same author, "Beethoven zum 26. März 1927," *Die Musik* 19, no. 6 (March 1927).

13. Arnold Schmitz, *Das romantische Beethovenbild: Darstellung und Kritik* (Berlin and Bonn: F. Dümmlers Verlag, 1927), 174.

14. Adolf Sandberger, "Das Erbe Beethovens und unsere Zeit," in *Neues Beethoven-Jahrbuch,* vol. 3, A. Sandberger and B. Filser, eds. (Augsburg, 1927), 28.

15. Hanns Eisler, "Ludwig van Beethoven: Zu seinem 100. Todestage am 26. März," in *Musik und Politik: Schriften I, 1924–1948* (Munich: Rogner and Berhard, 1973), 27 and 28–29; originally published in *Die rote Fahne,* Berlin, 22 March 1927, and *Die rote Fahne,* Vienna, 27 March 1927.

16. Dennis, D., *Beethoven in German Politics, 1870–1989* (New Haven and London: Yale University Press, 1996), 122.

17. Alfred Rosenberg, "Beethoven," *Völkischer Beobachter,* 26 March 1927, reprinted in *Blut und Ehre: Ein Kampf für deutsche Wiedergeburt: Reden und Aufsätze von 1919–1933* (Munich: Zentralverlag NSDAP Franz Eher Nachf., 1936), 225.

18. *Deutsches Beethoven-Fest Bonn,* from 21 to 31 May 1927 (Bonn: Corthaus, 1927), 5 and 7.

19. All of the official speeches delivered at the Vienna centenary events are to be found in their original languages in *Festbericht* (cited above, in note 3).

20. Ibid., 46.

21. *Le Courrier musical,* 29th year, no. 8 (15 April 1927), 240.

22. Quoted in Dennis, *Beethoven in German Politics,* 104.

23. *Festbericht,* 83.

24. *Internationaler Musikhistorischer Kongress* (cited above, in note 12), 392-94.

25. *New York Times,* 27 March 1927.

26. See the catalogue *Austellung der Stadt Wien, "Beethoven und die Wiener Kultur seiner Zeit": Beethoven-Zentenarfeier* (Vienna: Historisches Museum, 1927).

27. *Festbericht,* 49.

28. Ibid., 54.

29. Ibid., 51.

30. Ibid., 48.

31. Ibid., 50.

32. Édouard Herriot, *La Vie de Beethoven* (Paris: Gallimard, 1928); Serge Berstein, *Édouard Herriot ou la République en personne* (Paris: Presses de la Fondation nationale des sciences politiques, 1985).

33. *Gewissen: Unabhähgige Zeitung für Volksbildung,* 4 April 1927, quoted in Dennis, *Beethoven in German Politics,* 126.

34. *Festbericht,* 54.

35. Ibid., 57.

36. Ibid., 55.

37. See Helmut Goetz, "Die Beziehungen zwischen Pietro Mascagni und Benito Mussolini," *Analecta Musicologica* 17 (1976), 222.

38. *Festbericht,* 45.

39. Klemens von Klemperer, *Ignaz Seipel: Christian Statesman in a Time of Crisis* (Princeton: Princeton University Press, 1972), 289, 290.

40. Leo Schrade, *Beethoven in France: History of an Idea* (New Haven: Yale University Press, 1942), 247.

41. *Le Courrier musical,* 15 April 1927, 240.

42. *Die Fackel,* nos. 750-765 (June 1927), 6.

43. Ibid., 102.

44. Romain Rolland, "Actions de grâces à Beethoven," in *Internationaler Musikhistorischer Kongress,* reprinted in *Beethoven: Les grandes époques créatrices (1966)* (Paris: Albin Michel, 1980), 1505 and 1509.

45. Franz Werfel, "Der Gefeierte," *Neue freie Presse,* 27 March 1927.

46. Paul Bekker, *Beethoven* (1911; Berlin: Schuster and Loeffler, 1921), 283. See also, by the same author, *Neue Musik* (Berlin: Erich Reiss Verlag, 1919), 75.

47. Alban Berg, "L'Impuissance de la 'nouvelle esthétique' de Hans Pfitzner" (1920), and "Réponse responsable à une question frivole" (1926), in *Écrits* (Paris: Christian Bourgois, 1985).

48. Quoted in Andreas Eichhorn, *Beethovens Neunte Symphonie: Die Geschichte ihrer Aufführung und Rezeption* (Kassel, Basel, and London: Bärenreiter, 1993), 301.

49. Norman Del Mar, *Richard Strauss* (Philadelphia, New York, and London: Chilton Book Co., 1969), vol. 2, pp. 301-11.

50. Quoted by Ornella Volta in Erik Satie, "Parfait entourage," *Revue musicale*

*S.I.M.,* 8th year, nos. 7–8 (July–August 1912), 83; reproduced in *Écrits,* collected, edited, and with an introduction by Ornella Volta (Paris: Éditions Champ-Libre, 1981), 304.

51. Danièle Pistone, "Beethoven et Paris: Repères historiques et évocations contemporaines," *Beethoven à Paris,* special issue of *Revue internationale de musique française,* no. 22 (Paris and Geneva: Champion/Slatkine, 1987), 18.

52. Lionel Landry, "Le déclin de Beethoven," in *Beethoven: Numéro spécial de la Revue musicale,* Paris, 1 April 1927, 114.

53. Quoted by Boris Schwarz, *Music and Musical Life in Soviet Russia* (Bloomington: Indiana University Press, 1983), 53.

54. Quoted by Bärbel Schrader and Jürgen Schebera, *The "Golden" Twenties: Art and Literature in the Weimar Republic* (New Haven and London: Yale University Press, 1990), 179.

55. Otto Klemperer, *Écrits et entretiens* (Paris: Hachette/Pluriel, 1985), 104.

56. Landry, "Le déclin de Beethoven," 115.

57. *Le Courrier musical,* 29th year, no. 3 (1 February 1927), 68.

58. *New York Times,* 26 March 1927.

59. Daniel Gregory Mason, "Beethoven after a Hundred Years," in *Beethoven, 1827–1927: Centennial Essays for Beethoven Week, 20–27 March 1927* (New York, 1927), 4.

60. Felix Weingartner, "Sur le centenaire de Beethoven," *Le Courrier musical,* 1 April 1927, 183–84.

**CHAPTER TEN**

1. *Hymne supranational,* music by L. van Beethoven, words by H.-L. Follin, Founder of the Supranational Republic (Paris: Durdilly/Hayet, 1928); see also Henry-Léon Follin, *Les Conditions d'un mouvement individualiste et supranational* (Paris: Éd. Liber, 1922), and *A.B.C. du citoyen supranational* (Paris: A. Delpeuch, 1925).

2. Quoted in Leo Schrade, *Beethoven in France: History of an Idea* (New Haven: Yale University Press, 1942), 248–49.

3. Édouard Herriot, *La Vie de Beethoven* (Paris: Gallimard, 1928), 228.

4. Romain Rolland, "Actions de grâces à Beethoven," in *Internationaler Musikhistorischer Kongress,* reprinted in *Beethoven: Les grandes époques créatrices (1966)* (Paris: Albin Michel, 1980), 1489.

5. Raymond-Raoul Lambert, *Beethoven rhénan (Reconnaissance à Jean-Christophe)* (Paris: Les Presses françaises, 1928), 70–71.

6. Jean-Luc Chabot, *L'Idée de l'Europe unie de 1919 à 1939* (Grenoble: Presses universitaires de Grenoble, 1978), 442.

7. Richard N. Coudenhove-Kalergi, *Pan-Europe* (1923), introduction by A. Reszler, afterword by V. Pons (Paris: P.U.F., 1986).

8. *Paneuropa,* no. 2 (May 1924), 20.

9. *Paneuropa*, 5th year, no. 9 (November 1929), 23.

10. *Paneuropa*, no. 3 (June 1924), 7.

11. Alfred Rosenberg, "Vereinigte Staaten von Europa?" (1925), in *Blut und Ehre: Ein Kampf für deutsche Wiedergeburt: Reden und Aufsätze von 1919–1933* (Munich: Zentralverlag NSDAP Franz Eher Nachf., 1936), 267.

12. *Paneuropa*, 8th year, nos. 8/9 (November 1932), 232–34.

13. Lubar Jilek, "Paneurope dans les années vingt: La réception du projet en Europe centrale et occidentale," *Relations internationales* 72 (Winter 1992), 430.

14. Georges Duhamel, quoted by Élisabeth du Reau, *L'Idée d'Europe au XXe siècle* (Brussels: Complexe, 1996), 95.

15. Frederic Spotts, *Bayreuth: A History of the Wagner Festival* (New Haven and London: Yale University Press, 1994), 173.

16. Willi Hille, "Nationalisierung der deutschen Musik," *Die Musik* 26, no. 9 (June 1933), 666.

17. Fred K. Prieberg, *Music im NS-Staat* (Frankfurt: Fischer, 1982), 354.

18. William Shirer, *Berlin Diary* (1941), quoted by David Dennis in *Beethoven in German Politics, 1870–1989* (New Haven and London: Yale University Press, 1996), 163.

19. Hitler, 9 November 1939, quoted by Heribert Schröder, "Beethoven im Dritten Reich," in *Beethoven und die Nachwelt: Materialen zur Wirkungsgeschichte*, ed. H. Loss (Bonn: Beethovenhaus, 1986), 221.

20. Otto Klemperer, *Écrits et entretiens* (Paris: Hachette/Pluriel, 1985), 272.

21. Prieberg, *Music im NS-Staat*, 83.

22. Herbert Gerigk, "Ludwig van Beethoven," in H. Gerigk, ed., *Meister der Musik und ihre Werke* (Berlin: Rich. Bong, 1936).

23. Arnold Schmitz, "Zur Frage nach Beethovens Weltanshauung und ihrem musikalischen Ausdruck," in *Beethoven und die Gegenwart: Festschrift des Beethovenhauses Bonn: Ludwig Schiedermair zum 60. Geburtstag* (Berlin and Bonn: Ferd. Dümmlers Verlag, 1937), 274.

24. Herbert Birtner, "Zur deutschen Beethoven-Auffassung seit Richard Wagner," in Schmitz, *Beethoven und die Gegenwart*, 40.

25. Walther Rauschenberger, *Volk und Rasse* (1934), quoted by Joseph Wulf, *Musik im Dritten Reich: Eine Dokumentation* (Hamburg: Rowohlt, 1966), 240.

26. Arnold Schering, *Beethoven und die Dichtung* (Berlin: Junker and Dünnhaupt, 1936). See Schröder, "Beethoven im Dritten Reich," 214.

27. Erik Levi, *Music in the Third Reich* (London: Macmillan, 1994), 35.

28. *Völkischer Beobachter*, 11 November 1934.

29. According to Kurt Gerlach-Bernau (1934), quoted in Georg Ruppelt, *Schiller im nationalsozialistischen Deutschland: Der Versuch einer Gleichschaltung* (Stuttgart: Metzler, 1979), 30.

30. Schröder, "Beethoven im Dritten Reich," 218.

31. Hanns Eisler, "Mit Musik kämpfen" (1938), quoted in Andreas Eichhorn, *Beethovens Neunte Symphonie: Die Geschichte ihrer Aufführung und Rezeption* (Kassel, Basel, and London: Bärenreiter, 1993), 338.

32. H. J. Moser, in *Stuttgarter Neues Tageblatt* (1941), quoted in Schröder, "Beethoven im Dritten Reich," 197.

33. Prieberg, *Musik im NS-Staat*, 408.

34. Pierre de Coubertin, 16 August 1936, quoted by Jean-Marie Brohm, *Jeux olympiques à Berlin* (Brussels: Complexe, 1983), 141.

35. See Dennis, *Beethoven in German Politics*, 162.

36. Quoted in Brohm, *Jeux olympiques*, 85.

37. Elly Ney, "Bekenntnis zu Ludwig van Beethoven," in A. Morgenroth, ed., *Von deutscher Tonkunst: Festschrift zu Peter Raabes 70. Geburtstag* (Leipzig: C. F. Peters, 1942), 59.

38. Speech given by the organizer of a concert given at the University of Tokyo in 1944, quoted in Nicholas Cook, *Beethoven, Symphony No. 9* (Cambridge: Cambridge University Press, 1993), 97.

39. Waldemar Rosen, "Deutschland im europäischen Musikaustausch," in H. von Hase, ed., *Jahrbuch der deutschen Musik* (Berlin: Breitkopf und Härtel / Max Hesses, 1943).

40. *Völkischer Beobachter*, Vienna, 28 March 1938, quoted in Prieberg, *Musik im NS-Staat*, 355.

41. Lucien Rebatat, "Mozart à Paris," in *Je suis partout*, 21 July 1941.

42. Paul Valayer, "Warum die Franzosen Beethoven verstehen," *Zeitschrift für Politik* 28 (1938).

43. *Comœdia*, 12 June 1943.

44. Arthur Hoérée, "Le grand festival Beethoven,"*Comœdia*, 19 June 1943.

45. Louis Beydts, "La musique — La consolatrice," *Je suis partout*, 7 February 1941; Georges Duhamel, *La Musique consolatrice* (1944) (Paris: Éditions du Rocher, 1989).

46. Philippe Burrin, *La France à l'heure allemande, 1940–1944* (Paris: Seuil / Points, 1995), 302.

47. Conversation with M. Philippe Morin.

48. *Musique et radio: Revue mensuelle de l'industrie et du commerce de musique, radio, machines parlantes, télévision, cinéma*, no. 369 (June 1941), 93.

49. Marcel Delannoy, "Fin d'une époque ou seulement fin d'une année?" *Nouveaux temps*, 12 January 1941.

50. Letter from Robert Bernard to Glachant, Ministry of Foreign Affairs, Vichy, 28 June 1941; published in Myriam Chimènes, "*L'Information musicale:* Une 'parenthèse' de *La Revue musicale*," in *La Revue des revues: Revue internationale d'histoire et de bibliographie*, no. 24, "Des revues sous l'occupation" (Paris, 1997), 91–110.

51. Prieberg, *Music im NS-Staat*, 399.

52. Arthur Honegger, "Festival Beethoven,"*Comœdia,* 21 June 1941. All of the articles from *Comœdia* have been reprinted in *Écrits,* ed. H. Calmel (Paris: Honoré Champion, 1992).

53. Romain Rolland, *Beethoven: Les grandes époques créatrices (1966)* (Paris: Albin Michel, 1980), 866. See *L'Information musicale,* no. 112 (16 April 1943).

54. *L'Information musicale,* no. 127 (8 October 1943).

55. Dany Brunschwig, "Homage de la Société des concerts du Conservatoire au Maréchal Pétain, Chef de l'État," *L'Information musicale,* nos. 96–97 (22 December 1942).

56. *L'Information musicale,* i.e., Armand Machabey in no. 122 (25 June 1943) and Robert Bernard in no. 117 (21 May 1943).

57. *Jeunesses musicales de France: Bulletin officiel,* no. 1 (2 November 1943).

58. *Jeunesses musicales de France: Bulletin officiel,* no. 22 (11 April 1944).

59. Émile Vuillermoz, "Un chef," *Je suis partout,* 2 June 1944.

60. J.-L. Crémieux-Brilhac, ed., *Ici Londres, 1940 –1944* (Paris: La Documentation française, 1975), 205 and 295.

61. Quoted in Eichhorn, *Beethovens Neunte Symphonie,* 271.

62. *Musical Times,* June 1941, 216.

63. Fania Fénelon, *Sursis pour l'orchestre,* with Marcelle Routier (Paris: Stock, 1976), 164.

64. See Joza Karas, *La Musique à Térézin, 1941–1945* (Paris: Gallimard, 1993).

65. Simon Laks, *Mélodies d'Auschwitz* (Paris: Éditions du Cerf, 1991), 31 and 131. Laks quotes the Polish article.

66. Primo Levi, *Si c'est un homme* (Paris: Julliard/Pocket, 1987), 53.

67. Laks, *Mélodies d'Auschwitz,* 23.

68. Wilhelm Furtwängler, "La valeur universelle de Beethoven" (1942), in *Musique et verbe* (Paris: Albin Michel, 1979), 153.

69. Daniel K., "Singing the Ode 'To Joy' in Auschwitz: A Ten-Year-Old's Story," *The Beethoven Journal,* vol. 10, no. 1 (1995), 4. This account has been attributed to Otto Dov Kulka and is quoted, in part, in Karas, *La Musique à Térézin,* 166.

70. Quoted in Wulf, *Musik im Dritten Reich,* 222.

71. Thomas Mann, *Doctor Faustus: The Life of the German Composer Adrian Leverkühn, as Told by a Friend,* trans. H. T. Lowe-Porter (New York: Alfred A. Knopf, 1948), 478 and 487.

72. Thomas Mann, *The Genesis of a Novel,* trans. Richard and Clara Winston (London: Secker and Warburg, 1961), 178.

73. See Dennis, *Beethoven in German Politics,* 74.

**CHAPTER ELEVEN**

1. Edgar Morin, *Penser l'Europe* (Paris: Gallimard, 1987), 14.

2. Charles Melchior de Molènes, *L'Europe de Strasbourg* (Paris: Éd. Roudil, 1971), 182.

3. Report of the Secretary General, Council of Europe (1950), Doc. 85, Annex 2; quoted in René Radius, "Report on a European Anthem," Consultative Assembly of the Council of Europe, 10 June 1971, Doc. 2978 (noted hereafter as Radius Report).

4. Letter from Richard Coudenhove-Kalergi, Bern, 3 August 1955, Council of Europe archives.

5. Aloïs Larcher, "Le drapeau de l'Europe et l'hymne européen: La genèse de deux symboles," Council of Europe (Strasbourg, 1995), 2.

6. Letter from Paul Lévy, Chief of Information, to Richard Coudenhove-Kalergi, Strasbourg, 5 September 1955, Council of Europe archives.

7. The archives of the North Atlantic Treaty Organization (NATO) contain no trace of this initiative. Letter to the author from the Chief of NATO Archives, 13 October 1995.

8. *Der Spiegel*, 21/45 (30 October 1967), 166.

9. Speech by Willi Stoph, 16 December 1970, in *Hommage à Beethoven de la République démocratique allemande 1970* (Dresden: Verlag Zeit im Bild), 20.

10. Dr. Hajas, "Karajan und die 'Neunte,'" *Österreichische Zeitung*, 24 December 1947, quoted in Robert Bachmann, *Karajan: Notes on a Career* (London: Quartet Books, 1990), 159.

11. J. and B. Massin, *Ludwig van Beethoven* (Paris: Le Club français du livre, 1967), 781; emphasis in the original.

12. See Theodor W. Adorno, "Le style tardif de Beethoven," *Beethoven, L'Arc,* no. 40 (Paris, 1970).

13. T. W. Adorno, *Beethoven: Philosophie der Musik* (Frankfurt: Suhrkamp, 1994), 120 and 115. See Rose Rosengard Subotnik, "Adorno's Diagnosis of Beethoven's Late Style: Early Symptom of a Fatal Condition," in *Developing Variations: Style and Ideology in Western Music* (Minneapolis: Minnesota University Press, 1991), 32.

14. See, inter alia, Ma Tingheng, "I Was Poisoned by the Bourgeois Music of the West," *Guangming Ribao,* 4 March 1965; Jiang Qing; *Chinese Literature* (1967), quoted by Richard Curt Kraus, *Pianos and Politics in China: Middle-Class Ambitions and the Struggle over Western Music* (Oxford and New York: Oxford University Press, 1989), 118, 137, and 139.

15. Igor Stravinsky, "Beethoven ohne Weltanshauung," *Melos,* no. 14 (1947).

16. Richard and Edith Sterba, *Beethoven et sa famille* (Paris: Éd. Corrêa/Buchet-Chastel, 1955), 91.

17. Anthony Burgess, "A Clockwork Orange Resucked," preface to the new American edition of *A Clockwork Orange* (1962) (New York: Norton, 1986), ix.

18. In Burgess's novel, the Fifth Symphony is the work played during the character's treatment; the film concentrates all of the story's symbolism in the Ninth Symphony. At the end of the novel, the character recovers his pleasurable sensations derived from music and voluntarily rejects violence, whereas the film ends with his faked and hypocritical reconciliation with power. It is that difference that led the author, after an initial enthusiasm, to reject the film.

19. José Luis Alvarez, *Miguel Ríos ¿El rock que no termina?* (Gijón: Júcar, 1984), 91 and 188; Alvaro Feito, *Miguel Ríos* (Madrid: Édiciones JC, 1983), 23-24.

20. Speech by Kurt von Fischer, in *Beethoven-Symposion, Wien 1970: Bericht* (Vienna: Österreichische Akademie der Wissenschaften, Hermann Böhlaus Nachf., 1971), 21.

21. Frank Schneider, "Zur Kritik der Spätbürgerlichen Beethoven-Deutung," in H. A. Brockhaus and K. Niemann, eds., *Bericht über den internationalen Beethoven-Kongress 10.-12. Dezember 1970 in Berlin* (Berlin: Verlag Neue Musik, 1971), 181.

22. Heinz Klaus Metzger, "Zur Beethoven-Interpretation" (1970), in *Beethoven: Das Problem der Interpretation, Musik-Konzepte,* no. 8 (Munich, 1979), 5.

23. Roland Barthes, "Musica practica," and Claude Helffer, "Réflexions d'un interprète," *L'Arc,* no. 40 (Paris, 1970), 17 and 77.

24. Pierre Boulez, "Tell Me" (1970), in J. J. Nattiez, ed., *Points de repère* (Paris: Christian Bourgois/Seuil, 1981), 219.

25. Karlheinz Stockhausen, "Kurzwellen mit Beethoven: Opus 1970," in *Texte zur Musik, 1963-1970,* vol. 3 (Cologne: Verlag M. DuMont Schauberg, 1971), 121.

26. Werner Klüppelholz, *Mauricio Kagel, 1970-1980* (Cologne: DuMont Buchverlag, 1981), 17.

27. Mauricio Kagel, "Beethovens Erbe ist die moralische Aufrüstung," interview with F. Schmidt, *Der Spiegel,* 24/37 (7 September 1970); reprinted in F. Schmidt and J. J. Nattiez, eds., *Tam-Tam: Monologues et dialogues sur la musique* (Paris: Christian Bourgois, 1983). See also the documentary by Wilhelm Flues, *Kagels Beethoven: Die Dreharbeiten zu "Ludwig van"* (Cologne: Westdeutsches Fernsehen, 1970).

28. Hilde Speel, "'Ludwig van . . .' Kagels Anti-Beethoven-Film in Wien uraufgeführt," *Frankfurter Allgemeine Zeitung,* 30 May 1970.

29. "Beethoven: Abschied von Mythos," (unsigned article), *Der Spiegel,* 24/37 (7 September 1970).

30. *Hommage à Beethoven de la République démocratique allemande 1970* (cited above, in note 9), 25.

31. Ernst Hermann Meyer, "Das Werk Ludwig van Beethovens und seine Bedeutung für das sozialistisch-realistische Gegenwartsschaffen," in *Bericht über den internationalen Beethoven-Kongress* (cited above, in note 21), 583.

32. Jean de Solliers, "Le langage musical de Beethoven," *Europe,* no. 498, "Bicentenaire de Beethoven" (October 1970), 77.

33. Yves Florenne and Béatrice Didier, "Beethoven et l'imaginaire," ibid., 52.

34. Hans Sittner, "Beethoven in der Zeit," in *Beethoven Almanach 1970* (Vienna: Verlag Elisabeth Lafite, 1970), 9.

35. Bernard Fournier, "La modernité de Beethoven: Un défi au temps," *Europe* (cited above, in note 32), 90.

36. Hans Heinrich Eggebrecht, *Zur Geschichte der Beethoven-Rezeption* (1972) (Mainz: Laaber Verlag, 1994).

37. Massin, *Ludwig van Beethoven,* 802.

38. Ibid., 730 (note of 1967).

39. Maria Antonietta Macciocchi, "La culture européenne sur le chemin du XXIe siècle," in B. Beutler, ed., *Réflexions sur l'Europe* (Brussels: Complexe, 1993), 124, 145.

40. Letter from Jehan-Louis Gaudet to Paul-Henri Spaak, Lyons, 26 August 1949, Council of Europe archives.

41. Letter from the Service of Documentation and Studies to Jehane-Louis Gaudet, Strasbourg, 7 September 1949.

42. "Marche de l'Europe unie," M. Clavel, 1951; "An Europa," Ernst Hohenfeldt and Fritz Schein, 1953; "Marseillaise de la paix," M. L. Guy, 1953; "Europa vocata," Hanns Holenia, 1957; "Europa!" Paul Krüger; "Hymnus europaeus"; "Vereintes Europa," 1957; "Inno all'Europa," Ferdinando Durand and Adriana Autéri Sivori, 1958; "Europe, lève-toi," Léo Alban, 1961; "Paneuropa," Clarus Falk, undated; "L'Européenne," Jean Lafont, undated, Strasbourg, Council of Europe archives.

43. Radius Report, 2.

44. Letter from Paul Lévy, Director of Information, to the Secretary General of the European Movement, the Netherlands, from Strasbourg, 3 April 1962, Council of Europe archives.

45. *Hymnes de la Communauté européene*, recording by the Musique de la Garde républicaine, cond. P. J. Brun, 1958.

46. Nicole Hirsch, "La création de la 'Cantate de l'Europe': Une soirée de la foi et du coeur," *France-Soir*, 3 May 1957.

47. Press file concerning the *Cantate de l'Europe*, Council of Europe archives.

48. From the Secretary General of the Belgian section of the Council of European Municipalities, 1962, quoted in Radius Report, 3.

49. Statement by the President of the Consultative Assembly, January 1965, quoted in Radius Report, 4.

50. Radius Report, 7.

51. Resolution 492 (1971) of the Consultative Assembly of the Council of Europe, twenty-third ordinary session.

52. Radius Report, 6.

53. Ibid.

54. Ibid.

55. See, inter alia, the proposal by the Director of Information quoted in the Conclusions of the 206th meeting, 11–18 January 1972, and "Round Table for Europe Day," file TR (73) 3, 7 February 1973.

56. Letter from Secretary General Lujo Toncic-Serinj to Rose Martine Hirsch, 7 May 1974, Council of Europe archives.

57. "Hymne Européen," press release, Council of Europe, 19 January 1972, C (72) 1.

58. Respectively, Schott Edition 6488, ED 6489, and ED 5203; and Deutsche Grammophon LP DG 2 530250, cassette 3 300 246.

59. Files D.P.I. (72) 5 and 11, Council of Europe, 29 February and 22 June 1972, Council of Europe archives.

60. Since Herbert van Karajan's death, the Council of Europe has been considering a revision of the agreement with his heirs. However, as of April 1997, no change had been made in the 1972 terms.

61. Laurent Dalbecq, *Le Drapeau de l'Europe,* piano arrangement, Éditions Robert Marin, Charnay-lès-Mâcon, 1968.

62. "Hymne européen," internal document of the Committee of Ministers, Council of Europe, CM (72) 43, Strasbourg, 7 March 1972, Council of Europe archives.

63. Activities of the Council of Europe. Report of the Secretary General. Council of Europe, Strasbourg, 1973, p. 9.

### CHAPTER TWELVE

1. *Times,* London, 28 August 1974.

2. Cecil Rhodes, epigraph to "Imperialism," part 2 of *The Origins of Totalitarianism,* by Hannah Arendt (San Diego, CA: Harcourt Brace, 1979), 121.

3. Letter quoted in the verbatim record of the 5 September 1974 meeting, Office of the Consultative Assembly, Document AS/Bur (26) PV3, p. 16.

4. The term *apartheid* was not openly employed in Rhodesia, but similarities with the policy of South Africa meant that it was common outside of the country. See R. Kent Rasmussen, *Historical Dictionary of Rhodesia/Zimbabwe* (Metuchen and London: Scarecrow Press, 1979), 22.

5. Memorandum from the Director of Legal Affairs, 30 September 1974, Council of Europe archives.

6. Letter from the Secretary General, Council of Europe, to the National Chairman of the European Veterans' Federation (France), Strasbourg, 16 September 1974, Council of Europe archives.

7. "National Anthem Is Found at Last," *Rhodesian Herald,* Salisbury, 27 August 1974.

8. The records of cabinet meetings for 1974 are sealed until 1999; the Zimbabwe National Archives contain no documents regarding the Rhodesian national anthem (letter from Zimbabwe National Archives to the author, Harare, 12 October 1995).

9. Harold Nelson, *Area Handbook for Southern Rhodesia* (Washington, D.C.: American University, 1975), 332.

10. *Rhodesian Herald,* 28 August 1974.

11. Ibid., 27 August 1974.

12. Ibid., 28 August 1974.

13. Ibid., 29 August 1974.

14. Ibid.

15. Peter Goodwin and Ian Hancock, *"Rhodesians Never Die": The Impact of War and Political Change in White Rhodesia, c. 1970–1980* (Oxford and New York: Oxford University Press, 1993), 146.

16. *Herald,* 17 and 18 April 1980.

17. See Marc Fumaroli, *L'État culturel: Essai sur une religion moderne* (Paris: Éd. de Fallois, 1992).

18. See recommendation 56 (1953) of the Consultative Assembly to the Committee of Ministers and recommendation 94 (1956) of the Consultative Assembly to the Secretary General, quoted in René Radius, "Report on a European Anthem," Consultative Assembly of the Council of Europe, 10 June 1971, Doc. 2978.

19. Written question no. 1462/80 from Mr. Curry to the Committee of European Communities, 12 November 1980, *Official Journal of the European Communities* (henceforth *OJ*), no. C56/8 (16 March 1981). Office of Official Publications of the European Communities, Luxembourg.

20. Aloïs Larcher, A., "Le drapeau de l'Europe et l'hymne européen: La genèse de deux symboles," Council of Europe (Strasbourg, 1995), 8–10.

21. *Le Monde,* 23 May 1981.

22. Pierre Favier and Michel Martin-Roland, *La Décennie Mitterrand,* vol. 1, *Les Ruptures* (Paris: Seuil, 1990), 59.

23. *Le Monde,* 22 May 1981.

24. M. Tummers and colleagues, "Proposition de résolution relative à un hymne européen contemporain," 30 January 1985, Council of Europe archives, 352, Doc. 5353.

25. Vincent Ostria, "Le hasard et l'indifférence," *Les Cahiers du cinéma,* no. 471, Paris (September 1993).

26. "Report of the Ad Hoc Committee," *Bulletin of the European Communities* (henceforth *Bull. EC*), supplement 7/85, Office of Official Publications of the European Communities, Luxembourg, p. 32.

27. Picht Picht, "Vers l'assimilation culturelle? Plaidoyer pour une sociologie comparée de l'Europe," in B. Beutler, ed., *Réflexions sur l'Europe* (Brussels: Complexe, 1993), 149.

28. René Girault, "Chronologie d'une conscience européenne au XXe siècle," in B. Beutler, ed., *Identité et conscience européennes au XXe siècle* (Paris: Hachette, 1994), 19; italics in original.

29. "Discours de Jacques Delors: Cérémonie du drapeau européen," 29 May 1986, Office of Spokesman for the Commission President.

30. "Programme de la cérémonie," annex to the press communiqué "Cérémonie consacrant l'adoption du drapeau européen sur l'esplanade du Berlaymont à Bruxelles le 29 mai 1986," IP (86) 243, Office of Spokesman for the Commission President.

31. "L'Europe des citoyens: Bilan des travaux de mise en oeuvre des deux rapports du comité ad hoc sur l'Europe des citoyens," *Bull. EC,* 11-1985, pp. 42 and 44.

32. See *L'Art du jumelage,* undated pamphlet, European Council of Local Authorities, p. 14.

33. CD of the Chorus of the European Communities, *Choral Mosaic from Europe,*

Dirk de Moor, choirmaster, Pavane Records, 1991; Les Petits Chanteurs du Monde, cond. Francis Bardot, 1989; Nationalhymnen, *European Brass Band,* Delta Music, 1986; Europa: Donne un choeur à l'Europe, cond. Laurent Grzybowski, Paris, 1996; Les Fanas de l'accordéon, *Europe 2000,* Milan Musette, 1995; Orchestre de variété, Jean-Pierre Gautier ("musical saw"); Jean S. Berger, *St.-Denis Musical Force,* Neuilly, 1990.

34. Fanfare of the Garde Républicaine, *Hymnes nationaux,* Corélia, 1992; Paris Air Force Band, *Marches et sonneries de l'Armée française,* Corélia, 1996; Main Navy Band, *Cérémonial et tradition,* Corélia, 1995.

35. CD *L'Hymne européen,* European Commission/European Council, 1995, "Note for the attention of the Editors," General Directive X for audiovisual, news, communications, and culture, European Commission, Brussels, 1995.

36. Written question no. 2108/87 by Mr. Ernest Glinne (S-B) to the Council of European Communities, 28 January 1988, 88/C 121/63, *OJ* no. C 121/33 of 9 May 1988. Written question no. 84/88 by Mr. Luis Guillermo Perinat Elio (ED-E) to the Committee of European Communities, 10 June 1988, 89/C 180/05, *OJ* no. C 180/3 of 17 July 1989. Joint reply to written questions nos. 2107/87 and 84/88 by Mr. Ripo di Meana on behalf of the Commission, 23 September 1988, ibid.

37. Written question no. 403/89 by Mr. Ernest Glinne (S) to the Committee of European Communities, 3 October 1989, 90/C 9/44, *OJ* no. C 9/22 of 15 January 1990. Reply by Mr. Dondelinger on behalf of the Commission, 20 October 1989, ibid.

38. Conversation with Marcello Burattini, Chief of Protocol, European Union, Brussels, 26 June 1995.

39. Michael Hartmeier, "Difficultés allemandes par rapport à la symbolique nationale," *Revue d'Allemagne et des pays de langue allemande,* vol. 28, no. 4, Strasbourg (October–December 1996), 587.

40. Denis de Rougemont, *Vingt-huit siècles d'Europe: La conscience européenne à travers les siècles: D'Hésiode à nos jours* (Paris: Payot, 1961).

41. Written question no. 595/90 by Mr. Lyndon Harrison (S) to the Committee of European Communities, 16 March 1990, 91/C 115/03, *OJ* no. C 115/2, 29 April 1991.

42. Reply by Mr. Dondelinger on behalf of the Commission, 6 April 1990, *OJ* no. C 115/2, 29 April 1991.

43. Pierre E. Barbier, Program notes for the Beethoven cycle by the Orchestre de Paris, 1994–1998.

44. Ulrich Schmitt, *Revolution im Konzertsaal* (Mainz: Schott, 1990), 267.

45. David Dennis, *Beethoven in German Politics, 1870–1989* (New Haven and London: Yale University Press, 1996), 200.

46. *Ode to Freedom, Bernstein in Berlin, Beethoven Symphony No. 9,* CD DG 429-861-2.

47. *National-Zeitung,* Berlin, 28 December 1989, quoted in Dennis, *Beethoven in German Politics,* 243.

48. David Benjamin Levy, *Beethoven: The Ninth Symphony* (New York: Schirmer Books, 1995), 195.

49. Richard Taruskin, "A Beethoven Season? Like Last Season, the One Before . . . ," *New York Times,* 10 September 1995.

50. Leonard Bernstein, in the program for the concerts of 24–25 December 1989, quoted in Dennis, *Beethoven in German Politics,* 201–2.

## CONCLUSION

1. Quoted in Paul Nettl, *National Anthems* (New York: Frederick Ungar, 1967), 133.

2. *Le Monde,* editorial, 2 May 1998.

3. André Boucourechliev, *Essai sur Beethoven* (Arles: Actes Sud, 1991), 132.

4. Maynard Solomon, *Beethoven* (Paris: J.-C. Lattès, 1985), 349.

5. Nicholas Cook, *Beethoven, Symphony No. 9* (Cambridge: Cambridge University Press, 1993), 102.

# bibliography

## SOURCES

Beethoven, Ludwig van, *Ludwig van Beethovens Werke, Vollständige kritisch durchgeseheene überall herechtige Ausgabe,* 30 vols. Leipzig: Breitkopf und Härtel, 1884.

———. *Cahiers de conversation de Beethoven.* Translated and presented by J.-G. Prod'homme. Paris: Corrêa, 1946.

———. *Beethovens Tagebuch of 1812–1818,* ed. M. Solomon. In *Beethoven Studies,* vol. 3, edited by A. Tyson. Cambridge and New York: Cambridge University Press, 1982.

———. *Beethovens Briefe.* Edited by Ulbert Leissmann, Leipzig: Insel Verlag, 1912.

———. *Correspondance de Beethoven.* Translated and with an introduction and notes by Jean Chantavoine. Paris: Calmann-Lévy, n.d.

———. *The Letters of Beethoven.* Translated and edited by E. Anderson. New York: St. Martin's, Press, 1961.

Schiller, Friedrich. "À la joie," trans. Jean-Pierre Lefebvre. In *Anthologie bilingue de la poésie allemande,* edited by J.-P. Lefebvre. Paris: Gallimard/Pléiade, 1993.

———. "An die Freude," *Gedichte,* vol. 1. In *Sämtliche Werke.* Stuttgart and Berlin: Gotta'sche Buchhandlung Nachfolger, 1904.

———. *Œuvres,* 5 vols. Translated by A. Régnier. Paris: Hachette, 1859.

———. *Lettres sur l'éducation esthétique de l'homme. Briefe über die ästhetische Erziehung des Menschen.* Original text and French version by Robert Leroux. Paris: Aubier, 1992.

———. *Don Carlos, infant d'Espagne.* Translated by Sylvain Fort. Paris: L'Arche, 1997.

## BEETHOVEN, THE *ODE TO JOY,* THEIR RECEPTION

*Beethoven, 1827–1927: Centennial Essays for Beethoven Week,* 20–27 March 1927. New York, 1927.

*Beethoven, 1770–1827: A Selected Bibliography Prepared in Connection with the Beethoven Centenary Festival,* 22–29 March 1927. Boston: Public Library of the City of Boston, 1927.

*Beethoven Centennial, 1827–1927: The Life and Works of Ludwig van Beethoven.* Columbia Phonograph Co., 1927.

*Beethoven-Zentenarfeier, Wien, 26. bis 31. März 1927: Festbericht vorgeletgt vom Exekutivkommitee der Feier.* Vienna: Universal Edition, 1927.

*Beethoven-Zentenarfeier, Austellung der Stadt Wien: "Beethoven und die Wiener Kultur seiner Zeit."* Vienna, 1927.

*Beethoven-Zentenarfeier: Internationaler Musikhistorischer Kongress.* Vienna, 1927.

*Deutsches Beethoven-Fest Bonn,* 21–31 May 1927. Bonn: Corthaus, 1927.

*Beethoven.* Special issue of *La Revue musicale,* Paris, 1 April 1927.

*Beethoven.* Paris: Hachette, 1961.

*Hommage à Beethoven de la République démocratique allemande.* Dresden: Zeit im Bild, 1970.

*Beethoven.* Special issue of *L'Arc,* no. 40, Paris, 1970.

*Beethoven à Paris.* Special issue of *Revue internationale de musique française,* no. 22. Paris et Genève: Champion-Slatkine, 1987.

Abert, Hermann. "Beethoven zum 26. März 1927," *Die Musik* 19, no. 6 (Berlin, March 1927).

Adorno, Theodor W. *Beethoven: Philosophie der Musik.* Frankfurt: Suhrkamp, 1994.

———. "Le style tardif de Beethoven" (1937). *L'Arc,* no. 40, *Beethoven* (Paris, 1970).

———. "Alienated Masterpiece: The *Missa solemnis*" (1959). Translated by D. Smith. *Telos,* no. 28 (1976).

Arnold, Elsie and Denis. "The View of Posterity: An Anthology," in *The Beethoven Companion,* edited by D. Arnold and N. Fortune. London: Faber and Faber, 1971.

Barthes, Roland. "Musica practica." *L'Arc,* no. 40, *Beethoven* (Paris, 1970).

Bazzana, Kevin. "Berlioz's Musical Celebrations at Bonn." *The Beethoven Newsletter,* vol. 6, nos. 1 and 2 (San Jose State University, 1991).

———. "The Beethoven-Album: Supplement to the Beethoven Festival at Bonn, August 1845." *The Beethoven Newsletter,* vol. 7, no. 2 (San Jose State University, 1992).

Bekker, Paul. *Beethoven* [1911]. Berlin: Schuster and Loeffler, 1921.

Berlioz, Hector. *Beethoven.* Paris: Buchet-Chastel, 1979.

Bertaux, Pierre, and Gerald Stieg. "Beethoven et Schiller." In *Aspects de la littérature autrichienne au XXe siècle,* pp. 11–19. *Austriaca, Cahiers universitaires d'information sur l'Autriche,* no. 23 (December 1986).

Birtner, Herbert. "Zur Deutschen Beethoven-Auffassung seit Richard Wagner." In *Beethoven und die Gegenwart, Festschrift des Beethovenhauses Bonn, Ludwig Schiedermair zum 60. Geburtstag,* edited by A. Schmitz. Berlin and Bonn: Ferd. Dümmlers Verlag, 1937.

Bischoff, Bodo. *Monument für Beethoven: Die Entwicklung der Beethoven-Rezeption Robert Schumanns.* Cologne: C. Dohr, 1994.

Bloom, Peter. "Critical Reaction to Beethoven in France: François-Joseph Fétis." *Revue belge de musicologie* 26–27 (1972–1973).

Boucourechliev, André. *Beethoven* (1963). Paris: Seuil, 1983.

———. *Essai sur Beethoven.* Arles: Actes Sud, 1991.

Bouyer, Raymond. *Le Secret de Beethoven.* Paris: Fischbacher, 1905.

Boyer, Jean. *Le "Romantisme" de Beethoven: Contribution à l'étude d'une légende.* Paris: Didier, 1938.

Breidenstein, Heinrich Karl. *Erinnerung an Ludwig van Beethoven und die Feier der Enthüllung seines Monuments zu Bonn am 10., 11. und 12. August 1845.* Bonn: Verlag von B. Plenes, 1845.

———. *Festgabe zu der am 12ten August 1845 stattfindenen Inauguration des Beethoven-Monuments* (Bonn, 1845, facsimile). In *Liszt Saeculum,* no. 25 (Centre international Liszt pour la musique du XIXe siècle, 1979).

———. *Zur Jahresfeier der Inauguration des Beethoven-Monuments: Eine achtenmässige Darstellung dieses Ereignisses, der Wahrheit zur Ehre und den Festgenossen zur Erinnerung.* Bonn, 1846.

Breuning, Gerhard von. *Memories of Beethoven: From the House of the Black-Robed Spaniards,* edited by M. Salomon. Cambridge: Cambridge University Press, 1992.

Brisson, Élisabeth. *Le Sacre du musicien: Place et fonction de la référence à l'Antiquité dans le processus créateur de Beethoven.* Doctoral thesis in history, E.H.E.S.S., F. Escal and P. Vidal-Naquet, dir., 1997.

Buenzod, Emmanuel. *Pouvoirs de Beethoven.* Paris: Éditions R. A. Corrêa, 1936.

Burnham, Scott. *Beethoven Hero.* Princeton: Princeton University Press, 1995.

Chantavoine, Jean. *Les Symphonies de Beethoven.* With an introduction by A. Goléa. Paris: Belfond, 1970.

Chorley, Henry Fothergill. "The Beethoven-Festival at Bonn, 1845," *Modern German Music,* vol. 2, London, 1854. In *Liszt Saeculum,* no. 25 (Centre international Liszt pour la musique du XIXe siècle, 1979).

Comini, Alessandra. *The Changing Image of Beethoven: A Study in Mythmaking.* New York: Rizzoli, 1987.

Cook, Nicholas. *Beethoven: Symphony no. 9.* Cambridge and New York: Cambridge University Press, 1993.

Cooper, Barry, ed. *The Beethoven Compendium: A Guide to Beethoven's Life and Music.* London: Thames and Hudson, 1991.

Cooper, Martin. *Beethoven: The Last Decade, 1817–1827.* London: Oxford University Press, 1985.

Dahlhaus, Carl. *Ludwig van Beethoven: Approaches to His Music.* Translated by M. Whithall. New York: Oxford University Press, 1991.

Dau, Rudolf. "Friedrich Schillers Hymne 'An die Freude': Zu einigen Problemen ihrer Interpretation und aktuellen Rezeption." *Weimarer Beiträge: Zeitschrift für Literaturwissenschaft, Äesthetik und Kulturtheorie,* no. 24:10 (Weimar, 1978).

Debussy, Claude. *Monsieur Croche et autres écrits.* Paris: Gallimard, 1971.

Dennis, David. *Beethoven in German Politics, 1870–1989.* New Haven and London: Yale University Press, 1996.

DeNora, Tia. *Beethoven and the Construction of Genius: Musical Politics in Vienna, 1792–1803*. Berkeley and Los Angeles: California University Press, 1995.

———. "Beethoven et l'invention du génie." In *Actes de la Recherche en sciences sociales,* no. 110 (Paris: Seuil, December 1995).

Eggebrecht, H. H. *Zur Geschichte der Beethovens-Rezeption.* Mainz: Akademie der Wissenschaften und Literatur, 1972; reissued by Laaber-Verlag, 1994.

Eggli, Edmond. *Schiller et le romantisme français.* Paris, 1927; reprint, Geneva: Slatkine, 1970.

Eichhorn, Andreas. *Beethovens Neunte Symphonie: Die Geschichte ihrer Aufführung und Rezeption.* Kassel, Basel, and London: Bärenreiter, 1993.

Einstein, Alfred. "Beethoven's Military Style." In *Essays on Music,* edited by P. H. Lang. New York, 1956.

Fähnrich, Hermann. "Das Beethovenbild Romain Rollands." *Zeitschrift für Musik* 113, no. 3 (Leipzig, March 1952).

Floros, Constantin. "Zum Beethoven-Bild Schönbergs, Bergs und Weberns." In *Beethoven und die Zweite Wiener Schule,* edited by O. Kolleritsch. Vienna: Universal Edition, 1992.

Forbes, Elliot. "A Neglected Work in Beethoven's Choral Music: The Funeral Cantata." In *Essays on Music in Honor of Archibald Thompson Davison.* Cambridge: Harvard University, 1957.

———. "Stürzet nieder, Millionen." In *Studies in Music History: Essays for Oliver Strunk.* Princeton: Princeton University Press, 1968.

Fouque, Octave. *Les Révolutionnaires de la musique.* Paris: Calmann-Lévy, 1882.

Friedländer, Max. *Das deutsche Lied im 18. Jahrhundert.* Stuttgart, 1902.

———. "Das Lied vom Marlborough." *Zeitschrift für Musikwissenschaft,* vol. 6, 1923–1924.

Furtwängler, Wilhelm. *Musique et verbe.* Paris: Albin Michel, 1979.

Geck, Martin, and Peter Schleuning. *"Geschrieben auf Bonaparte": Beethovens "Eroica": Revolution, Reaktion, Rezeption.* Hamburg; Rowohlt, 1989.

Grove, George. *Beethoven and His Nine Symphonies.* 3rd edition, 1898; New York: Dover Publications, 1962.

Hartmann, Horst. "Zur Interpretation und aktuellen Rezeption von Schillers 'An die Freude.'" *Weimarer Beiträge* 5, no. 10 (Berlin and Weimar, 1979).

Herriot, Édouard. *La Vie de Beethoven.* Paris: Gallimard, 1928.

Hoffmann, E. T. A. *Écrits sur la musique.* Lausanne: L'Âge d'homme, 1985.

Huchet, Stéphane. "Beethoven et l'iconographie française." In *Beethoven à Paris, Revue internationale de musique française,* no. 22 (February, 1987).

Indy, Vincent d'. *Beethoven.* Paris: Henri Laurens, 1911.

Jäger-Sunstenau, Hanns. "Beethoven als Bürger der Stadt Wien." In *Colloquium Amicorum: Festschrift Joseph Schmidt-Görg zum 70. Geburtstag,* edited by S. Kross and H. Schmidt. Bonn: Beethovenhaus, 1967.

Jander, Owen. "Beethoven's 'Orpheus in Hades': The Andante con moto *of the Fourth Piano Concerto." In* Nineteenth-Century Music *8 (Berkeley and Los Angeles: University of California Press, Spring 1985).*

Janin, Jules. "Le dîner de Beethoven, conte fantastique." *Gazette musicale de Paris* 5, no. 1 (1834).

———. "Fêtes en l'honneur de Beethoven." *Le Journal des débats* (Paris, 13 and 18 August 1845).

Johnson, James. "Beethoven and the Birth of Romantic Musical Experience in France." In *Nineteenth-Century Music* 15, no. 1 (Berkeley and Los Angeles: University of California Press, 1991).

Jun'ichi, Yano. "Why Is Beethoven's Ninth So Well Loved in Japan?" *Japanese Quarterly,* no. 29 (1982).

Kahl, Willi. "Zur Geschichte des Bonner Beethovendenkmals." In *Beethoven-Jahrbuch,* new series, no. 2, vol. 1 (Bonn: Beethovenhaus, 1953–1954).

Keiler, Alan. "Liszt and Beethoven: The Creation of a Personal Myth." In *Nineteenth-Century Music* 12, no. 2 (Berkeley and Los Angeles: University of California Press, Autumn 1988).

Kerman, Joseph, and Alan Tyson. *The New Grove Beethoven.* New York and London: Norton and Co., 1983.

Kinderman, William. *Beethoven.* Berkeley and Los Angeles: University of California Press, 1995.

———. "Beethoven's Symbol for the Deity in the *Missa solemnis* and the Ninth Symphony." *Nineteenth-Century Music* 9 (Berkeley and Los Angeles: University of California Press, Autumn 1985).

Kirkendale, Warren. "New Roads to Old Ideas in Beethoven's *Missa solemnis.*" In *The Creative World of Beethoven,* edited by P. H. Lang. New York: Norton and Co., 1970.

Knight, Frida. *Beethoven and the Age of Revolution.* New York: International Publishers, 1974.

Kreutzer, Léon. "Grands festivals de Bonn à l'occasion de l'inauguration de la statue de Beethoven." *Revue et gazette musicale de Paris* 12 (Paris, 1845).

Kropfinger, Klaus. *Wagner and Beethoven: Richard Wagners Reception of Beethoven.* New York: Cambridge University Press, 1991.

Kunze, Stefan, ed. *Ludwig van Beethoven: Die Werke im Spiegel seiner Zeit.* Laaber: Laaber-Verlag, 1987.

Küthen, Hans Werner. "Wellingtons Sieg oder die Schlacht bei Vittoria, Beethoven und das Epochenproblem Napoleon." In *Beethoven zwischen Revolution und Restauration,* edited by H. Lühning and S. Brandenburg. Bonn: Beethovenhaus, 1989.

Ladenburger, Michael. "Der Wiener Kongress im Spiegel der Musik." In *Beethoven zwischen Revolution und Restauration,* edited by H. Lühning and S. Brandenburg. Bonn: Beethovenhaus, 1989.

Lambert, Raymond-Raoul. *Beethoven rhénan (Reconnaissance à Jean-Christophe)*. Paris: Les Presses françaises, 1928.

Lang, Paul Henry. "Beethoven in France." *Romanic Review* 35 (1944).

Levy, David Benjamin. *Beethoven: The Ninth Symphony*. New York: Schirmer Books, 1995.

Loos, Helmut, ed. *Beethoven und die Nachwelt: Materialien zur Wirkungsgeschichte Beethovens*. Bonn: Beethovenhaus, 1986.

Magill, Charles. "Schiller's 'An die Freude.'" In *Essays in German Language, Culture and Society*. London, 1969.

Mainka, Jürgen. "Beethovens Bonner Kantaten." In *Bericht über den internationalen Beethoven-Kongress*. Berlin: Verlag Neue Musik, 1971.

Martin, Uwe. "Freude Freiheit Götterfunken: Über Schillers Schwierigkeiten beim Schreiben von Freiheit." *Cahiers d'études germaniques,* no. 18 (1990).

Mauclair, Camille. "En écoutant Beethoven." *Les Héros de l'orchestre*. Paris, 1919.

———. "Le bienfait de Beethoven." *La Semaine littéraire* 35 (Genève, 1927).

Marston, Nicholas. "Schumann's Monument to Beethoven." *Nineteenth-Century Music* 14, no. 3 (University of California Press, Spring 1991).

Marx, Hans J. "Beethoven as a Political Person." In *Ludwig van Beethoven, 1770 – 1970*. Bonn–Bad Godesberg: InterNationes, 1970.

Massenkeil, Günther. "Die Bonner Beethoven-Kantate (1845) von Franz Liszt." In *Die Sprache der Musik: Festschrift Klaus Wolfgang Niemöller zum 60. Geburtstag,* edited by J. P. Fricke. Regensburg: Gustav Bosse Verlag, 1989.

———. "International Relationships in Beethoven's Life and Works." In *Ludwig van Beethoven, 1770 –1970*. Bonn–Bad Godesberg: InterNationes, 1970.

Massin, Jean and Brigitte. *Ludwig van Beethoven*. Paris: Le Club français du livre, Fayard, 1967.

———. "Beethoven et la Révolution française." *L'Arc,* no. 40, *Beethoven* (Paris, 1970).

Matthews, Denis. *Beethoven*. London and Melbourne: J. M. Dent and Sons, 1985.

Messing, Scott. "The Vienna Centennial Festival of 1870." *The Beethoven Newsletter* 6, no. 3 (San Jose State University, 1991).

Metzger, Heinz Klaus. "Zur Beethoven-Interpretation" (1970). In *Beethoven: Das Problem der interpretation, Musik-Konzepte,* no. 8 (Munich, 1979).

Müller-Blattau, Joseph. "Freude schöner Gotterfunken: Ein Kapitel deutscher Liedergeschichte." *Die Musik* (Berlin, October 1934).

Nottebohm, Gustav. *Beethoveniana: Aufsätze une Mittheilungen:* Leipzig and Winterhur: Rieter-Biedermann, 1872.

———. *Zweite Beethoveniana*. Leipzig: Rieter-Biedermann, 1876.

Palisca, Claude. "French Revolutionary Models for Beethoven's *Eroica* Funeral March." In *Music and Context: Essays for John M. Ward*. Cambridge: Harvard University Press, 1985.

Pannain, Guido. "La cultura di Beethoven in Italia." *Neues Beethoven-Jahrbuch,* vol. l Augsbourg: B. Filser, 1924.

Pass, Walter. "Beethoven und der Historismus." In *Beethoven Studien: Festgabe der Österreichischen Akademie der Wissenschaften zum 200. Geburtstag von Ludwig van Beethoven.* Vienna: H. Bohlaus, 1970.

Pioch, Georges. *Beethoven, Portraits d'hier,* no. 3 (Paris, 1909).

Pistone, Danièle. "Beethoven et Paris." *Beethoven à Paris, Revue internationale de musique française,* no. 22 (February 1987).

Prod'homme, Jacques-Gabriel. *Les Symphonies de Beethoven* (1906). Paris: Charles Delagrave, 3rd ed., 1909; reprint, New York: DaCapo Press, 1977.

———. *Beethoven raconté par ceux qui l'ont vu.* Paris: Stock, 1927.

Quinet, Mme Edgar. *Ce que dit la musique.* Paris: Calmann-Lévy, 1893.

Revault d'Allonnes, Olivier. *Plaisir à Beethoven.* Paris: Christian Bourgois, 1982.

Röder, Thomas. "Beethovens Sieg über die Schlachtenmusik: Opus 91 und die Tradition der Battaglia." In *Beethoven zwischen Revolution und Restauration,* edited by H. Lühning and S. Brandenburg. Bonn: Beethovenhaus, 1989.

*Rolland, Romain.* Beethoven *(1903). Paris: Édouard Pelleton, 1909.*

———. *Beethoven: Les grandes époques créatrices.* Paris: Albin Michel, 1980.

Rosen, Charles. *The Classical Style.* New York: W. W. Norton, 1972.

Rumph, Stephen. "A Kingdom Not of This World : The Political Context of E. T. A. Hoffmann's Beethoven Criticism." *Nineteenth-Century Music* 14, no. 3 (University of California Press, Spring 1991).

Ruppelt, Georg. *Schiller im nationalsozialistischen Deutschland: Der Versuch einer Gleichschaltung.* Stuttgart: Metzler Studienausgabe, 1979.

Schenk, Erich. "Salieris 'Landsturm'-Kantate von 1799 in ihren Beziehungen zu Beethovens 'Fidelio.'" In *Colloquium Amicorum: Festschrift Joseph Schmidt-Görg zum 70. Geburtstag,* edited by S. Kross and H. Schmidt. Bonn: Beethovenhaus, 1967.

Schenker, Heinrich. *Beethoven: Neunte Symphonie.* Vienna: Universal Edition, 1969.

Schindler, Anton. *Beethoven as I Knew Him* (1860). Edited by D. MacArdle, translated by C. Jolly. Chapel Hill and London: University of North Carolina Press/Faber and Faber, 1966.

Schmidt-Görg, Joseph, and Hans Schmidt. *Ludwig van Beethoven.* Bonn and Hamburg: Archives Beethoven/Deutsches Grammophon Gesellschaft, 1969.

Schmitt, Ulrich. *Revolution im Konzertsaal Zur Beethoven-Rezeption im 19. Jahrhundert.* Mainz, London, and Paris: Schott, 1990.

Schmitz, Arnold. *Das romantische Beethovenbild: Darstellung und Kritik.* Berlin and Bonn: F. Dümmlers Verlag, 1927.

———. "Zur Frage nach Beethovens Weltanschauung und ihrem musikalischen Ausdruck." In *Beethoven und die Gegenwart: Festschrift des Beethovenhauses*

*Bonn: Ludwig Schiedermair zum 60. Geburtstag,* edited by A. Schmitz. Berlin and Bonn: Ferd. Dümmlers Verlag, 1937.

Schrade, Leo. *Beethoven in France: History of an Idea.* New Haven: Yale University Press, 1942.

———. "On *Beethoven in France:* A Reply." *Romanic Review* 36 (1945).

Schröder, Herbert. "Beethoven im Dritten Reich." In *Beethoven und die Nachwelt: Materialien zur Wirkungsgeschichte Beethovens,* edited by H. Loos. Bonn: Beethovenhaus, 1986.

Schulz, Franz. "Die Göttin Freude: Zur Geistes- und Stilgeschichte des 18. Jahrhunderts." In *Jahrbuch des Freien Deutschen Hochstifts.* Frankfurt: Gebr. Knauer, 1926.

Schumann, Robert. *Sur les musiciens.* Paris: Stock/Musique, 1979.

Sharpe, Lesley. *Friedrich Schiller: Drama, Thought, and Politics.* Cambridge and New York: Cambridge University Press, 1991.

Solie, Ruth. "Beethoven as Secular Humanist: Ideology and the Ninth Symphony in Nineteenth-Century Criticism. In *Explorations in Music, the Arts, and Ideas: Essays in Honor of Leonard B. Meyer,* edited by E. Narmour et R. Solie. Stuyvesant, NY: Pendragon Press, 1988.

Salomon, Maynard. *Beethoven* (1977). Translated by H. Hildenbrand. Paris: J.-C. Lattès, 1985.

———. *Beethoven Essays.* Cambridge and London: Harvard University Press, 1988.

Sonneck, Oscar, ed. *Beethoven: Impressions by His Contemporaries* (1926). New York: Dover Publications, 1967.

Taruskin, Richard. "Performers and Instruments. Resisting the Ninth." *Nineteenth-Century Music* 12 (University of California Press, Spring 1989).

———. "A Beethoven Season? Like Last Season, the One Before. . . ." *New York Times,* 10 September 1995.

Thayer, Alexander W., and Elliot Forbes. *Thayer's Life of Beethoven,* edited by E. Forbes, 2 vols. Princeton: Princeton University Press, 1967.

Tiersot, Julien. "Beethoven, musicien de la Révolution française," *Revue de Paris* 17 (Paris, 1910).

Vaihinger, Hans. "Zwei Quellenfunde su Schillers philosophischer Entwicklung." Appendix 2, "Ein Freimauerliederbuch als Quelle des Liedes an die Freude?" *Kantstudien* 10 (Berlin, 1905), pp. 386–89.

———. "Schillers Lied 'An die Freude' und sein freimauerischer Ursprung," *Kantstudien* 11 (Berlin, 1906), p. 483.

Wallace, Robin. *Beethoven's Critics: Aesthetic Dilemmas and Resolutions During the Composer's Lifetime.* Cambridge and New York: Cambridge University Press, 1986.

Webster, James. "The Form of the Finale of Beethoven's Ninth Symphony." In *Beethoven Forum,* vol. 1, edited by L. Lockwood and J. Webster. Lincoln: University of Nebraska Press, 1992.

Wieland, Christoph Martin. "Schillers Lied an die Freude: Eine Vorlesung im Zirkel einiger Freunde aus dem Jahre 1793." *Monatshefte der Comenius-Gesellschaft,* new series, vol. 5, cahier 3 (1913).

Wilder, Victor. *Beethoven: Sa vie et son œuvre.* Paris: Charpentier et Cie, 1883.

Winter, Robert. "The Sketches for the 'Ode to Joy.'" In *Beethoven, Performers, and Critics,* edited by R. Winter and B. Carr. Detroit: Wayne State University Press, 1980.

Wyzewa, Théodore de. *Beethoven et Wagner: Essais d'histoire et de critique musicales.* Paris: Perrin, 1898.

Young, Percy M. *Beethoven, a Victorian Tribute.* London: Dennis Dobson, 1976.

## POLITICAL MUSIC

Antonicek, Theophil. "'Vergangenheit muss unsere Zukunft bilden': Die patriotische Musikbewegung in Wien und ihr Vorkämpfer Ignaz von Mosel." *Revue belge de musicologie* 26–27 (Brussels, 1972–1973).

Bartlet, M. Elizabeth C. "L'Offrande à la Liberté et l'histoire de la Marseillaise." In *Le Tambour et la harpe: Œuvres, pratiques et manifestations musicales sous la révolution, 1788–1800,* edited by J.-R. Julien and J. Mongrédien. Paris: Éd. du May, 1991.

———. "The New Repertory of the Opéra during the Reign of Terror: Revolutionary Rhetoric and Operatic Consequences." In *Music and the French Revolution,* edited by M. Boyd. Cambridge: Cambridge University Press, 1992.

Biget, Michelle. *Musique et Révolution française: La longue durée.* Annales littéraires de l'université de Besançon. Paris: Les Belles-Lettres, 1989.

Buch, Esteban. *O juremos con gloria morir: Historia de una épica de Estado.* Buenos Aires: Sudamericana, 1994.

Bunten, Alice Chambers. *God Save the King: Facsimiles of the Earliest Prints of our National Anthem.* London, 1902.

Charnoy, Thierry. "Énonciation et chanson révolutionnaire." In *1789–1989: Musique, histoire, démocratie.* Paris: *Vibrations*/I.A.S.P.M.-M.S.H., 1992.

Christmann, Pfarrer. "Einige Ideen über den Geist der französische Nationallieder." *Allgemeine musikalische Zeitung,* nos. 15–17 (Leipzig, January 1799).

Clark, Richard. *An Account of the National Anthem Entitled God Save the King.* London, 1822.

Cotte, Roger. *La Musique maçonnique.* Paris: Éd. du Borrego/Maçonniques, 1987.

———. "De la musique des loges maçonniques à celle des fêtes révolutionnaires." In *Les Fêtes de la Révolution: Colloque de Clermont-Ferrand.* Paris: Société des études robespierristes, 1977.

Cummings, William H., *God Save the King: The Origin and History of the Music and Words of the National Anthem.* London and New York, 1902.

Didier, Béatrice. "Stylistique des hymnes révolutionnaires." In *Orphée phrygien: Les musiques de la Révolution, Vibrations,* special issue (Paris: Éd. du May, 1989).

Donakowski, Conrad L. *A Muse for the Masses: Ritual and Music in an Age of Democratic Revolution, 1770 –1870.* Chicago and London: University of Chicago Press, 1972.

Dunning, Albert. "Official Court Music: Means and Symbols of Might." In *La Musique et le rite sacré et profane.* Strasbourg: Université de Strasbourg, 1986.

Estayer, Jacques, and Georges Bossi. *L'internationale, 1888 –1988.* Paris: Éd. sociales/Messidor, 1988.

Fiaux, Louis. *La Marseillaise.* Paris: Fasquelle, 1918.

Gessele, Cynthia. "The Conservatoire de musique and national music education in France, 1795–1801," In *Music and the French Revolution,* edited by M. Boyd. Cambridge: Cambridge University Press, 1992.

Grasberger, Franz. *Die Hymnen Österreichs.* Tutzing: H. Schneider, 1968.

Hansen, Hans Jürgen. *Heil Dir im Siegerkranz: Die Hymnen der Deutschen.* Oldenbourg, Stalling, 1978.

Hare, Robert. "Ceremonial and Festival Functions of Masonic and Revolutionary Music." In *La Musique et le rite sacré et profane.* Strasbourg: Université de Strasbourg, 1986.

Hudde, Hinrich. "L'histoire d'une fascination: *La Marseillaise* en Allemagne." In *1789 –1989: Musique, histoire, démocratie.* Paris, *Vibrations*/I.A.S.P.M.-M.S.H.,1992.

Jam, Jean-Louis. "Fonction des hymnes révolutionnaires." In *Les Fêtes de la Révolution, Colloque de Clermont-Ferrand.* Paris: Société des études robespierristes, 1977.

———. "Musiques populaires et musique du peuple." In *1789 –1989: Musique, histoire, démocratie.* Paris: *Vibrations*/I.A.S.P.M.-M.S.H., 1992.

———. "Marie-Joseph Chénier and François-Joseph Gossec: Two Artists in the Service of Revolutionary Propaganda." In *Music and the French Revolution,* edited by M. Boyd. Cambridge: Cambridge University Press, 1992.

Leclerc, Jean-Baptiste. *Essai sur la propagation de la musique en France, sa conservation et ses rapports avec le gouvernement.* Paris: Imprimerie nationale, Year IV (1796).

Luxardo, Hervé. *Histoire de la Marseillaise.* Paris: Plon, 1989.

Mongrédien, Jean. *La Musique en France des Lumières au romantisme, 1789 –1830.* Paris: Flammarion, 1986.

———. "La musique aux fêtes du sacre de Charles X." In *Recherches sur la musique française classique,* vol. 10 (Paris: Picard, 1970).

Nettl, Paul. *National Anthems.* Translated by A. Gode. New York: Frederick Ungar Publishing, 1967.

Pierre, Constant. *Les Hymnes et les chansons de la Révolution.* Paris, Imprimerie nationale, 1904.

———. *Le Conservatoire national de musique et de déclamation.* Paris: Imprimerie nationale, 1900.

———. *Musique des fêtes et cérémonies de la Révolution française.* Paris: Imprimerie nationale, 1899.

———. *Le Magasin de musique à l'usage des fêtes nationales et du Conservatoire.* Paris: Fischbacher, 1895; Geneva: Minkoff Reprint, 1974.

Place, Adélaïde de. *La Vie musicale en France au temps de la Révolution.* Paris: Fayard, 1989.

———. "Les chants et les hymnes de la Révolution française: Rôle moral et fonction sociale," In *Musique et médiations: Le métier, l'instrument, l'oreille,* edited by J. M. Fauquet and H. Dufourt. Paris: Klincksieck, 1994.

Porter, Cecilia Hopkins, "The Rheinlieder Critic: A Case of Musical Nationalism." *Musical Quarterly* 43, no. 1 (January 1977).

Robert, Frédéric. *La Marseillaise.* Paris: Imprimerie nationale, 1989.

———. "Art impulsé ou art dirigé?" In *1789-1989: Musique, histoire, démocratie.* Paris: *Vibrations/*I.A.S.P.M.-M.S.H., 1992.

Schneider, Herbert. "Der Formen- und Funktionswandel in den Chansons und Hymnen der französischen Revolution." In *Die französische Revolution als Bruch der gesellschaftlichen Bewußtseins,* edited by R. Reichardt and R. Koselleck. Munich: Oldenbourg, 1988.

Scholes, Percy. *God Save the King! Its History and Its Romance.* London: Oxford University Press, 1942.

———. *God Save the Queen! The History and Romance of the World's First National Anthem.* London: Oxford University Press, 1956.

Sonneck, O. G. *Report on "The Star-Spangled Banner," "Hail Columbia," "America," "Yankee Doodle"* (1909). New York: Dover Publications, 1972.

Tiersot, Julien. *Les Fêtes et les chants de la Révolution française.* Paris: Hachette, 1908.

———. *Histoire de la Marseillaise.* Paris: Delagrave, 1915.

Vega, Carlos. *El Himno Nacional Argentino.* Buenos Aires: Eudeba, 1962.

Vovelle, Michel. *Théodore Desorgues ou la désorganisation, Aix-Paris, 1763-1808* (Paris: Seuil, 1985).

———. "La Marseillaise." In *Les Lieux de mémoire,* vol. l, *La République.* Paris: Gallimard, 1984.

## OTHER MUSICIANS, OTHER MUSIC, THEIR RECEPTION

Adorno, Theodor W. *Essai sur Wagner.* Paris: Gallimard, 1966.

———. "Bach Defended against His Devotees" (1950). In *Prisms.* Cambridge, Mass.: M.I.T. Press, 1981.

Barzun, Jacques. *Berlioz and the Romantic Century.* 2 vols. New York and London: Columbia University Press, 1969.

Beaufils, Marcel. *Comment l'Allemagne est devenue musicienne* (1942). Paris: Robert Laffont, 1983.

Bent, Ian. "Heinrich Schenker et la missione del genio germanico." *Rivista italiana di musicologia,* no. 26 (Florence, 1991).

Botstein, Leon. "History, Rhetoric, and the Self: Robert Schumann and Music Making in German-Speaking Europe, 1800–1860. In *Schumann and His World,* edited by Larry Todd. Princeton: Princeton University Press, 1994.

Buch, Esteban. *Histoire d'un secret: À propos de la Suite lyrique d'Alban Berg.* Arles: Actes Sud, 1994.

Burrows, Donald. *Handel.* New York: Schirmer Books, 1994.

———. *Handel: Messiah.* Cambridge: Cambridge University Press, 1991.

Dahlhaus, Carl. *Nineteenth-Century Music.* Translated by B. Robinson. Berkeley and Los Angeles: University of California Press, 1989.

———. "Nationalism and Music." In *Between Romanticism and Modernism: Four Studies in the Music of the Later Nineteenth Century,* translated by M. Whittall. Berkeley and Los Angeles: University of California Press, 1980.

———. "Das deutsche Bildungsbürgertum und die Musik." In *Bildungsbürgertum im 19. Jahrhunderts,* edited by R. Koselleck. Stuttgart: Klett-Cotte, 1990.

Dean, Winston (with Anthony Hicks). *Haendel.* Paris: Éd. du Rocher, 1985.

Endler, Franz. *Karajan: Eine Biographie.* Hamburg: Hoffmann und Campe, 1992.

Escal, Françoise. *Aléas de l'œuvre musicale.* Paris: Hermann, 1996.

Eugène, Éric. *Wagner et Gobineau.* Paris: Le Cherche-midi, 1998.

Fulcher, Jane F. "Style musical et enjeux politiques en France à la veille de la Seconde Guerre mondiale." *Actes de la recherche en sciences sociales,* no. 110 (December 1995).

Gregor-Dellin, Martin. *Richard Wagner: Sa vie, son œuvre, son siècle.* Paris: Fayard, 1981.

Gut, Serge. *Liszt.* Paris: Éd. de Fallois/L'Âge d'homme, 1989.

Gutman, Robert W. *Richard Wagner: The Man, His Mind, and His Music.* New York: Harcourt, Brace and World, 1968.

Johnson, James. *Listening in Paris: A Cultural History.* Berkeley and Los Angeles: University of California Press, 1995.

Kallberg, Jeffrey. "The Rhetoric of Genre: Chopin's Nocturne in G Minor." In *Chopin at the Boundaries: Sex, History, and Musical Genre.* Cambridge and London: Harvard University Press, 1996.

Laks, Simon. *Mélodies d'Auschwitz.* Paris: Cerf, 1991.

Landon, H. C. Robbins. *Haydn: Chronicle and Works.* 5 vols. Bloomington: Indiana University Press, 1976–1980.

———. *Haydn: A Documentary Study.* New York: Rizzoli, 1981.

Large, David C. "Wagner's Bayreuth Disciples." In *Wagnerism in European Culture and Politics,* edited by W. Weber and D. Large. Ithaca and London: Cornell University Press, 1984.

Larsen, Jens Peter. *The New Grove Haydn.* New York and London: Norton and Co., 1983.

Levi, Erik. *Music in the Third Reich.* New York: St. Martin's Press, 1994.

Locke, Ralph. *Les Saint-Simoniens et la musique.* Paris: Mardaga, 1992.

———. "Liszt's Saint-Simonian Adventure." *Nineteenth-Century Music* 4 (Berkeley and Los Angeles: University of California Press, 1980).

Menger, Pierre-Michel. *Le Paradoxe du musicien: Le compositeur, le mélomane et l'État dans la société contemporaine.* Paris: Flammarion, 1983.

Merrett, Robert James. "England's Orpheus: Praise of Handel in Eighteenth-Century Poetry." *Mosaic* 20, no. 2 (Winnipeg, MB: University of Manitoba, 1986).

Morrow, Mary Sue. *Concert Life in Haydn's Vienna: Aspects of a Developing Musical and Social Institution.* Stuyvesant, NY: Pendragon Press, 1981.

Murphy, Kerry. *Hector Berlioz and the Development of French Music Criticism.* Ann Arbor and London: U.H.I. Research Press, 1988.

Newman, Ernest. *The Life of Richard Wagner,* vol. 4, *1866–1883.* New York: A. A. Knopf, 1946.

Prieberg, Fred K. *Musik im NS-Staat.* Frankfurt: Fischer, 1982.

Said, Edward. *Musical Elaborations.* New York: Columbia University Press, 1991.

Smith, Ruth. *Handel's Oratorios and Eighteenth-Century Thought.* Cambridge: Cambridge University Press, 1995.

Somfai, Laszlo. "'Learned Style' in two late string quartet movements by Haydn." *Studia musicologica,* no. 28 (Budapest, 1986).

Treitler, Leo. *Music and the Historical Imagination.* Cambridge, Mass.: Harvard University Press, 1989.

Turbow, Gerald. "Art and Politics: Wagnerism in France." In *Wagnerism in European Culture and Politics,* edited by W. Weber and D. Large. Ithaca and London: Cornell University Press, 1984.

Vignal, Marc. *Joseph Haydn.* Paris: Fayard, 1988.

Walker, Alan. *Franz Liszt.* Ithaca: Cornell University Press, 1988.

———. "Schumann, Liszt, and the C-Major Fantasie, op. 17: A Declining Relationship." *Music and Letters,* no. 60 (1979).

Walton, Chris. "Einleitung: 'Doppelagent oder' 'kläglicher Mensch'? Ein Rückblick auf die Furtwängler-Rezeption des vergangenen Jahrzents." In *Wilhelm Furtwängler in Diskussion.* Zurich: Amadeus, 1996.

Weber, William. *The Rise of Musical Classics in Eighteenth-Century England: A Study in Canon, Ritual, and Ideology.* New York: Oxford University Press, 1992.

———. "Wagner, Wagnerism, and Musical Idealism." In *Wagnerism in European Culture and Politics,* edited by W. Weber and D. Large. Ithaca and London: Cornell University Press, 1984.

Wulf, Joseph. *Musik im Dritten Reich: Eine Dokumentation.* Hamburg: Rowohlt, 1966.

Young, Percy. "The Indispensable Mr. Handel: Changing Perception of a National Composer." *Studia musicologica norvegica,* no. 12 (Oslo: Universitetsforlaget, 1986.

# index